# Religion and Politics in International Relations

# Religion and Politics in International Relations

## The Modern Myth

Timothy Fitzgerald

continuum

Continuum International Publishing Group
The Tower Building        80 Maiden Lane
11 York Road              Suite 704
London SE1 7NX            New York NY 10038

www.continuumbooks.com

**British Library Cataloguing in Publication Data**
A catalogue record for this book is available from the British Library.

ISBN: HB: 978–0–8264–2692–5
      PB: 978–1–4411–4290–0

**Library of Congress Cataloging-in-Publication Data**
Fitzgerald, Timothy, 1947-
   Religion and politics in international relations : the modern
myth / Timothy Fitzgerald.
      p. cm.
   Includes bibliographical references.
   ISBN-13: 978–0–8264–2692–5
   ISBN-10: 0–8264–2692–1
   ISBN-13: 978–1–4411–4290–0 (PB)
   ISBN-10: 1–4411–4290–8 (PB)
1. Religion and international affairs. 2. Ideology--Religious
aspects. 3. Religion and politics. I. Title.

   BL65.I55F58 2010
   201'.727--dc22
                        2010024405

Typeset by Fakenham Prepress Solutions, Fakenham, Norfolk NR21 8NN
Printed and bound in Great Britain

For my granddaughter Mia

# Contents

# Acknowledgements

Most of this book was written in Kyoto, Japan, while I was engaged in various research activities during a year's release from normal duties at the University of Stirling. Between July 2008 and January 2009 I was Visiting Research Professor at The Institute of Humanities [Jinbunken], Kyoto University, and I express my deep gratitude to both the Institute and to Kyoto University for their generous invitation. I am especially grateful to Professor Masakazu Tanaka for his kindness in inviting me and in helping to make my stay so pleasant and productive. I am also grateful to Professor Tanaka and his colleagues and research students for giving me the opportunity to explore some of the ideas in this book in a preliminary way at the Anthropology Research Seminar in November 2009.

My gratitude also to Professor Akio Tanabe of Kyoto University for interesting comments on my paper, and for his observations on religion in India; and to Masahiko Togawa for his generous invitation to give a paper in the Graduate School of International Development and Co-operation at Hiroshima University.

I am also grateful to the organizers of the International Workshop, 'Forms of Modern Knowledge in East Asia: Methodology and Perspective', held by the Academy of East Asian Studies at Sungkyunkwan University, Seoul, Korea, on 23 October 2009, for their invitation to explore some of these ideas in an East Asian forum.

From April to September 2010 I was offered the six-month Numata Scholarship by Ryukoku University, Kyoto. I am deeply grateful to Ryukoku University and to Professor Jusho Wakahara for his generosity, and for being so kind to me during this period. I am also grateful to other distinguished members of the research committee, especially the Chair, Professor Nobuko Nagasaki, and her distinguished colleagues, Professor Chisui Satoh, Professor Shoryu Katsura, and Professor Hisashi Nakamura. A special word of thanks to Professor Miwako Shiga for her invaluable organization and help. The research group provided valuable opportunities for exploring issues around 'religion' and 'politics' in Japan, India and more globally, combined with the opportunity to develop my ideas in a special lecture at Ryukoku University. Under their auspices I was also able to visit Delhi and Lucknow in July and August for research on Dalits, Ambedkar Buddhism and Bahujan Samaj.

While in Delhi I was able to have unscheduled meetings with several professors at Jawaharlal Nehru University (JNU) to discuss some of the ideas in this book in relation to Bahujan Samaj discourse and Indian debates on secularism and religion more generally. I am grateful to the following professors for their time in the middle of their own busy schedule (listed in the order in which I met them) Chinna Rao, Vidhu Verma, Nandu Ram, Valerian Rodrigues, Manindra Nath Thakur, Y.S. Alone, and Tulsi Ram. I also had the privilege to meet scholars, writers and professors in Delhi including Sukhadeo Thorat, D. C. Ahir, Late Bhagwan Das, G. Aloysius, Raj Kumar, Smita Patil, and Veeramani. I was also fortunate to have the opportunity of presenting some ideas in the seminar at Centre for the Study of Social Systems (CSSS), School of Social Science, JNU, thanks to the Chairperson Professor Susan Visvanathan and to Dr. V. Sujatha.

In Lucknow I met several professors at the Babasaheb Bhimrao Ambedkar University where I was invited to give a formal lecture on Ambedkar Buddhism and the globalizing religion-secular discourse. My gratitude to the Vice-Chancellor Professor B. Hanumaiah, Professor Kameshwar Choudhary, Dr. B. B. Malik, and several others with whom I had useful discussions. There were many other Buddhists and Dalits I met, including politicians and bhikshus, who gave me valuable insights into the contested Anglophone discourse on religion and the secular, and the problems of translating these categories in the context of power relations in Uttar Pradesh. I should in particular mention Bhikshu Bhante Chandima at the UP government sponsored Vihara; and Dr. B. Suresh of Chhatrapati Shahuji Maharaj Medical University. My warm gratitude and respect is also due to Shiv Shankar Das, PhD candidate at JNU, Delhi, my companion, interpreter, and organizer, who helped me in so many ways.

The period in Kyoto with Ryukoku University coincided with a one-semester sabbatical provided by the University of Stirling. I owe a debt of thanks to all my colleagues in the University's School of Languages, Cultures and Religions for their help and cooperation in supervising PGs, teaching and lecturing, and various administrative responsibilities. I am fortunate to work with such colleagues, all of whom have their own intense schedules and research demands.

I am grateful to Trevor Stack at Aberdeen and Naomi Goldenberg at Ottawa for their collegiality, inspiration and friendship in organizing the series of workshops and conferences on critical religion and the religion-secular binary at Stirling, Aberdeen, Ottawa and the British Academy in London. Thanks to the British Academy for funding the international conference in January, 2010. Thanks also to Dr. Fiona Barclay at the University of Stirling for her help in organizing the workshops at Stirling. It goes without saying that the success of these various workshops and conferences depended in the end on all the participants, and the many interesting papers that were read.

I also want to thank several people who read all or part of the manuscript and gave me their comments. The original unpublished article of which this book is an extension and elaboration was read by Julie Russell and Bill Cavanaugh. The book's manuscript itself, or various parts of it at different stages of drafting, was read by Jeremy Carrette, Mariachiara Giorda, Naomi Goldenberg, Alison Jasper and Tisa Wenger. I am grateful to them all for their labours.

Finally I would like to express my warm appreciation to David Eunice, Kyoto translator and Sign-painter to the Stars, who through that year in Kyoto found time in his busy schedule to share his knowledge of Kyoto, and to eat, drink, argue and laugh with me, and who helped lighten some of the darker symptoms of trauma inflicted on me unexpectedly. Whether or not he or any of the other people I met during this year agree with the views expressed in this book, I am grateful to all of them for their conversations, comments and insights.

T. Fitzgerald, Kyoto, August 2010

# Chapter 1

## Introduction:
## Religion is not a Standalone Category

This book is a critique of *discourses* on 'religion' and 'religions', not a description or analysis of any 'religion' as such. I am especially concerned here with such discourses as they appear in International Relations literature, and in texts closely related to IR such as Politics and the Social Sciences. This is admittedly a broad interpretation of the term 'international relations', but not much broader than the comparable content of the Special Issue on Religion and International Relations published by the journal *Millennium* (2000: 29(3)).

When we talk unreflexively about a religion such as Hinduism or Christianity we assume that it exists as a distinct entity in the world, and this tendency to reification or misplaced concreteness is strengthened by wide discursive forces around us, such as the media, academia and the publishing industry. The combined force of these discursive agencies tends to construct the belief that Religion itself, or specific religions, exist in the world as empirical objects of investigation with distinct characteristics which can be described and analysed. This reification of 'religion' is evident in recent stories told in IR, politics and the social sciences of religion's 'resurgence' or 'return from exile'. Quite often, as I will show in detail in this book, such writers even represent 'religion' as an agent acting in the world with malign intention. If challenged, they might defend themselves by saying that this is merely metaphoric language. But perhaps all mythology starts in metaphor before it becomes transformed into a powerful figment of the imagination projected onto reality and determining decisions about action. For the myth of religion and religions as essences and even intentional agents in the world has many ramifications, some of them potentially dangerous ones, for example in directing homeland security operations, or in foreign policy decision-making by state agencies.

It is not obvious in what sense any particular 'religion' exists at all. We all know, when we are pushed into thinking seriously about it, that religions are not things that exist in the world in the same sense that, say, chairs and tables seem intuitively to be such empirically encountered objects. Religions are classifications designed to indicate a distinct kind of institution, experience or practice. Yet religions are spoken of, written about, described, analysed and compared *as though* they are phenomena that can be observed. That religions are not themselves the objects of empirical investigation, but collective acts of the imagination, does not mean that they have no kind of reality.

The same might be said about other collective acts of the imagination, such as institutions – churches for example. What we actually observe are people behaving in certain ways in a certain kind of environment and buildings, and we have few problems in referring to the church at the end of the street, or in saying that the neighbours go to church every day. However, if we claimed to have observed the Universal Church, that would obviously be more problematic, because the Universal Church exists at a much more abstract level. It is an ideological construct which is much more difficult to locate. This does not mean it has no reality as such. Historically the idea of the Universal Church has been given such power that many generations of people have lived and died in the belief that it is a reality. In that sense it *is* a reality. One could say that the Universal Church has been a powerful myth celebrated in the Mass and the anointing of kings, and defended by armies and ecclesiastical courts. But it would be very difficult for anyone to claim to have seen the Universal Church, and to write a description of it would be to write a description of how generations of people have imagined it, including those who have had power in producing authoritative representations of it.

Religion is an even more abstract category, and right from the start there is a problem about the relation between 'religion', 'a religion' and 'religions'. The claim that we have observed and can describe the Universal Church is problematic enough. But to make a similar claim about this family of terms is arguably even more problematic. Religion in English has for centuries (since the Reformation) referred mainly to Christian Truth, especially in the form Our Protestant Faith. To find out the meaning of this complex claim to truth would require consulting a whole range of experts in English, German, Dutch, French and some other languages – theologians, liturgists and church historians, for example. Religion as Protestant Truth was (and by many still is) contrasted with the superstitions of Catholics and other pagans, which I suggest would only have been referred to as 'religion' in an ironic sense. If religion has referred to truth, and in English has been almost always used to refer to Protestant Truth, then any other claims to truth would not have been considered 'religion' in any real sense, since by definition these have been considered to be false. To study 'religion' would therefore be to study Protestant ideology in its historical formations and its claims to truth about the meaning of the world and the ends of human existence. However, what constitutes religion in this sense has always been disputed. Others would argue that Christian Truth is really truth according to Catholic (or Orthodox) theology and practice. To claim to observe or research or describe 'religion' in this sense would be an elusive goal. One could not easily say that 'religion' exists except as a complex history of contested ideas and discourses about Ultimate Truth.

It would also be quite different from the modern idea that one can study 'a religion'. On the above idea of religion as truth, few Christians would have accepted the idea that 'Christianity' is 'a religion'. The idea of 'a religion' implies one of a kind or class of objects of investigation, and this is a modern idea with its own history. There is an important semantic difference between studying Christian Truth and its vast complexity of theological, liturgical and juridical contestation, and studying 'a religion' as one of a kind. For the modern idea of 'a religion' is the classification of 'secular' sociologists, historians and court judges. One would first have to know what to include as 'a religion', and what to exclude. The idea of 'a religion' as one of a class of things would require studying the history of a modern idea and how it came into being historically, and the much wider context of ideas within which it has operated as a system of classification. One would need to be able to give an account of the relation between any particular religion and the general category of religion. This in turn would be to exclude, either implicitly or explicitly, a whole range of claims about truth and a whole range of beliefs and practices and institutions which are deemed to be 'non-religious' or 'secular' in the modern sense, such as political or economic. To do this, one would have to research what certain kinds of authorities have deemed to constitute a religious practice or institution as distinct from a non-religious or secular practice or institution. Such authorities would include the 'scientific study of religions' as an academic discipline since the eighteenth or nineteenth centuries, and the decisions of modern secular courts in many different countries. And since what constitutes a religion and what doesn't is the topic of continual contestation, it is as or more difficult to claim to study 'a religion' as it is to study the older meaning of 'religion'. Both terms operate in different semantic contexts, have a different logic of use, and are inherently contested according to significantly different criteria and by people with different purposes.

Religion, a religion and religions in the plural together form a general modern category or family of categories used for classifying a kind of practice and institution, not something which has any clear, empirical referent which can be observed. Furthermore it is a category that can easily be confused with the older usage of 'religion' as Christian truth, which has also been deeply contested but according to a different system of criteria. Yet in modern discourse the term religion is used as though it is obvious what is meant. Though there is a modern history of debates about the proper definition of religion, many of which are entirely contradictory, few people doubt that religions exist. There are standard lists of religions and world religions. There is a vast publishing industry claiming to offer descriptions of these supposed entities. They are taught in schools and universities. They have been constructed since the late eighteenth century and have increasingly become the objects of empirical knowledge. And religion is a special and distinct area of interest for some academics in IR, sociology and politics.

Religions, while not things that exist in the world as empirical objects of experience, have been imagined in ways that have huge power over all of us. The belief in the existence of religions has become an intuitive item of common sense, and is propagated by a range of powerful agencies such as constitutions, courts, the media, the rhetoric of politicians, and in the theorized research of academics, for example in religious studies, the social sciences and IR. This is still true despite the critical deconstruction of the category especially within religious studies over the last 20 years. The vast academic and non-academic publishing industry on religion and religions still churns out books on the religions of the world such as Hinduism, Buddhism, Judaism, Islam, Christianity, Confucianism, Shinto, Zoroastrianism, African traditional religions, pre-historic religions, religions in Ancient China, Roman religion, Greek religion, or the religion of the Pacific Islanders. The effect of this industry is to generate the illusion, often made theoretically explicit, that religions exist in the world as distinct kinds of things; and that these religions are manifestations of religion itself, a kind of universal essence which incarnates in all human groups, in all languages, at all periods of history and pre-history. The religious essence is also believed to manifest itself in special kinds of experiences and to be detectable in the 'religious' dimensions of life. It is this whole discourse on religion, religions and the religious with which I am critically concerned, and which I argue constitutes a globalizing modern myth with its own ideological work to do. And it is this wider myth that is being taken up and propagated over the last 15 or 20 years by IR and political science.

However, the critique of the category 'religion' leads us inevitably into a critique of all those categories deemed to represent the 'non-religious' secular. There could be no secular 'politics', for example, without 'religion'. Indeed, there could be no secular discipline such as IR without 'religion', a point acknowledged by some of the IR writers discussed in this book. The two categories are parasitic on each other. This is a historical and a conceptual claim about collective imagination. We could not imagine the non-religious secular domains such as 'politics' without the category religion operating as its binary other. Many scholars working in IR, politics and various other secular disciplines may claim to have no interest in religion, or to see it as marginal to what they do. Yet the marginalization of what is imagined to be 'religion' is simultaneously its inclusion by negation. I am arguing that the formation of any secular domain imagined as 'non-religious' is historically dependent on the conceptualization of religion as a distinct and different domain, even where this is unacknowledged, or where the scholars, journalists, lawyers or politicians are simply unaware or uninterested.

The secularity of those scholars who *do not* take an interest in religion is as dependent on the modern category 'religion' as those who do take an interest. However, the claim to be studying religion, or describing it, is obviously necessary for its re-inscription as part of the furniture of our world. When we claim to be researching, studying or describing some religion or other, or some religious experience or aspect of existence, we do so on the implicit or explicit assumption that our object of research is essentially different from 'politics' or from our own research activities. The latter, being imagined as 'secular', are deemed to be essentially different from what we are researching. Religion and politics, religion and the state, or religion and the secular university are typically represented as separate and distinct domains that at certain points come into contact with each other. In these representations, religion and politics, or religion and secular social science, are imagined as having nothing *essentially* to do with each other. When the political scientist studies politics, she does so with the same assumption that politics and the secular state has nothing essentially to do with religion, even though religion might in specific circumstances impinge on politics, and become an issue and even a problem. One frequent variation on this construction, propagated by IR specialists and social scientists, is that when religion and politics get mixed they become volatile and dangerous. But this is the same principle found in constitutions such as the US Constitution. There is the idea that a wall must be constructed to ensure that these distinct substances do not come into collision with each other. They have become essentialized as two different substances with distinct essences that must be kept separate. In the language of the IR specialists reviewed in this book, religion 'returns from exile', or 'resurges' irrationally and fanatically and threatens the calm, rational and only reluctantly violent liberal state.[1]

The argument here is that, historically and conceptually, the idea of religion as a universal essence manifesting in specific religions, and the idea of politics as a distinct, non-religious domain, emerged (in English at least) in the late seventeenth century and did not become powerfully institutionalized until the American and French Revolutions and their respective proclamations of a new world order. But the meanings of the key terms in these proclamations are deeply ambiguous, for the revolutionaries were appropriating older Christian discourses of religion as Christian truth and transforming them in the context of a new Euro-American world order. The new terms and meanings proclaimed in these seminal moments were hotly and violently contested, but gradually they won the day and became the basis for the contemporary globalizing myth of religion and secular domains. The continuation of the same words 'religion' and 'secular' from the old regime to the new one has acted to disguise the fundamental transformations in the meaning and typical use of these terms, and has facilitated the illusion of an essential continuity. One deeply embedded assumption made by historians and many others is that the modern distinction between religion and the secular is a continuation of a distinction that has always existed in 'Christianity'. I shall argue that this is a fallacy, a backward projection of a new distinction which was probably first articulated in the late seventeenth century and which has come to constitute a fundamental constituent of modernity. Even 'Christianity' is a reified modern invention that is continually recycled as a historical essence.

One way or another, 'religion' has become a special kind of attribute, practice or institution essentially different from non-religious ones. In this sense 'religions' and 'world religions' are modern inventions. It is in this sense that it seems relevant to point out that no-one has ever seen a religion, any more than they have seen a 'state' or a 'nation' or a 'market'. This is also true about a large range of other general categories, and without them we would not be able to say very much at all. But categories of the kind I focus on in this book have become invested with great ideological weight in modern Anglophone theories about the world. They have been invested with misplaced concreteness. They lend themselves to myth. We act *as though* they are in the natural and inescapable order of things. These categories of modern ideology stand over and above us as though they have an independent existence, and as such have become alienated from our own collective productivity. Much of the globalizing Anglo-American world is organized according to these imagined entities or domains.

'Religion' and its proclaimed separation from the non-religious 'secular state', for example, is a matter of constitutional and juridical importance. The distinctions between religion and politics, or between religion and science, are fundamental to modern institutions and practices. Such terms have been elevated in significance beyond merely abstract categories without which we could not speak or write, into fundamental beliefs about the world. Globalized categories such as 'religion', 'politics' and 'nation state' have become the reified objects of the contemporary world order. These are more than abstract categories, but powerful rhetorical constructs or even myths that we believe in. These categories are invested with powers and indeed define powers of great historical and contemporary significance. In this book I want to show how 'religion' and 'religions' are invented or re-invented by a sample of writers in International Relations. Some of these writers unquestionably believe in 'religion' and 'religions'. Others see that religions are modern inventions, and attempt to question them as such. But a key point is to notice how the invention of religion and religions is also the invention of the non-religious secular domains of natural reason that constitute our common sense experience of the world.

Religion is generally understood as a universal and distinct kind of human practice and institution. Though it is frequently (though not always) defined by 'belief in the supernatural', religion is generally seen as a natural aspect of human experience and action. Also, religion in general has some problematic relationship to religions in particular. These 'religions' have been set up in modern discourse as things that exist in the world, things which belong to a general class but each with their own essential characteristics. These essential characteristics can be listed and compared with the essential characteristics of other similar things (Hinduism, Buddhism, Christianity, Confucianism, Shinto, Sikhism, Roman religion, Greek religion, Native American Religion and so on). I shall suggest that these are all modern inventions that have been transformed through the power of rhetoric into distinct figments of the imagination. They serve both specific and more general ideological requirements.

The invention of religion and religions has also been the modern invention of the non-religious 'secular' domains such as the nation state, politics and economics. These domains are mutually parasitic, and we could have no modern idea of a non-religious state (for instance) without the idea of a distinct and separate domain of 'religion'. For example, imagined as a specific religion, 'Hinduism' is an idealized, colonial construct that masks the actualities of power relations in colonial and postcolonial India. As a member of the universal class of 'religions', Hinduism serves as a myth that simultaneously constructs the myth of the secular state.

'Politics' is widely assumed to be an obvious feature of the ancient and modern worlds in all cultures everywhere. Politics is ubiquitous, and to claim that politics is a modern invention will also seem counter-intuitive. However, I would suggest that, typically, politics as an Anglophone category has two significantly different modes of deployment. In one it refers specifically to a distinct domain of non-religious rational action separate from another domain, 'religion'. This usage emerged only in the late seventeenth century, and 'politics' seems to have been invented around that time as a word. Yet politics is also used in the far more general sense of 'power'. As such, everything can be political. If politics merely means power – and it is often ambiguously used in this way – then historical and ethnographic universality is acquired but at the expense of specificity and meaningfulness. Power in human relations is probably one of the few genuine universals, like hunger or fear; but as such it carries little analytical weight. Yet, in modern rhetorical constructions, 'politics' has also been invested with the different and more specific meaning of non-religious rational action. In modern usage, 'politics' is 'secular', and therefore stands as separated from 'religion'. The predominant modern usage of 'politics' refers to a domain of rational, problem-solving action separate and distinct from the irrationality of religious superstition. In the *imaginaire* of modernity, if religion and politics mix, then the result is thought to be unstable and dangerous, leading to fanaticism and terrorism. Therefore in modern discourse 'religion' ought not to be involved in power, which is the proper domain of rational politics.

This ambiguity in the meaning of 'politics', either 'power' in a very general sense or power in the more specific sense of secular, provides the category with a flexible, ideological deployment. The modern assumption – that religion in its real nature is (and therefore ought to be) uninterested in power/politics and merely concerns itself with salvation in some 'other world' – is tacitly projected backwards into the past and horizontally into other cultures. Thus kings are secular and non-religious but priests are religious – a modern fabrication that bears no relation to historical evidence – and ideally excluded from the power structure. If priests are, or have been, involved in power, then that is an over-extension of their legitimate interest.

I am not a trained historian, but I cannot find a sustained discourse on 'politics' in English in the sense of a domain of rational action separated from 'religion' before 1680. Probably more expert historians than me can prove me wrong. But if I am right, then we have an extraordinary and misleading flexibility in the category 'politics', on the one hand as a distinct domain separated from another domain called 'religion', and on the other hand a vague reference to power which exists universally between humans. The rhetorical illusion generated by this ambiguity is that the modern distinction between two domains, religion and politics, is inherent to all human groups at all periods of history.[2] This Anglophone discourse not only cognitively colonizes the non-Anglophone world through globalization but also colonizes the Anglophone or more generally the Europhone past.

This book, as with my previous published work, is not an attack on those theorized practices, commonly classified as 'religious', which many people hold to encompass what is truly valuable in our personal and collective lives.[3] It is a critique of the modern practice of classifying 'religious' as against 'secular' domains as though these categories are part of the order of things. It is a critique of the religion–secular binary and its function in sustaining the myths of modernity. It is a claim that such a classificatory practice is itself ideological. By classifying a specific range of theorized practices as religions, faiths or spiritualities,[4] it thereby exiles them and simultaneously constructs the domain of the secular as in accordance with natural reason. One of the unintended effects of these acts of classification is that they marginalize a range of different ways of representing moral and metaphysical dimensions of existence into an irrational or at best non-rational sub-category, a hived-off basket of other-worldly fantasies, while simultaneously legitimating another range of representations such as politics, economics and the nation state as inevitably in accord with 'natural reason' and common sense. The kinds of collective and personal moral vision thus classified as 'religions' and 'spiritu-alities' become effectively emasculated and cordoned off from the public space and confined to the realms of private 'faith' in tacit distinction from the hard realities of factual science and rational secular politics. In this way the metaphysical assumptions, acts of faith and value commitments underlying secular domains tend to be relatively hidden from scrutiny. Secular institutions and the natural rationality that supposedly legitimates them stand over against us as the common-sense reality, the natural order of things, the way the world is.

It is frequently held that the separation of religion and politics originated historically in the second half of the seventeenth century as a movement in favour of toleration, and when this separation is considered at all it is still often legitimated in contemporary society in this way. Toleration is indeed an important virtue. But I shall argue at various points in this book that, while there is some historical truth in this narrative of origins, it is exaggerated. The idea of religion as a distinct and separate category of practices arose in part and initially as a tool of the Christian administration of colonized subjects, and became increasingly entrenched through the emergence of new class interests as a way of legitimating not only scientific knowledge but also new concepts of ownership, new forms of labour and productivity, and new concepts of rationality. This imagined separation was not only about toleration for a new emerging class of entrepreneurs and industrialists, but also about the needs of colonial rule.[5] These were presumably connected, and it would be a mistake in my view to see toleration only as an issue internal to Europe. Christian Europe was subjected to change through the processes of overseas colonization as much as were the overseas colonies. One product was the invention of Christianity as 'a religion', a thoroughly modern idea projected back in the mythical reconstruction of our own collective past. Another product was 'political economy' or the science of economics, which represents itself as the description of real and natural forces in the world – the non-religious and factual. This is also the emergence of a supposedly essential distinction between faith and knowledge, between the natural and the supernatural, or between hard science and metaphysical belief.

I will argue in the final chapter that Marx's critique of political economy is still of fundamental importance to the demystification of modern ideology. This book is partly an experiment in applying critical Marxist theories of mystification and alienation to belief in 'religion' and 'religions'. Marx did not do this. When he critiqued religion as mystifying and alienating, it was almost always the Christian churches and church-states, and the particular myths that sustained them, that he had in mind, and their function in legitimizing the feudal order and the bourgeois capitalist order. Marxists have tried to apply similar analyses to other so-called 'religions' such as Buddhism, Islam, Hinduism, or Confucianism, and so on. I want to distinguish what I am doing in this book by looking critically at the modern belief in the existence of 'religions' as such and in general, and thus at the parasitic other of 'religion', the secular. My attempt to deconstruct the myth of religion and religions is equally an attempt to deconstruct the myth of the secular. These two are joined at the hip, and constitute a single, two-faced category carrying a message that says 'we are essentially different'. Belief in 'religion' and 'religions' as objects of secular knowledge (and by extension of control and even suppression) is shared as much by Marxists as by non-Marxists.

Therefore my analysis, which is indebted to Marx in significant ways, does not conform to the usual Marxist path of analysis, because I shift attention away from the ideological function of Christian churches, church-states and the myths they propagate, and their Buddhist, Hindu, or Muslim presumed equivalents, to the ideological function of the whole mythical discourse on religions in general. In general, the existence of religions is not itself normally treated as a myth or even as a problem. Religions are thought of as complex phenomena that include a mythical aspect or dimension. Buddhism, Islam or Sikhism, for example, are usually assumed to contain myths or even tacitly to be mythological constructions of the world; but the *descriptions* of these phenomena by secular scholars are taken as factual rather than mythical and derived from empirical observation rather than 'faith'. We 'know' that religions exist because we observe them, describe them, analyse them, compare them, praise them or denounce them. But what we do as secular people has nothing essentially to do with religion. Religious studies and the social scientific study of religion, for example, are widely assumed to be non-theological, empirical, secular disciplines. Most Marxists, who think of themselves as secular social scientists or economists, share this belief. There is a Marxist tradition of analysing the ideological function of specific 'religions' such as Buddhism, Confucianism, Islam or so-called African religions in legitimizing political or economic power; as such they are treated as specific kinds of ideology, distinct from secular ideologies. Such and such is a religion, as distinct from a secular ideology, even though they share similar functions. In contrast, I am analysing the very idea of religion and religions, and yet borrowing from Marx to do that. So I could say that I am refocusing the object of the Marxist analysis away from particular religions to the discourse about religions as such. And I want to show that this discourse is itself a myth, not *essentially* different from any other myth, with important ideological work to do in the legitimation of the 'secular'.

Hopefully, it may be clearer to the reader that the ideology that mystifies us is not the invention of religion and religions as such, but the religion–secular binary. The secular domains and their supposed essential difference from religion and religions are an integral part of the myth. The invention of religions has facilitated the invention of natural reason that transforms modern rhetorical constructs like the rationality and inevitability of capitalism and 'politics' into common sense. The mythological nature of our belief in self-regulating markets, self-maximizing individuals and private property has been mystically transformed into the inherent nature of things, the real world of facts and rational decision-making. These myths, which have been invented by largely male elites with specific interests at specific historical moments, have become transformed into a dominant and globalizing view of the world that appears to us as inevitable and incontestable.

My argument, however, is derived not only from Marx, but from other sources too. One source is an ironic one. It is the observation that Marxism as a tradition could be (and sometimes has been) seen as a religion itself, despite the claims made by Lenin and many other Marxists that Marxism is a scientific analysis of history and economics. There is a strong resemblance between Marxism and Christianity, a point argued for example by Bertrand Russell in his *History of Western Philosophy*. Though Marxism is sometimes referred to in religious studies books as a 'pseudo-religion', 'quasi-religion' or 'religion-like phenomenon', not many Marxists would see it as such, and many such as Lenin have viewed it as secular science and as the foundation of the secular socialist state.

But I want to extend this idea to the observation that *liberal capitalism* and its theorization by liberal economists is itself very similar to what is widely thought of as a religion or a religious ideology.[6] Liberal capitalism and liberal economic theory are rarely referred to as a religion, but on the contrary are hardly seen as an ideology at all. Capitalism is generally assumed to be part of the 'natural' order of things, and secular scientific economists would see what they do as essentially different from what theologians do. Of these three – Marxism, Christianity and secular capitalism, only Christianity is normally classified as 'a religion'. Yet all three have strong resemblances. For example, they all offer a final resolution to the problems of human existence. They are all significantly founded on metaphysical beliefs that are not derivable from empirical observation. They can all be seen as *soteriologies* based on acts of faith, that is, as doctrines of human liberation from a condition of ignorance, suffering or lack of true freedom and self-realization. In this way I want to question the supposed essential distinction between 'religion' and the modern world of global capital, the nation state and the 'secular' social sciences. The whole range of human practices and institutions are better thought of in terms of overlapping resemblances, similarities and dissimilarities in their characteristics. The idea that all the practices and institutions of the world can be classified into this Anglophone (or more widely Europhone) *either–or* religion–secular binary is an astonishingly implausible idea. The real task is to try to understand how such an idea can ever have gained ground and become so important in the definition of modernity.

Another source of my approach is the anomalies in the classification of what counts as a religion and what does not, and the problem of defining religion.[7] I go into this issue in greater detail in other chapters. It needs to be born in mind that I began in religious studies and so I came at the problem from the 'religion' side of the binary, and was for a long time unconscious that the problems I encountered with the category of religion from within the field of the study of religion could equally be approached from the other side of the binary division, say from the point of view of the secular study of politics or IR, or from the point of view of constitutional history and the arbitrary interpretations by courts, in countries as diverse as India or the USA or France, as to what does and what does not constitute an essentially religious belief or practice. To briefly indicate just one example of such an anomaly, traditional practices such as yoga or vipassana meditation are normally classified as religious and as parts of the 'religions' Hinduism and Buddhism. They are taken to be characterized by faith in unseen forces or entities or states of being such as 'pranayama', 'kundalini', 'karma', Brahman, gods and goddesses, Buddhas and Bodhisattvas, and unconditioned insight (mukti, moksha, nirvana, satori). Yet people who are experts in yoga and meditation say they are based on empirical observation and experiment. They are in the first place *practices*, and these practices confirm experimentally the claims about their truth. They are 'look and see' philosophies. But in this sense they arguably share more with the empirical sciences than with Christian faith in the Resurrection, the Virgin Birth, or the Trinitarian God. That experienced yogis can stop their own hearts beating or can be buried alive for a week without fear or damage to their mental or physical health are taken by their practitioners as empirically observable signs that their theories of human nature are true. To say that these are not true science and that therefore they are acts of religious faith is a piece of arbitrary dogmatism based on a simplistic and unsubtle binary opposition imposed from outside.

This is merely one example of many which can be cited from my own and other people's research. Another example, again taken from India, is whether 'caste' and untouchability are religious or merely social institutions. This was one of the earliest perplexities I had in my studies of the so-called 'religion' of Hinduism. It was not until much more recently that I came to realize that this is a problem which Indian courts have been struggling with for several decades, a problem which they in turn inherited from the Anglophone classification systems of the British colonial administrators. This is one example of the more general problem courts have had, in countries as different as the USA and India, in determining what constitutes a secular as distinct from a religious practice.

I have now come to realize that the history of court decisions in India (to continue with the example with which I am more familiar) on relations between 'religion' and the secular state runs side-by-side with a vigorous public debate among the intellectual elite about the meaning of 'secular' and 'secularism'. So contested is this term that some participants have argued that secularism in India has its own meaning and cannot be equated with 'Western' secularism. Some Hindutva theorists have argued that much of what has been included in the religion Hinduism is really not religious at all but secular, the traditional customs of the Hindu nation, and that the Westernized 'secularism' of Nehru and its legacy in Congress is a pseudo-secularism. These debates show that what constitutes religion and what constitutes secular domains such as politics or 'society' in India are so hotly contested that it makes no sense to deploy these categories as though they usefully describe any stable realities in the world. These are widely disputed modern colonial constructions that do not seem to translate well into Indian (or other non-European) languages.

Constitutions simply announce the nation state and its separation from, and relation to, religion and religions. This announcement or proclamation provides the rhetorical context for a discourse on 'freedom of religion' as a right, and non-interference by religions in the affairs of the state. The courts then have the task of deciding the cut-off points in specific cases. But the courts' decisions are largely arbitrary and based on highly imprecise criteria that change over time. And besides, there are good arguments for claiming that the secular courts themselves are not essentially different from religious institutions. The resemblances between what are typically classified as 'religious' institutions and the sacralizing procedures of secular courts in their pursuit of the realization of justice are strong. I have argued elsewhere, and will argue again in this book, that there are so many anomalies in the distinction between religious and non-religious institutions, practices, and experiences that the whole discourse becomes too problematic and loses its power to convince.

Why, then, do we continue to assert this distinction, and to embed it into so many of our theoretical constructs and everyday beliefs about the world? What does it mean to claim, as IR writers are doing, that religion has returned from exile and is resurging? The binary distinction between religious and secular is powerfully institutionalized in universities and parliaments and constitutions. But what kind of narrative can we construct which provides us with a plausible reason for its successful institutionalization in the first place? This question has to be answered at least in part by historical contextualization. But I have already suggested its ideological function in constituting modernity. By inventing a distinct, ideally privatized, sub-rational domain of 'religions' based on belief in the 'supernatural', or in another unseen 'spiritual' dimension, we have simultaneously been able to invent an equally imaginary 'real world' of natural reason which is assumed to underpin the material and factual domains of the state, politics and economics. This is a largely masculinist invention of a tough-minded realism where solutions to practical problems are sought through confrontation with the facts, logical analysis, strict measurement, rational bureaucratic organization and negotiation; a domain arrived at through progressive recognition of the world 'as it really is'. In this way the enchantments of the modern world – the upward march of Progress towards Self-Realization through mastery of Nature, the liberal Secular State as inherently peace-loving and democratic, Individuals as self-maximizing entrepreneurs endlessly raising all living standards through harmonies of self-regulating markets, Private Property as the natural condition of rational living, and Scientific Paradigms such as evolutionary biology as descriptions of the way the world actually is in itself (what Kant referred to as the dogmatic delusion) get transformed into unchallengeable realities and common places. In contrast, powerful competing ethical and metaphysical paradigms have been mass-labelled and emasculated as religions, or associated through propaganda with some innate propensity to irrational violence. Many economists, who themselves work with mythical postulates masquerading as hard-headed, factual, empirical science, would be outraged by the idea that what they do is not *essentially* different from what 'religious' folk do.

The invention of the fantasy world of religion, and its function in transforming a historically-specific secular ideology into the inescapable nature of things, has parallels in the invention of 'tradition' and its function in the invention of modernity. Like religion and the secular, tradition and modernity are the same two-faced coin. The illusions of modernity such as the march of progress are parasitic on the simultaneous invention of tradition.

My critique of discourses on religion is also partly derived from the academic postcolonial and orientalist critique of the colonial constructions of world religions. Not much postcolonial discourse critiques its own secular positionality, and much of this kind of writing continues to deploy the category religion with little critical consciousness of its parasitic relation to the myth of secularism. Yet at the same time there is now a considerable literature which argues that religions such as 'Hinduism', 'Buddhism' and 'African tribal religions' are the reified inventions of missionaries, colonial administrators and European scholars, albeit in cooperation with indigenous colonial subjects, usually a section of the literate male elite of the colonized countries.[8] My own addition to this observation is that these complex processes of inventing 'religions' as objects of secular knowledge has simultaneously been the invention of the idea of the non-religious secular in its various formulations, including belief in disinterested secular scholarship itself, as though secular scholarship is itself objectively factual and non-ideological. Though I cannot here go deeply into the postcolonial literature, it seems fairly clear that Orientalism is characterized typically by the opposition between *our* secular rationality and modernity as against *their* traditional, religious irrationality.

Belief in these non-religious secular domains is not *essentially* different to belief in religion, but is ideologically constructed *as if* it is. This indicates the expression used in the sub-title to this section – *religion is not a standalone category*. It exists in binary opposition to the category of the secular. They are mutually parasitic, in much the same way as 'supernatural' and 'natural', 'spirit' and 'matter', or 'faith' and 'knowledge' are mutually parasitic categories. Religion and the secular are really two sides of the same categorical coin, and whenever we claim knowledge of religions we are engaged in an ideological practice which simultaneously and tacitly asserts the natural rationality of the secular.

Some readers will have noticed that, given what I say about the ideological nature of belief in secular objectivity, then my own position becomes problematic, not least because I am employed in a secular university and receive my salary from secular funding agents. Where do I stand? What are my own commitments? This is a fair question and in principle an important issue, and I try to deal with this partly in Chapter 4, which sketches my own research background; and partly in the final chapter. But, in the first place, I would only say here that the critical deconstruction of the myth of modernity and its dependence on the religion–secular binary is an argument like any other argument, and will stand or fall depending on its reception by a readership.

But there is fairly obviously an intention to raise some moral issues about our responsibilities as academics, whether we work in International Relations, the Social Sciences, Politics, or Religious Studies. One part of the argument concerns the value and purposes of the vast accumulations of secular knowledge recorded in the never-ending proliferation of books and journals which we academics compete to produce. How does all this knowledge production improve the quality of life, virtuous living, or further the ends of justice? Or are these issues irrelevant? Do our universities, in their search for fame, prestige, money, students and glittering careers, do anything worth doing at all, apart from re-inscribing the categories of the status quo? Do we really believe that the radically unequal current distribution of the world's resources is inevitable, and anyway not really our business? Is there or is there not a connection, however indirect it might appear, between our discoursing on religion and religions, on the one hand, for example the facile linkage of 'religion' with irrational terrorism; and on the other the use of economic theory to justify the brutal conditions of sweatshop labour, not much different from slavery, operated by vastly wealthy capitalist corporations and corrupt elites?[9] The arguments underlying this book do not definitively reveal such a linkage, but raise the subterranean connection of religion as a classification with the naturalization of capital and economic theory. I do at least hope to encourage a more explicit debate about the relationship between world disorder and our functions as teachers, knowledge-producers and competitive seekers after funding opportunities.

To put it bluntly, I do believe that the current ethos of Western universities, the way they are funded, the values of market competitiveness which they increasingly promote, the use of profitability as the main criterion for judging the value of academic achievement, are wrong. But it is more than this. Universities, on my argument, have become (perhaps they always were?) ideological state apparati, agencies for the relatively indirect and disguised legitimation of the state, which has as one of its most pressing functions the management of corporate capital. Therefore, according to the views expressed in this book, universities should be a sacrosanct space for reasoned democratic dissent without fear of a managerial class whose own ideological and ethical inclinations may be closer to the views of a commercial corporation.

These possible connections between power and moral accountability of academic knowledge production seem even more directly pressing in the case of a discipline such as International Relations. This is not a personal matter about the moral and intellectual integrity of individuals in a specific academic discipline. I have no reason to doubt that personal standards of moral integrity are as high there as anywhere else, and it is certainly not my concern to set myself up as any kind of moral exemplar. It is an institutional and structural matter. These ideological commitments, according to my arguments, gain their efficacy because they are not fully conscious or disclosed. The production of discourses on religion appears innocent and disinterested, as though we are only describing and analysing the facts. But IR as a discipline, its journals, its theories, its senior personnel, are closely connected to powerful agencies and presumably has far more influence on the way people in important national and international agencies construe the world and conduct policy. I cannot help assuming, therefore, that even those academics from the discipline of IR who do not agree with my arguments will see that the issues they raise, for example about the uses of 'religion' for classification purposes, and the way that we represent other people and their so-called 'religions', have significant implications in terms of the uses and misuses of power.

Even in the event that these ideas (which are of course not mine alone, yet are still very much a minority position) should influence debates already taking place, they are likely to change little outside the critical self-reflexivity of some sections of the intellectual community. The powerful agents of ideological reproduction will presumably continue. Furthermore, there is nothing to 'put in its place' such as a ready-made counter-ideology. My proposal is anyway an attempt to deconstruct 'politics' as a supposed domain of non-religious rational action, not to enter into that domain and extend it. In that sense my project is a negative one. 'Politics' is part of our problem. Unlike in the time of Lenin and the cadres who founded the Russian Socialist party, and who were able and willing to deploy and organize an anti-capitalist tradition of theorizing and establish a socialist state through revolution, no such situation exists today. The idea of a secular socialist state is as vulnerable to critique as any other kind of secular invention. If there is going to occur any kind of transformation in collective consciousness, it can only be the result of quiet and non-confrontational subversion, and the systematic critical deconstruction of the categories and discourses which mystify the contemporary world [dis]order. That is a moral commitment, not a 'political' programme. There is no reason why universities should not be sites for a critical, democratic debate on our own institutionalized self-images and self-legitimations; the purposes of our 'research' and the accumulation of secular knowledge; the real or supposed innocence of our work; and its intended or unintended consequences.

## Notes

1.    See Cavanaugh (2009), for a powerful and extended critique, including some good historiography concerning the modern invention of religion. See also Cavanaugh's essay in Fitzgerald 2007b. Germane to this whole discussion is the influential work of Russell T. McCutcheon; see for example McCutcheon, '"They Licked the Platter Clean": On the Co-Dependency of the Religious and the Secular', *Method and Theory in the Study of Religion*, 19, 173–199

2.    I have discussed this issue in Fitzgerald 2007a and given examples of how this confusion of different logical deployments of 'politics' operates in the texts of historians and others.

3.    I was recently accused of this at a conference, by someone who clearly never read any of my publications. I had a very similar reception from a political scientist when I suggested at a seminar that 'politics' is a modern colonial invention as much as 'religion'.

4.    I agree very much with the arguments of Jeremy Carrette and Richard King in their powerful book *Selling Spirituality: the Silent Takeover of Religion* (2005). One crucial point for them and me is the following: if, as they and I argue, capitalism, as imagined by neoliberal dogma, is not essentially different from what would typically be classified as a

religion, then where has the 'secular' disappeared? Is the production of secular universities essentially different from a form of ritual? And hasn't 'religion' become such a universal container that it loses its point?

5.  See Cavanaugh (2009) for some additional historical analysis.
6.  More recently Robert Nelson (2001) has argued that economics is a religion, in his *Economics as Religion*. However, see Cavanaugh's (2009: 108/9) critique of Nelson. See also Carrette and King (2005).
7.  I have given many examples of the problems of defining religion and connected issues in *The Ideology of Religious Studies* (2000).
8.  I cannot give full details here of this literature since it would take me too far afield and take up too much time and space. Two books that can take the reader into the issues quickly are King (1999) and Bloch *et al.* (2010).
9.  Consider for example John Pilger's documentary on *The New Rulers of the World*, available online at http://www.youtube.com/results?search_query =john+pilger+new+rulers+of+the+world&aq=1/. This documentary is not concerned ostensibly with 'religion'. It is solely my argument that the invention and discoursing on religion and religions is a constituent ideological factor in legitimating a view of the world that considers such mass exploitation for the purposes of 'profit at any cost' the inevitable result of market forces and 'naturally' self-maximizing individuals. When Muslim or other groups band together to oppose this they are labeled as 'religious fanatics' or irrational 'religious nationalists'.

# Chapter 2

## *Summary of the Contents of the Chapters*

The tendency towards mythological representation of 'religion' is attested by two notably different images of 'religion' in public discourse. One is that religion is essentially barbarous, violent and irrational, a malign agent in the world, causing conflict and mayhem and threatening the essentially peace-loving and reasonable nature of the non-religious secular state. The face of this masked construct has been well exposed by William Cavanaugh in his *The Myth of Religious Violence* (2009). Is violence and terror the true face of 'religion'? Or is it a mask hiding a deeper identity inside? For the other image is that 'religion' is [or ought to be] essentially peace-loving, non-violent, non-political, concerned with the inner spiritual life and the other world. Religion has nothing to do with power. Religion is kind, gentle, non-political and non-profit-making. Religion is a matter of personal faith and piety, essentially separated from the non-religious rough-and-tumble of practical politics and economics. The ambiguity of this two-faced imaginary begs for historical clarification. The images themselves are important. But even more fundamental is the assumption lying behind it that 'religion' could be either violent or peaceful, as though religion is some clearly identifiable agent in the world. Here I give a summary of the contents of the chapters, so that the reader can quickly get a sense of what the book is about.

In chapter 3 I introduce the reader to an attempt in international relations studies to statistically prove that 'religion' has a special relation to irrational violence. I am using the term international relations quite widely, because it is so closely related to the social sciences and politics, which themselves have wide scope. One of my concerns has been the way data are gathered, classified and interpreted in order to prove statistically that religion has a special relationship to violence. On close inspection, though, we find the category 'religion' and its supposed distinction from, say, 'ethnicity' or secular politics or secular nationalism, to be virtually empty of any clear content. Yet databanks that classify and interpret in this way are located in prestigious universities, and funded by US State agencies. Theories about so-called religious violence based on these databases are presumably used to make informed decisions on homeland security and foreign policy. Through this intellectually unsound route, secular agencies and the military can justify their own violence on the pretext that they are defending us against irrational religious bigots. Standing large over this whole process is the myth of 'religion' as a diabolical agent in the world, threatening the natural order and peace of natural (secular) reason and enlightened self-interest.

Chapter 4 provides a brief sketch of the intellectual trajectory of my own research background as a way of explaining more clearly to the reader how I arrived at the present arguments and method of analysis. There is no presumption that my own personal experiences have any interest in themselves, and I am not interested in contributing to the self-serving aspects of autobiography. However, understanding where a writer comes from intellectually can be useful in helping the reader orient herself or himself to the purpose of the argument. This seems especially true in a book which is seeking engagement with specialists in International Relations and Politics, as well as Religious Studies, and who would therefore not necessarily be familiar with the kind of research I have been engaged in.

Chapter 5 provides a fuller introduction to the argument that lies behind the book, an argument that gets more treatment in the final chapter, Chapter 11. These chapters all have the cumulative effect of clarifying my own theoretical and moral commitments.

Chapter 6: I begin an analysis of specific texts by identifying the underlying binary structure in Christopher Hitchens's book *God is Not Great: How Religion Poisons Everything* (Hitchens 2007). I critique this text early in the book because I want to draw attention to the way in which the same ideological structure of the religion–secular dichotomy, which I will go on to analyse in more serious academic production, also informs populist writing. By trading on the rhetorical force which 'religion' unleashes in the popular imagination, Hitchens achieves various goals. One is to legitimate his own rational superiority and civility as a secular devotee over those barbarous others he designates 'religious'. Another may be to ingratiate himself with his US hosts (Hitchens was born and educated in the UK but now lives in the USA). I do not blame Hitchens for wanting to be rich and famous if that is a motive. It is the lack of generosity towards those he uses for his own self-promotion that bothers me. It is the exploitation and popularization of powerful and prejudicial clichés that drown out the voices of those he classifies as religious barbarians that is my concern.

I have argued in my previous work on English historical texts (Fitzgerald 2007a) that through the history of Protestant rhetoric there runs a discourse concerning the rationality and civility of Protestant nations as against the irrational barbarity of non-Christian heathens. This attitude has for centuries been taken by missionaries into 'the field' – the field often meaning a people subjugated, colonized and 'civilized' by a superior invading power. This self-representation of civility and rationality as against the irrationality and backwardness of the natives has in many ways been adopted into the rhetoric of Euro-Americans who represent themselves as 'secular'. It is a binary construction that has operated throughout the era of colonialism and played a significant role in colonial classifications of the practices and institutions of subordinated peoples. It has been strongly linked to the superior rationality of European technology, government, law, language, philosophy, concepts of self, dress, diet, house design, and every other aspect of life. It has also frequently and explicitly been linked to modes of production and consumption, and the superior rationality of capitalism and 'free' markets. Hitchens is obviously not a Protestant Christian, but his contempt for those he deems to be 'religious' (whether they willingly accept that classification or not) and his idealization of US secularism, follow very similar contours. In a sense he is continuing the traditions of missionary proselytizing, whether of those converting others to Christianity, or to a specific ideology of trade, markets and wage labour, or to the belief that Europeans are more evolved, developed, rational and progressive. In all these cases a number of binaries are operating: rational–irrational; civilized–barbarous; reality–myth; genuine knowledge–wild faith.

I anticipate that I will be criticised for assuming that a single populist text by a self-publicist tells us anything significant about serious academic discourse. On the contrary, my point is that it is serious academic commitment to the same binaries under the sober appearance of neutral scholarly analysis that legitimates the wider and more populist representations of which the book in question is an example. When academics innocently recycle discourses on 'religion' as though this is a harmless and disinterested category, under the assumption that they are engaged in the production of objective description and analysis, they are inadvertently legitimating much more dangerous rhetoric of the kind found in Hitchens's widely selling book.

**Chapter 7:** I examine what, on the face of it, looks like a very different kind of text, Eli Berman's *Radical, Religious and Violent: The New Economics of Terrorism* (Berman 2009). The first point, which every reader will be compelled to notice, is the association in the title of 'religious', violent' and terrorism'. Though Berman has a more serious and interesting argument to make than Hitchens, the title alone ineluctably summons the suspicion that the author wishes to cash in on the emotive impact of such associations, thus promoting self-publicity and linking himself to media sensationalism.

Berman is an economist and proud of his association with the distinguished Chicago School of Economics. He believes that, as an economist and social scientist, he can offer compelling reasons why *religious* radical groups are more successful at violence and terror than non-religious ones. He provides an ingenious argument to account for this, and his book contains considerable and interesting research data. The problem is the way the data are classified in order to convince the reader that 'religion' really is a dangerous something in the world, while the secular remains blameless, natural and transparent.

In this work, non-violent religious radicals are exemplified by such groups as the Amish, Hutterites, Mennonites and ultra-Orthodox Jews. Violent religious radicals are exemplified by such groups as Hezbollah, al-Qaeda, Taliban, Hamas and the Mardi Army. Berman also discusses or mentions some other violent groups, including 'secular' ones such the Basque Separatists (ETA), the National Liberation Army and the Revolutionary Armed Forces (FARC) in Colombia, the Shining Path in Peru, the Kurdistan Workers Party (PKK) in Turkey, and the Liberation Tigers of Tamil Elam (LTTE) in Sri Lanka.

Berman says he hopes his analysis might be useful for democratic secular governments and their security agencies in their fight against terror. It leads him to make some specific policy proposals about the best way to disarm these groups, reduce their influence and win over the local populations that 'harbour' them. In this way, resistance to the truths of secular capitalism can be reduced. Some of his arguments are based on statistics provided by the US State Department. Presumably he is therefore using the same official classifications that they use to determine what counts as 'religious' and what as 'secular'.

Berman fails to discuss in any comprehensive way why so many groups, violent or peaceful, whether classified as religious or secular or Islamicist, with different histories and ideological self-representations, are so strongly opposed to mainstream consumer capitalist society and its agencies. Berman identifies a whole range of groups in different parts of the world that, though distinct at the doctrinal level, share a collective desire to distance themselves from mainstream US capitalist market values, and that share many significant organizational attributes. But we therefore need to understand and assess the commonalities and differences in their critiques of main-stream consumer capitalism. Taking their reasons seriously means reviewing our own standpoint as academics who, while we strive for impartiality and accurate representation, yet are located in the career structures of secular universities, and our salaries and research financed by the secular state, by the markets, and by special interests. Yet it is the principles and practices of the dominant mainstream against which many of these groups apparently stand opposed. It seems to me to be one of the major lacunae of Berman's book, that the secular which he himself represents as an economist and social scientist remains a simple given, a largely hidden substratum outside the range of critical enquiry, rather than itself a competing ideology of global power against which these other groups stand with varying degrees of tension. He never, for example, draws direct and sustained attention to the massive violence of secular states in pursuit of public or private corporate interests.

The lack of analysis of the supposedly reasonable and peace-loving secular state, or of the superior secular ground of rationality on which Berman

himself assumes he stands as an economist and social scientist, is facilitated by a lack of serious attention to the problem of demarcating the
'religious'. The central argument, that it is specifically *religious* groups as
distinct from *secular* ones that are especially successful at violence, presupposes a convincing distinction between the meanings of these classifications.
But Berman fails to make any convincing grounds for the distinction. His
unanalysed, theoretically naïve binary opposition between the religious/
theological/spiritual aspects of existence and the non-religious/material/
secular ones – virtually identical to Hitchens in this respect – is built into
his descriptions and summaries from the beginning, but never addressed
in any convincing way. Though more scholarly than Hitchens's, and with
some interesting and sympathetic analysis of Ultra-Orthodox Jews and other
groups, Berman's book exemplifies the rhetorical construction of 'religion'
as a dangerous and irrational agent in the world, destructively set against
the blameless normality of the secular in its various manifestations either as
capital, the nation state or the academy.

The two books discussed so far, though of significance to International
Relations, were written by authors who are not specifically located in IR
departments. I now go on to consider several books and papers published in
a more formal sense under the auspices of IR and Politics, and whose authors
are located in IR and Politics departments.

**Chapter 8**: I analyse the introduction and some of the individual contributions by different authors in a book edited by Fabio Petito and Pavlos
Hatzopolous, *Religion in International Relations: The Return from Exile*
(Petito and Hatzopolous 2003), and also in a special edition of the IR journal
*Millennium* (Petito and Hatzopolous 2000), edited by the same authors and
titled 'Religion and International Relations'. In both the book and the journal
special edition, the editors and at least some of their contributors try to
show that the modern formation of IR as a discipline has been historically
dependent on the exclusion or marginalization of religion which, since 9/11
and after a period of absence, or at least of reasonably good behaviour, has
once more returned from 'exile'.

I do not have the space to analyse all the contributions to this book. My
main focus is on the editors' introduction which frames the problematic of the
book; and also on separate chapters by Vendulka Kubálková (2003) in her
chapter 'Toward an International Political Theology'; Carsten Bagge Laustsen
and Ole Wæver (2003), 'In Defence of Religion: Sacred Referent Objects for
Securitization'; and Anthony D. Smith (2000), 'The "Sacred" Dimension of
Nationalism'. (One of the contributors to both the book and the journal, Scott
M. Thomas, has also written his own book on 'the resurgence of religion' and
its return from exile, and I analyse that separately in Chapter 9.)

On the first page of *Religion in International Relations* the editors claim
that 'religion was the object that needed to vanish for modern international

politics to come into being'. This is a potentially important insight, one apparently shared – as we will see in the chapters that follow – by Scott Thomas and Elizabeth Shakman Hurd. It is a view that converges with what Thomas calls 'the modern invention of religion' and its ideological function in the simultaneous imaginary of the secular state and IR itself as a secular discipline. These ideas indicate a convergence with developments in other disciplines too.

However, this critical viewpoint is not only lost sight of, but is contradicted by a more dominant tendency to essentialize religion as though it were a real object or even agent in the world. Religion is represented by Petito and Hatzopolous as a distinct kind of thing, globally present, and identifiable by certain essential characteristics. Specific kinds of practices and institutions are decisively *religious*: for example, there is religious law and there are religious communities. But not only is religion a distinct kind of thing in the world, they claim that religion is a global, 'worldwide' agent with work to do. Religion resurges, generates, imposes, persecutes and drives. They even play with the idea that religion should be considered a 'victim'.

As analysis of the texts in Petito and Hatzopolous's book shows, its editors are not alone in this kind of global reification of religion and religions. Nor is it IR specialists alone who fall into the trap of misplaced concreteness. For example, the discipline of the science of religion, founded by scholars such as Max Müller in the nineteenth century and now generally known as Religious Studies, has arguably been one of the agencies responsible for transforming 'religion' into an essence, which in turn is manifested in empirical 'religions' found globally. One characteristic of the wider reifying discourse is that the essential difference between religious and secular practices is typically communicated 'below the radar' – quietly and tacitly. But some of the contributors in this collection explicitly attribute an essence to religion, which they try to specify.

For example, Vendulka Kubálková (2003), in her chapter 'Toward an International Political Theology', argues *explicitly* for an ontological distinction between religious and secular thought (p. 87). This author makes wild generalizations about what 'all religions, western and eastern' share. In their chapter 'In Defence of Religion: Sacred Referent Objects for Securitization', Carsten Bagge Laustsen and Ole Wæver (2003) make the interesting and potentially fruitful remark that 'IR is not the neutral observer it pretends to be; it is implicated by its own secularist self-perception' (p. 175). However, this does not lead them to deconstruct religion and its supposed essential differences from politics and international relations. For these authors too, religion has an essence, a belief that is conveyed in many very explicit ways.

Anthony D. Smith (2000), in 'The "Sacred" Dimension of Nationalism', writes a learned and sophisticated argument concerning the characteristics of nationalism, and the continuities and discontinuities between what he refers to as traditional religions and those modern nationalisms which share many of the characteristics of 'religion'. Within the various kinds of nationalism he detects differences between religious and secular nationalisms, and also sacral features such as rituals, liturgies and ceremonies which suggest that both types of nationalism bear similarities to religions. I argue that the formulation of nationalism in these terms has two contradictory tendencies. One tendency is to question the essential difference between what is represented as 'religion' and what as 'nationalism'. The other tendency is to maintain problematic distinctions – between religion and secular, or religion and politics, or tradition and modernity – in the sociological description and analysis itself, thus perpetuating the problem of representation by giving these categories objective, sociological legitimacy. In this way sociology appears as part of the same mythical imagining as religions and nation states themselves.

Throughout Petito and Hatzopolous's book, the binary opposition between 'religion' and the non-religious secular is transformed from a rhetorical construct born in specific historical and power contexts into an uncritical and universal presupposition. While in some papers there are attempts at critical historicization, by authors such as Anthony D. Smith and Scott M. Thomas, some such as Vendulka Kubálková, and Carsten Bagge Lausten and Ole Wæver, actually and explicitly theorize these supposed essences, while others merely assume the reality of the essential distinction and proceed to re-embed it in their descriptions and analyses.

One of the effects of these arguments is that the secular positionality of the authors, which is itself an ideological position, is obfuscated. Furthermore, theological arguments for an essential definition of religion become confused with claims that 'religions' can be the global objects of empirical investigation. One problem with these kinds of representation is that 'religion' in general is not an object amenable to empirical investigation. Religion is a general and disputed category conveyed in persuasive discourses in a specific European language (in this case, English) with a specific contested history. What arguably can be investigated empirically are the procedures, in different places, contexts and languages, which determine what will be considered (in legislation, for example, or in media and politicians' rhetoric) to be a 'religion' and who will be considered 'religious'. But there is no possible evidence of anything or any agent called religion existing in the world which is susceptible to empirical observation and which could be the referent of this general category.

**Chapter 9:** Scott M. Thomas, who is one of the contributors to Petito and Hatzopolous's book (Petito and Hatzopolous 2003), has been widely praised for his own book *The Global Resurgence of Religion and the Transformation of International Religions* (2005). He refers to 'the modern invention of religion', to 'the invention of religion as part of the rise of western modernity', and to 'the concept of religion … as part of the political mythology of liberalism'. He insightfully suggests that both the modern secular state and international relations are part of the same process as the modern invention of religion, suggesting a symbiotic and mutually implicated relationship between them. But for most of the book, far from treating 'religion' as a rhetorical invention with a crucial part to play in the 'mythology of liberalism', and far from critiquing an understanding of 'religion' that constructs it as a real and present danger to liberal reason and freedom, Thomas energetically re-inscribes the category along with its ideological binary 'secular liberalism' as a fundamental organizing principle of his book. This is indicated partly by the title itself. The possibility of taking the expression 'the resurgence of religion' in the title as a metaphor, rather than as an example of the fallacy of misplaced concreteness, is made almost impossible by the reinforcing reifications throughout his text. Thomas imagines 'religion' as though it is an agency that can 'resurge' globally in different manifestations. It is thus part of the stuff that myths and metaphysics are made of. These categories are not themselves inductions from empirical observation, but the *a priori* categories of modernity still being asserted in a work that claims to question them. They are arguably themselves the basis for a system of classification that constructs the sacred canopy of global capital.[1] Thus, while Thomas laudably aims to critique modern ideology, the stronger and contradictory effect is to further embed modern ideological assumptions.

**Chapter 10**: Of the books reviewed here, Elizabeth Shakman Hurd's *The Politics of Secularism in International Relations* (Hurd 2008) is the most focused and sustained in its attempt to critically historicize the religion–secular dichotomy as an ideological power formation deriving from Christendom and underpinning modernity. There are many reasons for saying this, but I stress four strands. One is her insight that the 'division between religion and politics is not fixed but rather socially and historically constructed'. Second is her helpful distinction between two different models of Euro-American secularism, which she refers to as *laicism* (based on the French tradition) and *Judeo-Christian secularism* (typically instantiated by the US). Third is her discussion of secularism in Turkey and Iran and relations between these two polities and Euro-America.

This latter discussion potentially and suggestively opens the wider issue of the way a doctrine of secularism, and its parasitic binary invention of 'religion', has been institutionalized in other polities such as India, China, Japan and Iraq, and indeed its globalizing impact on communities everywhere. India in particular has been the subject of intense scrutiny in a large number of books, papers and conferences,[2] and the meaning of religion, secular and secularism has been part of an on-going debate there for several decades. The Indian case highlights the role of colonialism in this regard. By taking a detailed look at secularism in Turkey and Iran, Hurd opens up a useful way to connect the discussion more widely.

Fourth is her recognition of the mutually parasitic binary construction of an essentialized religion, 'Islam', as an irrational and backward Other against which European perceptions of its collective self as rational and progressive have been facilitated. Where Euro-America is secular, rational, progressive and democratic, Islam is religious, irrational, backward and prone to tyrants and arbitrary dictatorships. These self-serving binary oppositions are therefore an exercise in power. By understanding secularism as itself a form of 'productive power', Hurd brings secularism into view as a project or ideology or power formation, after which it cannot remain veiled and hidden from critical sight, or as the transparent, neutral substratum of academic description and analysis.

In these ways Hurd's book represents a serious scholarly attempt at critical deconstruction. However, the ambiguities are there throughout her text. The first paragraph of the book indicates that, while intending to critique modern categories, 'religion' and 'politics' are being recycled simultaneously into the text as though they are unproblematic descriptive and analytical categories. In this way Hurd (in many ways like Thomas) re-inscribes into her own text the problematic categories which she is attempting to critically disembed.

Another problem, I would argue, is with her historicization of the terms religion and secular. Hurd, influenced by William E. Connolly, for example in his work *Why I am not a Secularist* (Connolly 1999), has persuasively identified Kant as one crucial and possibly definitive stage in the emergence of the modern religion–secular dichotomy in the eighteenth century. Hurd's history of the English word 'secular', while useful and insightful in some respects, is surely contestable in others. In particular I will argue that it is a mistake to conflate medieval and early modern distinctions between the religious and the secular with the analytically separable distinction between sacred and profane; and that her historicization of the term 'secularization', and her claim that the Treaty of Westphalia of 1648 exemplified 'secularization', is crucially unclear, both indicating and yet obscuring the radically changed meanings of these terms.

Another problem is that, despite her exposure of the secular as an ideological power formation, Hurd's own positionality as a secular scholar is obfuscated. This is perhaps the most basic and most difficult problem for all of us, who are financed and disciplined by secular universities, sources of funding, and career structures, to bring into explicit focus. Whereas (to take one possible analogy) the early medieval writer the Venerable Bede was able to construct an interesting and insightful narrative of the history of early England, while making his own Christian commitments highly explicit, it seems to be a characteristic of modern secular writers to conceal our own faith commitments. But the logic of Hurd's own insights seems to point to the need for a more explicit articulation of the author's own positionality.[3]

**Chapter 11**: These issues bring me to the next and final chapter, where I attempt to work out and bring more consciously into view my own positionality and my own agenda. This has been the most difficult chapter to write, because it is here that I feel compelled to practise what I preach. But I can find no clear, ready-made and substantively explicit ideological position which can stand as an alternative to the dominant status quo, and which will convincingly and automatically appeal to a pre-articulated constituency. It is this problem that I suspect inhibits writers such as Thomas and Hurd from following through the logic of their own critical insights. For one thing, it tends to impose on us something like a personal confession of faith, which runs counter to the strongly entrenched academic practice of erasing ourselves from our own texts. We can probably all confess to a commitment to 'freedom' and 'democracy', but part of our problem is that this discourse has been comprehensively and powerfully appropriated (I would say misappropriated), not merely by individual writers such as Hitchens (explicitly) and Berman (implicitly), but by powerful ideologists of liberal capitalism such as Milton Friedman and his influential theorization of economics as an objective science, by the spokespersons for corporate capital, by the media, by politicians, or by the US military. Nor is it at all clear in what way modern universities are either free or democratic. On the other hand, if I adopt the self-designation 'socialist', those same powers will rhetorically force me into bed with Marxist-Leninism, Stalinism and Maoism, where I certainly do not want to go. And those who see the modern distinction between religion and the secular as a good, in that it appears to provide a constitutional and legal protection for tolerance of minorities, may assume that this critique leads ineluctably to intolerant authoritarianism. If I appeal to anarchism, then I will be charged with a militant disrespect for law and order, or alternatively a naïve belief in the natural human propensity for goodness and love. And if I appeal to 'God' or the 'supernatural', then I will be seen as a crypto-theologian, and recycled back into the 'religious' classification that I am trying to subvert. The problem for all of us who find many aspects of modern liberal capitalist ideology to be destructive, alienating and disempowering, is that we need to further open up a debate within academia and across the disciplinary divides about 'where do we go from here?'.

# Notes

1.  This is a deliberate if oblique reference to Peter Berger's *The Sacred Canopy: Elements of a Sociological Theory of Religion*, [Garden City, NY: Doubleday, 1967]. I have discussed Berger in various contexts in this book on p68, 162, 189, 210/1. See also Fitzgerald (2007a:98-100).
2.  For example, the 'Rethinking Religion in India' five year series of conferences beginning in 2009 in Delhi and organised by Professor S. N. Balagangadhara of the University of Ghent and his research students. See Balagangadhara (1994) and Bloch et al (2010).
3.  There are many other authors claiming to write about politics and religion or IR and religion which I have not had the space to consider. Two which I have on my desk beside me are by Jeffrey Haynes, *An Introduction to International Relations and Religion*, [Pearson Longman, 2007]; and Steve Bruce, *Politics and Religion*, [Polity, 2003]. However, while these books have strong scholarly features, I believe they are vulnerable to a similar kind of critique as those considered in detail here.

# Chapter 3

## Why the Focus on Religion in International Relations?

I was partly prompted to turn my attention to the topic of religion in International Relations by an article written by a specialist in that field, Robert M. Bosco (2009), 'Persistent Orientalisms: the concept of religion in international relations'. Bosco was driven by an interdisciplinary impulse to connect recent discourses in religion in International Relations, especially since 9/11 and concerns with Islam in that field, to the critical discussions about the category 'religion' which have been going on for some years now in Religious Studies. I thought this was a productive article which gave a good summary of some of the ideas that religion scholars have been debating, and which attempted to demonstrate the relevance and the need for interdisciplinary collaboration on such an important topic. Bosco's article also implies a critique of his own discipline for its lack of interest in what we in the study of religion were saying. A similar critique could be made of those of us in religious studies (or arguably in several other disciplines) for ignoring IR, which is after all a vitally important discipline, not least because of its close connection with centres of power: government policy, political think tanks, political and economic analysis, and international agencies of various kinds.

One of my own motives for investigating IR as an agency for the reproduction of the modern myth of religion is the way religion is strongly linked in that discipline with conflict and violence.[1] This is especially true since 9/11, which has been the most powerful source of the belief in IR that 'religion' has recently returned from its 'exile' on the safe margins of rational politics, but is now violently 'resurging'. The images of 'religion' acting as an agent of malign disruption of the peaceful work of rational secularists seemed to me especially striking and suggested the language of myth, which tends to invest abstract categories with volition and intention.

But the belief in the special connection between religion and conflict has a much longer history than 9/11. Some of the writers discussed in this book argue that, after the Treaty of Westphalia in 1648, which brought the bloody Wars of Religion to a close, religion was safely quarantined by the new secular states[2] which also came into being as a result. The idea is also mooted that

International Relations as a rational secular discipline for the analysis of world politics derived in the long run from these same historical sources. Once irrational and violent religion had been tamed and put into its proper place at the margins of government, at least in Europe and North America, then International Relations could emerge as the science of statecraft.

Jonathan Fox (2004), in his article "The Rise of Religious Nationalism and Conflict: Ethnic Conflict and Revolutionary Wars, 1945–2001" makes some pertinent summaries of the dominant paradigms in IR and related disciplines such as Politics and the Social Sciences:

> For most of the 20th century, the dominant paradigm in the social sciences on this topic was that religion would have no role in modern society and politics. The political science version of this paradigm, modernization theory, posits that processes inherent in modernization should inevitably lead to the demise of primordial factors like ethnicity and religion in politics. These processes include urbanization, economic development, modern social institutions, growing rates of literacy and education, pluralism, and advancements in science and technology. While this literature tends to focus on ethnicity, it is also clearly meant to apply to religion … In contrast, secularization theory, the sociological analogue of modernization theory, does focus on religion. It posits that the same factors cited by modernization theory will lead to the demise of religion, which is to be replaced by secular, rational, and scientific phenomena (Fox 2004: 716).

Writing specifically about IR, Fox argues that, until quite recently, that discipline basically ignored the topic of religion. He cites Philpott's finding that, between 1980 and 1999,

> … in about 1,600 articles in four major international relations journals (*International Organization*, *International Studies Quarterly*, *International Security*, and *World Politics*), only six articles 'featured religion as an important influence'. Only *Millennium* devoted a special issue to the topic (*Millennium* 29(3), 2000) (Fox 2004: footnote 4, 717).

Two issues arise. One is why 'religion' was so comprehensively ignored by IR theorists as an important factor in world politics before around 1980. The other is why it suddenly became such a major concern. Fox answers the first question in the following way:

> Rather than having a theory as to why religion was not important, international relations tended to focus on factors that did not include religion. Paradigms like realism, liberalism, and globalism placed their emphasis on military and economic factors as well as rational calculations, all of which left little room for religion … This trend can be traced to the fact that the

academic study of international relations was founded upon, among other things, the belief that the era of religion causing wars was over (Fox 2004: 716–17).

I note in passing that, according to this passage, paradigms that focus on rational calculation, and on military and economic issues, leave 'little room for religion'. This seems to imply that 'religion' is (in the IR and social science literature) not connected, or is (ideally) no longer connected, to war or to economics, and is not characterized by rationality.

Why, then, was there a dramatic upsurge in the place of religion in international affairs in the thinking of IR specialists? All of these assumptions began to be questioned from the late 1970s and early 1980s as a result of such events as the Iranian revolution, the rise of the religious right in US politics, the events in Waco, Texas, in 1993, and of course 9/11. These events had a galvanizing effect such that,

[b]y the beginning of the 21st century, a considerable body of theory developed, positing that religion remains important in the modern era. To an extent, this body of theory was inspired by the facts on the ground. Simply put, real world events have disproved the theories of religion's demise. Such events, to name a few, include: the acts of Osama bin Laden's Al-Qaeda, including the terrorist attacks of 11 September 2001; the Iranian revolution; the worldwide rise of religious fundamentalism; religious rebellions and opposition movements throughout the Islamic world including, but by no means limited to, Egypt, Algeria, and Afghanistan; religio-political movements like the liberation theology movement in Latin America; and ethno-religious conflicts like those in Chechnya, East Timor, Tibet, Sudan, and Sri Lanka. The core element of this body of theory posits that religion is an essential element of modern political and social phenomena. Religion is said to be among the essential foundations of civilization ... as well as one of the bases for modern political phenomena like nationalism ... and the Westphalian state system ... For many it is still an influence on individual ethical and political choices ... (Fox 2004: 717–18).

One thing that becomes apparent from Fox's summary is that, in IR and related disciplines, and presumably for Fox himself, 'religion' is 'a fact on the ground'. Empirical observation tells us that religion is still alive and active, and that the previous empirical data that religion had met its demise have proved illusory. This is expressed as a witness statement. We saw what we thought was a body lying on the ground, either asleep or dead. But suddenly it started moving. Then it sprang to its feet and attacked us. Furthermore, this living corpse wears many masks. It is a fact on the ground that Islam is a religion which inspires rebellion and terrorism in multiple locations; Al-Qaeda is a religious terrorist organization; the Iranian revolution was a religious revolution; and so on.

Religion according to this view is a piece of observation data. Furthermore, this empirical sighting establishes scientifically that religion is strongly associated with conflict and violence. But 'religion' is surely not an observable phenomenon? It is a general category of classification. We see people behaving in various ways and then we apply one or a number of our general categories, such as 'religious behaviour', political behaviour', 'economic behaviour', or the assertion of 'ethnicity'. But more than this, 'religion' is a highly contested ideological category of classification. What counts as 'religion' or 'paganism', for example, has for centuries been contested by Catholics and Protestants; or what counts as a 'religious' movement as distinct from a 'political' movement is not a self-evident datum but a classificatory decision based on value judgement and on implicit or explicit criteria.

There are two expressions that Fox uses here which point to this problem of analysis – 'religio-political' and 'religio-ethnic'. They draw attention to a wider problem of meaning. Are 'religion' and 'politics' separate phenomena? If so, how are they distinguished and by whom and for what purposes?

I will argue throughout this book that such use of language reveals a social science paradigm which is itself a deeply mystified faith ideology masquerading as disinterested reporting of 'facts on the ground'. This will become increasingly apparent in the chapters that follow, for I will show that neither Fox nor any of the IR writers that I go on to discuss can give any clear meaning to the term 'religion', nor to how religion in its various incarnations can be distinguished from non-religious movements or groups.

Fox's summary is one part of a story that is widely told and believed in IR and related disciplines. The story goes something like this. The inherent violence of religion has been quarantined since the Treaty of Westphalia and transformed into a marginal, private right of 'faith', a purely individual matter of personal conscience separated from the rational business of world politics and nation states. Secular reason in its various manifestations became founded in Europe and North America and gradually extended its benign and peace-loving influence through processes of secularization, modernization and globalization. Though conflicts of interest between various kinds of 'actors' (especially nation states) still persisted, these were no longer mired in the irrational fanaticism of religion, and consequently became amenable in principle at least to rational mediation and resolution. But a series of violent events led social scientists to be confronted by their own mistake. Religion was not dead after all, but had only been in 'exile' and recently has been 'resurging', as though brought back to life or woken from a long sleep. A moment's reflection on these stories puts them fairly and squarely in the realms of myth.

Let me only comment briefly at this point – and I return to it later – that in his article Fox is not questioning that 'religion' is a special kind of belief and practice distinguished from non-religious beliefs and practices. Throughout his article he unquestioningly recycles distinctions between religious and non-religious nationalisms and between religious and non-religious ethnicities as though these are categories that simply refer to matters of observational fact. Yet I cannot find any discussion in his article about how 'religious' nationalism can be demarcated from non-religious nationalism, or how religious violence differs from non-religious violence. The distinction itself is simply assumed. Nor is he himself questioning that religion is an actor or agent in the world. Nor does he question the myth that 'religion' is especially prone to irrational malignity. On the contrary, his article attempts to prove this statistically. Fox's aim is not to critically question the basic elements of the discourse. His aim rather is to prove that the theories of modernization and secularization are wrong *only to the extent* that they assert that 'religion' will gradually wither away. On the contrary, religion is re-surging, and never really went away in the first place.

Fox points out that, while there is a long tradition of linking religion and violence, it has been asserted with especial fervour by a number of academics since the 1980s and 1990s. One example he gives is Mark Juergensmeyer, a religious studies specialist who until recently was President of the American Academy of Religion and whose name appears seven times in Fox's article, including three times as references (see Juergensmeyer 1991, 1993 and 2000). We will see that Juergensmeyer is one of those regularly cited and quoted by several of the IR writers discussed here.

Fox seeks to establish a significant connection between 'religion' and conflict using statistics from two databases, Minorities at Risk (MAR) and State Failure (SF). In his summary he states that:

> The analysis of the MAR dataset shows that until 1980 religious and non-religious ethnic nationalism caused a near-identical amount of conflict, but from 1980 onward, religious nationalist ethnic groups were responsible for increasingly more violent conflicts in comparison to non-religious nationalist groups. The analysis of the SF dataset shows a rise in religious violence beginning around 1965 (Fox 2004: 715).

Fox draws three conclusions from his analysis of the two datasets:

> First, they show that religion can influence conflict, but it is not the only influence. Second, the influence of religion on conflict can change over time. Third, religion's influence on conflict has been increasing. This contradicts modernization theory and secularization theory, which were the dominant paradigms in the Western social sciences for most of the 20th century and predicted the demise of religion as a relevant political and social force in the modern era (Fox 2004: 715).

Even if I had the space, I would not see any reason to go into any further detail of Fox's analysis that can easily be accessed by the interested reader. My main concern is with the classification problem. When Fox makes distinctions between religious and non-religious ethnic minorities, religious nationalism and non-religious nationalism, and religious violence as distinct from non-religious violence, then the reader needs to know what counts as 'religious' and what counts as 'non-religious'. This is fundamental. After all, in his Conclusion Fox claims to have some important positive knowledge of facts; but this knowledge can only be reliable if the basic premise – that religious practice is distinguishable from non-religious practice – has some clear and convincing content. Given that groups classified as 'religious' will be strongly associated with an inherent tendency to irrationality and barbaric violence, much is at stake.

At this point a defence of the scientific and statistical methodology might include the claim that we should look to the two datasets, MAR and Failed States, to check out what they mean by 'religion'. Since the data for Fox's analysis have all been provided by these, then it could be argued that his only fault was to forget to direct the reader's attention to that definition. It could also perhaps be reasonably argued that, if a social scientist is to do his or her work and produce useful conclusions, then it is simply impractical each time to have a theoretical discussion based on a considered philosophical position which takes into account some of the huge amount of published debate on the question of the meaning and definition of 'religion'. To be fair we should assume he has (albeit silently and without comment) conformed to the strategic definition of religion as against non-religion adopted by these organizations.

I personally could find no such definition or theoretical discussion on the MAR webpage,[3] even though 'religion' is one of the categories used to classify various groups and their practices in situations of conflict. So I e-mailed the MAR group (Minorities at Risk Project Center for International Development and Conflict Management at the University of Maryland) and asked them to provide me with their working definition of 'religion'. I did this because it directly effects how, for example, a 'religious' group could be distinguished from a non-religious 'political' group; or how 'religious' violence could be distinguished from 'non-religious' or secular violence. They were kind enough to give me the following reply:

> For our purposes, religion is defined as traditions of belief in a supernatural order and including some combination of ritual/observance, narrative, symbolism and moral codes. In the data, religion is one of the variables that we track which measures an ethnic group's distinctiveness from the majority group (personal email, 15 June 2010).

The definitive term here is 'supernatural order'. I say this because all the other criteria specified – ritual observance, narrative, symbolism and moral code – would unproblematically apply to a wide range of beliefs, institutions and practices including those which are typically classified as 'political'. I discuss this point in various places throughout this book. And it is a common assumption that 'religion' is essentially characterized by belief in the 'super-natural'. It is a typical definitional criterion that has been frequently used to distinguish 'religious' beliefs and practices from non-religious ones. Yet it is also a highly contested one, as familiarity with debates within anthropology, religious studies and Asian Studies can easily show. So I emailed the organization again about the criteria for 'supernatural order' and received the following reply:

> We follow the layman's understanding of 'supernatural order.' Our goal at MAR is not to understand religion, but rather, to understand the political mobilization of ethnic groups. Therefore, for our purposes subtleties in the definition of 'supernatural order' are irrelevant. If there is a specific ethnic group that you are looking at and have questions about, please let me know (15 June 2010).

This reply is obviously problematic for me, for a number of reasons. To say 'we follow the layman's understanding' might seem very democratic. But have they done any research to establish what the layman's understanding is? And does the layman's understanding include the laymen of all linguistic groups, or only the Anglophone? And given that their organization is providing professional people such as Fox with data on 'religion' as a distinct factor supposedly associated with high levels of violence, is it wise to assume that one knows that laymen or professional people have a coherent notion of religion or the supernatural as a distinct and analytically separable element from politics or ethnicity? To say that the goal 'is not to understand religion, but rather ... the political mobilization of ethnic groups' itself presupposes some understanding of how religion differs from politics or ethnicity.

The rationality of such a highly-funded database producing social scientific knowledge on sensitive issues to do with dangerous contests of power in multiple sites around the world is too robust, apparently, to be concerned with clarity in the deployment of key categories. It is 'irrelevant', merely a matter of 'subtleties'. This seems a surprisingly off-hand and dismissive approach to the use of highly contested categories as key criteria of classification.

It also seems relevant in this sensitive context that the MAR dataset on which Fox relies, which, as mentioned, is 'A Project of the Center for International and Conflict Management' at the University of Maryland, is also affiliated to 'The National Consortium for the Study of Terrorism and Responses to Terrorism', and to the US Department of Homeland Security. Like Eli Berman, discussed in Chapter 6, who offered his analysis of 'religious' terrorist groups as advice to anti-terrorist agencies, the objective and disinterested knowledge produced by MAR and relied on by Fox is closely connected to the US State and may presumably influence its strategies.

It is not a happy situation when the controllers and collectors of such data appear unaware of, or uninterested in, the intellectually problematic nature of these issues. This is especially true when they are acting as agents of the state. There is a widespread assumption among both specialists and non-specialists in these issues that they 'know' immediately and instinctively what terms like 'religion' and 'supernatural' mean. A moment's reflection, however, suggests that even if these English language terms and the distinctions they imply seem clear and obvious in Anglophone contexts – which I would seriously dispute – this would not mean that they translate into the understanding of people who think in different languages and categories. The problem of translating these volatile terms is contentious. There would therefore seem to be an especially pressing responsibility on social scientists engaged in the collection and classi-fication of 'data' related to complex situations of conflict, to be aware of these issues and to discuss them openly in their methodological justifications. This requires critical alertness and an inter-disciplinary interest.

I would ask the reader to consider the arguments about these problematic categories such as 'religion' and 'supernatural' as they accumulate throughout this book; to look at arguments I and others have published in other books and articles; and in general to look at the history of the disputes around the validity of the category 'supernatural' as a way of demarcating a universal domain of beliefs and practices which can be distinguished from 'natural' or non-religious beliefs and practices. My point here is that, without a very well-argued case based on an extensive interdisciplinary consideration of the arguments, it is dangerous to base a key term such as 'religion', which as I already suggested is itself a highly contested category even within Christian history, on such a problematic notion as 'the supernatural'. This seems especially true when 'religion' is being employed as the key criterion in organizing knowledge about which groups are, and which groups are not, more prone to irrational violence.

I argue that 'religion' has no essential meaning, and its distinction from 'non-religion' is empty and arbitrary. What goes into which box is more a matter of power than disinterested reason, and in this book I will try to demonstrate this. I will make similar arguments about the distinctions between the supernatural and the natural, and between faith and knowledge. I hope to convince the reader by the end of this book that a whole edifice of ideological assumptions is founded on these weak and shifting binaries, none of which have any clear or stable meaning. I *show* this through a close analysis of the way writers in IR and the social sciences more generally actually *use* these terms. An appearance of meaning is generated through (largely unconscious) rhetorical deployment.

One of the many rhetorical tricks that writers deploy (though this is not a conscious Machiavellian kind of trickery) is to bury the histories of contes-tation that surround key categories and use them as though they are obvious, innocent and harmless. A term like 'religion' is a matter of commons sense. It is obvious what it means, and obvious who is acting for religious motives. Furthermore, such a term can be applied universally without any regard for how it translates into the thinking and motivation of the actors who are being subjected to the classification. But I am not convinced that, whatever his conscious intentions, it is unquestionably obvious that Fox himself is an objective, neutral and disinterested social scientist who is merely trying to get at the 'facts on the ground'. That he never subjects his key term 'religion' to any sustained attention or explains to the reader how he is using the term, indicates my point.

The nearest that I could find to a definition was 'a truncated religious identity variable is used that defines religious minorities as those minorities who belong to a different religion' (Fox 2004: 720). Now, this struck me to be an empty tautology. This sentence evoked in me the image of a collapsing pack of cards, or an elaborate trolley without any wheels. It was then followed by another image, widely deployed in the IR literature, of 'religion' as a mad agent in the world who has been in exile but is now once more malevolently stalking the globe and disrupting the rational world order of nation states and capitalist corporations. These images made me want to pursue the idea that the discourses on 'religion' are inflations of a figure that has no reality, a fiction that nevertheless has the power (if you believe in it) to generate volumes of dubious analysis and to instigate foreign policy decisions and homeland security measures.

Technical expressions such as 'the combined impact of religion and separatism on ethnic conflict in multivariate analyses' (Fox 2004: 721) will only sound impressive if the term 'religion' is not entirely empty of determinate meaning in Fox's text. When reading his summary of the results of his research, I would request the reader to bear in mind the important-sounding yet empty tautology, 'a truncated religious identity variable is used that defines religious minorities as those minorities who belong to a different religion' (Fox 2004: 720), and then bracket all appearances of 'religion' and 'religious' while reading the next paragraph:

> In general, the results of this study show that religion can be an important influence on conflict. In fact, its importance has increased during the period covered by this study. While the specific results from two different datasets are not fully consistent on the timing of this trend, they both confirm that the trend exists. More specifically, results from the MAR dataset show that the religious element of religious nationalism, while not a significant influence on ethnic conflict between 1945 and 1979, has had an increasingly consequential impact on ethnic violence since the early 1980s. The results from the SF dataset show that religious conflicts were less violent than other conflicts until around 1965, when they became more violent. Thus, the evidence indicates that there was an increase in the influence of religion on conflict over the period covered by this study. This directly contradicts the assumptions made by the majority of 20th-century social scientists and confirms the general contentions of a growing number of recent arguments that religion is an important influence on conflict. These

results are especially consistent with those who argue that religion is experiencing a resurgence or revitalization in modern times ... (Fox 2004: 727).

I shall argue in this book that the most important function of discourses on 'religion' is to clothe the ideology of the secular social scientist and the state agencies she or he may be serving with an aura of factuality. This facilitates the conceit that the secular social scientist is on a higher footing than the people who – largely without being consulted – have been forced into the classifications.

The majority of social scientists are just like the rest of us academics, decent and hard-working people who are trying to produce useful knowledge for a variety of different purposes – in the case of Fox, peace and the resolution of conflicts. But even if my own argument is wrong, and that 'religion' can be given a clear and consistent meaning which is universally translatable and with an influence on events which can be scientifically measurable, some attention at least needs to be paid to its contested history. It should seem clear that 'religion' as a category is not an innocent one. What gets classified as 'religious' simultaneous gets classified 'scientifically' as having an in-bred tendency towards violence and irrationality. The category figures prominently in US foreign policy and strategies for security. Modern states use the term as a minority classificatory device. If the category is empty of any clear, operational definition, then the danger is that anything that social scientists or their political masters and funding agents think needs to go into it can easily be accommodated. This is not a conspiracy theory and I am not referring to fully conscious processes. Myths such as the myth of religion do not work at that level. They are powerful precisely because they seem so natural and unavoidable that to question them seems eccentric or even mischievous.

Yet we have seen how an author such as Fox can really believe that 'religion' and its distinction from 'non-religion' is an observable fact on the ground. Yet surely it is obvious that no-one has ever seen a religion or a 'religious' motivation? He can even believe that religion is a special agent that can appear simultaneously in multiple sites stirring up anti-US conflict and sowing irrational hatred. When one strips away the technical jargon, one finds beneath it a strip-cartoon character, a powerful evil demon who has come back from the dead, wears disguises, manifests like an avatar in different forms, and with no good reason disturbs the gentle peace of the rational secular state. It never occurs to Fox that his own beliefs and practices in social science seem to have many resemblances to those which are normally classified as 'religious faith'. Such an insight would threaten his own faith in social science as providing objective knowledge of the world, superior to the knowledge provided by those violent, irrational traditions he labels as 'religious'.

These worries about the arbitrary usage and content of 'religion' as a category in IR and social science have come together with that line of my own work that has a different and distinct starting point. In order to clarify for the reader how my perception of the problems arose in the first place, I now go on in the following chapter to say something about my own research background.

## Notes

1.    See William T. Cavanaugh, *The Myth of Religious Violence*, OUP, 2009, for an outstanding analysis of these issues, and including a useful and original histioriography of the category 'religion'. See also Cavanaugh in T. Fitzgerald, *Religion and the Secular: historical and colonial formations*, Equinox, 2007b.
2.    There is a significant ambiguity about the meaning of 'secular' in this context which I discuss in various parts of this book. One might say, rather, that the Treaty of Westphalia was one stage in a much longer process of change in the meaning of 'secular'.
3.    Minorities at Risk (MAR): http://www.cidcm.umd.edu/mar/about.asp/ (accessed 7 June 2011).

Chapter 4

*Contextualizing the Problem in the Author's Research Background*

I offer a summary of my research history here, not because there is anything especially interesting in my own activities themselves but so that the context of my criticisms of International Relations can be better understood. Much of my research has been done in India and Japan, and neither of these countries is much under consideration in the IR literature discussed here. The construction of 'religion' in these texts is focused (if that is the right word) more on 'Islam' than on, say, Hinduism, Buddhism, Sikhism, Zoroastrianism, Confucianism or Shinto. But I believe that the theoretical and methodological problems of analysis and representation can easily be seen to be more widely relevant, especially the simplistic classification of 'religion'.

## Religious Studies at King's College, London

In more general terms, this book is a continuation of a project that began when I studied Religious Studies at King's College, London, in the 1970s and early 1980s. The problem as I saw it then was with 'religion' as a standalone category. It took some time for me to realize that 'religion' is joined at the hip with the supposedly non-religious domains of the 'secular', such as 'politics'. During my time as a student, I became concerned with problems in the deployment of religion as a descriptive category. The idea that religion is an inherently problematic category has become far more commonplace today. But as a student studying for a degree in religion I do not remember much discussion of the kind. Though W.C. Smith's important book on the category religion, *The Meaning and End of Religion* (1978), was on our reading lists, Talal Asad's critique (1993, 2001) had not yet surfaced, and anyhow the full implications of Smith's arguments were obfuscated by his involvement in the World Religions programme at Harvard University, which seemed to construct what he was simultaneously deconstructing (see Fitzgerald, 2000:47). In the texts and lectures at King's College, London, there seemed to be an unquestioned assumption that religions exist, that all societies have religious aspects, and that religious experiences are universal and ubiquitous. No one was questioning the validity of the category itself.

Yet at the same time there has always been a long-running anxiety about the meaning of religion as a concept that was expressed in attempts to *define* religion. The proper definition of religion has been a preoccupation in sociology, anthropology and philosophy. We went through all the definitions of religion, or the theories of religion that implied some kind of definition – Hume Comte, Hegel, Marx, Feuerbach, Tylor, Frazer, Durkheim, Weber, Wittgenstein, Geertz, Spiro, Horton. But this concern with definition did not touch the category itself. These definitions were frequently incompatible and contradictory, but this did not lead to an interrogation of the discourse itself. The idea of questioning the category itself would have seemed rather a strange one to most people, as it apparently still does now. Surely, all societies have religions, and we know them intuitively when we see them?

This is a rather subtle point that I have found most difficult to grasp and to express. In a paradoxical sense the concern with definition had the effect of further embedding the category into the realm of the unquestionable. Religion is in some vague and unanalysed sense simply 'there', but we need to be more precise about its exact characteristics. To do this we must look at the 'religions' to see what they contain and then make the best generalization. And what are the 'religions'? Why typically Hinduism, Buddhism, Judaism, Sikhism, Zoroastrianism, Christianity, Islam, Confucianism, Shintoism, etc. This circularity was embedded in the exercise.

Yet religion is an Anglophone (or more widely Europhone) abstract category, not a thing in the world that can be empirically observed. This category is arbitrary, as the range of contradictory definitions suggests. Though arbitrary, we feel a compulsion to deploy the term in certain circumstances, in a range of typical usages, and this compulsion strengthens the sense that the category corresponds in common sense to things or aspects of experience that exist in the world. In other words, it is not merely an abstract category, but one that stands for something real and objective in the world. This sense of compulsion leads one to suppose that it is not arbitrary, and that attempts at definition are like attempts to focus a lens. They presuppose the reality of the lens and the reality of the independent object that we want to observe clearly. It is this feeling – that usage is not arbitrary despite the wide range of things that can be and have been described as religious – that I have subsequently tried to analyse.

One element of the problem is that we construct what we claim to find in a self-confirming circularity; but the construction is driven largely unconsciously by a discursive Christian history. The so-called world religions are themselves colonial products largely inflected with Christian-derived categories deployed and sometimes disguised in the classification of the practices of colonial subjects, yet are taken to exemplify what is normally meant by religions, thus strengthening the circularity of a self-confirming process. It should be added here that 'Christianity' as 'a religion' is itself a product of the same modern processes. Until quite recently in historical time, the idea that Christianity is *a* religion would have seemed unthinkable to most Christians.

The Wittgensteinian 'family resemblances' approach to definition, which was particularly popular among philosophers at King's, places the criterion of legitimate meaning on typical use, what is sometimes called the language game theory of meaning. Yet this conception of usage tended to exclude historicization of the term, and tended to exclude the significant control on meanings by powerful institutions. Present usages are the accumulation of past usage, and several centuries of police work controlling correct and incorrect meaning exercised by Christian church-states, by bishop-princes and theologians, by kings and queens, by powerful elites generally, do not simply disappear. Yet these philosophers tended to ignore the historical and contested usages of the term 'religion'. Power and the control of meanings by elites and institutions were not typically considered. They looked at 'religions' that already supposedly existed, and then derived their typical usage from them.

In those cases where, in anthropology for example, the term has been theoretically disembedded (relatively) from that wider, largely unconscious Christian history – for example in Tylor's 'belief in gods', or in Durkheim's sacred–profane definition – the category itself remains embedded, for example in special subject areas such as the anthropology of religion.

Nor was there much explicit discussion of the problems of translation, as though Anglophone or, more widely, Europhone concepts are immediately and unproblematically translatable into non-European languages and forms of life. I suppose that the specialists in Sanskrit, Tamil and Pali who taught us were aware of these issues, but they were not flagged up as significant issues at the undergraduate level. And in philosophical discussions about religion and its definitions there was rarely if ever any sustained discussion about possible links between our assumptions of the universality of Anglophone or more widely Europhone categories and the Euro-American colonial dominance of vast areas of the world. (These issues about cognitive imperialism are now widely and even centrally discussed in such disciplines as anthropology and Oriental studies, but 'religion' as a legitimate descriptive category is rarely questioned even within postcolonial critique.)

Some of these arguments seemed to assume that 'religion' is simply a fact about the world, or a fact in the world, or a fact about a distinct kind of human experience of the world, and definition constituted attempts to pin down the essential characteristics of that phenomenon in the most accurate way possible. Though some theorists question these assumptions today, at least when they are consciously theorizing, I suggest that the language actually used to talk about religion and religions or religious experiences reflects a deeply held and quite mystified assumption, based on an unconscious process of reification, which still underlies a great deal of discourse on religion. This can be seen not only in the rhetoric of politicians, journalists and travel writers but also in many scholarly texts in Religious Studies. And it is a discourse of misplaced concreteness that permeates some of the texts analysed in the present book.

## Wittgenstein and Family Resemblances

As already mentioned, the most powerful philosophical critique of essential-izing discourses on religion derived at that time from Wittgenstein (in the kind of Anglo-American analytical philosophy we were taught at King's College, London; the picture may have been different if we had studied continental philosophy). In contrast, and against this reifying stance, family resemblance arguments derived from Wittgenstein treated religion in terms of a language game theory of meaning. The meaning of religion (as with all other terms) does not derive from its correspondence to something that exists in the world, but from the way the term is ordinarily used. By looking at the range of typical uses, one could identify what is commonly regarded as religion or as religious, and on that basis map out a family of typical characteristics that is useful for organizing our experience while avoiding the fallacy of reification or essentialization.

Apart from the feminist critiques and deconstructions of gender categories, which unfortunately and perhaps unsurprisingly were hardly visible in the reading or lecturing at King's at the time,[1] it was Wittgenstein who provided the most powerful philosophical challenge to essentialist definitions of religion. This approach to the issue is still quite popular, and has been powerfully argued recently by the anthropologist Benson Saler.[2] I have made several objec-tions to the Wittgensteinian approach in a number of publications. I cannot repeat all the arguments here, and must ask the reader (if she or he is interested and does not know that particular literature) to pursue it and make up his or her own mind (see Fitzgerald 2000, 2003). But, put briefly, one objection is that those who use Wittgenstein to found a flexible and non-essentialist definition of religion do not take power and the institutionalized control of meanings into account. They do not look at the way categories such as religion have been used historically by powerful interest groups and institutionalized in different contexts. To give only one example, what constituted religion in early modern England, and what constituted pagan superstition, was a matter of life and death. The sovereign church-state adjudicated these matters. It was a fundamental duty of the civil courts to track down heretics and punish them, and of the ecclesiastical courts to decide on the precise nature of the misde-meanor in the first place. But what in the past constituted heresy as against religion understood as Christian Truth, and what in modern times a court, interpreting a constitution, determines to be a religious as against a secular (non-religious) practice, has radically different meanings. In modern nation states it is the secular (in the modern sense of non-religious) courts that have the power of interpreting the constitution and deciding what constitutes a bona fide religion. In these two different historical contexts both 'religion' and 'secular' have significantly different meanings, determined by the dominant authorities of the times working within different discursive paradigms. This radical difference in meanings is disguised by the continued usage of the same words 'religion' and 'secular'.

Language games are treated by family resemblance theorists as though they are free-floating natural systems abstracted from the domination of hierarchies and the contestations of minorities. Such theorists do not sufficiently consider the point that, on the logic of family resemblances, so much could be included as 'religion' or 'religious' that it would be difficult to know what to exclude. The 'family' of 'religions' would become so huge that both terms would lose their meaning. If ideologies like capitalism, fascism, communism, nationalism, Confucianism and secularism all share significant family resemblances to the ideologies which are usually singled out as typical religions (Judaism, Christianity, Islam, Hinduism, Buddhism, Sikhism, Zoroastrianism, Shintoism, etc.), which many people have pointed out that they do,[3] then where does the boundary between religion and non-religion end? Why are faith in democracy or in liberal capitalism, or belief in 'free markets' and in unending progress and material prosperity, or belief in the nation state, not included in books on world religions? Where do family resemblances begin or end? If everything can be included, then does the category 'religion' have any meaning at all? And a similar point could be made about the idea of *family* resemblances. The family is so large that it includes the whole range of customary practices.

If we are to be guided by the theory of family resemblances, and assuming we can identify the meaning of words from the context of their use, then it seems perfectly legitimate in ordinary English to make the following statement:

Our neighbour is an opera singer, is devoted to her art, and worships Mozart. She religiously practises the scales every day.

In this sentence, terms such as 'devotion', 'worship' and 'religiously' are perfectly normal English usage, and do not themselves obey the contours of any essential separation between religious and secular domains. If this is not the case, then opera should be classified as a religion and the neighbour who is a singer a religious devotee, one of the committed faithful. But opera is typically excluded from books published on the topic of religion.

Another variation in the approach to definition was (and still is) the idea that 'religion' is an arbitrary marker and that, provided we academics can define clearly how we intend to use the term, we can more or less do what we like with it. This seems to me to attribute too much power to the academy, and not enough to other agencies such as constitutions, courts, colonial administrations, non-conformist interests, the rhetoric of politicians and the media. The classification of English universities as secular in the modern sense of non-religious, and thus their transformation from Christian institutions of theology and the training of priests, was surely itself not a free choice of academics. No doubt scholars participated historically in the modern transformation of those institutions we call universities, but only in the context of much wider forces of change. Arguably, the modern secular university is itself as much the *result* of the emergence of the complex historical discourse on religion and religions as its creator.

The idea that we can use religion more or less as we choose, provided we make it clear at the start of our research article what we intend to mean, is a strategy adopted by some anthropologists and sociologists. Even Max Weber began his *Sociology of Religion* by stating that he would not attempt a definition of religion at the beginning of the study but would wait until the end. This left the field free for him to use the term as though he was *discovering* the objects corresponding to the category rather than constructing them.

Probably it was the study of social anthropology, wisely included as a course at King's by the philosopher H.D. Lewis who was one of the founders of that Religious Studies degree, which gave some ethnographic form to my early doubts. The concern with the problem of the definition of religion in anthropology at least had a basis in the problematic attempt to apply Europhone categories in the analysis and description of other cultures. At the time, anthropologists seemed a bit more critically aware of the limitations of Anglophone categories than did the analytical philosophers, though I did not until much later come across any fully critical confrontation with the ideological power implications of representing other peoples in the categories of colonial or former colonial powers. Edward Said's *Orientalism* was first published in 1979, but I was unaware of it until later. And as far as I know Said did not problematize terms such as 'religion' and 'secular politics' as themselves orientalist constructs.

# Hinduism

During the time that I studied Religious Studies I had developed a real interest in the so-called 'world religions' Hinduism and Buddhism, some of their philosophical schools, and theoretical problems in the Anglophone representation of these hypostatized systems. Texts and lectures on Hinduism and Buddhism in Religious Studies at King's followed a similar pattern to the textbooks we used at the time and which I began to reproduce in my own lecturing when I later became a lecturer in Religious Studies at a college of higher education. While I was there, Friedhelm Hardy took over from Geoffrey Parrinder in the teaching of Hinduism and Buddhism. Whereas Parrinder had been a missionary in Africa but had developed an interest in Sanskrit (he wrote a theological comparison of the Gita and the Gospels among other things[4]), Hardy was a trained Indologist with a deep and specialized knowledge of Tamil literature. Hardy was therefore – unlike Parrinder – not a typical ecumenical Christian theologian, and I suspect was sceptical about the World Religions paradigm; but it was difficult to think outside of that paradigm at the time when one was duty-bound to teach such courses. In the UK the subject of religion was at that time dominated by Ninian Smart and the World Religions paradigm. How else could he have approached it?[5]

In the case of Hinduism it was partly a history of ideas approach – more chronology than history – that constructed Indian religion more or less as the religion of the 'priest' or Brahmin, framed by the rise and fall of various dynasties but with little detailed study about how kingly power worked. The chronological frame worked its way from the ancient civilizations of the Indus Valley and the archaeological discoveries of public baths (for ritual purification) and small statuettes of goddesses and animals (presumed to be objects of 'worship'); the invasions of the nomadic Aryans with their original three-fold class system (*Varna*) of priests (*Brahmin*), warriors (*Kshatriya*) and traders (*Vaisya*), with an additional indigenous class the *Sudras* being vacuumed up from tribal areas and sucked into the gradually forming 'caste' system; the Veda and the old Aryan gods, with tantalizing mentions of *soma* as a drug that induced trance-like states; the Vedanta (Upanisads) and the 'quest' for transcendence; monism or non-dualism, pantheism, monotheism, henotheism; the Epics (Mahabharata – especially the Bhagavad Gita – and Ramayana); the Puranas; the Avatar doctrine with especial attention to Rama and Krishna; *bhakti* and the increasing influence of Tamil culture on Hinduism; *varnas-ramadharma*; the theological or philosophical systems of Shankara (*advaita Vedanta* or non-dualism), Ramajuna (*vishishadvaita Vedanta* or qualified non-dualism), and Madhva (*dvaita Vedanta* or dualism); the Muslim invasions and the development of forms of theological syncretism; British imperialism and Reform; the Arya Samaj and the Brahma Samaj; modern saint heroes such as Ramakrishna, Vivekananda, and of course Gandhi.

Caste (*jati*) was frequently mentioned, but only in relation to the ideal Varna system with passing mentions of untouchables (*chandalas*), but with no detailed anthropological ethnographic study of what 'caste' might mean in everyday experience. The British, it seemed, were traders who somehow fell into increasing colonial control almost by accident and then had to take up the civilizing burdens of democratic reform in law, education and religion, and rational classificatory practices such as the taking of the census. Caste, which was one of the categories the census employed along with religion, remained a shadowy topic in the lectures and textbooks of the time. It was unclear to me whether *jati* was a 'religious' or merely a 'social' institution.

Hinduism was thus a largely de-contextualized systems of beliefs and rituals in relation to God (*Atman-Brahman/Nirvana*), gods (*deva*), goddesses (*devata*), 'supernatural' or mystical powers (mantras such as AUM, the Kundalini in yoga, the fire sacrifice, and other brahmanic rituals); special inner experiences;

renouncers (*sannyasin*); doctrines of salvation of the individual soul (*moksha, mukti*); charismatic founders; 'priests' and 'monks' and 'nuns'; and organizations like ashrams and their gurus which, consciously or unconsciously, were imagined by analogy with modern Protestant Christian 'churches' as voluntary organizations tacitly separated from secular power; and abstract philosophical systems about the unconditioned, with a few glances at ethics. These religions were largely disembedded from their 'social' contexts through circularity. What made a religion different at core from a merely secular or social phenomenon was religious experience; however, what made an experience religious was that it was structured and interpreted within the context of the belief and doctrine of a particular religion (Hinduism). Usually what counted as a religious experience, a religious organization, a religious ritual, or a religious doctrine, was that it was connected to belief in god or gods, the supernatural, the sacred or the unconditioned.

Yet contradictorily it was also sometimes pointed out that the defining feature of a Hindu is membership of a caste and the following of the appropriate *dharma*, which in turn implied the ritualization of the whole of life. *Dharma* at the level of caste order and daily life was the microcosmic representation of the macrocosmic order of the universe as a whole. All beings, including gods, kings, and even animals, are governed by dharma. The cosmic law of the universe operated at all levels of reality. Furthermore, a system such as yoga and its philosophical theorization in samkhya looked far closer to an empirical science to me than a dogmatic belief in The Three Persons of the Trinity, the Incarnation, the Resurrection and so on. This made problematic all those Protestant Christian-derived concepts which seemed to be tacitly driving the classification of what counts as 'a religion' and a religious practice: supernatural as distinct from natural; God as distinct from human; other world as distinct from this world; 'religious' church and priest as distinct from 'non-religious' secular king; faith as distinct from knowledge. None of these distinctions fitted well with Indian self-representations. Not only did they not seem to fit well; I was struck by the power and coherence of Indian ways of constructing the world – and of deconstructing the world, too. I myself practised yoga and meditation, and found them un-amenable to classification in the *either–or* religion–secular binary.

In these ways, in studying and then teaching 'Hinduism' as a so-called 'world religion', I became aware of a tension between Christian-derived concepts of 'religion' which framed our ideas and the ideas which they claimed to represent. I do not want to over-use the expression 'Christian-derived' or 'Protestant Christian-derived' because I have more recently developed a scepticism about this widespread notion of Protestant Christianity as a determinative source of modernity. Much of what we refer to as Protestant Christianity may have been as much an effect as a cause of modern representations. But certain strands of Protestant Christian theology and ethics were implicated in the wider processes of Enlightenment representation that produced the modern ideology of religion and religions. The traditions of representation into which I had been inducted, and which dated back to Max Müller and others, in effect forced and distorted Indian self-representations into Christian categories and resulted in the invention of 'Hinduism' as a religion.[6] A very similar procedure – decontextualized ideas and institutions forming an essentialized system – was followed in the construction of 'Buddhism' as a religion.

Formulaic accounts of the essential features of these imaginary inventions called world religions were (and still are being) reproduced in hundreds of money-making textbooks designed for schools, colleges and universities. The 'secular' was (and is) rarely mentioned as an integral part of the modern ideology, but lies behind the whole enterprise of religion-construction as a vague, unarticulated background within the context of which the religions (and also our own scholarly endeavours of description and analysis) are assumed to exist. If the secular was ever mentioned, it would have been in relation to the supposed non-religious secular powers of the king as distinct from the religious offices of the priestly Brahmin, and more ambiguously the caste system, which was supposedly an accretion to (and possibly a deformation of) the 'religion' in some supposedly pure form, and so ambiguously both part of Hinduism and simultaneously outside the religion and located in 'society'. But since we were doing a course on religion, and not politics or society, these aspects were only touched on as non-essential to our topic.

I came to realize that I myself, through a psychological process of reification, thought of Hinduism, Buddhism and others as though they were actual, objective systems in the world which could be empirically observed, and which could either be studied as a single system, or could be compared to each other, their descriptions lined up like members of an organic species and analysed and compared under different headings such as doctrine, ritual, ethics, experience, organization or social dimension and so on. These kinds of textbook (there are other, better, more critical kinds of textbook available now, but I doubt if they are read by the school inspectors[7]) are still being prolifically reproduced, despite all the criticisms made of them. Then, as now, I wondered what was driving this discourse so insistently.

I became aware of, and frustrated by, the way these models – which turned what I assumed to be some kind of corresponding reality, out there in the Indian sub-continent, into neat objects of knowledge – had arbitrary boundaries and cut-off points. One phrase that was very popular throughout the 1980s was 'religion and society', as though these were two separate things in the world which had problematic external relations. The general nuance was that the private, inner, 'experiential' relation with 'god' was the religious core; that doctrines and myths about this god and his (or her) relation to the world 'structured' and 'expressed' this core experience; that these doctrines usually (though not always: for example, Hinduism) derived from the teaching of a founder; that rituals were religious (rather than merely ceremonial) to the extent that they externally expressed this inner core; that objects and relationships were sacred in so far as they were more or less directly implicated in these rituals; and that organizations involving founders, priests, monks, renouncers, churches, temples, shrines, mosques and so on guarded and transmitted the doctrine and the practice. This assumption about religion and its supposed relation to society permeates the IR and social science books I analyse in this text, and in some cases (one of the authors is an economist) it is entirely explicit. It is more or less the definition of religion given to me by MAR, the database discussed in Chapter 3.

In the case of Hinduism, to continue with one example, this 'religion' supposedly had a relation *with*, or an impact *on*, 'society', as though it was essentially separate *from* the social but nevertheless important *for* the social. Religious Studies was concerned primarily with the religious, even though it took note of the social dimension. In the Religious Studies texts it was difficult to find a clear and convincing explanation of whether or not 'caste' was included or excluded as 'religious' or merely 'social', or whether or not the traditional functions of the king were 'religious' or 'political', or how a religious ritual differed from a secular one, for example a village feast, or a marriage, or traditional forms of exchange in the *jajmani* or *balutedari* systems of exchange of goods and services, or the practices surrounding untouchability. And while the complexities of the Sanskritic category *dharma* were touched on, it was and is difficult to see how *dharma* can be divided in terms of the Anglophone religion–secular binary. Yet *dharma* was and is frequently taken uncritically to be equivalent to 'religion'.

This reification of religion has not only occurred through Religious Studies, but has also been promoted from the other, 'secular' side of the binary division. Even as the influence of social or cultural anthropology permeated religious studies in the late 1970s and through the 1980s, the distinctive traces of this distinction between the religious and the non-religious secular continued. Sociology and social anthropology were primarily concerned with the 'social', and from this standpoint some sociologists and anthropologists dealt with 'religion', either as a specialist interest or as *one* of those aspects of human society that in specific contexts required attention. But the discursive distinction between religion and the secular, or religion and the social, was rarely if ever questioned from this side either.

One classic collection of essays by anthropologists on the definition of religion which was required reading in the course at King's on anthropology of religion was *Anthropological Approaches to the Study of Religion* edited by E.M. Banton (1966). It contains interesting and influential essays by Victor Turner, Clifford Geertz, Melford Spiro and others. However, their overall effect has been, I would argue, to validate and reinscribe religion into the general academic discourse on which they have had considerable influence. While raising and discussing many of the problems of applying a Europhone category in the context of radically different languages and cultures, these essays did not interrogate the ideological power dynamics behind the discourse itself. The category 'religion' and its demarcation from the social or secular was not systematically questioned; only the best way to define religion for research purposes.

For example, Geertz (1966) famously defined religion as '[1] a system of symbols which acts to [2] establish powerful, pervasive, and long-lasting moods and motivations ... by [3] formulating conceptions of a general order of existence and [4] clothing these conceptions with such an aura of factuality that [5] the moods and motivations seem uniquely realistic.' But this definition arguably encompasses all powerful ideologies, and does not tell us how a religious ideology differs from a non-religious one. Nor does it sufficiently draw attention to the power of dominant institutions (such as preaching, courts, persuasive theories by educated elites, advertising or the media) to protect these symbols, to police their interpretation, and to promote the sense of their inescapable reality. A powerful analogy may be from feminist analysis of the way dominant gender categories become transformed into inescapable facts of biological nature, disguising the power relations inherent in the representations. The assumption that there is some essential distinction between religious and non-religious domains, which is still today a globalizing discourse, is an ideological construct that takes on an appearance of naturalness and inevitability.

Spiro's (1966) definition was a sophisticated reworking, in the context of his own interesting ethnography of Burmese Buddhism, of E.B. Tylor's definition of religion as belief in gods or superhuman agents. However, one of the problems with a definition in terms of gods or the supernatural or the superhuman is that these terms themselves are difficult to translate into many non-European languages. Even within European Christendom the meaning of God has been policed and contested by powerful theological agencies, and it is not at all clear that the Trinitarian God of the Aristotelian–Thomist synthesis is equivalent to what Calvin understood by God. The stretch may be even further to the conceptions of Unitarianism or Deism. Muslim theologians who believe in Allah have held that the Christian Trinitarian God is itself a form of idolatry. Given the histories of conflict between the so-called Biblical monotheisms, who – apart from a small number of ecumenical theologians and other well-wishers – could say that Yahweh, Christ and Allah are the same 'god'?

# Gods

If 'God' is problematic, the problems multiply with 'gods'. The term 'gods' is widely used in anthropology and across the humanities and social sciences as a neutral, generic category. Yet 'gods' has been used historically by Christians in the sense of false idols, pagan heresies, demons and devil worship. These theological misrepresentations do not engender confidence in their use as neutral descriptive and analytical concepts for representing non-European categories. This point is strengthened by the fact that, even today, some well-financed evangelical missionaries interested more in conversion than in dialogue still hold these beliefs and still use this kind of language. To take just two examples of non-European languages, Sanskrit and Japanese: it is problematic to claim that the term 'gods' provides a neutral translation for Sanskrit categories such as Brahman, deva, devata or Bodhisattva; or into Japanese categories such as kami, hotoke or bosatsu. It is equally problematic to attribute belief in the 'supernatural' and its supposed distinction from the 'natural' to non-European languages and cultures around the world. Some writers have substituted the term 'superhuman' as a way to resolve this problem of the 'supernatural' while retaining the term 'religion' as a distinct form of life. But if the term superhuman has any advantages, it tends to erode a distinction between 'religious' and 'non-religious' domains. In some Indian conceptions there is no ultimate distinction between the human and the superhuman, as the practice of kissing the feet of enlightened gurus and powerful politicians suggests. Many sadhus are believed to be 'living gods' in the sense that they have become one with the divine reality which permeates what we illusorily experience as a mundane world. This is not a pedantic distinction; the veneration given to a sadhu or a living bodhisattva is part of a total system of representations that defines the identity of billions of people. It is astonishing that experts in International Relations believe they can classify these complex ideologies without any real knowledge in simplistic English categories and then advocate foreign-policy decisions on their basis. In Japan the Emperor was *ikigami*[8] (usually translated as 'living god') at a time when the Meiji Constitution of 1889 constituted State Shinto as the Japanese equivalent of the secular state.[9] In 1946 the US Occupation forces rewrote the Constitution which declared that State Shinto is really a religion and should be classified as such; and that the Emperor is no longer *ikigami* but something more like a British constitutional monarch. Here it is clear that power decides what gets classified as a religious belief and what as a secular one.

But these objections were developed more fully at a later stage, so to some extent I am reading back into history my present understanding. I was still a religious believer, in the sense that I still believed in the existence of religion and religions, and my scepticism was incipient and emergent rather than consciously developed. That each persuasive definitional foray in this classic collection on the definition of religion edited by Banton was different, and was not necessarily consistent with the others, did not lessen the overall sense to me as a student that something important was being talked about, if only we could eventually hit on the key note which would bring order and compatibility to our diverse definitions. It did not occur to me at this stage in my career to question the whole discourse on religion and religions. Everybody else seemed entirely sure that religion and religions exist; or at least that religion is a necessary and indispensible, neutral, disinterested descriptive category. Otherwise why would so many eminent anthropologists (and philosophers) take so much trouble in working on its proper definition?

# Anthropology

However, despite that important limitation, anthropology provided the best way to contextualize ideas; and in the teaching of Hinduism and Buddhism that I went on to do at a college of higher education in the early 1980s I found the anthropological literature on India indispensable. Ethnography brought the reader away from the artificially-abstracted 'world religions' reifications of Religious Studies closer to the grass roots. Some of my own students, especially those who were training as schoolteachers, often grew restless with abstract theological and philosophical concepts and vast historical generalizations, and were – I think rightly – more interested in the details of everyday customary practices and human relations. The problem with the history of ideas approach to Hinduism and Buddhism was that it created internally coherent soteriological systems with only little relationship to concrete human relationships. Such an approach disembedded ideas and practices from living institutions and from power. Ethnography to some extent opened up the opportunities to subvert these unsatisfactory divisions by offering concrete descriptions about how people live, how they marry and die, how they differentiate between male and female, which groups or offices control power, how hierarchies are constructed, what different classes of people do or do not eat or wear, how they subsist and the kinds of productivity they are engaged in. Ethnography seemed to open up more interesting views of caste and gender, and what might be described as the daily disciplines of civility.

But the division still persisted, because anthropologists often inadvertently reified 'religion' themselves in their attempts to provide the other side of the dichotomy, the social context in which 'religion' was one aspect. So even here the contours of the seemingly arbitrary Western distinction between religion and society permeated the anthropological literature. 'Religion' and 'society' (or 'politics' or 'economics') as Anglophone categories were rarely consistently deconstructed. And both sides tended to divorce 'religion' from power. Even Marxist anthropology, which classifies religion as part of ideology in general, still generally fails to critically and fully subvert the category, though I think the critical Marxist tradition may have some of the theoretical tools to succeed in this, a point I touched on in Chapter 1 and which I discuss more fully in the final chapter. Religious Studies accounts of religions and world religions are today permeated by ethnography, but the idiom of religions and world religions is still largely entrenched, apart from a few pioneering departments which teach critical courses which deconstruct the category religion and its dichotomous opposite the non-religious secular and invite students to perceive it as a conceptual and historical problem.

## Ambedkar, Gandhi and 'religion' in India

In further pursuit of these problems, and once I had finished my PhD in Philosophical Theology, I studied social anthropology at the LSE in the mid-1980s as a part-time master's degree and around the same time went to Maharashtra in India to do fieldwork on Ambedkar Buddhism and the Dalit movement for social justice. I was not an expert in Marathi, but I wanted to expose myself as far as possible to the actualities of 'Hinduism' and 'Buddhism' which the books I was reading were describing. I wanted to find out at first hand, or as close to first hand as it was possible for a white, male, middle-class university lecturer, what terms like *dharma*, caste and untouchable really referred to. The problems of the referent of categories 'religion', 'society' and 'politics' deepened when confronted directly by Indian forms of life, and especially the attempt to understand why large parts of an untouchable caste were attempting to change their collective designation from Mahar to Buddhist, and why they were finding it so difficult.

One of the many reasons why I wanted to study this movement (if this is the best term) was because of Dr B.R. Ambedkar, the leader of the Dalits and a convert to Buddhism.[10] His was a name which I don't think ever came up in Religious Studies lectures and the textbooks on Hinduism or Buddhism which we read when I was a student. Why was it that, while Gandhi was always included in textbooks on the religion of Hinduism, Ambedkar's name was rarely if ever mentioned? Nor was he mentioned in religion books on Buddhism.[11] Ambedkar, I discovered, had provided a significantly different analysis from Gandhi on the issue of emancipation from British colonial rule. Himself an untouchable, he had posed a powerful challenge to Gandhi, both as a leader of the untouchables and as a public critic of Hindu practices. It also seemed significant that Ambedkar became the first minister of law in Nehru's government, and the chairman of the Constitutional Committee that designed the modern Indian Republican Constitution. This significance seems even greater when one considers that in 1927 Ambedkar had publicly burned the traditional Hindu law book Manu Smriti. Furthermore, in his 1936 Annihilation of Caste, Ambedkar had distinguished between the Religion of Rules, by which he meant Brahmanism, and the Religion of Principles, which he identified with the values of liberty, equality and fraternity. He then went on later to identify these principles with *buddha dhamma* as taught by Shakyamuni Gotama 2500 years ago. It is interesting to note how ambiguous these principles seem in terms of the religion–secular binary. They are usually associated with the French Revolution and the Goddess of Reason, became the basis for French *laicété* and the modern secular state in France. In Ambedkar's strategy, they are first the Religion of Principles, then the basis of the Republican Constitution, and finally the core values of *buddha dhamma*.

Why would students studying Hinduism graduate without even knowing his name? I think because he spoils the liberal ecumenical construct 'Hinduism' by revealing – as an untouchable himself – the exploitative power ideology of Brahmanism behind the theological idealizations. I had for some time been suspicious of the way Western, usually Protestant Christian, religionists seemed to fete Gandhi and adopted him as one of the patron saints of Christian ecumenical theology which underlay so much of the thinking in Religious Studies and comparative religion. One of the ways Gandhi has typically, and positively, been represented by Christian ecumenicals and comparative religionists is as the emancipator of the untouchables, who he referred to as *harijan*, and his claim that untouchability is a corruption of the original pure Hindu philosophy of the *varna* system, which he argued was a division of labour necessary for the proper functioning of society. On my research trips I discovered that the term *harijan* is rejected and even detested by many members of scheduled castes as the patronizing condescension of upper-caste Brahmanical consciousness. To them it is irrelevant that Gandhi was not a Brahmin; to them he was part of the Brahmin ideological complex, albeit a reforming part.

This approving attitude to Gandhi and his *harijan* in Religious Studies was one small element in my general suspicion that the study of religion was not the neutral and objective description and analysis of the world that it appeared to be. It was something of a surprise for me to discover that Ambedkar, himself an untouchable and for many the true leader of the emancipation of untouchables (whom he termed Dalits), was an outspoken critic of 'Hinduism' and Brahmanical ideology as a vast, mystified system of degradation and exploitation. He criticised Gandhi as a high-caste reformist and paternalist who exercised power under the deceptive guise of non-violence. For example, Gandhi used his powers of self-publicity and a vow to fast unto death to pressure Ambedkar – I am not sure if Dr Ambedkar used the term blackmail, but it certainly has been used by those close to him – into dropping his demand for separate electorates for untouchables (the Poona Pact), a demand for which the British Imperial power had some sympathy.[12]

I discovered quite a lot of interesting and sympathetic work published on Ambedkar and the Buddhists, by such authors as D. C. Ahir, D. Keer, N. D. Kamble, Vasant Moon, A. K. Narain, J. M. Mahar, Eleanor Zelliot, Owen Lynch, Gail Omvedt, and others. I have since come to realize the vast literature from inside India on Dr Ambedkar, the Constitution, and the Buddhist and Dalit movement for democracy and social justice which is even stronger today. I have cited and quoted the work of some of these authors in my own published work on Ambedkar Buddhism, some of which has been included in books and journals published in India. Some of this work has been published also in Japan in both Japanese and English.[13]

Ambedkar, in his *Annihilation of Caste*, argued that 'Hinduism' was really a system of Brahmanical and more generally high-caste exploitation, and that true emancipation must be, in the first place, emancipation from this institutionalized form of exploitation through a peaceful democratic revolution. As first Law Minister of India in Nehru's cabinet he attempted to provide the Constitutional means to achieve this. Eventually, feeling that he had failed, he turned to *buddha dhamma*. Ambedkar had PhDs from Columbia University in New York and the LSE in London, and had qualified as a barrister in London. He was a highly qualified economist and social theorist, much influenced by the anthropology he learnt at Columbia. He used his skills as a lawyer to fight for the rights of the depressed classes in India. He developed a highly articulate critique of Hindu ideology and developed a counter-ideology of social justice and democracy that has massively influenced the contemporary discourse on *bahujan Samaj* embodied in the Bahujan Samaj Party (BSP) which currently governs Uttar Pradesh, the largest state in India. His work on the modern Indian Republican Constitution established him as a considerable expert in the field of constitutional history.

But, despite his remarkable talents and achievements, he was struggling against deeply entrenched prejudice. For example, he remarked that, when he publicly addressed huge crowds as a member of Nehru's cabinet, at the end of his time on the podium Brahmin ritualists would come and perform purification rites to remove his pollution before a high-caste member of the panel could take his place on the podium. Once an untouchable, always an untouchable. Just before he died in 1956, he took Buddhist *diksha*[14] in public in Nagpur, along with about half a million other members of his own untouchable Mahar caste, proclaiming the *dhamma* revolution. He argued that *buddha dhamma* was more ancient and foundational as an Indian practice than Brahmanism, that it was inherently democratic and concerned with collective as well as individual liberation, that it was scientifically rational, and that it ought to provide the indigenous vehicle for modern social transformation in India.

The point that was beginning to become clear to me was that Dr Ambedkar's mission was both religious and political simultaneously, and that the notion that they must be *either* one *or* the other is a false dichotomy. This seems obvious and even banal as I write it, yet this *either–or* dichotomization of religion and politics, or religion and the secular state, is written into constitutions in their attempts to keep 'them' separate.[15] It is structurally embedded in the division of academic specialisms. And it is encoded in typical language use. Whenever someone comments – as they do in the media and in academia – that Dr Ambedkar, or the Dalai Lama, or this or that Muslim leader, is 'using religion for political ends', the tacit legitimacy of this *either–or* classification is established rhetorically. Much of the IR rhetoric I go on to analyse in this book encodes the same binary assumption in its narrative of the dangers of allowing 'religion' and 'politics' to mix. If kept separate and confined to its proper sphere, religion is harmless; but when allowed to mix with politics, religion tends to become transformed into irrational and barbaric terrorism. Needless to say, Ambedkar has been accused of 'using' the religion Buddhism – which is supposedly and essentially a peace-loving and quietist personal soteriology based on meditation and renunciation – for political ends. Yet one could make a similar claim about Gandhi and his relation to the construct Hinduism.

My research in the mid-1980s and early 1990s was in the urban centres of Maharashtra such as Mumbai, Pune and Nagpur, and also the villages in Marathawada. The Mahar untouchable caste members lived separated from the clean part of the village and had limited rights of entry and no right to enter the village temple (Maruti Mandir). But there was a high level of awareness of Ambedkar's leadership, his interpretation of Buddhism as a movement for democracy and social justice, and many Mahar-Buddhists had withdrawn from traditional occupations of servility such as clearing away dead animals and night soil. I met many articulate Mahar-Buddhist spokesmen (always men). Some referred to 'Buddhism' or *buddha dhamma* as a personal soteri-ology, and they went to specific viharas (where these were available) to receive traditional teaching on the sutras from accredited Theravada monks and other kinds of Buddhist mendicants and renouncers,[16] and to practise meditation. However, all Buddhists I spoke to saw personal emancipation as indissolubly related to collective emancipation, just as Ambedkar insisted. For the factors of suffering were and are identified as institutionalized exploitation and degradation of caste and untouchability; the cause as Brahmanical ideology which legitimates the caste system; the end of suffering as the annihilation of caste and its replacement by a democratic society based on justice, equality, dignity and similar virtues; and the means to attaining the goal as education, morality, collective up-lift, and organization. Ambedkar was never shy about his belief that the scheduled castes and other backward groups had to seize power, not through violent revolution that he explicitly rejected but through constitutional means. In general this was and is the meaning of Buddhism or *buddha dhamma*. Central modern idioms for all these combined goals were access to education and political organization. In this they were and are similar to other minority communities in India; but it was Ambedkar who provided one of the most powerful and consistent articulations of these combined goals, and his slogan 'educate, organize, agitate' was repeated to me again and again by Mahar-Buddhists.

Yet in Maharashtra most Buddhists belong to the same Mahar caste, and the movement has found it difficult to transcend the caste divisions that Ambedkar identified as the cause of weakness. This was at least the case in the early 1990s, and from what I heard from Dalits further north in Lucknow recently (always men) this still is the problem in Maharashtra and more generally. Caste divisions can only break down when people begin to ignore the rules of endogamy and inter-marry on a large scale. Even today one reads in the press about young men and women, especially women, being murdered by their own kin for contracting love marriages with members of another caste. When one of these is from an untouchable caste, then the problem and the reprisals can be even greater. If Buddhists want to break the marriage traditions of their own community, the members of other castes do not.

In such circumstances there is bound to be a less than perfect series of possible nuances about what it means to be a Buddhist. What is a Buddhist? Spokesmen (always men) ambiguously described Buddhism as a practice of salvation, as an anti-caste reform movement for democracy, or a little more narrowly as a means of liberation for all scheduled castes, or even more narrowly as a means for the uplift of their own Mahar-Buddhist community, or simply as their specific caste identity. None of these is strictly incompatible or contradictory, but there is an inherent lack of fit between aspirations and possibilities given the overall structures of power within which they have to live.

There is thus an inevitable gap between the ideal aspirations and the actual conditions and achievements. But it would be a mistake to underestimate the degree of passionate commitment, and the courage that has been required to make any impression at all on the dominant system. Buddhists have endured violent high-caste suppression and have suffered greatly in their struggle for justice and democracy. For them, it could be said that *political power is a religious principle.* [17]While Buddhists when speaking English use the terms 'religion' and 'politics', it is very unclear how the distinction is being made. I do not think they normally intend to make any distinction. The movement itself seems to me to undercut these categories. For example, there is no 'other-worldly' doctrine of salvation separate from the collective liberation from adverse living conditions; but there is a transcendental ideal and transcendental and indeed sacred values. The *dhamma* revolution is both a transformation of consciousness and a transformation of the order of human relations. It is freedom from the fetters of *karma*, but it is also freedom from the fetters of untouchability. In this sense, *karma* is not 'fate' but goal-directed action. And 'enlightenment' is found not only through meditation but even more through education and self-improvement.

I do not suppose that the identification of a doctrine of personal soteriology with a collective identity is itself especially modern or especially Ambedkarite or 'Mahar'. Identities that are classified typically as 'religious' are also frequently ethnic struggles for legitimate power. In Religious Studies representations, 'Buddhism' is usually understood as a doctrine and a practice of personal emancipation from suffering and delusion; in short, an individual soteriology, though with a 'social' dimension. However, when in English we refer to Sinhalese Buddhism, or Tibetan Buddhism, or Japanese Buddhism, it would be difficult to distinguish the collective, ethnic identification of 'Sinhalese', 'Tibetan' or 'Japanese' from the term 'Buddhism'. I am not saying that this distinction does not exist in Pali, Sanskrit, Sinhala, Tibetan or Japanese languages. In a sense it must do, because *buddha dhamma*, understood as the transmission and practice of the teaching of Gautama Shakyamuni, and the narration of the achievement of enlightenment by

Buddhas, Arhats and Bodhisattvas, inevitably points to individuals who have gained liberation, as distinct from the vast mass of beings who have not. Yet, as the Buddha himself pointed out, whether or not or in what sense 'I' exist in nirvana is a merely intellectual, speculative and un-answerable question. The 'I' or 'me' is a problem to be seen through in practice, not a speculative doctrine of belief. The practice itself, in Theravada at least, includes the idea of renunciation of an individual's personal ties to family and kin group. But it would be a mistake to confuse 'individual' here as equivalent to the Individual of Western Individualism. The latter ideological category does not translate at all well into the normal sense in which one person is distinct from another in the understanding of South Asia or East Asia. At the same time, ideas and philosophical formulations about liberation of the individual consciousness from *karma* and conditioned existence are always embedded in collective identity and institutionalized practice. The universal elements of soteriological practice are transmitted through and difficult to separate from collective practices.

While I was in India researching Buddhism in the mid-1980s and again in the early 1990s I met many different practitioners of, and spokesmen for, 'true' Buddhism (they were all men). One Sinhalese bikkhu of the Theravada Sangha I met said that Ambedkar was not a true Buddhist but really a 'politician'. He told me that it was in the Pali tradition of Theravada Buddhism that true *buddha dhamma* was to be found. When I asked him what he thought of Tibetan Buddhism he said (in English) that it was full of populist accretions such as the 'worship' of bodhisattvas who are like gods, so it is a corrupted form. Though he admitted ordinary people in Sri Lanka do 'worship' gods, he said this is not the true *buddha dhamma* as practised by the Sangha. Buddha was not a god but an ordinary man who had become extraordinary by discovering the way to enlightenment. Buddha should not be worshipped like a god but revered as a great man and a great teacher who discovered truth. Both Tibetan Buddhism and the kind of *buddha dhamma* taught by Dr Ambedkar were therefore, in this Theravada view, a somewhat corrupt version of the original teaching.[18]

On another occasion I met a Tibetan lama who said something very similar about Ambedkar – that he was really a 'politician' who was using Buddhism for 'political' ends.[19] When I asked the lama what he thought of the Sinhalese tradition of Theravada Buddhism, he took a different tack. He agreed that, as far as it went, there was much truth in that tradition, but it was a limited representation of Buddhist truth. He used the term *hinayana* or lesser vehicle to refer to Theravada of Sri Lanka and South East Asia. He told me that it was only in the *Mahayana*, the greater vehicle, and especially the *Tantrayana* of Tibetan Buddhism derived from the *Madhyamika* of Nagarjuna and other great masters, that the full truth of Buddhism came to light. He also added that it is problematic to translate the term 'bodhisattva' into the English word 'god'.

Later, when I went to Japan, I met bikkhus from Sri Lanka, Bangladesh, Vietnam and Korea who were studying with the noted Pali scholar Mayeda Egaku.[20] Professor Mayeda was revered by these students, but generally they rejected Japanese Buddhism as 'not true Buddhism', and said it was more about being Japanese than about being Buddhist.

These conversations illustrated the problems of identifying anything as the essential core of 'true' Buddhism, and the problem of separating a supposedly religious centre from matters of ethnicity, status and power. There is a long, rich and complex history of philosophical dispute throughout Asia about the proper interpretation and understanding of truth, and the schools of thought that are classified respectively as 'Buddhist' or Hindu' attest to this. One could say much the same about 'Confucian' or Daoist schools. But these profound philosophical discussions over many centuries and in many languages are always rooted in, and conditioned by, collective and institutional affiliations. To present even a text-based account of 'Theravada Buddhism' as a historical 'religion', with a doctrinally formulated soteriological core having only an external and contingent relationship with specific 'societies' and nothing essentially to do with power, is difficult enough. It becomes much more difficult in the case of a collective designation such as 'Sinhalese Buddhism'. The Sangha is inevitably involved in power relations, for example in who can and who cannot join the Sangha, in caste and gender issues, in internal disciplinary matters, in relations with government, in the accumulation of land and wealth, in attitudes to poverty and social status, and so on.

These conversations raised in my mind the problem about what constitutes the 'political' or 'social' as distinct from the 'religious', not only for Mahar Buddhist followers of Ambedkar but equally for Sinhalese, for Tibetans and for Japanese. Another issue was what constitutes 'worship' of 'gods' as distinct from respectful remembrance and veneration of a great but deceased person, or indeed from remembrance of ancestors in Japan. Ambedkar was and still is frequently referred to as a bodhisattva who acted from compassion to lead the suffering people to liberation. But were the people worshipping him or merely venerating his memory? And is this distinction itself imported into the situation by way of Christian-inflected European languages? Another point was that, while Mahars described themselves as Buddhist or Bauddha, the members of other castes rejected that self-designation, sometimes contemptuously, and told me they were not Buddhist but Mahar. Even some members of other untouchable castes such as Mang, who one might have thought would have an interest in joining forces with Mahar-Buddhists in becoming involved in a movement for democracy, and in subverting the dominant power of Brahmins and other high castes such as Marathas, interpreted the movement only as a 'Mahar' bid for higher status and greater power. Their concern – at that time at least – was more focused on local issues of relative status than in the more universalist questions of democracy and equality. Another issue was the contested interpretations of history, their uses in the rhetorical struggles and legitimations of different interests, and in what sense history differed from myth as a charter for action and bids for power.

Another difficulty was that all these conversations were in English[21] either directly on a one-to-one basis or through an interpreter. For all these reasons I was increasingly conscious that what was being said in English language categories may have distorted what would be said in Marathi, Sinhalese or Tibetan. The translation of 'religion' into either Sanskrit *dharma* or Pali *dhamma* seems very problematic and imprecise.[22] All of these terms are sites of contested power struggles and rhetorical deployment.

For these reasons my doubts deepened about widely disseminated discourses on 'Hinduism' and 'Buddhism' as 'religions' which were and still are being reproduced in Religious Studies textbooks. It is easy to see why one might begin to suspect that these neat soteriological systems, based largely on textual study, abstracted from the complexities of power, status and collective identities, are the colonial inventions of Anglophone or more generally Europhone Protestant Christian scholars, from Max Müller onwards and right up to recent experts. I say this even though there has also been a powerful counter-movement of deconstruction and critique within historical and anthropological studies influenced by critical Marxism, by European continental philosophy, by Foucault, by Edward Said's thesis on Orientalism, and by what has come to be called Postcolonial Studies. But the theoretical identification of knowledge with power and with colonial systems of classification has not had much practical effect on the broader Anglophone reproduction of representations, and apart from a handful of academics such as Talal Asad, David Chidester, Richard King and some others, has resulted in little critical reflection on the religion–secular binary as an ideological category.

In this context, I am especially concerned with the uncritically manipulated discourse on 'religion' and the embedded 'secular', which is what this book (and my three previous, though very different books) is focused on. I say 'embedded secular' in the sense that, while 'religion' and religions are constructed and reified as distinct objects of secular knowledge, the easy presumption of the neutrality and objectivity of secular knowledge is elided and mystified. Attention is systematically distracted from the total ideological project in which the scholar herself is engaged, usually unconsciously. I stress that this sketchy account of my own encounters with a complex Indian reality (if there is such a thing as an Indian reality) that I did not (and still do not) truly understand, is only given here so that the reader can see where my argument is coming from. I do not suppose that there is anything especially interesting about my personal biography outside of this aim. My research, for what it is worth, raised problems not only about 'religion' as a clear and valid category of description and analysis but also about related categories such as 'secular', 'society', 'politics' and 'economics'. I was struck by, and suspicious of, the way in which on the one hand 'religion and politics' or 'religion and society' were widely used as though their meanings are distinct, obvious and certain; and yet on the other hand the dividing line between them seemed arbitrary, provisional and contested. It then appeared to me that these are not obvious and transparent terms for universal realities that correspond with empirical observation, but are contested Anglophone or more widely Europhone categories with ideological work to do. They force and subordinate other peoples' realities into our Europhone classificatory demands. Indeed, I will go further in this book and argue that they force our own past and present realities into modern dominant ideological categories that no longer serve our wider democratic aspirations.

Coming as I did from Religious Studies and problems with the category 'religion', my experience of researching in India forced me to be more conscious that the problem does not lie only with religion but with the secular categories which are deemed to be non-religious, such as society and politics. This has more recently led me to consider the whole issue of secularism which has been debated a great deal both in the West and in India. The problems with secularism, either in general or in any local variant of a globalizing Anglophone category, are the other side of the problem 'religion' with which I began. My suggestion is that they are joined at the hip, and the deconstruction of one side of the term cannot be accomplished without the simultaneous deconstruction of the other. This leads to the observation that the religion–secular binary is itself a basic modern ideological formation. But again I am now stating what has subsequently become more clear to me, but was only emergent in the research processes I am narrating.

## Japan

These critical and deconstructive tendencies became stronger when I went to live and work in Japan. Japan is a profoundly different country from India, and the idea that they are both 'Asian' or 'Oriental' seems to lack clear meaning. Japan is as different from India as it is from the UK or the USA. I feel it with my body and my posture as soon as I pass through immigration control. It has been especially in Japan that I have come to see my embodied identity as itself an ideological construction (to put it crudely) rather than some pre-given biological lump of organic 'matter'. But, despite the immense differences between India and Japan, they share something in common with each other and with most of Asia. They have both been confronted, in specific historical ways, with Euro-American imperial power. It has been in confrontation with imperial power that both India and Japan developed a collective self-representation as modern nation states. Of course, Japan was never directly and substantively colonized in the way that India was colonized by the British; but Japanese modern history since the end of Edo in the 1860s up to the present has been predicated on its confrontation with the power of Euro-America. One of the first things my Japanese colleagues told me when

I arrived in Japan to teach at a university there, shamefully ignorant about Japanese history (I went because my Japanese father-in-law asked me to), was that the US Commander Perry sailed into Edo Bay in 1853 in a formidable ironclad warship referred to as the Black Ship (*kurofune*), and demanded entry. The Japanese were overwhelmed by this display of power. Even handmade samurai steel (still reputedly the best steel in the world) was no defence. (Only about 50 years later, the Japanese navy shocked Euro-America by destroying the Russian navy.)

The term *kurofune* is one way to use a historical reference point to talk about another term that Japanese frequently used – 'outside pressure' (*gaiatsu*). Much of Japanese modern history is only explicable when understood as an attempt to avoid colonization. The Japanese ruling male elites have in many ways been highly successful in marshalling traditional forms of defence – linguistic, cognitive, organizational, ethical, and traditions of craftmanship – against invasions from an overpowering outside, especially Euro-American imperial power. One of the many influences that Japan has been unable to resist entirely has been the discourse on 'progress', 'development' and 'rationality'. These are closely connected with capitalist modes of production and consumption that arguably have driven the violent and exploitative expansion of Western power, colonization and, until quite recently, the slave trade. Yet even the irresistible globalizing force of capitalist interests backed by modern nation states such as France, Germany, Britain and the US has been filtered through, and contained by, Japanese non-Western forms of life and values.[23] This force of globalizing 'political economy', a discourse that arguably only emerged in the early nineteenth century from problems and categories in Christian moral theology, brought with it the associated discourses on scientific rationality, progress, democracy and freedom, and the ideology of individualism, much of it clothed in rhetoric deriving from Protestant Christianity about Western civility as against pagan barbarity.

One of the rhetorical levers the Western powers used to enter Japan was the demand of advanced, civilized nations for 'freedom of religion', accusing Japan of being backward, inward looking, static and semi-barbarous. To be considered as civilized, the Japanese would require a written constitution separating 'religion' from 'politics' and the state. Did the Japanese not realize that 'religion' is a private right to be protected by a secular state? That this manipulation of categories was arguably still contested in European countries such as England until well into the twentieth century did not alleviate the demand for the civility of 'freedom of religion' in Japan by the colonizers of much of the world. For it was one of the preconditions for unopposed entry of Christian missionaries, traders and other colonial personnel in a country that had been closed to Christians for the whole of the Edo period.

Originally, through a Shogunate policy called *sakoku*, Japan had closed itself to outsiders (*gaikokujin*) in the seventeenth century after expelling the Jesuits and other missions who were seen as subversive of native power relations and customary forms of legitimate authority. The Japanese were now, 250 years later, virtually forced to open up to Christian missions again, and more generally to Euro-American capitalist interests. The debates about the meaning of a 'constitution' that followed among the literate male elites of Japan included a great deal of discussion about how to translate 'religion' and the non-religious state into the Japanese language. It is evident from the mere existence of these debates that the Europhone term 'religion' is not a self-evident, transparent category with an instantly recognizable and universal meaning, but is highly contentious and destabilizing. The same can presumably be said about the idea of a secular, non-religious state. If 'religion' means 'Christianity', which was its major referent to the Japanese reforming elites, then which Japanese indigenous practices or institutions could be considered 'religious'? Furthermore, what does 'secular' or 'non-religious' mean in Japanese? Japan had its own highly sophisticated view of the world, and these Europhone terms were alien. After much debate among the elites, the Meiji Constitution of 1889,[24] in its search for an indigenous, Japanese formulation of Christian-derived, modern ideology, translated 'religion' into Japanese as 'shukyo'. It is of special interest how they decided to incorporate the idea of the non-religious secular state on the basis of National Learning (kokugaku).[25] For the debate, embedded in the struggle to maintain independence from the colonizing powers, led to the invention of State Shinto (Kokka Shinto).[26]

Thus Kokka Shinto (State Shinto) was not originally classified as a 'religion' in the Meiji Constitution, but as the equivalent of the non-religious secular nation state. 'Religions' were virtually invented by transforming existing shrine and temple organizations (some of which had acted as extensions of Shogunate administration and did not stand in a simple modern relationship as 'religion' to 'secular' governance) into private, voluntary associations (shukyo hojin). Meanwhile, national shrines were constructed (such as Meiji, Yasukuni and Heian) or existing shrines transformed (Ise and others) into ceremonial sites of the 'secular' state.

It seemed logically to follow, at least for many members of the Japanese literate male elites, that if to be civilized meant colonizing large parts of the world, then it was reasonable for the Japanese to do the same. Attempts were made to follow the European colonization of large parts of Asia and the Pacific with its own empire, and to exploit its own colonies as markets and sources of labour and raw materials. This led to the Pacific World War, the subsequent bombing of Tokyo, Nagoya, Nagasaki and Hiroshima, and occupation of Japan by the US under General Douglas McArthur. One result of this occupation was the new 1946 Constitution, written originally in English by US expert advisors. This constitution did various things, one of which was to re-describe State Shinto as an illegitimate form of 'religion' and make it illegal, privatize all forms of Shinto, re-assign the status of the Emperor from living god to constitutional monarchy along British lines, and outlaw Japanese armed forces except for self-defence purposes. Once again, the contested and power-related definition of what constitutes religion and what constitutes a legitimate secular state and civil society becomes apparent. It depends on which powerful elites, thinking in which languages, are dominant.

I have made a series of arguments in other publications about the way 'religion' as a distinct domain of belief and practice has been constructed in Japan.[27] My view is a minority one, but then that is true of my arguments generally. It is mainly by considering the case of Japan (or any other country) in the wider historical and ethnographic contexts that I have so far indicated that the argument gathers substantial weight. These arguments about Japan in particular are too complex to repeat in detail here, and I would ask the interested reader to follow them up and if necessary contest them. This is why I believe that interdisciplinarity is a necessary requirement for the disembedding of the globalizing 'religion' discourse from its disguised ideological configuration. There is no doubt that the Eurocentric discourse about 'religion' that developed in the colonial era has been translated into Japanese and to some extent internalized into the Japanese language and consciousness. 'Religion' (*shukyo*) is a special category of organization and practice separated from the secular state in the modern Japanese constitution. There are also today several university departments that study 'religion' (*shukyogaku*), though these are sometimes combined as departments of religious and Buddhist studies. There are Religious Studies journals and organizations. There is a lot of published and on-going research by Japanese and non-Japanese scholars of 'new religions' (*shin-shukyo*) which are voluntary organizations with the juridical status of *shukyo hojin* (religious juridical person). Some of these are well known. Sokka Gakkai ('value-creating society') has branches in many countries. Aum Shinrikyo is notorious for the sarin gas attack on the Tokyo subway in 1996. There are several much older ones. There is also a fairly widespread popular discourse on religion and religions in Japan.

The Japanese Wikipedia has several articles on the study of religion and the history of religions that I have recently translated for my own needs. These seem to have been written by obviously competent professional academics. In these on-line articles one finds an approach to the subject very similar to quite traditional approaches in Anglophone religious studies. There is no doubt that 'religion' as a distinct discursive domain is well established in Japan at various levels.

Yet my general experience of talking to Japanese people, both in English and in Japanese, has been that religion or *shukyo* is not something about which they know very much or in which they have much interest; that it is associated mainly with 'Christianity' or, sometimes, with 'Buddhism'; and that Japan is not a 'religious' country. One Japanese anthropologist said to me 'we do not *do* religion in Japan!' Many – I would say most – of the students I spoke to about this issue at my university did not see 'religion' as having much to do with Japan or with their lives. Religious Studies books on Japanese religion invariably classify Shinto as 'a religion' and Shinto shrines as centres of religious activity. There are many local and national festivals which typically involve parading a special palanquin containing *kami* (usually, and problematically, translated as 'god') from the local shrine around the neighbourhood. They are replete with ritualized behaviour. I have seen many of these and read ethnographic accounts of many others, and it seems obvious to me that the vast majority are concerned with parading local hierarchies, conferring prestige on donors, marking out the boundaries of administrative districts, promoting tourism and trade, renewing local solidarities, and having fun. There is also a sub-text that the festivals renew *Japanese* solidarities. Sometimes one can find a local expert who can give a history of the festival, but rarely is there anything like a theological belief system, and the vast majority of people (including the highly educated) are not aware of which *kami* is being paraded or what the festival means in such 'theological' terms. This is not because the Japanese people are ignorant of things we assume they ought to know, but because they have their own epistemological traditions and priorities. I frequently asked my Japanese students if going to the Shinto shrine at New Year or participating in a festival was religious or connected to *shukyo*; almost all said that these had nothing to do with religion; these are traditional Japanese customs. I asked specifically about these activities because they are widely included as 'religious' activities in English language books of religious studies.[28]

On the other hand I have always been struck (as have many other people) by the intense degree of ritualization in everyday behaviour in Japan. This is true of the home, the school, the university, the corporation, and just about every department of ordinary life. I have given many examples in my other publications. Let me give only one here to indicate briefly what I mean. One of the greatest national achievements in Japan is the transport system. Anyone who has experienced and regularly used the vast and complex train networks in Tokyo or the Kansai region will share with me a sense of wonder at their precision, cleanliness and convenience. The timetabling, punctuality, courtesy of staff, and correct behaviour of the passengers (despite all the stories of the hell of rush hour) provides an important insight into the workings of this vast nation in a wider sense. When the Shinkansen from Tokyo bound for Hakata arrives at Kyoto station, the cleaning staff, neatly uniformed and with identically constituted sets of equipment neatly at hand, line up at their pre-designated stations along the platform and, in precise unison, bow low to the train as it arrives. This bowing (similar to the saluting of a national flag) is an act of sacralization, a public display of deep respect, both towards the wonderful train itself, understandably an object of national pride, to the 'captain of the ship' driving the train and responsible for its safety and punctuality, and to those who travel in her. This ritual performance indicates an attitude of reverence to a major symbol of the collective identity of the nation. On the train itself, the neatly uniformed ticket-checker bows low as he or she enters each carriage, before respectfully proceeding down the aisle. I could multiply the details of these rituals of reverence – for example, where even on a relatively local train an inspector bows low to a virtually empty carriage before moving along down the aisle.

One way of thinking about this ritualization of the rail networks and arguably of all institutions in Japan is to say that Japan is a 'Confucian' country. Some scholars have claimed that 'Confucianism' is a 'religion'. The teaching of Confucius, referred to in Japanese as *jukyō*, entered Japan many centuries ago from China, was adopted (like the teaching of Buddha) by the elites as a mark of cultivation and civility, and gradually percolated through society. Though there are great scholars of *jukyō* in the universities, and though most ordinary people know the term, the ritualizing practices of everyday life in Japan are not a 'belief' system or a consciously adopted system of moral precepts (though moral precepts are included). If we are to use the term at all in this wider behavioural context, it would be more true to say that *jukyō* is a code of civilized practice of embodied gesture, social distance, hierarchy, and respect language which is taught as a practice by example and precedent in the school systems, and which continues throughout all stages of life and throughout all institutions. It becomes the largely unconscious practice of civility without which it is difficult to live in Japan, and without which we cannot understand a major cause of Japan's extraordinary success as a productive, technological nation with a GDP equal to Germany, France and the UK combined. Nor can we understand other experiences that visitors to Japan usually have, such as the levels of honesty and courtesy towards neighbours, the low levels of petty crime, the lack of graffiti, the punctuality, and the general attention to detail that characterizes production and consumption.

Is the ritualization of the train networks, or of Japanese institutions more generally, 'religious' behaviour? I cannot see why not. That the train services are generally privatized in Japan makes no difference to the attitudes displayed and promoted. The attention to the details of correct behaviour, to cleanliness and purification, to right timing, to things being in their proper place, to the reverence of the greater whole and to the transcendental principles of the Japanese nation itself, have most of the hallmarks of what people usually deem to be religious in other contexts. If one can see some similarities with military order and discipline, then such an understandable analogy merely raises the further question: why should we not describe the military as a religious practice? One problem arises because of the determination of Western analysts to assume that 'religion' and 'religious practice' is directed towards 'supernatural' agents or 'gods', is other-worldly, and is separated from secular society. But I suggest that these terms do not successfully demarcate any distinctive domain of human action. These vague terms are at best problematic even in English. Is the nation state not a god? Or a sacred canopy? Or a transcendental value to be defended if necessary with the ultimate sacrifice? It is even more difficult to translate these terms into non-European languages (are people who are revered by devoted followers 'gods'?), and leave as ambiguous many of the objects of devotion of ordinary people which are far more important in terms of commitment, and run much deeper emotionally, than a Protestant Christian-derived concept of the so-called 'supernatural'.

The problem is compounded by the fact that, at the constitutional level, the workings of commercial companies, schools, the state bureaucracies, everyday public purification rituals, the use of respect language, and all those disciplines of civility that go to make up 'Japanese identity', are not 'religious' but 'secular' organizations or practices. But this is an arbitrary line of exclusion that is better explained by the ideological demands of Anglo-America that historically has supposed that for a nation to be 'civilized' it must have a written constitution which provides for 'freedom of religious worship'. This in turn depends on the prior distinction between 'religion' and the 'secular'.

There also exists the idea of *nihonkyo*, sometimes referred to as the Japanese 'religion' or the religion of Japaneseness. This idea of *nihonkyo* is closely associated with *nihonjinron* theory, that is, a theory about the uniqueness of 'we' Japanese.[29] One small indication of what kind of myth may lie behind this reverence for the Japanese collective identity may be found in a short newspaper article (*Japan Times*, 3 July 2010) on opposition to suffrage for foreigners who live in Japan permanently. The article reports that the ruling Democratic Party of Japan advocated the introduction of limited suffrage for certain classes of long-term foreign residents, but this is a contentious issue even within the ruling party and is facing 'strong opposition' from the Liberal Democratic Party and other smaller parties, including those in the governing coalition. The article reports that the leader of a citizens' group in Nagoya opposing the rights of foreigners to vote said such a measure would 'threaten Japanese tradition and national security'. He is reported as saying that 'The pride of this country which has been built up by the Yamato (Japanese) race must be passed down to our children, otherwise there will be no future for our country.' The ancient historical Yamato polity is one of the sources of the myth of Japanese uniqueness (*nihonjinron*) which, as most long-term foreign residents of Japan are only too aware, corresponds to a widespread and deeply-rooted conviction which bears many family resemblances to those 'faiths' usually classified as religions. To try to isolate such a collective faith from a putative non-religious secular domain makes little sense, since it pervades all institutionalized practices in Japan, including sports and productive industry.

I have tried here to give a brief description of the problem I have encountered, while living and working in Japan and struggling with the language (very imperfectly; I am not a trained Japanologist, and am largely self-taught), in representing Japanese customs and forms of life in Anglophone categories such as 'religion' and secular domains. On the one hand, outside categories have been internalized and institutionalized at various significant levels such as the constitution, the classification of certain kinds of organization as *shukyo hojin ho* (religious juridical person), the idea of secular education, and the establishment of departments of Religious Studies. On the other hand, I have indicated how Japanese institutions that at the formal level would be classified as 'secular' are permeated by forms of behaviour which might equally be classified as 'religious'. I gave one example as the transport system. In my publications I have given many more examples, including the schools and baseball (*yakyu*).[30] What this is intended to indicate is the intercultural mimesis (to use Charles Hallisey's felicitous phrase) resulting from partial internalization and partial quarantining of Euro-American categories.

## Religion and the Secular as Mutually Parasitic Imaginaries

Beginning with problems in the deployment of 'religion', I have increasingly been obliged by the sheer logic of the discourse to look at mirror-image problems in the deployment of secular non-religious categories such as 'society' or 'politics'. Most Western academics seem to find no problem with the deployment of 'religion' as though it constitutes a stable descriptive concept providing reliable knowledge of the world, on a kind of 'you know what is meant' basis. But the problems that I have indicated with 'religion' cannot, I suggest, be separated from the problems with the meaning of secular and secularism, which have recently been discussed by writers such as Talal Asad, Charles Taylor and many others in the West, and have long been debated by Anglophone-educated Indians.[31]

What constitutes 'religion' and what constitutes the 'secular' has been a bone of contention for the literate classes of India for many decades. The courts, in interpreting the constitutional right to freedom of religion and non-interference of the secular State in religious matters, have to decide whether or not the minute regulations of caste practice, untouchability, sub-caste endogamy, polygamy, separate dining, temple entry prohibitions, are an essential part of the 'religion Hinduism' and therefore outside the jurisdiction of the courts. What has been constructed as Hinduism since the colonial era is a potentially vast and varied system or collection of systems governed by traditional laws of convention and authority, sometimes summarized in law books such as the Manu Smriti. If these law books and customary practices were protected under a Freedom of Religion clause, they would constitute an alternative and competing legal system to the courts themselves. What constitutes 'Hinduism' in public discourse has therefore come to be decided as much by the secular courts as by any other agencies. Different court decisions have limited the definition in different ways and to different degrees. The history of court decisions about what constitutes a Hindu religious practice that is protected by law, and what must be considered 'non-essential' to the religion, reveals considerable arbitrariness.[32] Furthermore, from the point of view of a Hindutva nationalist writer such as Atal Behari Vajpayee, the version of secularism that he attributes to Nehru and the Congress party is 'pseudo-secularism'. A true secularism for India is defined by the customary practices of 'Hinduism' or traditional Hindu law![33]

I now believe that the history of law and constitutions is one essential location for the deconstruction of the myth of the religion–secular binary. I argue throughout this book that this distinction is a modern Anglophone, or more widely Europhone, invention which, by insisting that all the world's practices and institutions can somehow be classified in terms of this simplistic binary opposition, has had the effect of blinding Anglo-Americans and those who have adopted Anglophone mythology, and severely limited our ability to comprehend much of the world. This ideologically-driven binary clothes modern institutions such as the state, capital and self-regulating markets with an aura of factuality in accordance with 'natural' (universal) reason. It is in this ideological context that it now seems 'natural' for secular scholars to produce knowledge about 'religion' and 'religions'. Not only does this inhibit a realization that, to take Japan again as an example, Japanese industry is motivated by a collective intensity and fervour for supreme achievement that can match the fervour and intensity of any Christian evangelical group. Belief in this ideological binary also hides from view the religious-like practices[34] of the scholars themselves.

While living in Japan, and since returning to the UK where I now live and work, I have developed arguments (historical and ethnographic) in a number of publications that the religion–secular dichotomy in its various forms – such as religion–society, religion–politics, religion–economics and religion–state – is an ideological construct which has had the effect of reifying religion as though it is a distinct universal category fixed in human nature and common to all peoples in all languages and all historical periods. When a definition is required, then one favourite is 'the supernatural' or 'gods', which merely substitutes two equally empty and arbitrary categories for the first. If the idea of the *non-religious* secular is equally empty and parasitic on whatever is put into the 'religion' basket, so it can be argued that 'nature' only has meaning to the degree that it is deemed separate from 'supernature', and so on. (Just as no-one has ever seen a religion, so no-one has ever seen 'nature'. These are not derived from empirical observation.) I have critiqued the construction of religion, supernatural, gods and so on, and also 'secular' categories, in several different contexts, including the academic literature of religious studies, philosophy and anthropology, arguing that the idea of religion as an objective category corresponding to some distinct reality in the world quietly and stealthily legitimates the nation state, the science of political economy, the secular reason of academic productivity and its assumed objectivity and neutrality. In other words, the invention of religion and its reproduction in academic and non-academic discourses conceals a massive sub-stratum of power beneath an illusion of objectivity and factuality. Yet this is also its weakness, for the belief in 'religion' and 'religions' creates a peculiarly narrow and distorted perspective on the world. I have also analysed Anglophone historical texts since the sixteenth century in order to suggest how and why this modern binary between religion and the non-religious secular was constructed in England and Euro-America more generally.

This reifying effect of religion as an ahistorical something which cannot be satisfactorily defined is built into the secularization thesis too; I have argued this point (Fitzgerald 2007a: 96–100) in relation to the sociologists Bryan Wilson (1990: 587–8), and Peter Berger, another influential exponent of this thesis and whose powerful book *The Social Reality of Religion* (1973) was on several of our student book lists at King's. I suggest that this tacit but elided construction of the secular by means of the reification of 'religion' is also more recently reproduced in Berger's claim that the world is now becoming *de-secularized* (see Berger 1999). Narratives about 'religions' as processes of constructing sacred canopies tacitly builds in the claim that secular sociology can reveal a higher truth in a neutral, objective way, thus eliding the ideological nature of sociology and the social sciences generally. When Berger now changes his mind and says he was wrong, the world is not becoming secularized but de-secularized, he is still positioning himself on the superior vantage point of the social scientist making predictions about the behaviour of an illusory reification that he himself continues to create! This reified – I would say mystified – way of constructing the world, which mirrors the disciplinary divide in the university, continues to be widely reproduced today, as I will show in the literature discussed in this book. As such, the religion–secular dichotomy is itself a substantial part of the 'sacred canopy' of the so-called science of society.

I mentioned before that, in the Religious Studies literature, the construction and reproduction of these reified systems such as Hinduism, Buddhism, Confucianism and Shinto owed a great deal to liberal Christian presuppositions. Many of the twentieth-century postwar Religious Studies experts had been missionaries, or had come out of Christian theology, or had an interest in liberal ecumenical theology which posited 'religions' as different paths to the One God.[35] It is true, on the surface at least, that many of the twentieth-century founders of Religious Studies repudiated the earlier and grosser characterization by their nineteenth- and early twentieth-century predecessors of 'oriental religions' as heathen superstitions. And some were uncomfortable at the suggestion that missionaries were agents of the imperial power and capital. Many missionaries were uncompromisingly opposed to imperialism, yet they still availed themselves of the colonial privilege of special entry and propaganda among subjugated peoples of their own alien beliefs. I speculated that some may have themselves wondered, in an existential moment of crisis in the postwar period of decolonization, what they were doing in Africa or India or China or the Pacific. Some wanted to find a common core of theological belief (different paths to the same [Christian] God) that would bring peace to the world through 'inter-faith' dialogue. Other originators of the study of religions were positioned as either atheist or agnostic – themselves arguably categories which have been developed in close relation to Christian theism and thus, again, difficult to translate into Hindi, Sanskrit, Pali or Japanese. One way or another, whether atheist, agnostic or theist, the claim to be discovering the world's religions was an illusion, for these objects of secular knowledge were actually being invented.

Throughout the twentieth century and still today, texts have been, and are being, produced by scholars in Religious Studies that contain many of the same tropes as their nineteenth-century predecessors, and it is only comparatively recently that there has been any critical reflection on the fact that the founders of secular disciplines have mainly been Europhone, white, privileged, middle class, male representatives of rapacious colonial powers which had created our conditions of wealth and privilege.

## Feminism

As more women came into the Religious Studies scene, a more critical element also appeared, especially because the problematization of gender categories by feminist scholarship and theory has been a crucial basis for the possibility of the critique of other categories. By questioning the supposed naturalness of the male–female binary, feminists opened up the possibility of questioning other categories which seem to be 'in the nature of things' but which can better be understood in terms of power relations. Yet even here the tendency in the study of religion was not to deconstruct the whole ideological enterprise and to question the relationship between 'religion' and its supposed distinction from secular reason, but to talk more about the importance of the 'goddess' as an alternative to the Christocentric male God or phallocentric 'gods' generally. And while this has been an important project, it is perhaps equally important for feminists (women and men) to investigate the invention of religion and its relationship to secular modernity as itself a phallocentric project (I discuss this further in the final chapter).[36]

This embedded ideology of the religion–secular binary in its various forms is also being produced in International Relations. There is now a healthy debate about these issues within the domain of Religious Studies, and it is being broached also in the IR literature. However, in both domains the critical work is swimming against the mainstream. Much writing on 'religion' still continues as though the writer occupies a neutral, non-ideological and objective view of a distinct and given aspect of the world, and in this way perpetuates what is better seen as a concealed ideological enterprise. This situation suggests what has been noticed by growing numbers of people, that colonial relations are still embedded in the supposedly postcolonial production of knowledge about religion. 'Religion' is constructed as though it is a distinct thing in the world, or a distinct form of experience, or a distinct kind of institution, or a natural aspect of human existence, or even a biological reality corresponding to a distinct gene. There is of course a sense in which religion is very distinct – as a discourse and a collective *imaginaire*. It is, after all, a matter of constitutional and juridical importance, and religion and its supposed difference from non-religious secular practices (not only academic, but also constitutional and juridical) has become a globalized 'fact' through the adoption of this Europhone-dominant discourse and its translation into non-European languages. How far the Europhone discourse has been translated and indigenized, and how far it has been adopted for strategic purposes by elites who must think in English as well as their own languages, is a point at issue. These processes are mixed up with complex histories of colonial and neo-colonial relations, and with local issues of communal and national identity. But this distinction and separation of 'religion' has been ideologically instrumental in the naturalization of secular rationality as though it is universal and inescapable, fundamental to the march of progress and the realization of the good life in material consumption.

One significant feature of this modern system of representations is that 'religion' appears mystifyingly as a standalone category, disguising its discursive power and veiling its function in the naturalization of the non-religious secular and its various formations. I have argued that we cannot properly understand either its historical genesis in the seventeenth century or its ideological function except in the context of the formation of capitalism as theorized by political economy, the legitimation of colonial interests, and the needs of the colonial powers to classify indigenous forms of life. Nor can we truly understand why it has been so widely adopted by non-European peoples except as a function of dominant power interests.

## Toleration

It is easy to point to positive functions of the separation of religion from secular domains. It seems to offer secular states a way to disarm 'fanaticism'; to accommodate different and potentially conflicting identities; to manage differences; to create a tolerant and democratic peace. Yet it can surely also be argued that 'secular' nation states are the perpetrators of massive violence, a point explored with insight by Cavanaugh (2009). The journalist William Pfaff has listed some of the weaponry owned and deployed globally by the US Navy alone, including '... 11 large nuclear carriers groups patrolling the seas ... 57 nuclear missile carrying submarines ... 79 Aegis defensive missile ships carrying 8,000 vertically-launched missiles ...' The list continues. Pfaff comments

> Out of this titanic American power, no peace is being produced. Americans have, during the 65 years since World War II, been spending more than the military spending of the rest of the world combined, with the avowed intention of pacification and global democracy. It has fought wars or carried

out military interventions in Korea, China (via Kuomintang mercenary forces and Tibetan tribesmen), Cuba (via exiles), Laos, Vietnam, Cambodia, Lebanon, Libya, Iraq (twice), Iran, Somalia, Afghanistan (twice), Pakistan (with drones and special forces), Nicaragua (via 'Contras'), Grenada, Panama, Dominican Republic, Sudan and Kosovo (with NATO). It has also been involved with coups in Guatemala, Chile, Greece and elsewhere. My list, incomplete or otherwise, is not offered in indignation. Some of this was justified, most not; some has to be seen in the context of the times. The point of the list is this: Battles were won, but not a single war was won by the U.S. (*Japan Times*, 27 June 2010).

My own reason for reproducing this list, in the context of so-called 'religious' violence, is to remind the reader of the violence and irrationality of the secular state in pursuit of its 'natural' interests and the ideological function of the religion–secular binary myth in clothing 'politics' with an aura of factuality. My argument has been and will be that discourses on religions by academics, politicians, state functionaries and the media have disguised the constructed aspects of secular power, the conceits of natural reason and its presumed grip on so-called 'reality', legitimated new hierarchies of privilege and wealth, and therefore contribute to the alienation of those whose main purposes in life are not reducible to power, careerism and self-promotion.

As the brief summary of my own intellectual trajectory given here makes fairly clear,[37] I did not arrive at the critique of the religion–secular binary primarily and directly by way of 'the masters of suspicion', at least not in the first instance.[38] Of course, more recently it has become impossible not to encounter, and thus be influenced by, these important thinkers and the debates they have generated. Of European philosophers, the non-Positivist Marx and the tradition of critical Marxism has increasingly come to seem to me to offer the most powerful Eurocentric concepts for critiquing modern ideology, and exposing the (often unconscious) connection between the protection of categories and the interests of powerful classes. But it is not only a matter of abstract theory, it has also been the confrontation with the vast and powerful worlds of India and Japan that have led me to question these apparently neutral and objective categories of analysis. In the final chapter I say more about some of these issues of my own positionality. However, my own work merges into a more general (though still minority) stream of contemporary writers concerned with the ideology of religion and the secular. It should be taken as one of a number of different attempts to critically deconstruct modern ideology.

# Notes

1.    The late Grace Jantzen arrived just as I was leaving; Nancy Lindisfarne (then Nancy Tapper) inflected her wonderfully comprehensive

anthropology lectures with feminist insights but, given the timetabling constraints placed on her (she only taught part-time and the course, which was virtually an introduction to social and cultural anthropology, lasted only one year), could hardly have been expected to make major inroads into such a male theological bastion. For two of her papers germane to the relation between orders of power and the control of categories, see Nancy Tapper (1987); and Nancy Lindisfarne, (2002). Kate Loewenthal taught us psychology.

2.   Benson Saler 2000.
3.   On economic theory, see, for example, Robert H. Nelson (2001).
4.   G. Parrinder 1970, 1972. He also wrote several books that developed the world religion paradigm.
5.   Hardy was a leading expert on Krishna devotionalism in both Sanskrit and Tamil (see especially 1983.)
6.   I do not mean by this that the world religion Hinduism was solely the invention of Europeans, since it has become obvious from much scholarly study that some powerful sections of the Brahmin and other higher castes were very active in collaborating in this project. There are many substantial scholars of South Asia such as Robert Frykenberg (1989) and Heinrich von Stietencron (1989) who, in pointing to the invention of Hinduism in the colonial era, have noted the collaboration or at least mutuality in this venture. An excellent summary of some of the main issues is given by Richard King (2010). See also King (1999). See also Oddie (2006) on missionaries and 'Hinduism'.
7.   An example of a more recent and excellent textbook with a good edited selection of readings from significant authors, along with well-informed historical introduction and commentary, is Ivan Strenski (2006a, 2006b). I use this textbook (volumes 1 & 2) in my own classes on theory and method. However, I do have some reservations. Strenski does not fully disembed the discourse on religion from its wider emergence in relation to other problematic categories, but tends to treat religion as a standalone category that is simply there, rather than as a category in the process of invention and re-invention. See also two excellent volumes of short essays, Mark C. Taylor, *Critical Terms for Religious Studies*, University of Chicago Press, 1998; Willi Braun & Russell McCutcheon (eds.) *Guide to the Study of Religion*, Continuum Press, 2000.
8.   Alternatively, *akitsu mi kami* (divine emperor) or *arahitogami* (*kami* in human form). See Helen Hardacre, *Shinto and the State, 1868–1988*, Princeton: Princeton' University Press, 1989:40.
9.   'The Meiji Constitution of 1889 granted Japanese subjects freedom of religion to the extent that religion did not interfere with fulfilling their duties to the state. At the same time the state increasingly took the position that Shinto was not a religion. On the basis of this view, it was possible to make participation in shrine rites obligatory … Not being

religious observances, it was held, shrine rites could be categorised as obligatory duties of a Japanese subject.' Hardacre, 1989:39.

10. Though I say 'a convert to Buddhism', an Anglophone expression used widely by Buddhists themselves when speaking English, it would perhaps be truer to say that he took '*diksha*', and that he practised and advocated *buddha dhamma*. Though I do not have the space to explore that more deeply here, I think there is a crucially ambiguous point here which affects how we understand Dr Ambedkar himself and how we understand practitioners of *buddha dharma* more widely (See, for example, Joseph Loss (2010)). Israeli practitioners of *buddha dhamma* explicitly distinguish *buddha dhamma* from the 'Buddhist religion'. Of the groups which he researched, Loss says, 'Those who say that they practice Dhamma distinguish between Buddhism as a religion and Dhamma as not religious. Those who say they practice Buddhism refer to Buddhism as not religious' (Loss 2010: 85). This chimes with what many Asian 'Buddhists' have told me over the years, that 'Buddhism is not a religion but a way of life'. Also relevant here is Goenka (2003), the famous teacher of Vipassana meditation. See the interview conducted by the journal *Buddha Dharma: The Practitioner's Quarterly* with Goenka, on why he is not a Buddhist even though he attributes the meditation to Gotama Buddha, and why meditation is a science of observation (See http://www.thebuddhadharma.com/issues/2003/spring/goenka_pure_attention.html/). In the case of Dr Ambedkar it is complicated because he used the term 'religion' in several different ways; and (like Goenka) he also wanted to establish that *buddha dhamma* was scientific.

11. In fact there has been a lot of research published in English by Western scholars since the 1960s on what – for shorthand, and rather problematically – I have referred to as 'Ambedkar Buddhism', and it has continued to increase in volume. This has been anthropological and historical. However, the Western literature is small compared to the writing, much of it of a very high quality, by Indian Dalits and Buddhists on Ambedkar, on Buddhism, on *buddha dhamma*, on Brahmanism, on Hindu, on Hinduism. It is only gradually that I have come to realize that these problematic categories, widely and uncritically deployed by Western scholars in Religious Studies and other disciplines, have been the subject of intense debate and analysis in India for many decades. All of these terms are contested and subject to struggles of power and control.

12. However, many Dalit and Buddhist writers and those who identify with the Bahujan Samaj discourse have followed the critical lead of Dr Ambedkar, for example in his *What Gandhi and the Congress Have Done to the Untouchables* (Ambedkar 1945). Of the many important works that could be mentioned here, worthy of note are: G. Aloysius 1997 and 2010; and Valerian Rodrigues 2005. I cannot give a comprehensive reading list here.

13. Fitzgerald, 1994a, 1994b, 1996a, 1997, 1999a, 1999b, 1999c, 2004.

14. This is usually – and in my view problematically – referred to as his 'conversion to Buddhism'.

15. One irony is that Ambedkar built such a separation into the Indian Constitution. Yet it is difficult to draw a clear separation between his Buddhist principles and his principles of morality and social justice. For Ambedkar *buddha dhamma* became virtually identical with good governance, morality and scientific rationality. In various publications I have analysed Dr. Ambedkar's writings in English and have tried to show that his different deployments of 'religion' sometimes presuppose and sometimes subvert the religion-secular binary'.

16. One active organization that aligns with Dr Ambedkar and that also teaches meditation and performs more traditional *puja* is Trilokya Bauddha Mahasanga (TBMSG), which has *dharmachari* rather than bikkhu. TBMSG was not very evident in the remoter parts of Marathawada but has a big temple in Pune and several establishments in other places, and a well-organized retreat centre near the Bhaja caves.

17. The implication of this would be that religion and politics are insepa-rable. One could, for example, say that political principles are a form of religious power.

18. The claim by English-speaking elites that 'worship' of Buddha is a corruption of true Buddhism seems to presuppose a Christian mono-thestic concept of worship and may derive from colonial orientalist discourse. More recently (2010) I have been to Lucknow, where there is a strong identification of buddha dhamma with the UP State Government of Mrs Mayavati and her ruling Bahujan Samaj Party. Indian monks with Theravada ordination from countries such as Burma are installed in the official state *vihara* in Lucknow and are fundamentally identified with the Dalit and Buddhist anti-caste movement for democracy and social justice.

19. Ironically, I recently (2009) found a news item in the *Japan Times* on the Dalai Lama's then prospective visit to Taiwan. This visit was strongly opposed by the Chinese government on the grounds that the Dalai Lama is really a political figure hiding behind a religious disguise and is intent on creating instability. In response, the US State department was reported to have assured all concerned that the Dalai Lama is a purely religious figure and has nothing to do with politics.

20. Professor Mayeda included me in his international 'Buddhist' circle in the kindest and most generous ways. It was very different from a circle of 'believers' in the Christian sense.

21. At around the time that I began my research in India, the move to Japan inevitably shifted the priority to Japanese language.

22. Other words which have been suggested as translations for 'religion' are *sādhana* ('realization' or discipline), *sampradāya* (school or sect or tradition of practice), *mārga* (path). See Klaus K. Klostermaier, *A Survey of Hinduism*, Albany, NY: SUNY, 1994:49.

23.  See the well-informed arguments of David Williams, in *Japan: beyond the end of history* (Williams 1994), where he posits that the Japanese state and political economy radically challenge the basic assumptions of all the main schools of Anglo-American economic thought.

24.  For edited versions of relevant documents relating to the Constitutions of 1889 and 1946, see Mark Mullins et al (eds.), *Religion and Society in Japan*, [Nanzan Studies in Asian Religions], Berkeley, Calif: Asian Humanities Press, 1993, especially "Background Documents", pp. 81–105.

25.  See Hardacre, 1989:76/8 and passim. See also Junichi Isomae, 'State Shinto, Westernization of Japan, and the Concept of Religion and Shinto' in T. Fitzgerald (ed.) *Religion and the Secular: historical and colonial formations*, London: Equinox, 2007:93–103.

26.  Toshio Kuroda, 'Shinto in the History of Japanese Religion', *Journal of Japanese Studies*, 7/1, 1981:1–21.

27.  Fitzgerald 1993, 1995; 2000 (chapters 8, 9 and 10), 2002.

28.  I explored these ideas in 'Japanese Religion as Ritual Order' (Fitzgerald 1993); I should add that I would write this differently now, but it shows a stage in my thinking after living in Japan for a few years. Some years later I further developed these ideas in an article called '"Religion" and "the Secular" in Japan: problems in history, social anthropology, and the study of religion' (Fitzgerald 2002). John Breen, in his article '"Conventional Wisdom" and the Politics of Shinto in Postwar Japan' (Breen 2010), shows how contested the category religion and its Japanese constitutional equivalent *shukyo* is in Japan, especially with regard to Shinto shrines and practices. Breen's knowledge of the Shinto establishment is considerable and illuminating. For example, courts, members of the public and a powerful Shinto organization all disagree on whether or not, or in what sense, a shrine and its practices are 'religious' rather than 'custom' or 'tradition'. My reservation about this article (and this point holds more widely for the journal in which it is published, and the Centre which publishes it) is that, while on the one hand Breen effectively shows how unstable the binary distinction between religion and secular politics is, the same categories tend to be uncritically recycled for descriptive and analytical purposes.

29.  Peter N. Dale (1991).

30.  See Fitzgerald, 2000:204–210 where I have compared US and Japanese baseball as a problem of cultural translation with implications for the meaning of 'religion'.

31.  See, for example, Rajeev Barghava (1998).

32.  D.E. Smith in Bhargava 1998: pp. 177–233.

33.  See Atal Behari Vajpayee (2007). There is an interesting parallel between this identification of the primordial Hindu way of life as equivalent to the modern nonreligious secular state and the Japanese case of Shinto, seen by National Learning scholars and many shrine priests as the

deep, nonreligious substratum of Japanese identity and values. In both cases there is a tendency to see 'religions' as foreign ideologies – for Hindu nationalists, especially Christianity and Islam, and for Japanese Christianity and Buddhism.

34.  This observation could be extended to the more recent tragedy that befell the Tohoku region as a result of the tsunami and the danger to the Tsushima nuclear reactor. This has been widely viewed on TV screens. Typically viewers have expressed admiration for the calm, cooperation, courage, orderliness and self-sacrifice evident in the response from Japanese technicians and members of the general public.

35.  Geoffrey Parrinder, mentioned earlier, who had been a Methodist missionary in Africa and who was involved in founding the Religious Studies department at King's College, London, was one of these prolific writers on world religions.

36.  My point here is that the transition from the male hierarchies of the medieval church-states to the 'representative democracy' and formal equality of the modern secular state has consisted largely of a rivalry between dominant male elites. In the earlier male order, Religion as Christian Truth has been a male construction with women filling male-imagined ideal symbolic roles such as the virgin mother of god. In the contemporary male order, 'religion' is largely associated with other-worldliness, emotional irrationality, benign (ie non-interfering) morality and [possibly] purity of heart or harmlessness. The ability to marginalize a range of moral communities with alternative values to capitalism and nationalism as 'religions' can be interpreted as one more way of marginalizing any potentially critical rival to the contemporary male secular order.

37.  The single most important influence in my life has been the teaching of Jiddu Krishnamurti. However, I have found it impossible to discuss Krishnamurti's teaching here. Nevertheless, one point of Krishnamurti's influence which has relevance for this intellectual project of the critique of ideology is his radical scepticism of the value of knowledge and its production in the realization of goodness and human flourishing.

38.  Though we read Freud at King's in the Psychology of Religion course, Freud's influence came to me more strongly through my Kleinian analyst.

# Chapter 5

## *Summary of the Argument*

## Two Images of Religion

There are two notably different images of 'religion' in public discourse. One is that religion is essentially peace-loving, non-violent, non-political, non-profit-making, concerned with the inner spiritual life and the other world. Religion has nothing to do with power. Religion is benign and gentle. Religion is a matter of personal faith and piety, essentially separated from the non-religious secular state, from the rough-and-tumble of practical politics, and from economics.

The other image of religion is that it is essentially barbarous, violent and irrational, causing conflict and mayhem wherever it raises its ugly head. This view of religion as essentially violent and irrational is popular today, especially since 9/11, and in this discourse the irrational violence of 'religious' terrorists and 'religious' nationalists around the world threatens the essentially peace-loving and reasonable nature of the non-religious secular state.

Both of these opposite images depend on the assumption that 'religion' is essentially different from the non-religious secular. They are like oil and water; or like two chemical elements which, when confined in their proper domains, are safe and harmonious, but when mixed become dangerously unstable. If 'religion' (which is essentially non-political and uninterested in power in this world) mistakenly becomes involved in 'politics' (which is the worldly arena of rational action) then it ceases to be true religion and becomes a dangerous and unnatural hybrid. In much academic and popular representation the hybrid takes on agency and becomes a cunning monster, pretending to be religion but in reality something more sinister, something that wears the mask of religion but reveals another identity in its illegitimate desire for power. Again and similarly, if religion is thought to be profiting, and pursuing some activity for its own economic gain, then it is a perversion of its true self. Religion is charitable, builds credit in heaven, and does not aim for this-worldly economic profit.

Various binaries step in to underwrite this construction of the essentially different natures of religion and secular politics: public and private, natural and supernatural, empirical and metaphysical, this world and the other world, soul and body, spirit and matter, faith and knowledge, fact and value. It may also be the carrier of gender constructions, for example, religion being essentially private, domesticated, feminine, passive, powerless and harmless, compared to the rough, tough public world of masculine politics and economics. There is also the matter of rationality: science and politics, manly pursuits, are decisively rational and clear in decision-making; whereas religion is at best non-rational, vague, mystical, with a tendency to emotion like a woman. Whereas science and politics are rational and in touch with the real world, religion is arbitrary, emotional, and has a tendency to violent hysteria.

These contrary images have a historical pedigree going back to the seventeenth century. Religion has been commonly assumed to have been the cause of the Wars of Religion in seventeenth-century Europe, as a result of which reasonable men (women had little to do with it, apparently) had to expel religion from politics and establish the non-religious state as the essentially rational and peace-loving arbiter of violent religious disputes. From this tradition comes the idea that, whereas religion is violent, barbarous and irrational when allowed to overstep its proper boundaries, the secular state is reasonable, peace-loving and only reluctantly violent. To be tolerated and tolerable, religion must be tamed, disciplined and domesticated, and confined to its proper sphere like the angel in the house.

It is important to notice how, in these metaphorical constructions, 'religion' is imagined here as though 'it' is something that exists in the world with essential characteristics that demarcate it from the domains of secular reasonableness. I will show that the metaphors used to represent religion even imagine it as an agent with volition. We will also see that religion, like a metaphysical essence, incarnates in specific 'religions' and 'world religions', with Islam since 9/11 being the most dangerous avatar that stalks the globe.

# From Religion to Religions; from Secular Priests to Secular States

There is a historical link between these apparently incompatible views, alternatively the angel in the house or the irrational maniac threatening to destroy the rational secular order. Seventeenth-century philosophers such as John Locke and William Penn, in reaction against the suppression of Non-conformity, and the attempts of Catholics to suppress Protestants and Protestants to suppress Catholics, argued that violent and irrational religion was not true religion, but a barbarous impostor responsible for despotism and bloody warfare, a perversion of true religion. Religion in its true nature, they argued, is (and therefore ought to be) essentially private, personal, non-political, tolerant, concerned with the saving of the soul and with the life after death. Churches should be emasculated from the church-state and transformed into voluntary associations with no power to coerce. Only the 'magistrate' (the ruler or governor, usually the prince or monarch) ought to have the power to coerce. Only the public domain of civil society could be governed by rules binding on everyone, and obedience to the legitimate ruler was a duty that had nothing essentially to do with religion at all.[1]

Penn in 1680 is completely explicit that true religion is an inner relation of the conscience with God and has nothing necessarily to do with the public domain of law and order. He even goes as far as to say that the magistrate is not necessarily a Christian. In contrast, and only 30 or so years earlier, the Treaty of Westphalia of 1648, which concluded the Wars of Religion, clearly assumes that all the princes involved were Christian (either Catholic or Lutheran).

This attempt at defining the nature of true religion as a private matter, one essentially different and separate from the non-religious magistrate or governance, was partly an attack on the dominant meaning of religion at the time. After the Reformation, when Latin came to be replaced in the literate cultures by the vernaculars in Protestant countries such as Holland, England and some of the German principalities, the dominant meaning of the term 'religion' – in English at least – referred to Christian Truth. Religion therefore did not refer to some putative object in the world, but to the Revealed Truth about the meaning of the world. There could only be one Truth. This Truth, revealed through the Bible, the life of Jesus Christ, and the doctrines formulated and controlled through the proper authorities, was not only about priests, churches and the salvation of the individual soul, but encompassed all aspects of life, including the sacrality of kings, the hierarchical ordering of estates, marriage, gender, inheritance, dress, diet and rationality. To become baptized, confirmed and married into and by the church was not only to follow the prescribed path of individual salvation, but simultaneously (ideally) to become a subject, a citizen, and a rational human being – though women achieved a lower state of rationality than men.

# Disciplines of Civility

I have used the expression 'disciplines of civility' to indicate this encompassing notion of Religion as Christian Truth, as opposed to the irrational barbarisms of pagan darkness. The opposite of religion was not the non-religious secular, which would have been almost inconceivable before the seventeenth century, but pagan falsehood and heathen superstition. Of course, what precisely constituted Christian truth was the issue of contention between Catholics and Protestants, with Protestants accusing Catholics of pagan barbarity (the whore of Babylon) and Catholics accusing Protestants of heresy. In so far as 'religion' was used in English, it usually meant Protestant Christian Truth. However, on all sides, Christian Truth was not a private matter separated from some notion of a non-religious state and society; to give two examples, the Anglican establishment was as much a 'church-state' as a state church, and the Treaty of Westphalia was fundamentally concerned with the legitimacy of Christian princes and principalities (whether Catholic or Lutheran).

We could also refer to Christian church-states as theocracies or confessional states. Whatever terminology we use, it is the encompassing of all aspects of life and the presumptions of what constituted fully human civility which characterized Religion, at least as it was understood by the European literate male elites.

It was against this holistic encompassment of all aspects of life by the Christian establishment of literate male elites that a new discourse developed which argued that religion was a matter of individual conscience and not essentially the business of the prince or magistrate. Locke and Penn, for example, both criticised the Roman Catholic and Anglican establishments on the grounds that they illegitimately totalized power and suppressed the rights of individuals to freedom of conscience. Indeed, it was arguably in the cauldron of seventeenth-century post-Reformation dissent that the idea of the rights of the individual in the modern sense first developed into a powerful and persuasive discourse. Partly as a result of the influence of writers such as Locke, Penn and others on the framers of the US Constitution (1790), religion and politics came to be imagined as two distinct domains, a separation also commonly expressed as the separation of church and state.

# Varieties of Secularism

Elizabeth Shakman Hurd, discussed in considerable detail in Chapter 10 of this book, drawing partly on the work of William E. Connolly has usefully distinguished between laicism and Judeo-Christian secularism as two different forms of secularism. Laicism derives from, and is best exemplified by, French *laïcité*. Judeo-Christian secularism is best exemplified by the United States. This is a useful distinction because it indicates that there are secularisms in the plural and helps to set up her analysis of secularism in twentieth-century Turkey and Iran. However, she also points out that 'Elements of both laicism and Judeo-Christian secularism compete and coexist in both European and American discourses on religion and politics' (Hurd 2008: 47).

This suggests that laicism and Judeo-Christian forms of secularism are more like different emphases within the context of the wider historical construction of secular politics and the nation state, and the 'othering' of 'religion'. However, underlying both these emphases lies a common binary opposition that, in separating the 'religious' from 'the secular', at the same time invents them.

It is the invention of the non-religious that I suggest is as important as the invention of the religious. I do not deny the importance of this analytical distinction in specific contexts. I only suggest that they can be understood as different emphases within a more general modern dichotomy, and that, as Hurd suggests, these different emphases can be explained in relation to the contingent differences between Anglophone and Francophone history leading up to, and continuing from, the American and French Revolutions respectively. The close historical relationship between American and French revolutionaries might be taken to indicate the importance of the commonalities as well as the differences between these formulations.

I have suggested, very briefly, one way to track the emergence of a modern discourse on religion as essentially private,[2] voluntary, and separated from power. In England this new domain of rhetoric was a minority view associated with non-conformists who were hardly tolerated by the Anglican church-state, but the situation in the colonial states of North America was different. James Madison and Thomas Jefferson may be thought to have expressed similar views that religion and politics are (and ought to be) essentially separated in their Virginia Statute of Religious Freedom (1786),[3] that influenced the US Constitution. I would suggest that the modern separation of 'religion' and 'politics' is indeed the modern, subversive kernel of that document. Yet the degree to which Christian Theist or, alternatively, Christian *Deist* language still encompasses it is remarkable, and it is hardly surprising that de Tocqueville argued that secular values were framed by a Christian civilization (see also Connolly 1999).

Another point I would like to draw to the reader's attention is that, in both of these analytically separable discourses, 'religion' is not a standalone category. In the older discourse, Religion as Truth always implies, and stands in opposition to, pagan falsehood and barbarous irrationality. In the modern discourse religion is conceived in opposition to the non-religious (much later to be referred to as the 'secular').

## A Politick Analysis of 'Politics'

Locke in particular uses the term 'politics' as something that is in its essential nature (and therefore ought to be) clearly distinct from 'religion'. He provides one of the earliest examples of a new Anglophone discourse on 'politics' as an essentially distinct domain from the separate domain of 'religion', a discourse that is today deeply embedded in the modern understanding of the world. Today, the meaning of 'politics', like the meaning of 'religion', is widely assumed to be self-evident, and is deployed with little critical scrutiny. We all use these terms instinctively in our everyday conversations without stopping to consider what these categories 'do' – their unintended consequences, for example.

In contemporary public discourse there is no doubt that 'politics', like 'religion', is somehow in the order of things, a universal domain of human practice, and distinguished from true religion by the latter's supposed lack of interest in 'worldly' power. Often Anglophone or, more widely, Europhone 'politics' refers specifically to representative government, elections, competition between two or three parties, and various forms of policy-making in liberal democracies. But the term gets extended to virtually any set of relationships between human beings in institutions, groups and nations. In this way it takes on a much more general meaning that is little more specific than 'power'. But my point here is that, in modern discourse, *secular* politics has been invented as something which is made possible by its separation from religion, and is therefore itself *non-religious*. This imagining of the non-religious is as fundamental as imagining the religious, its reverse mirror image. In this way a specifically modern category gets universalized, thus inadvertently smuggling modern presumptions into our analyses of other cultures or our own past. 'Power' may be ubiquitous, and thus may be one of the true universals of human relationships. Yet as such it is a virtually empty category. But then, once unmoored from specific Christian theological contexts, so is religion. The power of the categories lies ironically in their empty universality and their simultaneous specific moorings in Christian Truth.

This seems to me to be an interesting feature of our use of both 'politics' and 'religion' as categories of universal description and analysis. We assume instinctively that we know what we mean when we use the terms. We tend to assume that they are essentially different. We tend to assume that they are ubiquitous domains, in principle in all human individuals and their private experiences; and in all groups in all languages and cultures at all periods of history. Thus the Anglophone or, more widely, Europhone words 'religion' and 'politics' appear to be instantly translatable. And yet in English at least we can find through historical reading of texts that the binary opposition between religion and non-religion (whether secular politics, the state, economics or science) is a modern, post-Reformation and especially an Enlightenment invention that, in the long run, as a specific discourse or family of discourses, challenged and subverted the older dominant Christian discourse which made no such distinction. This, at least, is the gist of the argument in this book in relation to international relations.

Both Locke and Penn had connections with, and interests in, North American colonies, both wrote bills of rights, and both had a significant influence in the long term on the development of North American Constitutionalism through the eighteenth century, culminating in the US Constitution, which both guarantees freedom of religion as a private right and protects the state from religion. The term 'secular' was not used much, if ever, until well into the nineteenth century to stand for those domains separated from religion (in England the term secular, like its Latin counterpart in the Catholic church-state, referred mostly to the secular priesthood). By imagining a situation in which the authority of the ruler requires protection from religion, a crucial modern binary became thinkable. It is the emergence of this binary opposition between 'religion' and 'non-religion' that is the fundamental organizing trope of modern ideology, because it provides the basis for our transformation of a modern myth into a commonplace.

There are a number of points that flow from the rhetorical reformulation of the meaning of religion which should be briefly mentioned. One is that Religion understood as an encompassing truth about the world, the opposite of which was pagan darkness and irrationality, became transformed into multiple religions on a global scale, the objects of description, analysis and comparison. The binary opposite of this new category, inscribed into written constitutions and forming the basis of a modern view of the world, was the non-religious secular.

It is true that in the seventeenth century one finds reference to 'religions' in the plural. In the Treaty of Westphalia, for instance, there is a reference to the two religions, but here it refers to the two Christian confessions, Lutheran and Catholic. Yet several decades before, the term 'religions' was used in the description of the practices and traditions of non-Christian peoples, reports of which were circulating in increasing numbers as plantations and colonies multiplied. One author who refers to religions and the religions of the world was Samuel Purchas (1626/1613). However, close analysis of Purchas shows that his use of 'religion' and 'religions' to refer to pagan practices was ironic, for he constantly makes clear that these are not true religions, but irrational substitutes (see Fitzgerald 2007a). Nevertheless, I have argued that this need of early colonization to describe and classify indigenous non-Christian practices is significant in the long term for the emergence of the modern generic category. Yet this ambiguity between True Religion and the multiple false religions, which are not really religions at all, is still evident even in the writings of the nineteenth-century founders of the Science of Religion such as Max Müller and continues a little below the surface in much of what passes for the study of religion today.

Second, in the medieval and early modern period, and in most of Europe until much more recently, Christendom, in both its Catholic and its early modern Protestant formulations, encompassed what we separate out as church and state. There was no dominant discourse of a non-religious (in the sense of non-Christian) sovereignty in England or Europe, for example, until after the French and US Revolutions. The transformation of meanings led to the modern assumption that religion is equivalent to 'church' and the non-religious secular is equivalent to 'the state', 'politics' and other modern domains such as 'economics' and secular sociology. However, in medieval Christendom and in early modern Religion, the distinction between priest and prince or church and governance was not equivalent to religion and non-religious secular. The King[4] was anointed explicitly following Old Testament precedent.

Third, unlike the concept of religion as Truth, of which logically there can only be one, modern constructions of religion are reifications, objects of secular social scientific inquiry with essential characteristics which make them religions and not something else. Though no-one has yet been able to come up with a satisfactory definition of what those essential characteristics are, despite the almost obsessive attempts by many writers in different disciplines to do so, the assumption that religion does have an essential difference from non-religious secular domains is unavoidably implied by the policing of the boundaries between them. If, for example the state were not assumed to be essentially different from religion and therefore itself non-religious, it would be unable to enforce laws that demarcate religion from the state or from politics. If courts were not deemed to be essentially secular, non-religious institutions, they would be unable to make believable judgements about which groups can legally be classified as religious and which cannot. That such judgements are made on the basis of criteria that to a great extent are arbitrary or at least unclear does not contradict the assumption of essential difference embedded in the procedures. This is in contrast to the older distinction within the Christian Commonwealth between ecclesiastical and civil courts. Ecclesiastical courts did not decide what is and is not a lawfully recognized 'religion'. The concern of these courts was with truth and heresy. Furthermore, the fundamental duty of the civil courts was to track down and punish heretics. The civil courts had relatively more *profane* duties than the ecclesiastical courts, but they were not *non-religious*. What this profound transformation of meanings in the use of terms such as religion, secular and civil ineluctably suggests is that the distinction between the religious and the non-religious secular is a powerful modern myth which, like other dominant myths, has come to be taken for de facto truths about the world, embedding largely unconscious assumptions about reality which appear intuitively self-evident and unchallengeable.

# The Rhetorical Construction of Categories in the Propagation of a Myth

The category 'religion' and its essentialized distinction from secular politics, economics, the nation state and other rhetorical constructions is basic to modern Anglophone thinking about the world. I draw the reader's attention to the fact that these are English language terms, admittedly with close approximations in some other European languages, but not necessarily in any non-European language. Anglo-American views of the world tend to get confused in the minds of Anglo-Americans for universal and obvious truths that are intuitively inherent in the way things are. These categories have historical origins in specific power conditions in early colonialism, and have become transformed into an Anglo-American mythology that takes on the appearance of intuitively obvious, universal truths. These Anglophone discourses have now become globalized and adopted into the thinking of many literate elites. It is however a moot point as to the degree to which Anglophone discourses on religion and the non-religious secular translate into Arabic, Persian, Urdu, Chinese, Japanese, Korean, Hindi, or any other language.

An important property of a dominant myth is that it seems to be undeniable and obvious to believers in the myth. This was true for medieval Europeans who accepted as undeniably true the vast corpus of Christian myths about the world, its origins, its purposes and the way it should be governed. There were of course heretics who tried to have different thoughts, lifestyles and practices, and they were generally considered as eccentric, mischievous or evil and were policed accordingly by the authorities of the time. We hear a great deal about witch-trials and burnings, but witches were an established part of rural life and were consulted for centuries much as doctors are consulted today. Whether or not individuals were considered a danger to the encompassing authority of church-states depended on the context. But it was only in the modern era that knowledge became classified as either 'religious' or 'nonreligious secular'.

Similar points apply within the mythic universe that IR experts share with academics in Religious Studies, Anthropology, Sociology and Area Studies; and the vast number of our fellow citizens in the UK and other Anglophone countries such as the USA. One trope that is underwritten by this binary is that we secular scholars and writers are free and democratic, while those religious maniacs are subjugated by superstition and arbitrary power. In this way the opposition between their religious barbarity and violence against our peace-loving and only reluctantly violent secular rationality becomes a partly unconscious nuance or presupposition. But a moment's reflection surely points to a very different set of possible inferences. The massive violence of the secular US State and its interventions in areas of strategic interest, and its support for several polities which have little or no democracy at all, tend to erode our essentialist dichotomous assumptions. Imprisonment without trial, without access to a lawyer, or even without being charged for any offence, is increasingly common practice in the UK and the US. Thus the differences between the Inquisitions of medieval 'religious' society and modern secular societies, or between the latter and contemporary non-Western or non-Christian societies, are not essential; it is a matter of degree and context.

This is not to say that, for instance, medieval and modern myths about the world are not different from each other in various important respects. The medieval concept of the church-state and the modern secular state are obviously and significantly different from each other in important ways. Though the present Queen of England, Elizabeth II, was anointed at her Coronation ceremony in 1953 by the Bishops as she sat in the Chair of Edward the Confessor, the Prime Minister at the time was elected. Furthermore, the Coronation had to be agreed in advance by the Houses of Parliament before it was allowed to take place. But the discourse on Religion as Christian Truth, and the discourse on the essential difference between religious and secular beliefs and practices, are both powerful myths. Nor – to take one non-European example – is there any doubt that the myths of Japanese uniqueness known as *nihonjinron* are different from myths about US manifest destiny, or that the myth that the Japanese Emperor is a living *kami* (*Ikigami*) is different from the myth of the sovereignty of the 'American' people. The most fundamental differences lie, not in the power of myth to spellbind us, but in the myths themselves, the different kinds of powerful interests which they serve, and the different agencies of control of the organizing categories which order the myths.

One modern myth that IR and other agencies uncritically recycle, and that some of the IR experts considered here have attempted to deconstruct, is that categories such as 'God', 'religion' and the non-religious secular are obviously meaningful and do not require critical reflection. To critically deconstruct these assumed essential differences between religious and secular agents and institutions threatens to unravel our own self-serving myths that depend on these binary oppositions.

However, as I will show in the pages which follow, even in those laudable attempts to problematize the category of 'religion' as a modern invention, and to lay bare the significance of this invention for its corollary the secular state and politics, the basic binary structure of the myth continues to reassert itself. This is evident, for example, in the way that the problematic categories continue to be deployed as though they are neutral descriptive and analytical concepts. This has the contradictory effect of protecting the Anglophone secular neutrality of the observer, and sets up an unresolved tension between the deconstruction of 'religion' as a power formation on the one hand, and the descriptions and analyses of the world in terms of those same deconstructed categories. For if, as some of the authors here assert (and in general I agree with them) that the modern nation state and International Relations as a secular discipline have been made conceptually possible by the modern invention of religion, then the authors' own positionality has also by implication been problematized. To talk in terms of the resurgence of religion, or the return of religion from exile, or the representation of religion as an agent that drives events, is to convert what might generously be described as a metaphor into a statement of empirical fact.

I therefore argue in this book that scholars in International Relations concerned with religion and its relations to world politics are in general and with varying degrees of awareness rhetorically constructing or re-constructing a powerful modern myth. One aspect of the myth which has become increasingly apparent in IR publications since 9/11 is that, whereas religion is prone to irrational and fanatical violence, the secular state is peace-loving and only reluctantly violent. The other side of this mythical construction is that, in its true nature, religion is (and therefore ought to be) peaceful, non-profit-making, and unconcerned with power in this world. Religious violence is the result of an illicit confusion of religion with power and politics, the legitimate domain of the secular state. But this myth rests on a more fundamental preconception, which is that the religious and the non-religious secular are essentially

different. They have mutually exclusive domains, ends and defining characteristics. Whereas religion is essentially concerned with faith and salvation in
another, unseen world of the spirit, the non-religious secular is concerned with
the real world of individuals and nation states in which contestations of power
and material interests are resolved pragmatically in accordance with natural
reason. Underpinning this dichotomy between religion on the one hand, and
secular politics and the state on the other, are a number of supporting binary
oppositions; for instance, between faith and knowledge, God and the world,
the supernatural and the natural, metaphysics and empiricism, theology and
science, soul and body, inner and outer, a future life after death and this life in
the here-and-now, and so on. These binaries so deeply underpin the dominant
modern *imaginaire* of liberal capitalism that they have acquired the status of
universal truths, and have been virtually removed from systematic critique.

This process of essentialization can be clearly seen in a number of recent
books in IR which represent religion as a kind of universal essence which
incarnates in many forms, specific 'religions' and 'world religions', its recent
most dangerous avatar being 'Islamic terrorism'. Religion is not only widely
represented in IR as an object with its own nature but even as an agent with
its own volition. 'Religion' has become transformed through the power of
rhetoric into an agent that acts, resurges, threatens, returns from exile and
even disguises itself by hiding its true identity behind masks of subterfuge.
Furthermore, I will argue that these representational tropes, which occur and
recur not only in IR but throughout academia, the media, and the rhetoric of
politicians, cannot easily be read as an extended metaphor.

As with other powerful myths, a collective act of the imagination has
become transformed into the inherent and immutable order of things. In this
modern myth, 'religion' appears as a force of nature out of control, or even
as itself a god with its own intentionality and moods, a force which from
time to time restlessly stalks the globe to threaten the rational Euro-American
order of human civilization. According to this mythic narrative, the order
of natural rationality – embodied in secular science, politics, economics and
the university – has for centuries been disguised, perverted or hidden by
religious superstitions but painstakingly and progressively uncovered since
the Enlightenment. The increased momentum of this enlightenment march of
progress has liberated individuals from the grip of religious hierarchies and
tyrannies and ushered in an era of democratic secular nation states, individual
rights, private property, and the relatively unencumbered flow of knowledge
and information. Closed tribal societies and oriental despotisms, lost in the
darkness of irrational prejudice, have given way to global markets that follow
the natural logic of free trade, private property and the maximization of self-
interest. Recognition of these fundamental facts about human nature liberates
us while simultaneously providing us with the tools for further progress and
security. Thus a fundamental condition for the establishment and flourishing of
secular reason has been the gradual confinement of religion in its proper place,

transforming it from an intolerant and oppressive dictatorship into a private right to be tolerated by a beneficent non-religious state. In this condition of confinement, religion paradoxically finds its own true nature in purely devotional concerns with another unseen world fundamentally different from such rational and this-worldly concerns as politics and economics.

Unfortunately, according to this myth the progressive realization of perpetual peace and plenty through the global triumph of political economy and the natural logic of enlightened self-interest has been stubbornly resisted by irrational 'religions' represented by classes of fanatics with vested interests, such as priests, mullahs and other 'spiritual' demagogues. Despite the heroic efforts of generations of reasonable Euro-Americans who have struggled to liberate others from their own backwardness, religion has in some quarters refused to exile itself to the margins, clinging stubbornly to its outworn myths, resisting reason and progress, and periodically resurging in dangerous ways. In this recent version of a dominant myth, in which secular civility is once again threatened with religious barbarity, the essential distinction between irrational religion and rational secular politics appears as an unquestioned preconception on the basis of which policy is conducted, developmental aid offered to backward regions, failed states punished and corrected, countries invaded and wars fought.

The propagation of the myth of the religion–secular binary provides one side of the binary – the secular – with the superior standpoint in rationality and reality. Some would argue that this superior standpoint is based on science and natural reason, which tells us how the world really is. Scientific disciplines provide the most powerful models or representations of the world, and the same natural rationality that governs science also governs modernity more generally. Rational individual subjects make empirical observations and infer-ences about an objective world – in biology, politics, international relations, economics and so on – and then propose pragmatic solutions to problems on the basis of that knowledge. Those same rational 'players' produce, exchange and consume in markets which have a natural overall propensity to self-stabi-lization. The natural pursuit of individual self-interest through enterprise and entrepreneurship is assumed to result statistically in an overall satisfaction of material wants through the natural logic of supply and demand.

This picture of the logic of capital is complicated by the existence of nation states, corporations, and various international agencies, and it seems difficult to understand how these can fit into or be consistent with the myth of free markets. But the myth provides the underpinning for dominant Euro-American conceptions of representative democracy, the rational secular state, and the tolerant arena of political debate. The glaring inconsistencies in the myth are defused and the myth protected by secondary elaborations. The tolerant secular arena that is protected (one might say managed) by a benign state recognizes difference and gives a comfort zone to minority identities, views and practices. Global migrations of labour, especially from the 'under-developed' to the 'developed' world, test the latter's benign and generous societies and place a strain on the limits of tolerance. Much of the current public discussion about secularism in Europe and North America is concerned with how it can be modified to take account of the greater range of differences that result from the constant influx of new minorities and their forms of life; and how it can be protected from irrational and ungrateful religious fanatics.

It is true that only one of the texts I analyse consciously and deliberately frames the issues in these ways (Hitchens 2007). The other texts I read here apparently distance themselves from this binary of secular civility as against religious barbarity. They do this by adopting the neutral descriptive language typical of the social and economic sciences. Yet the implications of the problematization of religion and the secular as a modern power formation logically implies that secular, social scientific knowledge which the authors are offering the reader is located within a domain of power. There is thus repro-duction of the power relations embedded in the descriptions themselves, as though the authors, their universities, their careers, their salaries, stand outside the ideological binary formations which they also want to reveal.

'Religion' and 'religions' are the most powerful of these, and for good reason. As all the IR books which I analyse here make clear in their different ways, 'religion' is both the greatest threat to secular rationality and also simultaneously its most significant other or binary opposite. Some of the authors here describe and analyse the various categories used by the secular state to classify minority practices. The task of classifying all the different kinds of states, communities, organizations, agencies, or movements in the world is highly complex, as we can see from the texts analysed in this book; but clearly the distinction between those that are religious and those that are secular is fundamental for the authors. It becomes especially apparent in the rhetorical linkage of 'religion' with 'terror'. For example, Hindu nationalism or Sikh 'fanaticism' are classified as 'religious' and thus as dangers to the secular state of India. The conflict in Northern Ireland between Catholics and Protestants is described as a 'religious' conflict. Islamic groups such as Hamas and the Taliban are described as 'religions' with unrealized theocratic inten-tions. 'Religious' groups such as the Amish, Mennonites or Hutterites which emerged in sixteenth-century Germany with theocratic dreams and in violent contention with existing authorities, now exist in benign transformation in North America as constitutionally licensed 'religions' tolerated by the secular state and the surrounding dominant society. All of those institutionalized practices that accept confinement in the space of 'religion' without desiring to become a holistic (or totalitarian) government of unification cease to be a threat to secular civil society and simply persist in its benign and tolerant margins. When totalizing visionary discourses of justice and the good become transformed into 'religions', they can be domesticated by the secular state and made obedient and submissive to its power and forms of bureaucratic cognition. For example, the Anglican church-state that encompassed much of English society for several centuries is now 'a religion' too, concerned with saving souls and imparting moral guidance to families. Its attempts to give moral guidance to government are severely policed and interrogated by the media. Others might say the Anglican Church is a pathetic vestige of itself, limping along with its own survivals, like the monarchy that, as Head of Church and Head of State, is a shadow of its former power and dominance.

# Spirituality

'Spirituality' is another term that steps in for 'religion', even though discourses on spirituality are different in some less important respects, such as emphasizing the inner individual as against the ecclesiastically organized. Various modern ideas and practices of 'spirituality' divorced from power and politics have been made available to those who search for a higher self-realization or transcendental truth. The literature on alternative religions or alternative spiritualities is vast, reflecting a large marketplace. Some have uncritically adopted a modern discourse as if its fundamental binary categories stand in a one-to-one relationship with real, ontologically separate domains. From the side of religion, or spirituality, a higher ground of purity, wisdom and healing is imagined to have been achieved. An alienating dualism that divides the consciousness between spirit and matter, between the disenchantment of banal existence in this world and the promises of something rarer that transcends politics, is adopted as though a higher level of consciousness is available through one side of the dividing binary. These anaemic residuals of a dismembered consciousness are the virtues that sell spirituality in the globalizing markets (see Carrette and King 2005).

Yet, simultaneously and paradoxically, many of the movements and communities frequently classified as religions or spiritualities are explicit protests against the alienation of capitalism, or of mind–body dualism, or of rapacious environmental degradation. Some widely disseminated so-called *spiritual* discourses on holism in fact demand embodiment – the whole person – and thus reintegration with the material. This suggests a deep human protest against the alienation of modern essentializing discourses, and thus tacitly at least a rejection of a spirit–matter binary. To put it crudely, a faint but heartfelt cry can be heard for the reintegration of spirit and matter, of prayer or meditation with research, of authentic human relations with monetary transactions, of morality with economics, of democracy with power, of values with facts, of religion with the secular. There is a tendency to find a new, holistic discourse on love as a real power in the world. Wherever 'spirituality' implies an acceptance of an image of truth or self-realization in the inner as distinct from the outer, in an unseen world as distinct from the world of empirical observation, in the apolitical divorced space into which the 'secular' has confined it through its powers of classification, then I suggest it is a fantasy of alienation. However, among those groups that look for collective transformation and self-realization through a vision of the common good, and work to realize that vision in the here-and-now, then the locus of concern moves to subvert the categorial distinctions that under-gird the power of the secular state.

There are the beginnings of a trend in IR, in the conceptual domain if not yet in the domain of commitment and self-critique, to question the religion–secular binary classification. Some of the books I analyse in the next pages are concerned especially with the modern invention of religion as a privatized domain since the seventeenth century, and the ideological function of this new classification in the simultaneous construction of the idea of the modern secular nation state. It follows from this that some of this IR literature is concerned to critique the established categorical binary opposition between religion and the secular. It is at this point that my own work in philosophical theology, anthropology and religious studies seeks inter-disciplinary solidarity with writers in IR. In recently published pioneering work, some IR experts have begun to destabilize and subvert the smoothly-worn rhetorical grooves of the religion–secular binary, and to reveal its ideological functions in the service of the status quo.

Yet there is a deep reluctance and even resistance to taking this critique to any logical conclusion, and a significant number of these texts are mired in contradiction. Despite the stated intentions of some of the authors to investigate the modern invention of religion and its ideological function in the birth of modern politics, the continual reproduction of images of religion as though it is a metaphysical essence with manifest empirical forms, or even as an intentional agent acting in the world, re-embeds in mythic form the ideological constructions that are being problematized. Recent discourse in International Relations on 'the resurgence of religion' and its 'return from exile' constitutes a mythical transformation of a general category into a kind of thing in the world and even an agent. Yet (as I will argue) it is the reification of religion as an object of research that disguises the ideological and constructed formation of the secular domain, including the social sciences. IR writers have noticed and discussed the dependence of the conceptualization of the modern state on the modern invention of religion, and hinted at the implications for IR as a secular discipline. These texts are thus caught mid-stream between deconstructing the religion–secular binary (and thus cutting the neutral positionality of the academic writer from under her feet), and yet simultaneously representing the global events which have caused this awareness in terms which reinstate 'religion' as a thing in the world, or an agent, with defining characteristics that make it essentially different from the secular.

## Ambiguity: Religion as Agent? Or Religion as a Myth?

There is thus a deep ambiguity about the status of 'religion' as a problem in IR. Is religion being reinstated as an agent in world affairs and thus as an object of concern within an International Relations field which has traditionally and mistakenly ignored religion? Or, more radically, is religion and its supposed distinction from the non-religious secular domains – which is to say the religion–secular binary as a two-sided category – being deconstructed holistically in order to expose an ideological function that has hitherto appeared to be simply there 'in the nature of things'? This latter project is significantly different from the first one, and moves in a different direction. The first project changes little, because it simply attempts to correct a blind spot in the explanatory options available for understanding world events by reaffirming 'religion' as a valid causal force in international affairs, something which was unfortunately lost sight of for a while. This limited position has the effect of reasserting what has anyhow already been tacit, that secular domains such as IR and the social sciences are essentially distinct from religion, and are consequently equipped to give authoritative descriptions and analyses of religion and its agency in world affairs. In contrast the second project is far more radical and with unclear outcomes, for it problematizes not only the modern historical construction of 'religion' but also the 'secular' which, as a binary pair, has been the conceptual basis for IR, for the modern academy more widely, for the state, and for virtually the entire ideological apparatus of modern Western civility and its supposed rational superiority and progress.

The dangerous lack of clarity of the second aim is obvious. It leaves little standing ground to those of us who pursue it with critical and deconstructive determination. It appears to threaten the secular rational legitimacy of the institutions which pay our salaries and which generate and legitimate supposedly objective, disinterested knowledge in the various disciplines. And it runs up against powerful interests which are served by the mystification of secular reason as natural common sense, the way things are, rather than as a historically originated ideology.

But I argue that there are so many flaws in the classification of the world, and all its different nations, groups, organizations and movements, into two great emotive classes, that the second aim is necessary in terms of moral and intellectual integrity. IR, like religious studies, politics, sociology and economics, has to bite the bullet and confront the intellectual and ethical challenge posed by the contemporary unravelling of this article of modern faith. My critique of these texts gives me greater participation in a debate in which I am already committed in other neighbouring disciplines such as religious studies and anthropology. But it makes my own positionality vulnerable in obvious ways.

## Toleration

One of the many objections I anticipate to my position is that the separation of 'religion' from 'politics' derived in the first place from a legitimate demand of oppressed non-conformists for toleration. It has subsequently provided the conceptual and legislative basis for a pluralistic society that gives rights to minorities. I do not doubt that the modern invention of religion and the secular state has benefited non-conformist minority interest groups by providing them with a kind and degree of freedom from oppression. Historically, the demand for toleration for non-conformist groups that resisted the hegemony of the Catholic or Protestant confessional church-states – theocracies by any other name – eventually, after much trial and tribulation, won rights and in doing so helped to invent a new conception of a state separated from 'religion'.

However, I would argue that this licensed toleration of non-conformist groups and their practices should not be taken at face value. A historical transformation of the kind that produced the modern world of common-sense factuality required more than goodwill or diplomacy to bring it into being. It has involved a transformation of those practices in the very act of classification itself. What arguably began as toleration for non-conformist Christian confessions has extended into a vast category of 'religions', tacitly imputing to diverse practices, conceptualized in many languages and cultural contexts, an essential identity, or a number of putatively shared core attributes that makes them all exemplars of the general category religion, and thus all essentially different from the non-religious secular and the presumed higher rationality of that domain. Toleration of non-conformism or simple difference creates a generic and essentialized 'other' that strengthens the secular state and other presumed non-religious domains such as economics by partial emasculation of alternative epistemological and moral viewpoints. And this whole process is tied in with a circular discourse, now increasingly being challenged, on a progressive liberation of the individual and the markets from 'religious' tyranny. Increasingly, and for many, it is the dogma of individual self-interest, markets, private property, capital, and wage labour which seems tyrannous, and the claims of a tolerant and benign liberal democracy seem, to more and more potential voters, a shallow cover for the power of vested corporate interests that control neo-colonialist governments, make alliances with authoritarian states, and cynically subvert democratically-elected governments that resist US hegemony through the use of clandestine CIA operations, renditions, torture and prison camps such as Guantanamo Bay.

If academics are to contribute to the collective development of a new and more honest democracy, both within the nation state and on the international arena, then the entrenched assumption that we are defined by our neutral and benign non-religious secularity will inevitably need to be challenged. To strip away the facade of natural reason that mystifies real relations of power, the ideological processes invested in the mythical distinction between religion and secular have to be disembedded from the realm of unconscious assumptions. Modern 'secular' consciousness, far from being the epitome of enlightened progress, is itself the counterpart of the mythical construction of religion as its problematic other. Secularity, understood as the non-religious domain of natural rationality, is a discursive representation which in Anglophone history seems to have gathered momentum from the late seventeenth century as a radical non-conformist challenge to the Anglican church-state, a new discourse emerging from the meltdown of much established thinking during the English, French and North American revolutionary periods, and eventually becoming transformed into a commonplace through a process of elective affinity with new emergent interests of educated male elites. The supposed essential distinction between religious and secular institutions and practices is uncritically embedded in public discourse and underpinned by substitute binaries (faith–knowledge; supernatural–natural; metaphysics–empiricism; God–world; mind–body; spirit–matter; etc.) which stand in for each other in a never-ending circularity of displaced meaning, protecting the whole series from exposure as an ideology pretending to be a simple description of what exists in the world.

A moment's reflection on the terms of these binaries indicates that, even in English, and setting aside the vast problems of translation required to render them into the languages of cultures where 'religions' are assumed by Anglophone writers to exist, none of them has any essential meaning, and all of them taken singly are complex, contested, and historically unstable. As soon as we stop to think seriously about words like 'god' or 'the world', 'mind' or 'matter', 'supernatural' or 'natural', we begin to see that these are so contested in European languages, and often so difficult to translate into non-European languages, that they have no clear meaning. This raises a seriously interesting problem, which is that such empty categories nevertheless have huge rhetorical power. These points will emerge as the book proceeds. When placed in chains of binary oppositions they construct an appearance of two essentially distinct domains that are unconsciously embedded in texts across the humanities and social sciences. From this illusion derives various ideas about religion and the secular which, when carefully considered, are irrational and arbitrary yet are seriously assumed and sometimes even explicitly stated, not only in popular media discourse, not only in the shallow rhetoric of politicians, but even in scholarly texts written by highly-ranked academics: for example, that religions are defined by belief in 'God' who exists in some other world separate from this one, whereas secular rationality is located in the real, material, objective world that exists independently of the observer; that religions teach that the invisible and unextended soul is detachable from the extended body and survives death; or that religion and politics in their true respective natures don't mix, because religion is not concerned with power, and when 'religious' people try illicitly to gain power then disasters occur, like the Wars of Religion in seventeenth-century Europe, or more recently like 9/11; or that religion is essentially charitable and betrays its own true nature if it behaves like a capitalist corporation and pursues business in order to make a profit.[5]

My argument is that these binaries form the discursive basis of a dominant modern myth that, by inventing generic religion as one side of a fantastic binary, simultaneously invents the secular as the domain of common sense and natural reason. This myth thus legitimates a range of ideological values of modernity as though they are the final truths about the real world. It conceals the self-interest of powerful elites and rapacious corporations whose restless search for profits is disguised as rational, normal, and in the natural order of things; and whose own rapaciousness is projected onto the mythical beast of 'religion'. The consumption of 'spiritualities', which we might like to imagine as harmless alternatives to dogmatic religions, and even as enriching practices that bring soul-depth to our weekends and peace to the world, are the alienating fantasies that help to mask the violence of the secular nation state and the other agencies engaged in the management of global capital.

This two-faced myth of religion, conceived either as a harmless individual spirituality with no interest in power, or alternatively as a dangerously violent autonomous force in the world, provides the foundation for faith in the rationality of modern liberal capitalism and private property, transforming a historically contingent discourse with multiple origins into a powerful set of global assumptions about the order of things. While this myth has multiple global origins, I am primarily concerned with its Anglophone formations that culminate today in the legitimation of dominant US power. It can be noted that ancient cultures such as Japan, Korea, China and India have been constructing forms of capitalism that are in some respects significantly different from the US variety.

As I intend to show in the pages that follow, some of the writers discussed in this book uncritically succumb to the seductions of this myth in one or other of its forms, and further propagate it themselves as a set of presumptions – sometimes conscious, usually unconscious; presumptions which organize their texts and their supposedly neutral and objective knowledge. However, some of the experts in IR discussed here are themselves attempting to get a critical handle on these historical ideological processes, seen for example in their own recognition that the concealed assumptions underlying the theoretical construction of IR as a secular discipline are intimately dependent on what some of them refer to as the privatization of religion in the construction of liberal capitalist modernity.

Since my own positionality is deeply conditioned by the same ideological processes as those of my colleagues in IR, I cannot and do not claim to occupy a transcendental standpoint from which to criticise a supposed blindness in their position. It is partly a matter of contingent biography (see Chapter 4 and Chapter 11). In those places I try to indicate briefly the research and theoretical/experiential trajectory that has led me to these conclusions. The issue of positionality begs the question how, if we are all contained within the shared parameters of the same myth, any individual can step outside of it in order to get a critical angle on it? No-one can do this easily, but living in non-Euro-American zones for substantial periods of time and learning non-European languages can help to relativize and thus to bring to consciousness deeply embedded presumptions. While global US capitalism and its insistent propaganda about 'democracy and freedom' now infiltrates every corner of every continent, yet there are deep pockets of resistance. Some of them are described by the authors discussed here, but the descriptions claim a tacit neutrality and lack of commitment, which by implication is a commitment to the secular status quo. By constructing Islam and Islamic terrorism as a reified *religious* force in the world impacting on the *secular* state, the struggle of specific Muslim communities to assert an alternative moral vision to dominant Anglo-American capitalism is already neutered; these others are already forced into the categories of the dominant global ideology which they may be wanting to question.

I would suggest that even Japan, with the world's second largest GDP and an obvious ally to US interests, only *appears* to be amenable to the same strategies of analysis as the US and UK economies, containing some deep oppositional values not normally seen by Anglophone economists. One can imagine that the growing power of India and China will increasingly reveal, and perhaps already do reveal, alternative values that challenge US hegemony. However, if we are looking for signs of popular resistance to US hegemony and to rapacious capitalism, the rise of alternative great powers may not be the best place to search. Most likely we will not find a new global basis for popular democracy but a new form of hegemonic power, and new clashes of self-interested male elites armed with nuclear missiles and chemical gases claiming to represent legitimate national interests. Ironically alternative conceptions of justice and the good may be found in those small groups and movements – both 'religious' and 'secular' – described in the analyses that follow.

Detailed analysis of texts suggests that extricating ourselves from the pervasive grip of modern categories that organize the myth is difficult for academics, for a number of reasons. One is that we work in universities which, being 'secular', are legitimated in terms of the same mythological narrative. Our salaries and research projects are largely financed either by the secular state or by the logic of political economy. Another point is that, so dominant and triumphalist is the myth of the natural rationality of global capitalism, especially since the end of 'socialism' in the former Soviet Union, that it has displaced alternative grounds for argument. It is difficult to see what alternative ideological positions and what alternative categories are available for the development of a democratic *imaginaire*. To make a metaphor, we are like flies standing with both feet in glue: to extricate one foot, we press down on the other foot, and inadvertently push that foot further into the glue. We search for, but cannot find, an alternative place-hold to provide traction so that we can extract ourselves and fly once again. The self-confirming circularities of our ideological system so deeply permeate all our institutions, practices and ways of thinking that it appears to us as unavoidable, natural, and in tune with common sense. This is true for all of us who are educated in, and consciously or unconsciously saturated by, Euro-American and especially the dominant

US Anglophone discourse. To question the very ground upon which we stand is confusing and disorienting. We are continually told that there are no alternative positions to occupy, and we believe this is true. We can only have faith that, if and as critical discourse gains a footing, a democratic consensus on the language we should use to construct our collective world will emerge from the parameters of a widening public debate.

As some of the authors discussed here have insightfully realized, the central problem for IR is that the return of religion from exile, by reminding them that their discipline was formed by religion's simultaneous invention and marginalization, therefore threatens the illusion of secularity which has been an essential ingredient in IR's conceptualization in the first place. The implications of this insight for the whole of the secular academy cannot be missed.

The discourse on 'religion' as it has emerged in IR is a peculiarly influential manifestation of a wider rhetorical construction that has also been reproduced by scholars in neighbouring academic domains. A tacit assumption that appears through close analysis of a range of texts is that, whereas secular reasonableness attests to the final emergence of humankind into the light of fair-minded objectivity, religion is some dark and irrational force that needs to be contained, limited and deprived of its dangerous powers. Since its first development the practitioners of the discipline of IR have shared this more general self-image of secular reason as a fundamentally peace-loving and problem-solving ground of enlightenment, and religion has been represented as something only tangential to its remit, an ancient power intent on illegitimate world domination but finally exiled by the march of secular progress. The events of 9/11 especially have now led to a flurry of texts claiming that this dark force has returned from exile with a vengeance. The appearance of this myth in IR has special significance due to the discipline's influence on government think tanks, international agencies and policy-makers. Wherever discourses on 'religion' are being reproduced, the myth of the non-religious secular is also tacitly constructed as the universal domain of rational human action, providing circular legitimation for an ideology that serves particular interests.

This academic production is in turn a significant part of a broader array of agencies for the reproduction and dissemination of the myth, including constitutions, courts, state agencies, advertising and the media. IR in particular gives academic respectability to this rhetorical construction to those who hold powerful positions with the ability to influence policy.

In agreement with some IR experts I argue that religion as a privatized right is a modern invention which is ineluctably connected with the parallel invention of the non-religious state and politics. The modern categories of 'religious', as distinct from 'secular', practices are underwritten by a series of mutually parasitic binaries which form a circular ideological system which has generated an appearance of self-evident confirmation. One can see that the same structures of thinking underlie the evangelism of some evolutionary biologists, who frequently seem to commit what Kant articulated as the dogmatic fallacy, by which he can be interpreted to mean the error of confusing representations of the world for the world itself. It is of course true that the faith in progress that underlies much of science and technology, or faith in the perfectibility of the world through the accumulation of knowledge, or faith in the rationality of the state to achieve harmony and peace in some future time, are different from faith in the Christian doctrine of the Trinity. But they are not *essentially* different.

This critique of IR texts is not an inherently hostile project, since I am myself searching for an alternative standpoint from the circularity of a self-confirming system of representations. Like some of the authors I discuss here, I have an interest in a historical contextualization of those dominant categories that legitimate the current world order, in the hope that this might contribute in the realm of ideas to the development of a new democratic *imaginaire*. I do not believe that an intellectual debate of this kind can have much influence or importance unless these ideas can come to be perceived to have an elective affinity with wider changes in power relations, and a new vocabulary of democratic practice which goes further than the two-party system of representative government largely controlled and funded by corporate interests, the media and wealthy individuals.

Modern historiography is itself arguably a product of these same ideological structures, in the sense that, paradoxically, the categories that are themselves the products of modern historical processes are recycled and projected retrospectively to shape our own view of the past. Our view of the historical past, the place we imagine we have come from, is itself deeply moulded in terms of the same categories which are the product of that past. Yet, like some of my colleagues in IR, I share the view that, in part at least, we can only extricate ourselves from the grip of the presently-constructed past through a critical historiography itself.

# Origins

In the search for the origins of our modern system of representations, there is disagreement among IR experts on the historical emergence of secular modernity and its claims. One historical event frequently invoked as the crucial transitional point of the transformation of discourses on religion and the secular nation state is The Treaty of Westphalia (1648). I will be examining that claim at certain points in this book. Elizabeth Shakman Hurd, influenced by William E. Connolly, has persuasively identified Kant as one crucial and possibly definitive stage in the emergence of the modern religion–secular dichotomy in the eighteenth century. I gladly accept their insight about the crucial significance of Kant as a major stage in the formative process. However, as indicated earlier in this chapter, I have myself argued for a slightly earlier origin for the modern invention of religion and the secular state, dating this pair from around 1680 in the writings of powerful and well-connected non-conformists such as John Locke and William Penn.

The importance of these writers does not contradict the importance of Kant or any other individual. To achieve a thorough genealogy we would probably need to go back at least to writers such as Machiavelli, Bodin and Hobbes, but there is also the danger of an infinite regress. A concerted programme of research needs to be coordinated on the multiple Euro-American origins of the invention of religion and the non-religious secular as essentially distinct domains in modern ideology in languages other than English.

And if it is true, as I argue, that this modern ideology arose in the context of plantations and colonies, slavery, early nationalism, and the birth of modern capitalism in colonial sites, then the exclusive focus on Anglophone history is problematic. There are strong arguments for supposing that it was in the colonizing encounters with non-European peoples, whether in the West Indies or the East Indies, in the Americas, Africa, Asia and so on, that modern Christocentric Europhone categories of classification were developed. However, there cannot be much doubt that since the late sixteenth century, and especially during the seventeenth and eighteenth centuries, English and Scottish writers had a significant influence on the development of North American representations. These men (and they were mainly men) were part of a wider Christian European process at a time of growing competition between Portuguese, Spanish, French, Dutch and English colonial interests. The hugely significant role of the slave trade in these competitive struggles, and the debates over the classification of Africans and other non-Christians as human, semi-human or animal, were surely crucial factors in the birth of the discourse on modernity. Writers such as Locke were influenced by European discourses on the fanatical violence generated by the clash of different confessions or 'religions' during the Wars of Religion, to which the Treaty of Westphalia is deemed to have brought a peaceful solution. But Locke was also concerned with rights of property, both at home and in the plantations. Again, as Connolly (1999) has insightfully argued, Kant himself can be seen as the most important single philosophical recipient of these seventeenth-century streams of thought, representing a further eighteenth-century stage in their clarification and powerful reformulation in the context of his critical philosophy. Yet one of the consequences of Kantian rationality was that it continued the Christian propensity to delegitimize non-European modes of being (according to Connolly 1999). These influences no doubt flowed powerfully from Germany and France as well as from Scotland and England, especially and increasingly during the eighteenth century. Again, the invention of economics as a distinct theorized domain of natural reason in the late eighteenth and early nineteenth centuries was a further powerful stage in the production of modern secular ideology.

Better historians than me may identify other and possibly earlier stages in the emergence of modern categories. I confine myself mainly to Anglophone evidence, but this does not imply that similar historical research in other languages may not turn out to be of equal or greater importance. The meltdown of English order in the mid-seventeenth century led to the radical questioning of all orthodoxies. My own proposition is that men such as Penn and Locke bring into explicit clarity an idea that requires the context of colonies and plantations to make that idea properly comprehensible. Long before modern generic religion and religions emerged as a modern category, 'Religion' in English referred almost exclusively to Protestant Christian Truth, though in the Treaty of Westphalia it refers diplomatically to both Protestant (Lutheran) and Catholic confessions. Yet, since the late sixteenth century in English, 'religion' was also being applied by analogy (and ironically) to 'pagan' practices, including Catholic ones, and increasingly to those in newly encountered societies which offered opportunities in trade, resources, production and investment. In these multiple contexts, religion as Christian truth opposed to pagan darkness became transformed and partially neutralized as a category in the new production of scientific (rational) knowledge, and thus slowly emerged as a generic classificatory term for any traditions that seemed incompatible with the progress and legitimation of colonial interests.

The point I am making here is that the emergence of modern categories such as religion, non-religious secular, politics, economics and the secular university has not been solely through internal European developments, as though these could be understood in isolation from the wider global processes of encounter with other imagined worlds. Yet today it is the Anglophone discourse that still dominates, and the search for its historical origins in England and North America must be one legitimate area for our research.

Arguably only the French Revolution, with its own unique trajectory and yet sharing many of the revolutionary ideas of the age with the writers of the Declaration of Independence and the US Constitution, has had a comparable impact on the legitimation of secularism as the ground of reason, and thus simultaneously the invention of 'religion' and 'religions'. Despite the different nuances of French as against Anglophone constructions of the religion–secular dichotomy, interestingly discussed by some authors in the texts under discussion here, I will argue that underlying both these formulations lies a shared myth of the essential distinction between religion and the non-religious state and politics.

Let me summarize some of the points mentioned above and with which I am concerned in this book:

1   That scholars in International Relations (IR) concerned with religion and its relations to world politics are in general and with varying degrees of awareness rhetorically constructing a powerful modern myth. The myth is that there is an essential difference between religion and politics, or religion and the modern state, which in turn rests on a

deeper preconception of the essential distinction between the religious and the non-religious.

2     That this myth is a foundation of modern liberal capitalist ideology, transforming a historically contingent discourse into a powerful set of global assumptions about the order of things. The myth of self-equilibrating markets and the rational self-maximizing Individuals who 'play' them appear as natural, common sense realities, obscured for centuries by irrational religious traditions. Liberal capitalism, as theorized by the science of economics, appears as inevitable and in the immutable order of the world.

3     That there were multiple origins of this myth, especially the encounter of Christian European powers with non-European peoples and the new needs of classification that arose in colonial sites. There is therefore no single starting point for its articulation. However, its Anglophone formation achieved crucial early clarification from around the late seventeenth century.

4     That the discourse in IR, and indeed the formation of IR as a secular discipline, is part of a wider rhetorical construction which is being reproduced by scholars in neighbouring academic domains such as political economy or economics, sociology, political theory, anthropology, religious studies and literary studies. Wherever discourses on 'religion' are being reproduced, the imagined veridicality of the non-religious secular is also tacitly constructed. Greater interdisciplinarity between IR and neighbouring disciplines such as religious studies is therefore necessary for a correct analysis of the categories involved and the unblocking of collective intellectual energy which might eventually give rise to a radically new *imaginaire*.

5     That this academic production is a significant if apparently small part of a broader array of agencies for the reproduction and dissemination of the myth, including constitutions, courts, state agencies and the media. Without a critical awareness of this broader context within which IR and the academy generally is located, IR experts, like those in neighbouring disciplines, will be unable to see the outcomes of their own contributions to the production of this myth.

6     In agreement with some IR experts, I argue that the discourse on religion as a privatized right is a modern invention which is ineluctably connected with the invention of the non-religious state and the secular domains, notably 'politics' and 'economics'. However, I offer an alternative historical view of the decisive emergence of both religion and the secular state as an Anglophone binary apparatus, dating this pair from around 1680 in the writings of powerful and well-connected non-conformists such as John Locke and William Penn, who were involved in a power struggle with established dominant interests, the colonial connection with North America, and the development of state

bills of rights culminating in the US Constitution near the end of the eighteenth century. This fills in a gap between the Treaty of Westphalia (1648) and the cluster of diverse, momentous events of the late eighteenth century, including the US Declaration of Independence, the US Constitution, the French Revolution, the Declaration of the Rights of Man and Citizens, the advances in science and technology, the articulation of economics and its transformation from moral theology into a technically neutral language of naturally rational processes. At the level of metaphysics and in very general terms is the invention of the concept of the world as a self-subsistent and self-explanatory system of matter that does not require the Trinitarian, Monotheistic God of Christian theology as a hypothesis.

7    Finally, an indication of the globalizing dominance of the religion-secular ideology is the reproduction of the basic form of the written Constitution every time a new nation is constructed or reconstructed, along with other indicators of Anglo-American civility, such as the destruction of pre-existing modes of authority and practice accompanied by the growth of 'rights', corporations, property markets, and the pool of wage labour.

All of these parts of the argument hang closely together. Those specialists in IR who are laudably attempting to adopt a critical stance towards their own discipline and its formation, and to connect with other neighbouring academic domains, will appreciate that all of these interrelated aspects have direct relevance to arguments already being pursued in their own books and journals. IR is one of the most influential academic specialisms because its expertise feeds more directly into the thinking of policy-makers and think tanks advising governments and corporate capital than that of most other fields.

I have included a final chapter in this book which describes as best as I can my own theoretical positionality. I do this in conformity with the increasingly widespread critique of the myth of secular objectivity, that the observer is absent from the text that is only concerned with the objective and disinterested presentation of neutral facts. It seems no longer tenable that the author's own position of relative power and affluence, located in Western universities funded by the state or by corporate capital, is irrelevant to the kind of 'knowledge' that he or she produces. From my own position, I offer this summary of a complex, joined-up argument as a contribution to IR's own important debates on these issues.

## Notes

1.    *John Locke* (1689: 8–9); *William Penn* (1680). I have discussed these works in my introduction to *Religion and the Secular* (Fitzgerald 2007b).

Also see my discussion in *Discourse*, (Fitzgerald 2007a: 20–3; 267–74; and throughout Chapter 9) on the development of these ideas in the North American colonies.

2.  By 'private' I do not mean that there was intended to be, or expected to be, no public visibility. Penn and Locke both believed that Christian morality was essential for the order and flourishing of the Commonwealth. The crucial point is that there is no compulsion. It is an individual choice. Such 'societies' on this understanding have no powers to compel or punish, powers reserved now for the non-religious state. 'Religious societies' or churches come to be imagined as purely voluntary. It is in this sense that one can say that, in the modern discursive *imaginaire*, religion became privatized. In historical reality, of course, this was far from the case in England and much of Europe.

3.  http://www.lva.virginia.gov/lib-edu/education/bor/vsrftext.htm/ I would however argue that an analysis of this text indicates a specific significant historical attempt at the on-going transformation from Religion as Christian Truth to the modern generic concept. There is no space to pursue this point here.

4.  This is still true; see the liturgy for Queen Elizabeth II's coronation of 1953.

5.  The forms of Christian preaching which exemplify the 'prosperity gospel' are adept at both kinds of discourse, being simultaneously Religion as Christian Truth set against Pagan darkness; and yet also being registered as religious charities licensed by a benign US nonreligious secular state. Salvation seems to be both by the grace of God and also by the grace of the Markets. Some US protestant evangelical missionaries in parts of Latin America identify the pagan village economy, its collective consciousness, and its lack of surplus value as 'lostness' (a state of sin and damnation); but the wider markets which potentially open up the village to the rational progress of modernity, appear as the paths of salvation for the disembeded Individual.

# Chapter 6

## *How Religion Poisons Everything*

If academics have a role to play in public life, it must surely be as critics rather than as caretakers of public discourse (see McCutcheon 2001). In the first place this means self-critique, because the production and reproduction of ideological categories as if they are merely pragmatic and neutral for descriptive and analytical purposes is in effect to mystify ourselves and to legitimate the mystification of wider public discourse. Christopher Hitchens's book *God is Not Great: How Religion Poisons Everything* (Hitchens 2007) is not a scholarly one, and nor does it claim to be. Though he says he teaches literature in a US university, the style of this book reflects his other profession as a journalist. It is written in populist style, appealing to widespread myths about 'religion' for what I imagine would be a variety of motives – making money, settling personal grudges, and I infer also a passionate desire to promote US secular republicanism and free markets. Therefore its importance lies less in any originality, but rather in the normality of its underlying assumptions about 'religion' and all those things that religion is deemed to be essentially different from; combined with the powerful promotional opportunities that have gained the book such widespread publicity. That is to say that the reproduction of discourses on religion tends to disguise the simultaneous tacit reproduction of the secular as the ground from which religion can be constructed in the first place. The book reveals a structure of assumptions in populist rhetoric which are virtually the same as those reproduced in IR and cognate disciplines such as sociology, religious studies, anthropology and history. These same assumptions are proclaimed in modern written constitutions, in the interpretations and enforcements of courts, the classificatory uses by state agencies in the pursuance of state policies, and in academic descriptions, analyses and definitions of religion.

But, as I have argued in the chapter summaries given in Chapter 2, this structure of representations in the mode of the religion–secular binary is strongly connected historically with a parallel discourse on civility and barbarity. In discourses on Christian Truth, religion implicitly or explicitly defined civility and rationality, as against pagan barbarity and superstition. In the discourse in which religion is opposed to the non-religious secular, civility has frequently been associated with secular rationality, and the religious with barbarity. The latter discourse is an inversion of the former. Yet ironically they run side-by-side and are sometimes appropriated by the same people, with for example Protestant missionaries advocating the superior rationality of Christianity as against heathenism, but also advocating the superiority of Euro-American liberal democracy, capitalism and scientific technology.

Hitchens's admitted aim in this book is summarized well in his title. It is that religion means belief in God, which is irrational; that such belief is typically characterized by fanaticism and barbarity; and that such irrational barbarity poisons everything that the world might be, if only Hitchens and like-minded secular people with a grip on reality were allowed to get on and order things according to their own unencumbered powers of reasonableness and discrimination. The rational secular ground that Hitchens believes he himself stands on is not as strongly forefronted as the supposed nature of 'religion', but it is stated, both tacitly, in opposition to those qualities which he attributes to 'religion', and explicitly, in his use of self-referential terms. Non-religious Hitchens and people like him can be inferred as rational, civilized, humanist, tolerant, democratic, republican, and patriotically US American.

A major part of his thesis about 'religion' is set out in his second chapter, entitled 'Religion Kills', and this chapter and its title reveal enough about the structure of underlying assumptions and their problems to justify my focus of critique. This chapter 'is a very brief summary of the religiously inspired cruelty I witnessed in six places' (Hitchens 2007: 18). Here he tells several depressing stories of the fanatical hatred that different groups in various regions of the world feel for each other, the violence, torture, death and destruction that they engage in, their atrocities, hypocrisies and blindness to their own wickedness and ignorance.

Hitchens concedes that 'religion' does sometimes appear to have positive qualities, but these are only superficial. For example, Hitchens has 'been to evangelical services, in black and white communities, where the whole event was one long whoop of exaltation at being saved, loved and so forth' (2007: 16). However, there is good reason for being suspicious. At his own first marriage, in a Greek Orthodox Church, he could hear, if not believe, 'the joyous words that are exchanged between believers', only to notice later that the archbishop who officiated at his wedding 'trousered two fees instead of the usual one' (2007: 16).

Hitchens himself has visited many of these scenes of 'religious' slaughter and mayhem as a reporter and journalist – Belfast, Beirut, Belgrade, Baghdad, Bombay, Jerusalem. 'Religion' acts in all of these places as a global trouble-maker, the cause of all barbarous mayhem, rearing its ugly head wherever the forces of enlightenment are weak or absent; inciting violence, clouding the calm voices of reason and tolerance.

'Religion' is frequently referred to as an agent: 'Religion poisons everything. As well as a menace to civilization, it has become a great threat to human survival' (2007: 25); 'religion does not, and in the long run cannot, be content with its own marvellous claims and sublime assurances' (2007: 17); 'religion must seek to interfere in the lives of non-believers' (2007: 17); 'religion was beginning to reassert its challenge to civil society' (2007: 28).

In the short chapter 'The Metaphysical Claims of Religion are False', which is a shallow excursion through some Christian philosophical theology (2007: 64–71), with a couple of mentions of Maimonides and Mohammed thrown in, Hitchens says:

> Many religions now come before us with ingratiating smirks and outspread hands, like an unctuous merchant in a bazaar. They offer consolation and solidarity and uplift, competing as they do in a marketplace. But we have a right to remember how barbarically they behaved when they were strong and were making an offer that people could not refuse. And if we chance to forget what that must have been like, we have only to look to those states and societies where the clergy still has the power to dictate its own terms. The pathetic vestiges of this can still be seen, in modern societies, in the efforts made by religion to secure control over education, or to exempt itself from tax, or to pass laws forbidding people to insult its omnipotent and omniscient deity, or even his prophet (2007: 67–8).

It should be noted that, though more extreme in its imagery, the underlying attributions of agency to religion are here in principle and essentially no different from those found in reputedly more scholarly books. For example Mark Juergensmeyer, in the abstract summarizing his article 'Is Religion the Problem?',[1] says:

> In the rubble following the collapse of the World Trade Center towers in the violent assault of September 11 lies the tawdry remnants of religion's innocence. In those brief horrifying moments our images of religion came of age. Religion was found in bed with terrorism. Whatever bucolic and tranquil notions we may have had were rudely replaced by those that were tough, political, and sometimes violent. Is this the fault of religion? Has its mask been ripped off and its murky side exposed – or has its innocence been abused? Is religion the problem or the victim?

From Juergensmeyer's abstract and from the title itself, we can immediately notice a number of tropes that are also being popularized by Hitchens. There is an unmistakable tendency to talk about religion as though it is a thing or even an agent with an essentially different nature from politics. Is religion a problem or a victim? Religion is innocent and tranquil (or so we imagined); religion was found in bed with terrorism; religion wears a mask; behind its mask religion is really not religion at all, but something quite different: it is tough, political and violent; religion has a murky side. The inescapable impression that is conveyed by these expressions is that religion is something we encounter in the world, some thing that acts in the world, something with its own autonomous nature, and while we may be mistaken about its real identity, there seems to be no doubt that it has one.

Juergensmeyer shares with Hitchens many reifying, populist images of religion as a universal agent, and I suspect that any attentive reader will treat his data and conclusions about 'religious terrorism' with scepticism. This is why I link these two authors, despite their other differences. Juergensmeyer is one of the cited authors in the IR literature from outside IR. He is director of global and international studies and a professor of sociology and religious studies at the University of California, Santa Barbara. He is also currently President of the American Academy of Religion, which unsurprisingly is the largest academic institution in the world for the promotion of the study of 'religion' and 'religions'. He is author or editor of 15 books on what he describes as global conflict between religious and secular beliefs and practices. Yet his characterization of religion as a dubious agent associated with terror and mayhem is not much different from that of Hitchens.

Hitchens, with his popularization of the myth of religion as an agent in the world, and its essentialized distinction from secular politics, can therefore be seen as bedfellow to writers such as Juergensmeyer and many authors in International Relations. Hitchens may not adopt the academic gravitas in his style of writing, but he is operating within a very similar set of presumptions. The troubles he witnessed in Belfast were caused by 'religious gangs' and 'rival religious death squads, often for no other reason than membership of another confession' (Hitchens 2007: 18). Terms such as confession, faith, belief and piety are used throughout to characterize 'religion' in all these places, in conjunction with such adjectives as fanatical, senseless, irrational and barbarous. Beirut's problem was that it 'suffered from a positive surplus of religions' (2007: 19). The tension and communal violence in India at the time of Independence was characterized by 'religious bloodlust' (2007: 20). The 'goons and thugs' of the Shiv Sena Hindu nationalist movement are described as 'co-religionists' (2007: 21). Ethnic cleansing in Bosnia-Herzegovina is (he claims) better described as 'religious cleansing' (2007: 21). The gangs under the control of the xenophobic nationalist, Milosevic, were made up of 'religious bigots' (2007: 21). Author Salman Rushdie was hunted by 'religious death squads' (2007: 30) sent by 'religious authority' (2007: 31). Hamas is described as 'still another religion' (2007: 24), as though the supply is endless.

Hitchens claims to be concerned with 'religion', but tacitly at least his book is also about its opposite, the non-religious secular. Hitchens never says how religious fanaticism and irrationality is distinguished from non-religious irrationality and fanaticism, and the clear implication is that there is no such thing as secular fanaticism, or secular irrationality, or secular barbarism. He hardly needs to discuss secularism at all, because it is always the implied opposite of everything attributed to 'religion'. If those religious people are barbarous, then Hitchens and his secular ground are by implication civilized. If those religious people are violent, then Hitchens and the secular are by implication peace-loving and only reluctantly violent in their defence of the higher truth. If those religious people are irrational and fanatical, then Hitchens and the secular are the calm voice of reason and tolerance. This tacit understanding, which is the understated implication of the forceful and dramatic focus on 'religion', rhetorically inscribes upon the reader's understanding the idealized qualities of secular humanism, implicit rather than explicit, the unstated stand of civility and reason from which the author himself is viewing religion's barbarisms.

However, we do get some explicit hints of his own position and the kind of man a secular humanist is. As a secular humanist, Hitchens has not had his 'faculties of discernment poisoned'. A decent man such as the author can, 'when the tempests of hatred and bigotry and bloodlust have passed away ... feel relatively unmolested in and around "Manger Square" ...' in Jerusalem (2007: 23). Hitchens might sound unctuously pious when he says: 'I once heard the late Abba Eban, one of Israel's more polished and thoughtful diplomats and statesmen, give a talk in New York ... with the authority of a former foreign minister and UN representative ...' (2007: 24). But this is not piety, presumably, because piety is reserved for 'messianic rabbis and mullahs and priests', 'hysterical clerics' and 'Armageddon-minded Christians'. A brief moment of hope that religion might redeem itself comes when 'a handful of priests and bishops and rabbis and imams ... put humanity ahead of their own sect or creed'. But, alas, 'this is a compliment to humanism, not religion' (2007: 27). As a secular humanist, Hitchens seeks to heal the wounds afflicted on others by religion, even on the religious themselves, wherever he can. The crises caused by religion cause him to 'protest on behalf of Catholics suffering discrimination in Ireland, of Bosnian Muslims facing extermination in the Christian Balkans, of Shia Afghans and Iraqis being put to the sword by Sunni Jihadists, and vice versa, and numberless other cases. To adopt such a stand is the elementary duty of a self-respecting human' (2007: 27–8). In the midst of all this religious fanatical violence and barbarism, 'anyone concerned with human safety or dignity would have to hope fervently for a mass outbreak of democratic and republican secularism' (2007: 28). One can almost hear the secular bugles of the cavalry blowing, or Wagner's Valkyrie in the helicopter gunship attack in Apocalypse Now.

As a secular humanist and American republican, contrasting himself to the religious fanatic, Hitchens says of himself:

> When I am not operating as a tentative and amateur foreign correspondent, I lead a rather tranquil and orderly life: writing books and essays, teaching my students to love English literature, attending agreeable conferences of literary types, taking part in the transient arguments that arise in publishing and the academy (2007: 28).

Here the secular academic is promoted as the epitome of modest and agreeable civility in contrast to the lurking barbarism of the religious. But this very model of a decent and civilized life (he does not mention it as a very privileged one) 'has been subject to outrageous invasions and insults and challenges' (2007: 28) by the religious fanatics.

One of the problems that Hitchens shrewdly notices is that the 'literal mind' of the religious believer does not understand the 'ironic mind' of the rational and civilized writer and academic (2007: 29). Believers, people of faith, do not have the sophistication and self-scrutiny of the secular academic. Unlike the US attorney John Ashcroft, who is an evangelical Christian, Hitchens and his fellow secular humanists are ones who are able to see 'the light of reason, and the defense of a society that separated church and state and valued free expression and free inquiry ...' (2007: 32). James Madison and Thomas Jefferson are two of the great saints of secular constitutionalism.

We can see that, throughout this chapter, and throughout the rest of the book, the world is divided into two fundamentally and essentially distinct domains. One is the irrational and barbaric domain of religion, and the other is the rational and civilized domain of the secular. However, when we consider Hitchens's observations of the areas of conflict under discussion, the matter becomes more complex, and the binary classification acts as a categorial strait-jacket into which the complexities of power relations are forced. The conflict in Belfast seems to Hitchens obviously and paradigmatically a 'religious' rivalry between Catholics and Protestants. But in what *sense* is it 'religious'? Hitchens tells an old Belfast joke. A man stopped at a roadblock is asked if he is Protestant or Catholic. When he replies that he is an atheist he is asked 'Protestant atheist or Catholic atheist?'. This seems to me (once I had stopped laughing) to undermine the use of 'religion' as an especially useful category for describing and analysing the situation. If religion and its fanatical barbarities are accounted for by the irrational belief in God, as Hitchens suggests at the beginning of his chapter, then this joke implies that the rivalry between Catholics and Protestants has little to do with such belief. Whether theist or atheist, you are still either Protestant or Catholic. But Hitchens draws a different and rather weak conclusion:

> The ostensible pretext for this mayhem is rival nationalisms, but the street language used by opposing rival tribes consists of terms insulting to the other confession ('Prods' and 'Teagues') (2007: 18).

Why does Hitchens say that this is only an 'ostensible pretext' for rival nationalisms? I assume it is because he has, *a priori*, decided that this is really about 'religion', and his observations and causal explanations must be fitted into the *a priori* category. Instead, he might have considered how or whether religious rivalry and nationalist rivalry can be clearly or usefully distinguished. Furthermore, he doesn't notice how little the reader's understanding is enhanced by the weakly defined sense of 'religion' as belief in God, itself a highly contested word with many different theological constructions even within the broad Christian traditions of Catholicism and Protestantism. Compare English or Scottish Quaker practice with the Latin Mass, or the early modern Calvinist church-state with the Calvinist entrepreneurial individualism of eighteenth- and nineteenth-century North America, and one can immediately see that there are incommensurables in what is meant by 'God'. These incommensurables multiply greatly when one tries to translate the Christian trinitarian 'God' into Muslim conceptions of Allah; and the problems become even greater in attempting to translate 'God' into non-European languages such as Japanese, Chinese, Sanskrit, or African languages, to mention but a few examples.

This conflict might better be described in the way Hitchens does in fact describe it some of the time as rival nationalisms or tribal warfare, disputes over territory and resources. Another possibility is that nationalism has many of the traits widely attributed to 'religion' and, if this problematic term is to be used at all, then arguably nationalism should be one of its prime modern examples. Nations are imagined communities, invented traditions, invisible transcendental entities which demand absolute loyalty and commitment, sacrifice even unto death, ritual worship and sacred objects such as flags, constitutions, mythologized histories, founding saints and heroes, marching meditations on the sacrality of boundaries, and so on. Talk of God may in certain contexts add legitimation, but in nationalism it is the nation (or tribe, or territory, or collective self-identity) that is the main focus of undying loyalty, and one would need to be a theologian with an axe to grind to separate belief in God from belief in the nation or the collective identity. For partisan theologians (rather than liberal ecumenicists) the Catholic God and the Protestant God are presumably not identical, for only one is the True God. For ordinary people who are not trained theologians, the meaning of God is deeply rooted in their emotional attachments to a particular nation or community. Notice also Hitchens's use of the term 'confessions'. I think that in Hitchens's mind there was a conscious or unconscious association with the confessional of the Catholic Church, which he then vaguely hopes can be extended as a defining characteristic of 'religions'. But 'confession', like 'faith', can be used in ordinary language in ways that fail to demarcate a special and separate religious domain. One can equally confess loyalty to a group, confess faith in the glory of the nation, and confess one's betrayal of the nation. One can confess one's crimes in court. One can confess one's love for a man or woman. One can confess one's faith in free markets. Indeed, this book is Hitchens's own confession, something like a secularists' liturgy. One can hear other members of the choir – Daniel Dennett, Richard Dawkins, and so on – chanting in harmony in the background. This is not intended entirely as a joke.

If, however, nationalism was included as a 'religion', this would cause some obvious problems, not least because Hitchens' whole argument is based on the essential difference between religion and secular humanism; between the violence of religious fanaticism and the tolerance and love of peace of the non-religious and reasonable humanist; between the bloodlust of crazed theocracies and his own faith in the non-religious secular state with its sense of justice and fair play, and its constitutional guarantees of rights. To describe all this as religion would tend to reveal how general the term is, to the point of having little clear content.

Despite the relative emptiness of 'religion' as a rhetorical construct, the structures of prejudice upon which his argument is founded show the uncritical assumption that it has a weighty meaning. An essentialized distinction between religion and the secular runs throughout his book as an implicit, and sometimes explicit, fundamental principal. Hitchens never discusses an alternative possibility – that belief in the nation is not *essentially* different from belief in God; that allegiance to the flag and the constitution is not *essentially* different from a religious duty; that unstinting patriotic service to the nation is an act of faith; or that dying for the glory and honour of one's nation is a kind of martyrdom; these examples tend to undermine the conceit that religious and secular practices and values are essentially different. This point would render it useless as an analytical tool, but is never seriously considered, let alone refuted. I suggest that Hitchens's guiding assumption here is actually no more valid than the theological discourses that he despises. This is because, despite his literary expertise, he does not consider the point that words gain their meaning from strategic use, rather than because they stand in a one-to-one relationship with some objective nature of the world.

In Beirut, the simplistic distinction between religion and the secular doesn't seem to work well either. What Hitchens calls 'a wide selection of serpents ... a positive surplus of religions ...' (2007: 19) is actually described mostly in terms of what might just as well be called communities with different languages, histories, collective identities and self-representations. He uses all the following categories to identify different identities more or less in a single paragraph: Shia Muslims, Maronite Catholics, Kurds, Lebanese, Jews, Israel, Palestinians, Iran, Lebanon, and Hezbollah. Are all these religions? Are some of them religions but others not religions? Are some secular? What use is the religion–secular distinction in such a complex arena of competing group identities and interests? There seems to be a significant lack of fit between his simplistic characterization of 'religion' and the actual human complexity on the ground. One feels Hitchens straining to impose his two-pronged ideology of religious fanaticism as against secular rationality onto human communities engaged in conflict over land, access to water, power inequalities and disenfranchisement.

Much the same point can be made about Mumbai (Bombay), his next case study. Hitchens simplifies the complex tensions at the point of Indian Independence – often described by others as a movement for national independence – and the separation between India and Pakistan as 'religious bloodlust' (2007: 21). But why religious? Why not ethnic, or communal, or nationalist tragedy? Here, instead of the simplistic fanatical religion rearing its ugly and barbarous head in the absence of some rational secular humanism, he has to resort to the names of groups such as Muslims, Hindus, Parsis, Jews, Congress and Shiv Sena. These are all names of different communities, institutions or, in the case of Shiv Sena, a Hindu-based nationalist party. Being Hindu-based does not make it self-evidently 'religious' rather than 'ethnic' or 'communal' or even 'caste'. There is, for example, a complex history of published debate concerned with whether or not 'caste' is a religious or a non-religious institution. Many orthodox, high-caste Brahmins are technically atheists, and even for those described as theists the concept of the world, ethics and Brahman (a problematic rendering into English as 'God', often represented as female, and usually ultimately beyond form or gender) are very different from Christian ones. Hindu is better understood as a general communal term, with limited and specific uses in certain contexts, as when distinguishing between Hindu and Muslim or Jain castes, or as a highly complex group identity.

Hitchens's analysis is very simplistic, since no mention is made of the impact on caste communalism of colonial rule, the introduction of capitalism, or industrialization. Hitchens seems uninterested in serious exploration in the historical and anthropological literature. For centuries caste had acted as a complex system of integration in which different identified groups had different occupations, duties, privileges and places to live. Muslims and Hindus and other groups lived fairly peacefully together, but became increasingly conscious of themselves as distinct essentialized groups in competition with other castes for the rights and benefits that were increasingly being made available by modern reforms. Call this progress or not, it was a fateful and complex process which generated many tensions and conflicts which had not existed before. To reduce this to a simplistic problem of an ill-defined and over-generalized Anglophone 'religion' which does not translate well into either Sanskrit, Tamil or Hindi, with a lack of critical historical reflection, does not help us understand very much.

The same problem arises again in the case of Belgrade. Here the terms used (again in the order in which they appear in his analysis) are southern Slav, Croat, Serb, Roman Catholic, Christian Orthodox, Nazi, Jew, and German, ethnic, ex-Communist, nationalist, Muslim, Greek, Russian, Ottoman, and Bosnia-Herzogovina. These terms stand variously for different kinds and sizes of identity, either as self-representations or representations imposed by outsiders. Some might be referred to as national, some as ethnic or communal. But Hitchens wants them all to fit into his simple idea of 'religions'. He insists that what Serbs themselves referred to as ethnic cleansing ought to be called religious cleansing. But why? Why are the gangs of 'bigots' referred to as 'religious bigots' rather than communal bigots or nationalist bigots? But despite this complexity, that so badly requires clear understanding, Hitchens is satisfied with the slogan 'once again, religion poisons everything'.

Much the same can be said about his representation of the complex situation in Palestine and its relation with Israel and other communities in the Middle East. Rather than running through them all, let me ask one rhetorical question. Why is Hamas described as 'a religion'? Hamas is an elected government. Does that make it religious, or political? I suggest that both these terms are inadequate for a popular movement of national liberation. This is another way in which the simplistic distinction between religious fanaticism and secular reasonableness has to give way to more useful categories of description and classification. But, even more importantly, it invites the spinners of the myth of the religious–secular dichotomy to reflect self-critically on its dangerous consequences.

## Notes

1.     Orfalea Center for Global & International Studies, University of California, Santa Barbara: Year 2004 Paper 21; available online at http://escholarship.org/uc/item/4n92c45q/ See also his *The New Cold War? Religious Nationalism confronts the Secular State* (Juergensmeyer 1993) which is widely and approvingly cited in International Relations.

# Chapter 7

## Radical, Religious and Violent

In his book *Radical, Religious and Violent: The New Economics of Terrorism* (Berman 2009), Eli Berman hopes to answer two leading questions:

1 With so many angry people in the world, why are there so few resilient terrorist organizations?
2 Why, among the few resilient terrorist organizations, are so many made up of *religious* radicals?

The brief answer to question 1 is that terrorist organizations are especially vulnerable to betrayal and defection. Defections and information leaks are the Achilles' Heel of such clandestine groups. The brief answer to the second question is that religious radicals are better at reducing defections and information leaks than the non religious ones. Why? Answering this further question is the heart of the argument of Berman's book and constitutes its substantive content. The explanation why such organizations, which he refers to as radical religious groups, are good at this is complex and, within the confines of an un-self-critical social scientific and economics paradigm, interesting.

In summary form, the argument goes like this. Violent religious radicals, most of them Muslim, share significant structural features with a range of non-violent radical religious groups, including Jewish, Christian and some other secular ones. These groups and their history and organization provoke the problem that the author hopes to solve, viz.: 'Why are religious radicals, who often start out appearing benign and charitable and generally avoid conflict, so effective at violence when they choose to engage in it?' (Berman 2009: 2)

The characteristic of all of these groups is that they provide mutual aid and social services that allow them to persist with relative autonomy from mainstream society. Membership of these mutual aid communities requires acts of sacrifice that symbolize loyalty to the group and make 'shirking' and betrayal more difficult. Such sacrifices are a kind of mutual investment that binds the group together as a working unit. These features also explain why the groups can persist apart from the mainstream culture and market economy.

It seems ironic that, according to Berman's argument, despite the importance he attaches throughout to specifically *religious* groups as the most effective perpetrators of violence, their survival and persistent flourishing is not essentially to do with their theological or 'religious' beliefs. He sometimes claims that theological commitment may be necessary but not sufficient (2009: 9). In general, success is explained more by common organizational characteristics:

> If we ignore the theological differences and concentrate on observable, day-to-day behaviour within communities, radical Islamists are actually quite similar to religious radicals among Christians and Jews. Religious radicals in all three religions share a common approach to mainstream culture: they fear it threatens their traditional values and dedicate themselves to an unrelenting effort to differentiate themselves from its insidious lifestyle (2009: 64).

In his final chapter, Berman reviews the role of religious or theological motives in his argument and frankly tells the reader that, on the whole, and apart from the issue of trust in leadership, 'religion' or theology is really not very important (2009: 212–14).

This immediately raises a problem. If the theological beliefs of the groups are what define them as religious, and if these are not central to their success and resilience, then why claim that specifically *religious* terror groups are the most successful, more so than *secular* ones? We will see that Berman does provide an answer to this – trust in the 'clerical' leadership – though in my view it is not strongly convincing as it stands.

The groups he terms non-violent religious radicals are exemplified by the Amish, Hutterites and Mennonites, and ultra-Orthodox Jews. Analysis of the organization of the non-violent groups provides a model for understanding the resilience of violent groups. His main examples of radical religious groups that practise violence are Hezbollah, al-Qaeda, the Taliban, Hamas and the Mardi Army. The author distinguishes these from 'secular' groups such as the Basque Separatists (ETA), the National Liberation Army and the Revolutionary Armed Forces (FARC) in Colombia, the Shining Path in Peru, the Kurdistan Workers Party (PKK) in Turkey, and the Liberation Tigers of Tamil Elam (LTTE) in Sri Lanka.

These latter violent groups share similar organizational characteristics as the peaceful ones – Berman borrows from Laurence Iannaccone the concept of the 'club model' to refer to such groups. Like their peace-loving similar types, these successful terrorist organizations provide mutual aid and social services that allow them to persist with relative autonomy from mainstream society. They also require acts of sacrifice from members that bind the group together and reduce 'shirking'. Crucially, this ability to reduce shirking works in situations of violent terrorism to reduce defection and information leaks, which are normally the Achilles' Heel of all groups involved in insurrection against established governments with counter-intelligence agencies.

Berman hopes his analysis might be useful for democratic secular governments in their fight against terror. It leads him to make some specific policy proposals about the best way to disarm these groups, reduce their influence and win over the local populations that harbour them.

What Berman fails to discuss in any comprehensive way is why so many groups, violent or peaceful, whether classified as religious or secular, with different histories and ideologies, are so strongly opposed to mainstream consumer capitalist society and its secular agencies. If there are a whole range of groups in different parts of the world that share a collective desire to distance themselves from mainstream US capitalist market values, and that share many significant organizational attributes with each other, then we need to understand and assess the commonalities and differences in their critique. Taking their reasons seriously means reviewing our own standpoint as academics who, while we strive for impartiality and accurate representation, yet are financed by markets and the secular state against which many of these groups apparently stand on principle. It seems to me to be one of the major lacunae of Berman's book that the secular, which Berman himself represents as an economist and social scientist, remains a simple given in this book, a largely hidden substratum outside the range of critical enquiry, rather than itself a competing ideology of global power against which these other groups stand with varying degrees of tension.

Many people attribute the shocking global inequalities of material wellbeing to US-style corporate capitalism, consumerism, neo-colonialism and the exploitation of cheap labour. This issue is never properly discussed in the book, and consequently one is in the dark about why these groups should exist at all. The author is a man of reason – calm, pleasant, objective, disinterested, and shocked by, but analytically curious about, the violence of terrorists. At the same time he seems completely innocent of the shocking secular violence of Shock and Awe.

The sub-title of the book, 'New Economics of Terrorism', reminds us that the author is an economist who intends to explain the variable success and failure rates of these various groups in terms of economic and social science concepts. Berman provides the reader with information on his research background. An important stream of inspiration comes from University of Chicago economists such as Gary Becker and Laurence Iannaccone. The author writes a short, self-congratulatory genealogy of intellectual legitimation underpinned by a Nobel Prize:

> University of Chicago economists are hardly a bunch that shy away from controversial ideas. On the contrary, they embrace iconoclasts who insist that there's an economic approach to just about everything. Chicago economist Gary Becker won the scorn and ridicule of other social scientists early in his

career by insisting that education is best thought of as an investment, rather than a noble intellectual and moral adventure, labeling it 'human capital'. By the time Iannaccone sat in Becker's lectures in the 1980's, though, human capital had gone mainstream. Becker was on his way to winning a Nobel Prize for introducing another initially controversial idea, the 'demand for children', into mainstream demography. Becker's graduate students were busy in those days analyzing crime, immigration, marriage, and divorce, among other topics, as decisions that practical, rational individuals made in cost benefit terms. Yet, when Iannaccone proposed applying those tools to *religion*, even Gary Becker hesitated (2009: 62; emphasis in original).

The values of this group are suggested by Berman's laudation to the Nobel Prize winner Gary Becker who, in Berman's words, thought that education is best thought of as an investment, rather than a noble intellectual and moral adventure, labeling it 'human capital'. What Berman seems to be suggesting is that, if you strip away the wordy conceit that education is noble and moral, you can instead see the underlying economic truth that it is an investment. It seems that secular scientists are gradually developing the analytical tools that progressively peel away the distorted ideas and values of earlier generations to reveal the empirical truth about the world.

'Religion' is thus one of a number of topics, alongside crime, divorce, immigration and so on, which stands to be explained by the progressive insights and inspirations of hard-headed scientific economists. Even for the inspired frontiers-folk of Chicago economic theory, religion is a reified and mystified term that, by its exotic elusiveness, offers an especially difficult topic of analysis ('... even Gary Becker hesitated'). It is as though 'we explode myths, but this is the big one!'. In contrast, I suggest that the real myth is the subtext that the science of economics is fundamentally different from religion with more fundamental explanatory power.

The assumption that 'religion' and economics are essentially different, and also that one of these can be explained in the terms of the other, is problematic. At first sight this radical distinction would seem to put religion outside the explanatory paradigm of economics. As Berman says, even the Nobel-prizewinning Gary Becker baulked at the idea that religion could be explained in terms of the explanatory paradigm of economics. Many readers, especially those who have any familiarity with the fields of religious studies or social anthropology, will be aware of the complex academic discussions about reductionism, but I cannot find any serious discussion of this literature in Berman's book. Given the wider public discourses on religion, the complex history of that contested category, and its array of referents and possible readings, one might think that there is nothing sufficiently clear in the meaning of 'religion' that *can* be reduced to economic analysis. There is no definition of religion that is not hotly contested. Furthermore, despite the technical terminology and the complex mathematical models, many people might feel that economics may be difficult to distinguish from a form of divination.

Berman thinks it is easy to say what religion is, and what economics is, and how they differ. Here we have a very plain statement of the supposedly essential distinction between religion and economics:

> Most people, even most economists, don't think that economics and religion mix well. Religion is at its core, after all, about spirituality and faith. Religions make bold statements that are inherently metaphysical, unverifiable, and irrefutable – about the immortality of the spirit, the existence of heaven, the goodness of man. Economics, on the other hand, is composed of much more mundane stuff: the demand for gasoline, how to invest your retirement savings, and why government should regulate banking. Furthermore, economics is an empirical science, drawing strength from its ability to refute or support those relatively mundane claims with data. What could economics possibly have to say about spirituality, faith, and irrefutable propositions? (2009: 62).

Berman never considers that the fundamental categories of economics, such as the spontaneous coordination properties of the market economy, rational self-maximizing individuals, and natural rationality of private property, are not themselves deductions from empirical observation, but the presupposed metaphysical postulates and contested value-judgements. He does not consider arguments of such diverse writers as Walter Benjamin (1921) or Robert Nelson (2001) that economics is a religion.[1] He does not consider the role of faith in the credibility of money or markets. This only becomes obvious at historical moments of emergency such as the Depression or the recent banking crisis. Yet one can surely think analogously in terms of the currencies of medieval Christianity – the trade in relics, the investment in special rituals for the remission of time spent in purgatory, the rituals of exchange and investment between sinful mortals and divine justice mediated by the priesthood, arguably a complex system of exchange and investment which lasted for several centuries but which suffered widespread losses of faith culminating in the Protestant Reformation. The Protestants institutionalized new forms of exchange and investment. This is only an analogy and there are many obvious differences between medieval Catholicism and modern capitalism. The question is whether they are *essentially* different, as is implied by the binary classifications between 'religious' faith and 'secular' scientific knowledge. Historians and anthropologists have shown that there have been many systems of exchange in different societies – one might think of the famous example of the Kula ring of the Trobriand Islanders in Malinowski's ethnography.[2] Nor does Berman consider the point that 'markets' are constructs, not empirically observable objects in the world. It is perfectly true that many people do assume that economics and religion don't mix well. There is a powerful public discourse that condemns religious groups that make profits from their services. Non-profit-making is a basic criterion for classification as a religious corporation or charity. True religion, according to this wide-spread view, has nothing to do with profits in this world. There is a similar, widely popular view of the dangers of mixing religion with politics. These popular assumptions are reproduced powerfully by various agencies including the media, the education system, the courts, and academic publications. Therefore it may seem unsurprising that these same suppositions constantly come to the surface throughout Berman's book, are basic to his analysis, and are never systematically questioned.

On the one hand Berman, on the basis of statistical evidence provided by agencies such as the US State Department, strongly links the connection between the success of 'terror' and 'religious' (rather than similarly secular) organizations. On the other hand, in much of his argument and with the main exception of his final chapter, Berman argues that theology as the religious element has quite limited relevance. Regardless of their theological or spiritual beliefs, it is the common characteristic of mutual aid societies that they strengthen solidarity and reduce shirking, leaks of information and defections. One problem here is that, beyond a restatement of popular assumptions, Berman nowhere provides a convincing account of the basis for classifying some mutual aid societies as religious and others as secular. At one point he relies on US State Department statistics to prove that groups classified as religious, such as Hamas or Aum Shinrikyo, are more dangerous than groups classified as secular. But this merely places the problem one step back, because he does not explain or justify how the US State Department determined these classifications. And when one looks carefully at various points in Berman's text, as I intend to do, we can see that there is no convincing boundary between religious and secular practices. Reliance on the validity of this binary for descriptive and analytical purposes unravels the argument and the interpretation of data.

The unanalysed binary opposition between the religious/theological/spiritual aspects of existence and the non-religious/material/secular ones is built into his descriptions and summaries from the beginning. The book starts with a reference to 9/11 and the 'global war on terrorism' (Berman 2009: 1), and Berman points out with statistics that the threat from terrorism has increased rather than diminished: 'The death toll has risen despite our monumentally expensive counterterrorism effort.' The 'our' here quickly and effortlessly incorporates the reader into the author's confidence, and reminds us which side we are on. He is an easy guy to like; the prose is that of a reasonable and humane American, with a friendly, no-nonsense, straight-talking style, no affectation or condescension here – in his case an economist, psychologist and social scientist, searching for ways to make sense of the barbarity. And having made sense of it, to see how to fight it through quick-witted counter-insurgency.

Berman names Hezbollah, Hamas, the Taliban and the Madhi Army as four 'radical religious organizations' which, even more than Al-Qaeda, have surprised 'the established militaries with both their resilience and their lethality' (2009: 2). He says that 'Muqtada al-Sadr has built a militia out of a religious charity and used it to become a kingmaker in Iraqi politics ...' (2009: 2). Berman does not mention whether their charity is 'religious' because al-Sadr claims that it is religious, or because it is classified as such by the (US or Iraqi) state authorities, or whether it is religious simply because Berman knows a religion when he sees one. The claim that al-Sadr 'used' such charitable activity as a kind of cover for the real goal of 'politics' implies that the work of religious charity is by definition different from politics, but can be illegitimately confused with politics. This kind of unanalysed discourse flows through public rhetoric and a great deal of academic writing.

Other expressions of 'normal' usage flow freely throughout. In the section summarizing the history and organization of Hezbollah, we find that it was formed by 'former seminary students', many of whom had studied in 'the Shiite holy cities of Najaf and Qom', had received generous support from 'the Islamist government of Ayatollah Khomeini', and subjected the city of Baalbek to 'religious radicalization' (2009: 3). This so-called *religious* radicalization was exemplified for the author by the wearing of the *burka* by women; and contrasted with a previous time when Baalbek 'had been tolerant enough to attract secular tourists of all denominations', and with the Hezbollah displacement of 'the *more secular* (my italics) Shiite *Amal* movement' (2009: 3).

In this summary of Hezbollah some widely held assumptions about the distinction between religious and secular are exhibited without analysis. Religious radicalization is exemplified by the wearing by Muslim women of *religious* dress, i.e. the *burka*. We are assumed to know what Muslim 'seminary' students are because we have the model of Catholic seminaries that train priests. The Muslim seminary students studied in Shiite holy cities (holy = religious), supported by an 'Islamicist' government. It is assumed without argument that 'Islam' is a 'religion', but the same kind of questions I asked above about religious charity can be put here. Does Berman call Islam a religion because that's what the US State Department says it is? Or because that's what Muslims (or those Muslims who speak English) say it is? Or because Berman knows this intuitively? However, if an Islamic government provides material as well as spiritual services, then would it not follow from Berman's own assumptions that that Islamic government is both religious and secular simultaneously?

The reader may notice also that these signs of religious radicalization are contrasted with the secular tolerance of tourism, that innocent pastime of enjoying wealth while spreading it to the less fortunate. The notion of the secular tolerance of tourism chimes loudly with the sister idea that, whereas secular governments are tolerant, religious governments are intolerant.

One early warning sign of a problem in the usage of these classificatory categories which might strike an attentive reader is this: if the distinction between the religious and the secular is so obvious that it needs no critical inquiry, then what do we make of the other points to which Berman draws to our attention: Hezbollah's dedication to social service provision, and their virtual establishment of 'a sort of alternative government'? On one reading he means religious social service rather than secular social service, and religious government rather than secular government. The binary opposition between these supposedly different types of practice and institution seems here to be quietly taken for granted. On the other hand, it is central to Berman's argument that mutual aid societies, both religious and secular, share some fundamental and common practices such as providing mutual aid and demanding sacrifices in order to reduce defections, and that these shared characteristics are therefore not essentially religious. These are material as distinct from spiritual. The importance of the religious element, whether in the context of radical mutual-aid groups, of Islamic states, or of the personal motivations of individuals, becomes attenuated by locating the 'religious' element in 'spirituality' or theology and contrasting this with the provision of material services. As Berman himself admits, for the largest part of his book there is really little or no role for 'spirituality' or religion as an explanatory factor in the groups' persistence. The theological element is only called on in a very specific and final part of the argument which appears in the concluding chapter.

A problematic usage in the distinction might be indicated by the expression 'the more secular Shiite *Amal* movement', because here 'secular' is being quantified as something more or less. If a movement or an organization can be more or less secular, then it can also presumably be more or less religious. This reminds us of something which may sound obvious, but which has implications, which is that the boundary between the religious and the secular can move depending on the context, not only of the actors (we do not know from Berman's account whether they think in these terms, especially if they are thinking in Arabic, Persian or Urdu for instance) but also of the writer's needs. The whole book is premised on the idea that religion and violence have a special relationship, and the subtext throughout is that secular states and their agents are essentially peace-loving, and only reluctantly violent. But the indication of a weakly delineated and shifting boundary tends to subvert the theoretical usefulness of this assumption.

Hezbollah displaced Amal 'as the leading representative of Lebanese Shiite Muslims'. Here again the distinction between the religious and the material is far from clear. In normal Anglophone discourse Shiite Muslims are 'religious'. So how come they had 'secular' leaders in Amal in the first place? One possible answer that Berman does not discuss might be that this displacement undermined the authority of Western-oriented governments, which suggests that 'secular' means Western, and therefore Amal's orientation towards Western governments implies a degree of secularity. This could mean that Amal showed a 'secular' face towards the West when they were negotiating in US English, and a Muslim face towards their own people when they were speaking in Arabic. If the leadership of a group finds itself caught between its own indigenous traditions of classification in Arabic and Muslim culture on the one hand, and the dominant classifications of external but threatening Western powers on the other, expressed in a foreign language (mainly US English), then it has no option but to mediate and negotiate the conflicting definitional terms. Arguably the problem of translation, of reconstituting ancient cultural and linguistic regions according to Europhone forms of civility and rationality, often with the purpose of colonial control and domination, has been ubiquitous throughout the colonial and global spread of US and more generally Euro-American power. The possibility that these historical processes of global power are likely causes, or partial causes, of the existence of groups violently (or non-violently) opposed to US global capitalism and consumer culture is not properly analysed in Berman's argument.

The author's prose has a common-sense logic and fluency about it, and yet if the reader is more alert than the author, who is rightly concerned about the facts but unfortunately not the classification of the facts, then the arbitrary and rhetorically constructed nature of 'religion' and 'non-religion' makes its presence felt in these ways.

The Taliban, like Hezbollah, were formed by 'another apparently benign group of clerics' who also began as 'seminary students' (2009: 4). Typically for 'religious radicals' they were 'pious', and provided services 'both spiritual and tangible'. They provided a safe haven in Afghanistan for foreign 'radical Islamists'. Their actions, organization and strategy 'demonstrated quite dramatically that a radical religious group has the potential to be an amazingly potent and violent force' (2009: 5).

Again we can see the easy construction of unquestioned identities: 'clerics' are or ought to be unproblematically like Christian priests and vicars – though presumably not like the Marxist-inspired liberation theologians of South America who are not considered. Piety, like 'holy', is considered unproblematically religious, as are radical Islamists. On the other hand there are two different kinds of service provided: 'spiritual' and 'tangible'. The spiritual services are presumably intangible, as contrasted to the materiality of the tangible. The supposed binary opposition between spirit and matter is integral to the structure of the whole argument. Berman's tacit meaning may be that groups that are or claim to be religious are really illicitly political in their aims, and are using the appearance of spirituality to achieve material benefits such as real political power. But this peculiar Anglophone way of dividing up people's motivations might unfairly reduce to a cynical bid for personal power what the actors see as a liberation movement from Western capitalism, and from the colonially-imposed and divisive structures of arbitrary nation states and their managers.

Yet behind the extremism it seems that the Taliban's material services were of the kind that most people would instinctively applaud:

In the Taliban's own version of their origins they organized to prevent school children from being abducted and raped on their way to school in the impoverished villages around Kandahar ... [L]ike many other radical religious groups, with noble aspirations and limited ambitions ... [t] hey sought to improve their own lives and those of the local community members through personal piety and local Islamic government (2009: 4–5).

When Berman uses expressions such as an '*apparently* benign group of clerics' and 'the Taliban's *own version* of their origins' (my italics) he conveys to the reader that things are not as they seem. Later in the book we will see that these good things might be understood, according to Berman's rational and scientific analysis, not as genuine religious ideals (whatever they might be supposed to be) but as useful power moves for consolidating the organization, especially with the aim of reducing defections and betrayals. Berman would probably not see his own work as a useful power move for the legitimation of the violence of the secular state, or for discursively inscribing secular reason as the ground of being.

Again, we can see here the assumed characteristics of 'religion' in the association with terms such as 'pious', 'seminary', 'spiritual' (as distinct from 'tangible', for they provided services of both kinds), and 'radical Islamicists'. When the author uses the expression 'both spiritual and tangible' to describe the services they offer, we again find the idea that spiritual means other-worldly, intangible, and not concerned with the things of this world, or at least not concerned with power.

In this summary of the Taliban, I don't think there is any explicit mention of the term 'secular', nor even of the degrees of secularity that Berman attributed to Amal. In the brief summary of the history and organization of Hamas, though, the term appears. As with the other groups, Berman is puzzled why this radical Islamic group has been so effective at violence (2009: 6). Their forerunner in the Gaza Strip, the Islamic Brotherhood, 'was a benign, non-violent religious organization' (2009: 6):

> Like other branches of the Brotherhood worldwide, they complemented the spiritual services provided in mosques with social and welfare services, delivered through a network of clinics, schools, charities, drug treatment centers, and even sports clubs (2009: 6).

Notice here that 'mosques' provide 'spiritual services', and that these spiritual services are 'complemented' by other kinds of services which are presumably not spiritual but material, not religious but secular. However, the more Berman relies on this distinction, the more arbitrary it seems to become. Services provided in mosques are religious; but those provided in clinics and schools are material and secular. I flag this up because I am looking for a pattern of religious or spiritual and non-religious or non-spiritual attributions of the kind we have noticed in the previous summaries of Hezbollah and the Taliban. It is never a distinction for which Berman (like so many other writers) ever produces any persuasive theorization, but one which runs unconsciously just beneath the surface of the text. It is popular discourse dressed up to look like serious analytical categories.

But then in 1988 something happened which changed the course of Hezbollah's apparently benign activities. The popular Palestinian Intifada began against Israeli occupation. The Intifada was led by 'the young *secular* leaders of the rebellion' (my italics), referring to Fatah, a major component of the Palestine Liberation Organization, and the Popular Front for the Liberation of Palestine (PFLP). This put the Brotherhood in a quandary, for their religious leadership was being undermined by a secular leadership. Here things seem to have been reversed. Here it is secular leaders who are popular and who engage in violent action, whereas the religious Brotherhood 'had traditionally treated the national conflict as secondary' (2009: 6). This led the Brotherhood to realize that 'it had to reinvent itself or become irrelevant. It established a militia, naming it *Hamas*. Almost overnight Hamas became the single most deadliest terrorist organization in the Israel–Palestine conflict.' (2009: 6).

Berman's problem is why it was that the religious Hamas, which had less experience in violence than its secular rivals, should have proved more effective. Here again, it appears to be the religious organization of the group that makes it more deadly. Yet, as we have seen with the spiritual–material distinction applied to the other groups, their effectiveness depends mainly on their provision of material and secular services!

Based on US State Department statistics, Berman states that 'radical Islamicists are particularly lethal terrorists' (2009: 8), far more so than their secular counterparts. This dependence on US State Department statistics pushes the analytical problem one stage further back. On what criteria did the State Department base its own classification? Berman's social science methodology then depends partly on the same criteria as those used by the secular state.

Which are the dangerous secular groups? The Basque Separatists (ETA), the National Liberation Army and the Revolutionary Armed Forces (FARC) in Colombia, the Shining Path in Peru, the Kurdistan Workers Party (PKK) in Turkey, and the Liberation Tigers of Tamil Elam (LTTE) in Sri Lanka. Berman does not question the assumption that we can distinguish between religious revolution and nationalist revolution. They are just different, that's all. But the secular groups cannot match the religious ones. In the 40 years between 1968 and 2007, the 'religious terrorists perpetrated fewer attacks ... but killed far more people' (2009: 8). Of the 20 religious terrorist organizations on the US State Department list, 18 are radical Islamicist. The other two are *Kahane Chai*, a Jewish group, and the Japanese *Aum Shinrikyo*.

Berman also comments that other, earlier secular groups of the 1960s and 1970s such as the Baader-Meinhof Group in West Germany, the Japanese Red Army, the Canadian FLQ, and 'even the Fatah under the young Yasir Arafat' were also far less lethal than the religious ones (2009: 8).

There is thus no doubt in Berman's mind that it is religious groups who pose the greatest threat as distinct from secular ones, even though he cannot convincingly distinguish between religious and secular practices or institutions, or between the 'spiritual' and 'material' services they provide. The US State Department figures 'reflect a general pattern in global terrorism over the past few decades: radical religious terrorists of the early twenty first century have become extremely dangerous to citizens and pose an existential threat to some governments. The threat from modern religious terrorist organizations is unprecedented' (2009: 8). But without knowing what distinguished a religious from a secular group, this is just rhetoric.

Berman's assumption that the core or essence of religion is essentially different from the social sciences is expressed by a number of popular binaries that underpin the religion–secular distinction, such as faith and knowledge, metaphysics and empiricism, belief in another world as against hard evidential data located in this world, the non-rational realm of transcendence as against the rationality of observation. Given the wide and popular dissemination of these assumptions, even those readers who are suspicious of this process of knowledge construction and its wide implications for global human relations may feel it is wrong to criticise Berman for his attempt to pursue its logic. But, on the other hand, one can see the reinforcing and self-serving power of ways of classifying others and (by contrast) oneself through these binary constructs.

However, it should be noted that belief in the essential distinction between 'religious' and 'secular' practices is not itself the result of empirical observation, or of historical investigation, but an *a priori* conceptual grid that provides the basis for the way the data are organized and interpreted. Nobody has actually seen a religion or a religious practice. What we observe is a range of human practices to which, in modern English, we apply with considerable arbitrariness the classificatory convention that some are religious and some non-religious or secular. What counts as a religious practice, when it is not simply a proclamation, has been and still is open to negotiation, for example through court interpretations of constitutions. To claim, for example, that economic practice is fundamentally different from religious practice depends on inherited Anglophone conventions of description and analysis that have a complex history of their own. It is an ideological construction of a distinct economic domain that first emerged arguably in the late eighteenth century. What constitutes the religious and what the secular is not fixed in nature but is the result of a historically-specific series of arguments which have emerged partly out of Christian moral theology and its own internal and external disputes. Yet these unstable categories in turn have been taken over by self-acknowledged empiricists as though they are semantic constants standing for inherently distinct ontological realities. The meaning and applicability of this binary is not historically researched either by Berman or, to be fair to him, by the vast majority of academics including historians. As in the work of many social scientists, these problematic categories are used to frame the data, construct the problem, and provide the solution.

I would ask the reader to consider the further idea that the ideological function of discourses on religion, represented as spiritual, immaterial and otherworldly, tacitly establishes secular rationality on the supposedly firmer and superior ground of common-sense observation of facts. Not only is 'religion' a given and essentialized aspect of human existence, but the true ground of understanding religion, as with understanding everything else ('there's an economic approach to just about everything'), is the secular, scientific, empirical method. What I propose is that Berman, while seeming to describe and clarify what the world is inherently like, is actually constructing, or helping to construct, the world, or rather a historically contingent view of the world – which coincides with US power and capital – by putting such fundamental categories beyond critical questioning.

Berman claims (2009: 62) that Adam Smith pioneered the economic analysis of religion in the *Wealth of Nations*. The last part of this section reads: 'The main point for now is this: Smith did not see his economic approach as inconsistent with spirituality or faith. When clergy and members of religious communities wander away from the spiritual – sanctuaries, prayer, and faith – and into the practical – markets, organizations, and politics – Adam Smith was convinced that the usual rules of economics apply' (2009: 63).

We can see here that the distinction between the 'spiritual' and the secular is maintained, but one can also see that, for economic analysis to apply, the clergy and members of religious communities need to 'wander away' from the spiritual to the secular, as though there might be two different physical locations, a religious location typically housed in a church, and a secular location typically discovered in a market. But surely a church is just as much an 'organization' as is a market? And do we not talk quite normally about church politics? Then perhaps, to find the distinction, we need to imagine two distinct functions of the brain, the religious function and the secular function. But of course this does not solve any conceptual problem but merely puts it one step back. The location of the religious or spiritual ('sanctuaries, prayer and faith') becomes progressively more ethereal and intangible until it is difficult to say what is being referred to.

Does this image of agents wandering between the intangible and the tangible not imply that it is only as practical, secular agents that the religious can be understood by economists? But what actually is being understood? If the essence of 'religion' – 'sanctuaries, prayer and faith' – can be distinguished from its 'practical' aspects – 'markets, organizations and politics' – then what Berman takes to be the core of religion seems to remain outside the explanatory paradigms of the social sciences. In trying to find a way to make religion susceptible to economic analysis, Berman has to leave an essential core behind in some inaccessible sphere of spirituality, prayer and faith, and treat markets, organizations and politics as the accessible aspects of the organizations. The idea that religion has an essential core ineluctably implies that the non-religious secular also has an essential core, and this is itself a kind of modern myth which also needs to be recognized.

This essential core meaning of 'religion' in 'spirituality' is also identified as the theological. This leads Berman to question the importance of theology in our understanding of such groups. There seems to be an assumption here that 'theology' is essentially different from other kinds of ideology because it is concerned with God, prayer, faith and spirituality. But none of these general categories has any essential meaning, since they can all be used in ordinary language in many different ways across a spectrum of contexts that can be classified as both secular and religious. Again there is a problem of language here that is not subjected to critical scrutiny.

Iannaccone followed Adam Smith's ideas, and in turn has influenced Berman's approach. Iannaccone asked the question: 'Why would anyone volunteer to join a group that required prohibitions and sacrifices?' (Berman 2009: 64). One of the most important shared features of all these mutual aid 'clubs' is sacrifices (2009: 66). To be a member of such a club one must do something that will be expensive or impossible to reverse later on. Circumcision is one example. But sacrifices are part of the life and include various typical methods used by these groups to distinguish themselves: special dress codes, use of beards, hair (or shaved heads), prohibitions on shaving, radical covering of the body, dietary restrictions, restrictions on sexuality, prohibitions on the use of modern technology and power supplies (e.g. Amish prohibit the use of electricity and cars), restrictions on wearing of jewellery, alcohol and meat:

> All prohibitions and sacrifices, even those in mainstream denominations, are a puzzle ... Some degree of prohibition is common to all denominations, though it is much more subtle among Methodists, say, than among Seventh Day Adventists. If we all ignored our upbringing and theology for a moment, doesn't it seem strange that anyone would volunteer to join a denomination that prohibits enjoyable activities? Religious radicals tend to impose more extreme versions of these prohibitions, insisting on stricter dietary standards, more stringent Sabbath observance rules, more restrictive dress codes, and more time spent in prayer, for example (2009: 67).

This is 'deeply puzzling' to Berman (2009: 67). His puzzlement is puzzling to me. This seems to me to be a strange question for anyone to ask, not least a sociologist. One would have thought that all social orders are based in part on prohibitions and sacrifices. Even mainstream consumer societies have laws and conventions on dress codes, diet, legitimate and illegitimate pleasures, domestic arrangements, who can and cannot raise children, which kinds of literature or film one can and cannot read or see, which kinds of public gathering or speech can or cannot be tolerated, and so on.

Are Native Americans religious or secular groups? Was their violence against white colonizers a case of religious or secular violence? One could turn that question around and ask if the violence perpetrated against Native Americans during the imperial expansion of the United States was religious, or secular, or both, or neither, or a mixture of the two? A moment's historical reflection would remind us that Native Americans were persecuted and massacred for their alternative, pagan, uncivilized practices – dress codes, public dancing, initiation rituals, relationship with animals and the environment, different ideas about property rights – by some of the Protestant and Deist founders of the American empire who also legislated the secular US state into existence. Resistance to – or just being in the way of – the progress of the American Destiny may not have been described as terrorism in the eighteenth or nineteenth centuries, but it met with similar response. It was savagery in resistance to the progress of civilization.

But Berman is apparently not interested in Native Americans. Indigenous Americans did not typically believe in Christian Truth, which is what the word 'religion' generally meant. It included assumptions of superior white civility and rationality. I suggested in earlier parts of this book that there is not one Christian idea of 'religion' in general Anglophone discourse but at least two quite different and even contradictory ones. North American Protestants and Deists such as Jefferson in the eighteenth and nineteenth centuries were themselves powerfully contributing to the development and reproduction of a modern generic concept of religion in which 'religions' are believed to exist in all societies at all times in all languages. Yet at the same time the leaders of American independence and empire building, including Jefferson, were deeply invested in the older discourse on Religion as Christian Truth and regarded infidels, pagans and heathens with some contempt. Indeed, Jefferson said he did not consider these savages to have any religion. Perhaps the more fundamental discourse underlying these discourses was one of civility and rationality as against barbarity and irrationality. There was also a discourse on progress, which in turn became linked with white European-ness, higher rationality, science and the secular state. Native Americans seem to have regarded 'religion' to mean Christian colonial power, and there is some interesting research on the unsure outcomes of submitting traditional practices (which make no distinction between the supernatural and the natural in Native American cosmologies) to classification by the courts as 'religious'.[3] Had Berman considered these groups and the contestations around the meaning of religion and whether or not such 'savages' have religion at all, I suggest he would have become entangled in many challenges to his own inherited metaphysical assumption that 'religion' has an essential universal core distinguishing it from the 'secular'.

The terror practised by the US state in the formation of its early empire, and the terror that the US state practises today in pursuit of its own gods of capital, markets, oil and mineral extractions, land ownership, and prestige is nowhere discussed by Berman. There is an assumption that runs throughout his book that the state does not do terror. The unstated assumption is that the state is inherently peaceful, democratic and concerned with justice, and merely reacts reluctantly to the violence of Muslims and other 'religious' discontents.

That some small, radical groups as diverse as the Mennonites, Ultra Orthodox Jews, Hamas and the Taliban, in their struggle to remain distinct from the dominant globalization of capitalism and consumerism, require more stringent and explicit prohibitions and sacrifices may turn out to have significant theoretical interest, but it does not seem like a major sociological insight.

Berman poses a problem here that seem to me to be central to this book, and worth quoting at some length. Given the economics of 'the secular market-place' and 'the value of time spent on working', then:

> With time at a premium, how do time-consuming religious practices, such as prayer, retain their appeal? Why aren't religions in general, and religious radicals in particular, disappearing? Mainstream religions are in decline in Europe, where church attendance rates have been falling for decades. The United States is an exception, though, with high and fairly stable church attendance from the early twentieth century to the present. Remarkably, the fastest growing religious denominations in the United States are the most time-consuming: evangelical Christians, Mormons, and ultra-Orthodox Jews, for instance, are experiencing rapid growth. In Central and South America evangelical Christianity is expanding quickly, at the expense of (less demanding) Catholicism. Anecdotally, radical Islam seems to be gaining an increasing following among Muslims, though denominational data on Muslims in most countries is generally unavailable ... Taken as a whole, not only are religious prohibitions and sacrifices a puzzle, they are a world-wide puzzle that applies both to ancient practices and to modern times.
>
> Iannaccone could not have known what he was getting into in the 1980's when he began asking these questions. He recognized that religious prohibi-tions and sacrifices posed a true challenge for the usual logic of economics, which implies that people will not volunteer to have their choices restricted – they might miss out on a choice they prefer. Yet the Christian version of that challenge, which he was most intimately familiar with, was only part of the story. Religious radicalism among Muslims would prove to be a major force in twenty-first- century history (2009: 67–8).

Berman's assumption here seems to be that, whereas in mainstream society such sacrifices are compulsory, in 'religious' denominations they are voluntary. But how convincing is this stark distinction between the voluntary nature of religious sacrifices and the compulsory nature of secular sacrifices? It is no doubt true that, according to the US Constitution, 'religion' has no coercive powers; these are reserved by the secular state. This, however, could not be literally true in the case of many mutual aid groups discussed by Berman, such as Hamas or the Taliban, who clearly have methods of persuasion, whether moral or physical. Even in the case of the non-violent clubs that Berman refers to such as the Amish and the Mennonites, it would seem strange if they had no persuasive mechanisms for encouraging mutuality and reciprocity. For one thing the children are presumably brought up with moral commitments to the group.

As a non-economist, I am surprised that the usual logic of economics supposes that people – even taxpayers, wage labourers and consumers in capitalist societies – will not sometimes 'miss out on a choice they prefer'. Consider, for example, the voluntary giving of one's own life to defend the secular nation state as a moral duty. Consider nursing or firefighting as professions. I am not an economist, but I cannot see how any theoretical discipline concerned with social orders could assume that only small groups are based on non-coerced sacrifices. Surely the very idea of a social order must assume that everyone has to miss out on some at least of the choices they prefer. Isn't all taxation based on the idea that we all have to sacrifice personal choices in order to pay for the functioning of the state and its policies? Are not the disciplines and prohibitions of the workplace, to which most people have to submit, a constant sacrifice made in order to survive and consume?

This point also leads to another observation in passing, though it is one I pick up again later. The term 'sacrifice', which is deeply embedded in the history of Christian theology, is apparently not so inaccessible that it cannot be used by economists and social scientists as an analytical category. Thus, helping someone build a barn (one of Berman's favoured examples) is an act of sacrifice for the Amish and Mennonites which is required for membership and solidarity. This shows that the idea of sacrifice operates regardless of the claimed distinction between religious and secular practices. Equally it would be perfectly meaningful in ordinary language to say that one sacrifices a significant part of one's income so that the state can pay for armed forces or old people's homes; to say that many people had to sacrifice their jobs and businesses or mortgaged homes in order to save the banks from collapse; or that the minister in charge of finance had to sacrifice the planned increase of expenditure on new prisons in order to subsidize the invasion of Iraq. This is completely normal language, and the examples are unexceptional and conceivably true. How could this be, if theological and scientific language occupy such essentially different domains?

Though Berman understandably hates terrorism, and the title of the book demands a special role for religion in relation to terrorism, he is not unsympathetic to the peaceful groups. For example, he gives the reader an interesting narrative of his own encounter with ultra-Orthodox Jews in Israel. Berman himself is Jewish American and has many happy connections with Israel. While spending a summer there between graduate school and his first academic job, an academic friend of his, Professor Ruth Klinov of the Hebrew University, asked the following question: 'Why were so many Israeli men not participating in the labor force (i.e. not working or looking for work)?'

This launched their research project. Some interesting statistics follow. Twelve percent of Israeli men of prime working age (25–54) were non-participants in the early 1990s. The comparable US rate of non-participation is 6%, which is typical of developed economies.

Berman and Klinov began doing research in Israel to try to find the answer to this intriguing question. 'What we found was shocking: *Among ultra-Orthodox men in Israel, 60% of those of prime working age were not participating in the labor force – not working and not looking for work*. The ultra-Orthodox accounted for about 5% of the Israeli population in the early 1990's when we first looked at these data, but they made up about a third of the male nonparticipants! If they weren't working, what were all these prime-aged ultra-Orthodox men doing? The survey data had an answer to that as well: nonparticipant ultra-Orthodox males were almost all full-time students in yeshivas – religious seminaries devoted to the study of the holy texts' (Berman 2009: 69; emphasis in original).

Berman points out that, in economic terms, full-time studying caused serious problems for these families. The 'average family with a father in yeshiva was large and very poor, with four or five children (so far), and was living in poverty according to official Israeli standards' (2009: 70). That such behaviour could be understood in purely economic terms is thus questioned.

On investigation, Berman met many men in their forties with large families who were studying full time in yeshiva and were proud of it (2009: 71). Berman also felt empathy for these men and their families. But the intellectual problem for him was to understand 'Why would anyone choose to study in a yeshiva when they had a family to support? Our calculations showed that at age thirty-five a yeshiva student could earn more than twice his monthly stipend by working, and would be eligible for child allowances regardless of yeshiva attendance. By age forty-five, he would be earning two and a half times the stipend with a decade of work experience ... So why choose yeshiva over work?' (2009: 72).

In trying to think of an answer to this question, Berman considered that it might be purely a matter of 'religious belief', but this didn't square with what he knew of ultra-Orthodox communities in North America, where equally devout yeshiva students do not usually remain in yeshiva after age 25. Another possibility was that these ultra-Orthodox men in Israel might be getting some high-paid jobs later in life as a result of their yeshiva training, but this did not make economic sense on the basis of the data. Another possibility was related to army draft deferrals; through various special historical agreements, yeshiva students could avoid military service as long as they studied, which might explain why so many were not working. But Berman discovered that this explanation, too, was wide of the mark:

> ... among ultra-Orthodox men with at least five children 66% were still in yeshiva between ages of thirty-five and forty, despite the fact that they were already draft exempt, in yeshiva or not ... So if it isn't draft deferral, or the economic returns, or the religious beliefs, or the lack of an alternative, then why was Israeli yeshiva attendance so high? That's what Iannaccone had figured out, when he was thinking about churches, prohibitions, and sacrifices (2009: 74).

In his attempt to explain this, Berman (following Iannaccone) further embeds the distinction between the spiritual and the material: 'The first key to Iannaccone's explanation of why religious radicals behave as they do is to realize how much collective activity – material as well as spiritual – goes on within radical religious communities …. What outside observers often miss are the nonspiritual services that radical religious communities collectively provide, in addition to the spiritual services' (2009: 75).

He gives the example of barn raisings among the Amish and Mennonites, in which individuals donate work time to the community. This kind of mutual cooperative service extends to most areas of life, such that the sociologist Julia Ericksen can say that 'the Amish society in Lancaster County can be likened to a very successful agricultural corporation' (Berman 2009: 75). This kind of mutual aid provision network, including education, healthcare, soup kitchens and even safe streets, is common to religious radicals, whether Christian, Jewish or Muslim. In the case of ultra-Orthodox Jews, according to the Israeli scholar Friedman, 'No sick member is without visitors; no child lacks food and clothing. No single member is without an arranged match … Cooperative stores provide essential food and household items at reduced prices' (2009: 76). Free services include visits to the sick, support and advice for mourners, and frozen meal services for the elderly, the sick, and for mothers after childbirth. The ultra-Orthodox even provide funds for emergency medical expenses not covered by medical insurance, 'as well as a decentralized system of voluntary donations'.

Berman points out that mutual aid has an ancient history, and there is evidence for it among the Jewish Essenes 2000 years ago. He fails to point out that mutual aid in one form or another is a necessary basis for the functioning of any group, whether a minority or the dominant formation. In the case of Islamic communities there is less evidence available to sociologists. On the other hand organizations such as the Muslim Brotherhood 'are famous for running religious schools, orphanages, soup kitchens, clinics, hospitals, and even youth centers and soccer clubs, all operated as charities' (2009: 77).

A study by Daniel Chen on mutual-aid funds in rural Indonesia organized by Koran study groups (Pengajian) showed that all community members donate to a common fund from which those in need can draw. The value of the contributions is calculated against relative income, such that poor members would have greater rights than more wealthy ones in times of need. Chen showed that 'Muslim religious communities play an especially important role in buffering community members against economic shocks when alternative forms of insurance are unavailable' (Berman 2009: 78).

But this formulation still leaves us with the conceptual problem of how to distinguish between these essentialized 'spiritual' and 'material' domains. One could surely point out that all social orders in one way or another provide services that in turn require prohibitions and sacrifices from its members. In one form or another mutual aid is surely an essential feature of any functioning society. The division of labour is a form of mutual aid. The division of labour in any society, including gender roles, redistribution of goods and wealth, care for children, pregnant women and the elderly, military service, the performance of rituals on behalf of the community, and all the other features of collective solidarity, are almost by definition the basis for any recognizable social order, from hunter-gatherer bands through semi-nomadic pastoral societies, hierarchical agricultural societies and across the spectrum to modern nation states. As far as I am aware, most social scientists take these things for granted. What is normally of interest to sociologists and anthropologists are the *different ways* in which these fundamental social processes are organized, how they are related to gender, status, prestige and power differences generally; whether mutual aid works through kinship networks, different forms of symbolic or material reciprocity, redistributive chiefdoms, sacred kingships, feudal hierarchies, taxation systems, socialist republicanism or modern capitalism.

Many of the general features he attributes to small mutual aid communities seem to apply (at the level of ideology at least) to Soviet socialism. While the authoritarian bureaucratic state apparatus may be absent in small groups, standards and processes of legitimating authority are presumably active especially in a situation where the ideology of the group is set against the dominant ideology of market capitalism. Though I think Berman is right to see these small communities as having a special interest, the interest does not lie in the general fact that they provide mutual aid or that they require sacrifices and prohibitions in order to function in terms of group solidarity, since in different ways this is true for all societies. What is of interest in his account is the way that these small radical groups provide radically *alternative* forms of social relations in the context of a world dominated by the values of consumer capitalism and technological progress. The point surely is not that capitalist consumer societies do not in their own ways provide mutual aid, or demand sacrifices and impose prohibitions. It could be argued that capitalism is a huge sacrificial cult of a particular kind, one that promises freedom but which produces enormous inequalities of well-being. Berman talks as though mainstream capitalist cultures, against which small mutual aid societies wish to define themselves, do not have their own versions of these systems and processes.

What seems of real interest is that so many of these small mutual aid societies exist on the basis of values that constitute an inherent critique of capitalism. While this appears to be the case from the way Berman represents these mutual aid societies – indeed it is a significant part of his analysis – Berman never confronts capitalism, consumerism or market ideology *as* ideology, that is, as a dominant system of representations and values competing against alternative ones, but simply takes them as given.

Another important aspect of sociological enquiry concerns the mechanisms for enforcing compliance and reciprocity. The anthropological ethnographies show a vast variety of different systems of enforcement of the rules of reciprocity in different kinds of social organization. Hunter-gatherer bands existed for many centuries with minimal levels of formal enforcement, maintaining their own traditions of distribution of goods, division of labour, child rearing and inheritance norms. Some complex African societies, known in the anthropological literature as acephalous (literally, without a head), had no formal authorities for enforcing rules of reciprocity, but relied on conventions of witchcraft, divine retribution, techniques of divination, or various forms of clan vendetta to solve conflicts of interests and ensure repayment of debts. Many societies developed complex symbolic forms of reciprocal exchange, including the exchange of women between different groups, to signify status, rights to goods and services, duties, and generally to bind the society or the segment together in a collective representation of common identity.

According to Berman, a problem for economists studying mutual aid groups or 'clubs' is how these informal and implicit mutual-aid contracts are enforced. This is indeed an important and interesting question, though not only for economists. It is only a special interest for economists, rather than for, say, political theorists, anthropologists, historians or any other person interested in human organization, if you assume with Berman that modern economics provides the crucial theoretical paradigm for making sense of these issues. To believe that economic theory is the fundamental explanatory paradigm is itself not a self-justifying supposition. It is not universally accepted that societies that have traditionally practised non-capitalist forms of exchange, ownership or authority can be understood by using analytical categories developed to analyse modern forms of division of labour, distribution of goods and services, rights and duties of reciprocity and aid.

For example, in his introduction to *Economic Anthropology* (1989) Stuart Plattner writes:

Economics grew up as a field of study in rapidly developing capitalist societies. Although the basic terms of economics are defined abstractedly, they fit best the capitalist, industrialized economy in which they were developed. The attempt to transfer them to the analysis of noncapitalist societies has created problems. Trying to comprehend the economic activity of an economy organised on the basis of corporate kinship groups, for example, is as difficult as it is for a speaker of English to understand the importance of tones in Chinese or Zapotec (a Mexican Indian language). The main problem is the 'embeddedness' of economic activities. ... The social and cultural matrix of our own economic behaviour is transparent to us so that, for example, heightened retail sales at Christmas seem 'just' economic, not religious. But the cultural context of economic behaviour in exotic societies is blatantly obvious. For example, *production* implies a discrete activity, a creation of economic value by changing the character-istics of a good. This activity is conceptually separate from *religion*, because in Western society, religious actors do not create economic production while they are doing religious acts. The closest we get occurs when religious leaders bless or certify the tools of production (for example, the priest blessing the fishing boats or the rabbi certifying that the food factory is kosher). This separation of spheres of behaviour creates a problem for the 'economic' anthropologist, who analyses something that looks like economic production but that is also clearly 'religious' (Plattner 1989: 10–11).

If what Plattner says is generally true – and it is surely a point that needs to be taken seriously – then modern economic theories are themselves configured by, and constrained by, the same basic assumptions that underlie modern capitalism. One problem with Berman's book, in discussing his history of the emergence of ancient communities such as the Amish, Mennonites and Hutterites from sixteenth-century German Anabaptism, is that he uncritically assumes that modern categories such as religion and economics can be universally applied to all periods of history and all contemporary contexts without any problems of meaning.

The concept of the economy as a distinct domain, and even as the fundamental explanatory domain, was arguably not articulated until the early nineteenth century in the work of people like Bentham and Ricardo. Berman makes much in his book of the insights of Adam Smith whom he refers to as the founder of modern economics (2009: 62 and passim). I agree with Berman's admiration for Smith, whose *Wealth of Nations* was surely a major stage in the emergence of economics conceived as a distinct domain of human practice essentially different from other domains such as the religious. However, this directs us back to a point I argued earlier, which is that Anglophone (and more widely Europhone) categories such as religion, secular, politics, economics, and constitutional law cannot be assumed to be natural kinds – generic and ahistorical. Kathryn Sutherland, in her explanatory notes and commentary to her edition of Adam Smith's *Wealth of Nations* (Smith 1776), says about the idea of 'political œconomy':

> The modern term 'economics' did not exist in Smith's time. ... Throughout the eighteenth century, the ... term 'œconomy' (subsequently 'economy', from the Greek oikonomia) retained as its primary significance 'the management of a house' or 'domestic regulation'. ... 'Political œconomy', cited in the OED from 1767, though it can be found in English in the late seventeenth century, is an extension from the domestic context, referring to arguments concerning the laws and management of a national economy as an aspect of the state (Sutherland 1993: 466).

Thus, three years before the American War of Independence, the new *Dictionary of Arts and Sciences* published in Edinburgh, the city of David

Hume and Adam Smith, does not record entries for either economy or politics as separate domains. Political economy is here, but is generally concerned with public safety, order and morals. The nearest the *Dictionary* comes to what in modern discourse we might think of as politics is under 'POLITY, or Policy':

POLITY, or Policy, denotes the peculiar form and constitution of the government of any state or nation; or the laws, orders, and regulations, relating thereto.

Polity differs only from politics, as the theory from the practice of any art.

By the edition of 1815, the entry for *economics* makes it part of 'political economy', which may reflect the growing influence of Adam Smith and others such as Ricardo and Bentham. Douglas Dowd argues that the arguments for free trade against mercantilism in Ricardo's *Principles of Political Economy and Taxation*, published in 1817, 'triumphed in Britain in the 1840's, after a bitter struggle over "The Corn Laws",' and that his underlying theory remains 'virtually intact today, both in form and content' (Dowd 2000: 31). Bentham published his theory of human nature and utilitarianism in 1780, in *An Introduction to the Principles of Morals and Legislation*. Dowd notes that, in this case as well, the effects of the theory took time to become influential, and 'first emerged in the 1850's, a full generation after [his] death' (Dowd 2000: 38). Perhaps this delay explains why there is no entry for economics as a science in the 1815 edition of the *Dictionary*.

Presumably this idea existed by that time, but only in narrow advanced circles. Waterman,[4] in his detailed historiographical work on the emergence of modern economics in the seventeenth, eighteenth and nineteenth centuries, has shown that the emergence of the idea of market equilibrium as a natural result of the concatenation of individual self-interest either as a good, or as a neutral description of 'human nature', developed from the ethical and theological concern of French, Scottish and English theologians with the meaning and legitimacy of cupidity as 'self-love'. These theological thoughts about how God's providential designs for human salvation and flourishing could have allowed the impulses of selfish desire to run rampant developed into the idea of a hidden providence guiding and harmonizing the clash of self-interests and bringing them to a harmonious equilibrium, an idea indicated by Smith's 'hidden hand'.

The answer to why theological thinking in seventeenth- and eighteenth-century France, Scotland and England was increasingly pre-occupied with the issues of self-love, markets and consumption makes sense in the context of the growth of overseas trade and colonies, the slave trade, the proliferation of imported consumer goods, increasing wealth and power of 'nations' (itself an old category in the process of acquiring quite new meanings); the development of the joint-stock company as a precursor to the modern corporation; the rise of 'politics' and the reluctant widening of the franchise; the new class wealth of the industrial bosses and the poverty and exploitation of the new classes of wage labourers. In short, economics as a discipline is itself a historically-specific representation of capitalism as an emerging global system. Historical analysis of these terms tends to raise a significant question-mark over these proclaimed essential differences between the religious and the secular, between God and nature, between divine law and natural law, and so on. To say that modern capitalist economics represents a new and different ideological power from the older dominant Christian ideologies is one thing. To say that there is an essential, ahistorical difference between 'religion' and 'non-religious' secular economics is a different kind of claim, and one that can be challenged on historical and conceptual grounds.

Looked at in this way, we might say that, rather than discovering the 'natural' laws of economics assumed to be universally distinct from all histori-cally and ethnographically specific forms of social relations, and rather than being the singular foundation of modern economics, Adam Smith's *Wealth of Nations* was one very important stage in the emergence of a new discourse on political economy which became definitive of modernity, more fully articulated several decades after he died. This was an idea of 'economy' separated from 'religion' and, in a different way, from the 'politics' of 'political economy'; and an idea of economic theory as a kind of science which describes and analyses 'natural' processes in which concrete human actors and their relationships can be accurately represented by abstract and impersonal mathematical models.

The belief of economists that the natural laws of spontaneous coordination of markets was 'discovered' by men such as Adam Smith should be set side by side with the alternative view of Marx, argued recently by the economist Michael Perelman, that markets were not discovered and did not arise sponta-neously. The emergence of capitalist markets in the era of Adam Smith and earlier depended on a series of violent acts of parliament that forced people with traditional means of self-subsistence off the land, and consequently created a cheap wage labour supply to run the mines and factories, and to labour without traditional rights on privately-owned farms. Perelman (2000) argues not only that this series was a sustained and deliberate policy, but that it is an inherent requirement of capitalism, and still occurs wherever people with traditional rights of land-use and self-subsistence impede the ability of corporations and enterprises to exploit the land and labour more profitably. However, this sustained violence of capitalism is mystified by the tacit or explicit claims of Chicago School economists such as Berman that economics represents natural realities which underlie and explain all 'social' facts.[5]

In so far as Berman is analysing contemporary mutual-aid communities that co-exist with the dominant capitalist modes of production and consumption, then an interesting theoretical problem arises. For, according to Berman's own analysis, these groups organize themselves in such a way that they constitute an implicit or explicit critique of capitalism. They offer an alternative moral vision of cooperation, sharing and mutuality. All of these groups therefore have a problematic relationship with mainstream society. In so far as some of these groups such as Amish, Mennonite, Hutterites or ultra-Orthodox Jews exist as constitutionally-defined religious charities in secular capitalist societies such as Israel or North America, then they are given certain rights to freedom of religion but also denied freedoms, such as powers of coercion, which are limited to the secular state.

I do not know precisely what coercive rights such groups constitutionally designated as religious communities are given by the secular state in countries such as the US and Canada. Similar problems arose with Native American communities, and I wonder why there is so little if any attention to these communities in Berman's book. Some of these communities rejected the designation of their traditional practices as 'religious' because they did not accept the Christian and imperialist associations with that word (eighteenth- and nineteenth-century white leaders who are today retrospectively referred to as secular used Protestant Christian rationalizations for the pogroms which wiped out many of the native tribes). At least some of the Native American communities did not accept the assumption that these practices were essentially separated from traditional coercive rights within their own communities, rights which the US Constitution had arrogated to the Federal and State governments. Alternatively, and under pressure, they strategically adopted the 'religious' designation for some of their own traditional practices in order to save at least some remnant of them (see Wenger 2005, 89–113; 2009).

Another point to make about Native American cultures is that, not only did Native Americans not make a distinction of the kind 'religion/nonreligion', nor did they make a distinction between natural and supernatural (Cooper 1988: 873–4). When Berman and many other writers assume a universally valid distinction for all societies at all points in history and even prehistory between religious and secular practices and institutions, they at the same time assume a corresponding distinction between nature and supernature. After entering 'native american supernatural' into Google, I got 'A Summary of Native American Religions' by David Ruvolo who says that, according to Raymond J. DeMallie, the Dakota world was 'characterized by its oneness, its unity… There was no separation of the natural world from the world of the supernatural' (Available at http://are.as.wvu.edu/ruvolo.htm). The second Google call took me to a National Humanities Center webpage called TeacherServe dedicated to Native American religion. Here Christine Leigh Heyrman of the Department of History, University of Delaware says 'Indians did not distinguish between the natural and the supernatural. On the contrary, Native Americans perceived the "material" and "spiritual" as a unified realm of being – a kind of extended kinship network' (http://nationalhumanitiescenter.org/tserve/eighteen/ekeyinfo/natrel.htm).

All three of these writers claim to write about Native American Religion and to define it by describing various beliefs in what they all refer to as the 'supernatural'. Yet they all also say that the Native Americans do not distinguish the supernatural as a distinct domain. As I have suggested in other parts of this book, this contradiction – whereby an object called variously Hinduism, Shinto or Native American Religion is constructed on the basis of indigenous beliefs in the 'supernatural' yet where the supernatural as a category may not exist indigenously – also arises in the application of this modern ideological binary to India and Japan. But this turns out to be a misrepresentation of many alternative visions of the moral universe expressed in the categories of non-European languages. It also raises general issues about the use of the term 'natural' in general discourse, which is widely used as though it is self-evident what is meant. But the category of the 'natural' has been constructed in modern ideology through a historical re-articulation of Christian 'nature' in opposition to the 'supernatural'. Both the earlier Christian discourse on nature and the modern transformed version are in their different ways tacitly parasitic on the category 'the supernatural'.

Berman contextualizes his historical account of the origins of modern communities such as Amish, Mennonite and Hutterite in the Anabaptist movements of the sixteenth century in what, retrospectively, we can reconstruct as the early beginnings of capitalist modes of production and exchange. But there is a different way of interpreting that history which Berman does not consider. The alternative would be to see that these processes were not the revealing of natural human economic understanding, but the very early beginnings of a family of new discourses that, as Waterman has pointed out, only began to emerge from theological moral debates later. Not until the late eighteenth or more likely the early nineteenth century was there a clear idea of a domain of economics as a natural science independent of moral theology. Berman retrospectively projects onto late medieval conflicts between German Reformation power formations, conceived by the actors in terms of moral theology and the legitimation of different concepts of confessional state, the categorical distinctions between religion and social science that did not become articulated until several centuries later.

Berman assumes that we can talk about religious communities and economic and political processes in sixteenth-century Europe in the same sense that we can talk about them in modern capitalist societies. He also describes the emergence of capitalist markets as though they happened naturally, like inevitable forces of nature driving the evolution of societies from primitive to modern. Tacitly, he buys into the wider ideological justification of capitalism that represents it as an evolutionary emergence of a higher state of rationality, finding its apogee in US consumer and corporate capitalism. Furthermore, he tends to represent these processes as only beneficial and liberating, a view which in my view indicates a lop-sided reading of history. The Anabaptists were violently against these processes, not because they had an alternative economic theory, but because they had an alternative moral and theological vision of the good life. Berman points out that their descendants in North America only became peace-loving through defeat, persecution and refuge in North America. However, this transformation was made possible by the separation between religion and state, not finally established until the writing of the US Constitution in the late eighteenth century, a new separation which did not exist at the time in Europe (though the French Revolution was presumably also a major instigator of this distinction) and which provided a legal space for their existence.

One could certainly argue that this state provision indicates the positive side of the invention of 'religion' as a special kind of belief and practice separated from the non-religious state. It was, after all, partly a response to demands for toleration within Christendom. It has provided a protective form of life for groups that might otherwise die. However, it necessarily does that at the price of emasculating and distorting their original vision of moral encompassment, of the social whole. Such groups as the Amish, once rooted in the peasant societies of late medieval and early modern Europe and representing a challenge to the authority of the Catholic and Lutheran church-states, became transformed into modern 'religions' in liberal capitalist North America. In that sense, not only has the emergence of the non-religious state been essential to their conceptualization, but the reverse must be equally true: the invention of religions has been historically essential to the invention of the modern nation state and capitalism as incontrovertible realities existing independently of human will.

It seems important to notice that these major historical events were not merely the restoration of some natural state of affairs that had previously existed but had irrationally been denied and suppressed by reactionary confessional states. These events *created* the idea of the 'state' as non-religious and independent of 'religion', and at the same time *created* the idea of religion as private, voluntary, even multiple (religions) and essentially distinct from the state. It was rational for those who believed that God encompasses all aspects of civilized (that is, fully human) life to have resisted the emergence of this new powerful discourse. This explains the resistance of the established Christian confessional states.[6]

In contrast, following Berman's data, groups such as Hamas and Hezbollah may have a more complex and tense relationship with the contemporary authorities, for, as Berman has suggested, they are like governments in waiting,[7] offering a vision of an alternative to the secular state derived from Muslim traditions, and identifying secularism with Western – especially French, British and US – imperialism, which they are prepared to resist by violent means. These kinds of communities may not have the same degree of legally-sanctioned coercive powers as those held by established states, but they often have deep and authoritative roots in the popular consciousness of the wider society in a way that the émigré descendants of the Anabaptists do not.

In the case of mutual aid communities with no coercive powers, Berman asks: How can members feel confident that their own voluntary donations of services, time, labour and money will be reciprocated? This is what Berman refers to as the problem of shirking. How can one trust that the other will reciprocate? This is a specially interesting problem for Berman, because the groups classified as 'religions' in states such as the US, Canada and Israel have no legal powers of coercion and must therefore rely on other forms of authority which are 'voluntary' and which cannot be enforced in the way that secular states can enforce obedience to the laws of the dominant society.

His answer is that, by voluntarily sacrificing time and energy to perform acts of service to the community as a whole, individuals become bound into a system of mutual obligation on which it is difficult to renege. As he puts it, 'Prohibitions distance club members from outside activities ... which makes members more available to help the community with its collective activities' (Berman 2009: 81). Are prohibitions a kind of coercion or not? It is another term that needs unpacking.

The coercion of voluntary 'clubs' (to use Iannaccone's and Berman's term) is not coercion in the same sense that the state can coerce with force. It is presumably a 'freely chosen' moral commitment. This is surely a legitimate distinction as far as it goes. But this raises a number of further questions that Berman does not deal with in a very convincing way. Moral obligation may not be coercion, but children brought up in such a system will presumably feel loyal to the group into which they are born and will be educated in the theological and moral thinking which underpins that sense of obligation. Berman's attempt to explain these commitments in functional terms (the perpetuation of group survival) avoids the reasons why individuals and groups act as they do. Or it claims to understand better than those who commit themselves to prohibitions the reasons why they do it. It reveals the assumption that, after all these centuries, at last social science can explain to us what the committed were themselves unable to properly understand.

One avenue that Berman might have explored is the concept of 'faith' or trust. People have faith in reciprocity, and act on that basis. If their faith wanes, then the system is threatened. But the same is arguably true of the value of capital and money in ordinary transactions in the dominant system. Without faith in the exchange value of money and the various agencies that are trusted with the maintenance of value, we end up with the Great Depression, with wheelbarrows full of virtually worthless currency in Germany's Weimar Republic, or with the recent threat of meltdown of the entire global banking system. On what grounds could we argue that faith in God, gods, the super-natural, or magic is *essentially* different from faith in the values of money and capital? If faith in the efficacy of sacrifice, in the ultimate providence of self-love, in market equilibrium, and in natural laws have historically been based on faith in God, then the historical transformation of their use in the modern construction of economics suggests less of an essential difference between theological and economic faith, and more of a transformation of old meanings in a new paradigm. Difference, yes; but not an essential difference. The difference is one of nuance and context.

This point could be illustrated by Berman's own interesting analogy from his experience as an academic running research seminars, which indicates that many of the characteristics of organizations classified as 'religious' share many with those usually classified as 'secular', a point which he himself makes in other places. He says:

> In my job, at a research university, collective production is critical in research seminars and classes, whenever challenging material gets presented. Everyone benefits from the wisdom of good citizens. They're the ones who come prepared, pay attention, and ask good questions, making learning easier and more enjoyable for everyone else in the room. They provide appropriate encouragement, constructive criticism, good answers, and new ideas. Presenting to a seminar full of colleagues and graduate students who behave like good citizens is a satisfying, fulfilling, collective-learning experience. It has a warmth and a unity of purpose to it – a little like praying in a dedicated congregation (2009: 79).

Berman briefly and suggestively extends this university analogy on mutual cooperation to the members of sports teams, the partners of a law firm, the surgical staff at a hospital, anyone who has run a business meeting, or the members of a fraternity. He suggests a set of rules which 'should be able to guarantee a high-quality seminar (or other collective product)' and which 'have direct parallels in the religious prohibitions imposed by religious radicals' (2009: 80).

One of his points is that the specifics of such rules in radical communities operate functionally to differentiate their moral vision and practical integrity from the mainstream capitalist society. But generally he only sees these rules as the enactments of tradition in a hostile environment. Berman points out (indeed it is central to his analysis) that these groups are all rejecting mainstream capitalist culture and offering an alternative vision of social justice. Yet despite Berman's rightly empathetic portrayal of the moral and redistributive achievements of ultra-Orthodox and other communities, these tend to be presented in his social scientific analysis not so much as good in themselves as functionally necessary to achieve mere self-survival and self-perpetuation. Listed in this way and abstracted from real life these rules seem just like that, 'rules', rather than constituting a coherent system of values. These rules might seem unacceptably severe to most people living within the paradigm of current mainstream culture in the US, with its daily bombardment of propaganda on the American Way of Life, the need to consume, the normality of wage labour, the unremitting burden of clock-time, the inevitability of globalization and progress, the incessant pressure to conform to the stressful and conflictual rules of the state. But, to the degree to which these rules are considered necessary for the survival of small, vulnerable groups, persistent separation from mainstream capitalist culture may partly be a function of mainstream capitalist culture itself, which with its hedonistic seductions and its naturalization of the norms of self-interest, personal profit, ruthless competitiveness and mass consumption powerfully erodes alternative modes of consciousness and democracy.

The negative characteristics of mainstream society are almost completely ignored in Berman's representations of capitalism, which he presents not as a conflictual and much contested norm underwritten by the mystifications of ideology and the violence of the secular state, but as the natural and largely benign growth of markets, individualism and free choice. In many ways Berman acts as the idealistic and uncritical spokesman for capitalist society. Nowhere, for example, in his discussion of radical violence of groups such as Hamas, Hezbollah and the Taliban does he offer any real consideration of the legacies of Western imperial and colonial interventions in the Middle East or other parts of the world, or of the artificial divisions and disruptions caused by the imposition of arbitrary nation states.

Furthermore, Berman's analogy with other forms of cooperative living that he classifies as 'secular' tends to erode his over-strong contrast between 'religious radical communities' and other kinds of community. He himself is at pains to point out that the theologies of all these groups in different parts of the world may be quite different, but their lifestyles and the structure of their organizations have striking features in common. This point tends to erode any supposed essential distinction between religious and non-religious groups. And this indicates a wider problem with Berman's theoretical assumptions, for while on the one hand the importance of theological differences is downplayed in order to bring out the many similarities of values and practices in mutual aid communities, yet his insistence that 'religion' and 'terror' have some special relationship still gets flagged up – in the title, in the claim that supposedly 'religious' groups such as Hamas are more successful at violence than 'non-religious' groups such as the Tamil Tigers,[8] and in his continuous deployment throughout of an essentializing discourse on the religious and the secular.

Berman does try to provide a justification for the distinction between religious and non-religious radicals in his claim that, despite the broad similarity of values and organizational principles of many communities across the spectrum, regardless of whether they are classified as religious or secular, nevertheless the 'religious' ones have the edge in successful violence. He does this in his final chapter (chapter 8) by appealing to the relationship between beliefs in the 'supernatural' and the effectiveness of pious Mullahs as trusted leaders. Here, he says:

> Previous chapters have deemphasized or dismissed the spiritual and theological aspects of terrorism ... Yet despite the accumulated evidence that incentives within organizations matter, altogether ignoring the theological and spiritual aspects of radical religious violence cannot be right either. If al-Sadr's militia, the Taliban, Hezbollah, Hamas and others are successful

mainly because they have adopted a club structure, then why wouldn't secular organizations succeed in the same way? Why couldn't a club organize around Marxism, or environmental activism, or a profit motive, or no particular ideology at all, like a street gang does? To be sure, there are broad organizational similarities between street gangs, mafias, Marxist rebels, and radical religious terrorists – as we have seen. Why are radical religious clubs more effective than secular clubs? (2009: 212).

Berman claims that belief in the supernatural (which without any real evidence he says is typical and universal) provides clerics with a special motive to be pious and trustworthy. It is belief in the supernatural, that for Berman is synonymous with religion, spirituality and theology, which finally comes into its own here. One point to note about the just-quoted passage is that Berman is distinguishing between 'incentives' on the one hand and 'spiritual or theological aspects' on the other. Again we find this problematic distinction between the religious and the non-religious, in this case between 'spiritual' aspects represented by 'clerics' and *economic incentives* that operate in the secular domain.

Berman's book, with its title *Radical, Religious and Violent*, utilizes throughout an analytical distinction between the religious and the secular, and on that basis promotes a special relationship between violence and 'religious' groups. Yet at the same time the book reduces and even marginalizes the explanatory power of theological commitments (it is mainly in the final chapter that the author turns his attention to the attenuated 'religious' element) and stresses the commonalities of a broad range of communities regardless of their conventional classification as religious or secular.

It also seems to this reader significant that many of the communities Berman discusses, along with other protest and anarchist groups which he does not mention, define themselves in opposition to the mainstream values of capitalist society in terms of an alternative concept of what it means to be human. For me, the most valuable part of the book lies in Berman's positive representation of the extraordinary ability of small vulnerable groups such as the Amish and Mennonites to organize successful cooperative societies functioning on values at odds with the dominant capitalist ones; in his interesting and sympathetic portrayal of the ultra-Orthodox Jews in Israel; and also in his imaginative grasp of the analogy between a successful 'religious' community and a successful seminar group. Berman empathetically portrays groups such as the Amish, Mennonites and ultra-Orthodox Jews, which are all typically classified as 'religious' by mainstream society, as offering successful and visionary alternatives. Though his representation of violent groups such as Hamas is understandably less sympathetic, even here Berman points out their commitment (even before turning to violence) to serving the community in times of great hardship and thus strengthening bonds of reciprocity for survival.

My own feeling is that, had Berman treated the uncritically-assumed religion–secular distinction as part of the analytical and descriptive problem rather than its solution, an even more interesting analysis would have emerged. The attempt to continue working with an essentialized distinction between religion and secular aspects of human life works against the perhaps more radical insight that there exists in the world a whole range of different groups who resist the relentless march of globalizing capitalism, whether derived from the complexities of Christian, Muslim, South or East Asian history; whether indigenous groups of North America or other continents protecting traditional forms of life; whether anarchists, socialists, communists, environmentalists, goddess-worshippers, naturists and so on.

It is therefore a pressing question why Berman should be so concerned to provide some analytical value for the designation 'religious' and to link it with lethal violence. To be frank, I suspect that one reason is that he has wanted to cash in on the selling power of this widely-perceived connection. But it is not merely a matter of selling power. Berman shares the wider and often unconscious need to be able to identify 'religion' as a cause of the world's problems because this deflects attention away from the massive violence of secular states in the prosecution of capitalist interests. He is mystified. This, I would suggest, is why the modern invention of religions as essentially different from non-religious secular practices is invested with such importance. The effect is to clothe secularity in the appearance of the natural, the rational, the inevitable, and the unremarkable. On this widely disseminated view, the secular is not, like religions, a metaphysical construction, an ideology, or a faith. The secular is the way the world really is once the illusions of 'religion' have been finally outgrown by progress. And capitalism, as part of this natural order, is merely a term for the 'natural' economy of free markets and rational self-interested individuals. Social science and economic theory are based on, legitimated by, and give further circular confirmation to, this same set of knowledge claims. They provide knowledge of the world 'as it really is'. Berman's own positionality as an economist and social scientist, like this ideology of modernity in which it is embedded, is never questioned. To question the natural reality of 'religion' and to see it instead as an ideological construction of modernity would simultaneously be to question the superior secular basis of the social scientist.

These so-called religious groups may only be religious because they are classified in English as such by the 'secular' constitution and law courts, by the media, and by social scientists such Berman. Did Berman ever ask Hamas or Hezbollah if they considered themselves to be 'religious' rather than 'secular'? Their answer might depend on which language the question was asked in. If the distinction is taken to imply the same kind of thing that it implies in modern Western discourse, with its inscription of religion as a personal right and a voluntary practice, essentially distinguished from the legitimate and compulsory power of the secular state, then the answer would seem to be no, since on Berman's own evidence these groups see themselves as governments in waiting legitimated by popular mandate. Even established governments in Muslim and many other non-Muslim societies around the world which may represent themselves in English as secular for strategic reasons may not think in these terms in their native languages. Even in India, with its secular republican constitution and its long history of official English, there is good evidence that the term 'secular' has significantly different resonance to that which it has in the UK, France or the USA.[9] There are complex problems of translation and hermeneutics involved in these questions, usually originating in the historical context of Western colonialism. Categories such as religion and secular are not fixed in nature but have had and still have strategic relationships to power.

Could it not be argued that it is precisely in their moral vision of a mutual aid society and an alternative to 'secular' government that such groups may not acknowledge or value this modern Western distinction? Methodologically, would it not be more interesting and productive to place mutual aid communities who reject mainstream capitalist society on a wider continuum, and disencumber the analysis from the imposed essential distinction between 'spiritual' and 'material' which itself is part of mainstream capitalist ideology? There exist a wide range of communitarian groups, and the way different anti-capitalist communities decide on and 'impose' rules may be more flexible and wide-ranging than Berman acknowledges.

I mentioned above that what mutual aid communities see as moral commitments and a vision of the good life that rejects mainstream capitalist culture tends, in Berman's social scientific quest for objective knowledge, to become interpreted as functionalist 'rules' for mere self-perpetuation. The moral principles and practices shared by individual collectives tend in Berman's social scientific analysis to be transformed into mere mechanisms for separation from other human groups. I do not deny that the moral codes of these groups may have such an effect, but what Berman does not sufficiently consider is that these moral commitments imply a critique of the self-interested, profit and consumer oriented values of capitalism, and of the value of social science 'knowledge'. What Berman refers to as mainstream society remains in his analysis hidden from critical scrutiny, normalized and naturalized. This rather functionalist orientation is reminiscent of the way an entomologist might describe the functioning and evolutionary self-perpetuation of ant communities. Their behavioural norms function only to survive and reproduce, rather than as commitments to a better way of living. This tendency to transform moral practice into mere rules for self-perpetuation comes out rather clearly in the way Berman summarizes the theoretical purposes of his mentor, Iannaccone. Referring to the latter's 'remarkable insight about religious radicals', he says:

He had wondered why people would submit to religious prohibitions and how groups that require them could survive. The answer he discovered is that religious prohibitions are productive for the community because they increase the availability of members for collective activity such as mutual aid, an essential part of what makes radical religious communities cohesive. His approach is called the 'club' theory of religious radicals, a term suggesting that these communities are organized around collective activity (such as mutual aid) from which members benefit, but that nonmembers can be denied ... Prohibitions distance club members from outside activities ... which makes members more available to help the community with its collective activities (Berman 2009: 81).

There is a tendency to circularity in this statement. By representing the moral vision of human good, with its implied critique of mainstream capitalist values, in terms mainly of 'prohibitions', then we get a model of communities merely perpetuating themselves. Prohibitions and the sacrifices entailed by service to the community make the communities cohesive by distancing them from the outside mainstream capitalist society; the greater availability of its members for serving the community increases the cohesion of the community, which perpetuates the community's separation from the mainstream society, which serves the community's survival and self-perpetuation. There is a kind of circular banality in this account, because it fails to explain the most crucial issue, which is why people are prepared to make such sacrifices in the first place.

The representation of sacrifices made by community members in such economistic terms as 'investments' and 'efficiency', while not without some use, does not meet the objections that Berman is honest enough to mention from 'people of faith' (2009: 99–100). As Berman himself points out, some of the people of faith are themselves economists. The expression 'people of faith' is slightly ambiguous in this context. I am sure Berman means that some economists have 'religious' faith, not that economics is itself a matter of faith. He does not see that he himself is a man of faith. In general, 'people of faith' are 'religious' and are thus tacitly distinguished from people of science who are non-religious. Personally I would have thought that economists *are* people of faith, and that economics as a practice is not *essentially* different from various forms of divination that are usually classified as 'religious'. This does not mean that economics, like other systems of explanation with a high degree of internal logical consistency, is not useful for guiding collective or individual decision-making. The philosopher Peter Winch (1970) pointed out that the anthropologist E.E. Evans-Pritchard, in his classic account of *Witchcraft, Oracles and Magic among the Azande* (1937), found his subjects' system of witchcraft beliefs and the divinatory role of the poison oracle to be as satisfactory a way of running his life while living with them as any other which he knew. He pointed out that, to the Zande, there was nothing miraculous or strange about belief in witchcraft or the powers of the poison oracle. It was a matter-of-fact commonplace that it would be absurd to question. The system was based on an unquestioned faith in the system and its metaphysical components and, when oracular predictions failed, there existed a sophisticated system of secondary elaborations that could explain the failures and protect the overall system of explanation from sceptical erosion. As a layman, I am not convinced that the modern system of economic theory is essentially different in these respects. By referring to 'people of faith' in this way, Berman tacitly excludes social science from the faith paradigm, inscribing himself and his colleagues as people of rational knowledge rather than mere belief. By choosing this form of expression, Berman recycles the largely unconscious assumption that scientists like him better understand why people make such sacrifices than do the sacrificers themselves. This in turn further embeds the uncritical assumption that science and secularism are not themselves forms of faith, a self-justifying and circular dichotomy between faith and knowledge that coincides with a list of corresponding binaries: spirit as against matter, faith as against knowledge, metaphysical speculation as against empirical rationality, other imaginary worlds as against this objectively encountered world, and so on. These binaries have become so embedded in modern consciousness that they are hardly conscious any longer, but assumed as ahistorical universals.

To claim as an insight that 'a sacrifice can usefully exclude shirkers' (2009: 97) is, arguably, to miss the point that a sacrifice is a commitment to a moral order which may be superior to the chosen values of cynical calculation, shallow careerism and competitiveness of capitalist mainstream society and its intellectuals. It also fails to mention that capitalism and nationalism, as historically modern fetishes, could also be viewed as vast sacrificial systems based on devotion to transcendental values, metaphysical beliefs and an array of ritual practices which only appear to be essentially different from other cults classified as 'religious' through the deep power of rhetoric and propaganda. Taking such a view requires resisting the denial mechanism provided by the illusions of secular reason; and instead acknowledging the faith-based, ideological commitments and enchantments of capital.

Yet great social scientific advance and insight is attributed to this circularity of functional features. Berman proclaims rather triumphantly that '*The idea of an efficient religious sacrifice is Iannaccone's second great insight into religious sects*' (2009: 99; emphasis in original). What does the great insight tell us? That sacrifice 'allows people to demonstrate their commitment' (2009: 99). Is this really a great insight? Notwithstanding the supporting reference to the great Jewish philosopher Moses Maimonides, most ordinary people will be surprised to know that people who make sacrifices are unaware that it signals a commitment, and that we have had to wait for a late twentieth-century social scientist to explain that to us. What society in human history has not required sacrifices from its members as a sign of commitment?

What Berman does not consider sufficiently, even as an idea that requires refutation, is that capitalism itself is based on collective faith in unseen powers that operate markets and determine the value of capital and money; and on vast human sacrifices. This fact may be obvious to anyone on minimum wages employed at a supermarket check-out on an hourly basis without social security; and is presumably obvious to members of radical mutual aid societies who critique the values of commoditized human labour. But it is disguised from modern economists by the unconscious power of ideology, which transforms profit value into an ineluctable force of nature. One of the values of Berman's work is that it helps us to realize that it is not only Marxists who have understood that capital and the nation state are modern gods imagined as reified forces of nature or even supernature that require the devotion of an array of ritual institutions. The radicals themselves, in their own terms and in different ways, seem to have understood it and reject it!

Insinuating that Iannacone's insight may be science of the kind in which Galileo was engaged when he made experiments from the Tower of Pisa to disprove Aristotle, Berman lists a number of testable predictions that Iannaccone's theory generated:

> His approach generated a number of novel predictions about religious radicals that lent themselves to testing. Radical religious communities will be tighter socially than other groups, minimize outside contacts, have smaller congregations and higher attendance at services (making enforcement easier), have less education and earn less (increasing their demand for mutual aid), but donate a greater proportion of their income to charity because they are more committed (Berman 2009: 81).

It seems important to notice how many of these predictions are already embedded in the theory itself. The so-called predictable outcomes are not much different from a restatement of the theory. Having decided that one is looking for self-perpetuating groups that reject the values of the dominant consumer society, and that make sacrifices by committing the members to mutual aid, then it follows that outside contact will be diminished, that members, in their rejection of the self-interested maximization of profit and consumerism, will be more committed to a materially poorer life (by the standards of US mainstream culture), and that separation from the mainstream capitalist society will in turn increase commitment to, and dependence on, mutual aid. This is a very restrictive circle of propositions from within which to generate new insights about things we do not already know. It is virtually a tautology.

Berman's theory has a number of problems that need addressing. These are of course interrelated, but it is worth listing them as separate parts of an overall theoretical problem. Berman's social science does not pay much attention to the point that the rules, prohibitions and sacrifices of a range of groups are much more than the mechanical strivings of the species whose only purpose is perpetuation. What the social scientists call rules and prohibitions are also moral commitments, and they imply at least a concept of the potential of human nature which is incompatible with the values of capitalist market society. Alternative moral communities will undoubtedly have important differences between them, but on Berman's own account they all imply a critique of the mainstream values of capitalist society. In this way not only do we get a rather mechanistic and functionalist picture of the communities as something little more than merely self-perpetuating entities, but the mainstream values and institutions of capitalism remain as taken for granted, as though simply part of the natural order of things, much like the rationality of social science. One might at this juncture ask, what are the values and moral imperatives of the disciplines of economics and social science, beyond perpetuating the dominant institutions of capitalist society by making them appear as morally-neutral and rationally superior?

A related point that Berman does not consider much (though see him on subsidies on fertility rates – 2009: 116) is that the severity of the rules of inclusion and exclusion of such communities is itself partly conditioned by the power of mainstream capitalist society and its agencies to subvert and destroy the alternative values which the community adheres to. These communities do not simply perpetuate themselves in a neutral environment. They survive (or otherwise) in an environment of power relations, where their own alternative values are under constant threat. The different ways that such communities do this will, of course, depend partly on the different traditions from which they have originated. For example, as Berman points out, not all groups deny the validity of using modern technology in the way that the Amish do, and this may be partly explained by origins, tradition and specific ideological formations. We do not know what the Amish would look like as a community if useful technologies, which are now being produced by capitalist corporations, were instead being produced by a wider society generally committed to similar values as their own, such as cooperation and mutual aid rather than the religion of self-interest and corporate profits. Nor can we know what forms of authority and decision-making might emerge in these communities if they were located in a wider environment in which new forms of democratic participation were allowed to emerge.[10]

Another problem is that, on the one hand throughout the book Berman uncritically insists on an essentialized distinction between 'religious' communities and the non-religious secular mainstream in which secular social science is embedded; yet at the same time he reduces the significance of one part of the totality, which he classifies as religious, theological and spiritual, in order to highlight the supposedly distinct aspects he classifies as secular, material and practical. This distinction, I argue, has the effect of protecting the secular from scrutiny as itself a specific historical ideology masquerading as the natural order of things; and protecting from scrutiny the rhetorical constructions of representative government, and consumer markets as 'freedom' and 'democracy'.

Another effect of the uncritical assumption of the religion–secular distinction is to discourage the analytical construction of a wider continuum of different groups both historical and contemporary. Berman does to some extent acknowledge a wider range of 'nonreligious' groups that share some of the features of those he classifies as religious radicals. He mentions the Mafia, gangs, criminal organizations, military units, sports teams, communes such as the Israeli kibbutz, the Shakers and the Essenes, nineteenth-century Utopian communities such as Shakers, Amana, Oneida, Harmony, Zoar and Jerusalem. I also have in mind a range of communities such as millenarians, anarchists, socialists, levellers, communists, utopians, trade union cooperatives, and other alternative communitarian enterprises. Some of these groups have, to different degrees and in different ways, tried to put themselves effectively outside the dominant mainstream. Others have emerged in revolutionary situations and have hoped to impose their own vision on everyone. Some have chosen to operate within capitalist markets but on productive principles of cooperation and mutual aid. Trade unions have existed not only to protect their members directly in wage negotiations with employers but also to develop socialist, communist, cooperative or communitarian alternatives. The reader gets the uneasy feeling that Berman has chosen his mutual aid communities mainly to prove his interesting but rather limiting social science theory.

Providing advice to counter-intelligence and counter-insurgency forces in order to save lives seems a valid aim. And Berman's insistence that this aim can better be achieved through the peaceful provision by governments of better social services is a potentially creative one that deserves respect. The problem with it is that, just as the moral commitments of mutual aid communities are made to sound like mechanisms for self-perpetuation, so his recommendations become tinted with a merely tactical purpose in capitalism's desire to wipe out opposition to its advances. Is the unacknowledged purpose of social science really to win strategic advantage for dominant power? More attention to the historical contingencies of their different positionalities would surely help us understand why some groups remain peaceful and others resort to armed struggle. For historical reasons, a group such as the Mennonites and another group such as Hamas, both of which, as Berman has suggested, share so many humanitarian commitments, nevertheless are confronted in ineluctably different ways by the power of US capital and the general ideological thrust of capitalist ideology and propaganda. This different positionality might help us to understand why the Mennonites and ultra-Orthodox Jews are able to survive and persist in relative peace, despite their tendency to moral opposition to mainstream capital and nationalism, while groups such as Hamas, who are also committed to mutual aid and welfare, take to armed struggle.

The two leading questions which Berman is concerned with and which I summarized at the beginning are not, on the face of it, concerned with the reasons *why* there are so many angry people in the world in the first place. Perhaps reasonably, Berman appears to take it simply as a fact with which inevitably we have to live. Some questions cannot be reasonably answered, and this may be one of them. Probably there have always been a lot of angry people in the world, and we cannot reasonably expect anyone to know all the reasons for human discontent all the time. Most of it would be irrelevant speculation. Berman is an economist and social scientist who clearly believes in the rational pursuit of disinterested empirical knowledge based on accurate observation and evidence, and the development of useful typologies and analytical categories through which to make sense of, and interpret, the evidence.

Of course, as a competent social scientist, Berman (like all of us with similar aspirations) is no doubt perfectly well aware that the selection of what counts as valid evidence and its interpretation depends on choices, on the prior paradigms and hypotheses that are brought to bear on the selected data, on what the author (and his publisher) hopes to achieve in writing and marketing the book, and even sometimes on the ability to write successful funding applications in order to be released from other academic responsibilities. These are all obvious points which most professional academics would be well aware of; they are the junctures where the ideals of objective knowledge and disinterested analysis can become subordinated to considerations of funding, marketing, career ambitions, ideological and emotional commitments both conscious and unconscious, and moral choices. This is not only Berman's problem; it is one we all share; but it is especially a problem for social scientists whose claim is to produce objective explanations for the behaviour of groups while marginalizing explanations for their own practices. This problem, therefore, inevitably raises a further one concerning the positionality of the writer, especially when, as with Berman, the writer's main concern is with factual accuracy, objectivity and neutrality. This is why sociologists claim to be social scientists.

Further than this, Berman has the added hope that his book and its recommendations might be useful for some outcome which he clearly specifies, in a domain of great public interest including policy decision-making. That intended outcome is to help counter-insurgency agencies to defeat terrorist groups by competing effectively with them in the provision of services, and in that way to deprive them of their local covering support. To have a preference for one outcome rather than another moves one immediately into the realm of motives, values, ethics and allegiances. Does Berman himself see his own advice to US agencies and policy-makers as merely a technique for perpetuating the existence of dominant liberal capitalism? Or does he see it as a moral commitment to values that he considers inherently good, and worth defending *because* they are inherently good?

If the existence of angry people in the world is one fact, the existence of terrorist organizations is another fact – or seems to be. However, that some organizations are *terrorist* while others are not is *not* itself a simply fact, because the distinction inevitably depends on a definition of what constitutes terrorism, as distinct, for example, from legitimate resistance to occupation. The UN, for example, has been debating for 30 years in order to define terrorism, and has not yet come to an agreed result. The webpage of 'Eye on the UN' ('There is no UN definition of terrorism: A Project of the Hudson

Institute New York and the Touro College Institute for Human Rights') provides the following:

> The UN General Assembly's Ad Hoc Committee (AHC) on Measures to Eliminate International Terrorism concluded its 15th Session on April 15, 2011 without reaching agreement on the draft Comprehensive Convention on International Terrorism (CCIT). Working from the 2007 version of a package and on the premise that 'nothing is agreed until everything is agreed,' Member States struggled with questions on the scope of and exceptions to the definition of terrorism. The AHC's report of April 15, 2011 states that 'several delegations reiterated that the convention should contain a definition of terrorism, which would provide a clear distinction between acts of terrorism covered by the convention and the legitimate struggle of peoples in the exercise of their right to self-determination' (available online at http://www.eyeontheun.org/facts.asp?1=1&p=61).

The problems involved include both complex conceptual considerations and the conflict of strategic interests. It would seem odd, therefore, if the social scientist who wishes to throw light on what it means to be a terrorist and from whose point of view the preferred definition is salient should not at least include some discussion of the complex issues in order to provide the reader with a justification for his or her own approach.

The index of Berman's book contains one entry for the definition of terrorism, and it comes late, much more than halfway through:

> First we need to be clear about terms. The definition of terrorism is controversial, but most people agree that if you target civilians – or more generally non-combatants – in pursuit of a political goal (as opposed to a purely criminal goal), you're a terrorist (Berman 2009: 158).

He distinguishes terrorists from 'insurgents', who 'use violence but target military, police, or government officials, rather than civilians, generally with the immediate political goal of controlling territory, and with the final goal of controlling a country' (2009: 158).

This definition seems manageable for Berman's purposes. It avoids the more complex issues that have made an agreed definition of terrorism impossible for the UN General Assembly's Ad Hoc Committee. Berman generally avoids discussing the legitimacy of the struggle of people in the exercise of their right to self-determination under foreign occupation and colonial or alien domination. Berman forefronts the violence of some small groups which resist occupation but avoids the moral problem of the violence of invasions by secular states. Berman manages to embed into his argument an unanalysed assumption that secular states, like Western secular science, are inherently peace-loving, reasonable and only reluctantly violent in the defence of higher values such as freedom, truth and democracy.

And again, that the majority of these terrorist organizations are made up of *religious* radicals is not a simple fact either, for that, too, depends on a clear understanding of what distinguishes a religious from a non-religious organization, whether terrorist or not. This question about the nature of religion in a generic sense (rather than an exclusive reference to Protestant Christian truth) is a peculiarly modern one. One of the earliest writers to imagine 'religion' as something which can be studied from an objective, non-religious position was David Hume in *The Natural History of Religion*. Hume was a friend of Adam Smith, another illustrious member of the Edinburgh Enlightenment, to whom Berman refers frequently. The idea that 'religion' can be explained naturally, for example as an irrational belief in gods and magic based on psychological facts such as fear or awe, or the pre-scientific need for explanation of the universe, or as a technique for the maintenance of social order, became even more explicit during the nineteenth and twentieth centuries within the developing field known generally as the study of religion, which is also sometimes referred to as religious studies, the comparative study of religion, the history of religion, and the science of religion. This field also has branches in the philosophy of religion, the sociology of religion, the anthropology of religion, the psychology of religion and others. The relation between this diverse and amorphous field and Christian theology on the one hand, and the social sciences on the other, is a complex historical and theoretical problem that has also been debated for many decades. Any argument which claims to be about religion or the religious aspects of life, and which wishes to be taken seriously, would need to know something about the range of these debates in so far as they affect the issues. And when the issues are about terrorism, then the definitional problem takes on added importance.

What distinguishes a religious from a non-religious organization in Berman's theory? Apart from his unexamined appeal to other binaries such as spiritual–material, there is no clear discussion of this point in the book, presumably because Berman thinks the answer is too obvious to need addressing.

# Notes

1.  Some other writers who problematize the relations between 'economics' and 'religion' or 'spirituality' include R. Laurence Moore (1995); David Loy (1997); Philip Goodchild (2002); Jeremy Carrette and Richard King (2005).
2.  See my reference below on p132 to Stuart Plattner's *Economic Anthropology* (1989) which accurately expresses the problem of applying modern categories such as 'religion' and 'economics' to non-Capitalist societies.

3.  See Tisa Wenger (2009). See also Arvind-Pal Mandair in his book *Religion and the Spectre of the West: Sikhism, India, Postcoloniality, and the Politics of Translation* (2009), where he describes as an act of epistemic violence the classification of Sikh practices as 'religious', and of 'Sikhism' as 'a religion', by both the British colonial government and the Indian State.

4.  A.M.C. Waterman (2008). See also a more elaborated discussion in Chapter 11 of this volume.

5.  Michael Perelman (2000). See Chapter 11 of this volume for more discussion. Perelman's view is supported by David Harvey in his *A Companion to Marx's Capital*, (Verso, 2010)

6.  The historian David Cannadine (2001) seems to suggest in his work *Ornamentalism* that England remained in many ways a confessional state into the early twentieth century.

7.  Thanks to Naomi Goldenberg of the University of Ottawa for this expression.

8.  When Berman published his book, the Tamils of Sri Lanka had not yet been destroyed by the Sinhalese state and its armed forces.

9.  See my discussion of Anthony D. Smith in Chapter 8 of this volume.

10. These would have been interesting questions to put to members of different communities.

# Chapter 8

## The Return from Exile

In this chapter I comment on several articles taken from two volumes edited by Fabio Petito and Pavlos Hatzopolous: 'Religion and International Relations', a special issue of *Millennium Journal of International Relations* (2000); and *Religion in International Relations: The Return from Exile* (2003). Some authors, such as Vendulka Kubálková, Scott M. Thomas, Carsten Bagge Laustsen and Ole Wæver, contribute to both volumes. One striking feature of these two volumes is that some authors take explicitly Christian theological positions in their approach to 'religion'. In one sense I admired this openness to theology, and the willingness to try to step across normally taboo disciplinary boundaries. But, as I will show in my discussions of Vendulka Kubálková, and Bagge Laustsen and Ole Wæver, there are severe difficulties in doing this.

The relationship between Christian theologies and the global discourse on religion and religions is complex and no longer especially direct. 'Religion' and its definition has for long been within the province of constitutions, courts, academia, the education system, the media and other agencies. There is a vast publishing industry on the 'religions of the world' which represents itself as non-theological, secular, neutral and objective. Many of the theorists of the study of religion or the science of religion have explicitly tried to distance themselves from theology in order to establish their belief in religions as objects of comparative study. One can argue that they have not been very successful, but that would depend on the criterion of success. On the one hand many universities have departments of religious studies, either as separate schools with Theology, or as completely separate departments distanced from Theology.

The work of Religious Studies scholars tends to be ignored by international relations scholars, as can be seen from the dearth of references to Religious Studies authors in these two volumes. Furthermore, different Christian theologians themselves have taken different attitudes to 'other religions'. Historically, and until quite recently, other 'religions' were not Religion in the sense of Truth but superstitious and pagan substitutes for Truth. Some Christian evangelicals still hold this view. During the twentieth century a liberal ecumenical theology developed which has held that all 'religions' are equal paths to the one God. Tillich, for example, was more amenable to this kind of theology than Karl Barth. The contribution of Christian theologies to the historical invention of religions and their systematic study and classification is highly complex. There is no clear referent to the term 'religion', just as there is no clear referent to the term 'secular'.

## Fabio Petito & Pavlos Hatzopolous

In their 2003 book, Petito and Hatzopolous' try to show that the modern formation of IR as a discipline has been dependent on the exclusion or margin-alization of religion – what they describe as its exile. In the first paragraph of the introduction, the editors say the following:

> The worldwide resurgence of religion seems nowadays to generate repression – at times through the imposition of religious law upon a community of people, at other times, through the association of religion with 'terror', through its supposed inclination to generate extreme – even indiscriminate – political actions; or even in scenarios involving the persecution of other religious communities; or, more apocalyptically, as the driving force behind a coming 'clash of civilizations' (Petito and Hatzopolous 2003: 1).

Though there is a sense in which the editors intend to go on to challenge this view, I would first ask the reader to notice how their statement sets religion up as a powerful agent and an object in the world. Religion resurges, generates, imposes, persecutes and drives. Religion is also a distinct kind of thing, a *religious* kind of thing: there is religious law and there are religious commu-nities. The assumption that these are essentially different from non-religious laws and non-religious communities is quietly communicated 'below the radar', tacitly. And I draw the reader's attention also to their claim that religion is a global, 'worldwide' agent, and a global, 'worldwide' kind of practice and belief. This is itself a proclamation, a statement of faith, rather than an induction from empirical observation.

The next paragraph introduces a switch point. The switch, however, is not a critical reflection on the metaphoric use of language. It is an extension and further embedding through simple reversal:

> But what if in order to study the role of religion in international relations we need to reverse the picture? To treat religion not as the generator of repression, but as the 'victim'? (2003: 1).

Here religion continues to be represented as an agent, but as a damaged agent; rather than 'the generator of oppression', as itself a victim. This idea is immediately followed by what appears at first to be a disclaimer: 'This reversal should not be understood necessarily in literal terms'. This would seem to invite the reader to consider that the language being used is merely an extended metaphor. But this is not what they mean:

> Instead religion is a victim insofar as it was *exiled* from the modern constitution of international relations; religion was the object that needed to vanish for modern international politics to come into being. Religion has been, and largely remains, what the discipline of International Relations can speak about only as a threat to its own existence (2003: 1; emphasis in original).

This important insight into the mutually parasitic discursive relation between 'religion' and IR is obscured by the reifying effects of language. Here religion continues to be a victim, a damaged agent that has even been exiled. Religion is also explicitly an 'object' – 'the object that needed to vanish'. Furthermore the exiled agent and object has been replaced by another object that came into being and has 'its own existence' (2003: 1), viz. the discipline of International Relations. But is it really true that IR is an object with an existence? We might in ordinary language say that IR as a discipline, or as a discourse, or as a recognised theoretical domain, came into existence historically, but we would surely not want to imply by that that IR is an 'object'. Sometimes, the logical level at which we use words is understandably ambiguous, but the tendency to misplaced concreteness and to reification becomes progressively overwhelming throughout the book, and arguably that is what rhetoric and the construction of myths do: they transform an *imaginaire* into a literal truth. And further, since the existence of IR depends on the exile of religion (e.g. its absence or separation), then by clear implication IR is essentially a *non-religious* being. This absence of religion is an essential characteristic of IR: 'The rejection of religion ... seems to be inscribed in the genetic code of the discipline of IR' (2003: 1).

The language used here about religion and IR does not seem to me to be essentially different from theological language about God. They are all objects of the imagination that, through the power of mythical language, have taken on the appearance of real entities and agents in the world. Belief in the myth of God acted as a rationale for the medieval church-state; so, in a similar way, the myth of the editors' metaphysical agents and objects, widely believed by a host of other academics, journalists, politicians, philosophers and ordinary people, has acted as a rationale for the organization of our own world in significant ways, including the invention of the modern nation state, the organization of the academy, and the invention of International Relations.

Yet there is surely an important insight in this story. It is that, in order to invent the myth of the non-religious secular in tune with natural reason and common sense, the world as it 'really is', the myth of religion as a separate, different kind of experience, emotion and commitment concerned with another kind of supernatural world, had also to be invented. There is a difference between saying that the existence of non-religious IR is dependent on the exclusion of religion to the margins, or into a separate category of existence, and saying that the conditions for conceiving of IR as a theoretical domain have been historically dependent on the ability to conceive 'religion' as an essentially distinct domain. But unfortunately this is not what they say.

The problem is that nowhere do the editors clearly theorize their own language, or what 'religion' or 'non-religious secular' mean. They nowhere show any critical suspicion that the binary opposition that they are inscribing into the text and the reader's reception, far from being a literal rendering of what is in the world, is a rhetorical construction aimed to persuade us to imagine the world in a particular way. How are we to understand the logical and semantic level of analysis in their assertion that the non-religious secular – they refer to politics and international relations, but the same principle applies to the nation state, economics, law and so on – depends for its existence on the exclusion of religion? What is being excluded from what? And what kind of agent is 'religion' when it is being posited as the 'object' of secular analysis?

The idea of religion as a global agent that 'resurges', or as a special and distinct kind of state, experience, practice, law system, belief and institution is part of a widespread Anglophone rhetorical construction which embeds an essentialized dichotomy between the religious and the non-religious as though it is part of the order of things. It also implies a metaphysics, such that religion, which is an unseen essence, manifests in specific religions, which are ubiquitous empirical objects of investigation found in principle in all societies everywhere, in all languages and at all times in history and even prehistory. These mysterious agents, imbued with the metaphysical essence of 'religion', are further asserted to be essentially distinct in kind from a non-religious essence. This myth is circulated by various agencies including constitutions, law courts, the media and academia.

This idea of religion as an essence, as a special kind of force or agent acting in the world, and of religions as things in the world which manifest this shared essence in particularistic ways, simultaneously inscribes the non-religious secular as its innate opposite, not always and everywhere apparent, sometimes suppressed and covered up by religion, but there and waiting to be revealed through the progress of human rationality. If we shift our attention to this as discourse or rhetorical construction, we can immediately see that it is itself a modern myth, a fundamental part of the modern *imaginaire* that convinces us that this fictitious essentialized dichotomy is in the nature of things. This myth has huge power and it is difficult for us to get free of the language that constructs it, because to do so has radical implications for the whole structure of our vision of the world, the warp and woof and texture of our common consciousness. To deconstruct this mythical world in which we ourselves live, as some writers in this book have noticed, problematizes the very discipline of IR itself.

The result of a shift of focus from religions as objects and agents in the world, essentially different in kind from the secular state and politics, to the discourses that rhetorically construct this dichotomous Anglophone *imaginaire*, is that the terms themselves lose their efficacy as descriptive and analytical categories. We saw in a previous chapter how little clarity Hitchens's descriptive and analytical use of religion and its assumed distinction from the secular and the ethnic achieves when confronted with the complexities on the ground. The present authors have tried to push the agenda forward but they fail to get the problem into clear view. If one is critically problematizing terms such as 'religion' and everything that is deemed to be its 'non-religious' binary opposite, such as politics, the state and international relations, then all these terms become interconnected parts of the problem that needs solving. It then becomes imperative to refrain from recycling them. The writer of a text who, while attempting to critically and historically problematize 'religion' as a category of discourse, yet simultaneously continues to use terms like religion, religious, faith and spirituality as though they unproblematically describe real aspects of the world, is still caught up in the secular illusion whose spell he or she is trying to break. They are recycling the key beliefs of the myth.

# Vendulka Kubálková

Vendulka Kubálková, in her chapter 'Toward an International Political Theology' (Kubálková 2003: 79–105) argues *explicitly* for an ontological distinction between religious and secular thought (2003: 87). What is interesting in this argument is that, while claiming to be able to identify the essential characteristics of 'religion', and therefore of all 'religions', the author already knows that they exist. But she provides no evidence for this. Her whole argument therefore exemplifies tautological metaphysical reasoning from intuitively cognized premises, and the conditions for the possibility of empirical verification or falsification of her vast generalizations are absent:

> It is infeasible to discuss religion in IR without appreciating that the difference in religious and secular thought is ontological, that is, in what each of them 'counts for real'. All spiritual communities, all religions, Western and Eastern, share a distinction between ordinary and transcendental reality ... According to most religious thought, the structure of the ordinary world, with its assumptions of separate and distinct cause and effect, the spatial arrangement of objects, and the linearity of time does not exhaust reality. Most religions share the idea that the world as revealed to the temporal senses is only one item in a hierarchy of being ... Human

experience is seen as only one dimension of a multidimensional reality that is ordered by design rather than chance (2003: 87–8).

The first sentence is not a claim to empirical knowledge. It is a rhetorical proclamation, a mere assertion which sounds close to what she calls the 'assertive rules' which she also claims are typical of 'religion'. The rest consists of astonishing claims to almost superhuman knowledge of all the putative religions of the world that themselves can hardly be based on induction from empirical observation. The author repeatedly uses such expressions as 'all spiritual communities', 'all religions', 'most religions', 'most religious thought', as though she is an authority who can penetrate into the essences, many of them wrapped in languages very different from English. Some scholars spend their lives just studying one putative 'religion' in Tibetan, Chinese, Japanese, Sanskrit, Pali or some other language, as also non-literate traditions. Some of those scholars are themselves involved in complex published debates about the relevance or validity of the term 'religion'. The sheer size of the claim, that one can make such generalizations about all systems of belief and practice that might be or have been classified in English as religions, is itself an act of faith, a sheer assertion of belief. Kubálková also claims that all religions believe in 'a hierarchy of being', and that the world is 'ordered by design rather than chance'. But how does she know this? Even if this was a genuine matter of empirical study and observation, and religions really were empirical objects in the world available for inspection, it would be almost superhuman to be able to make such authoritative pronouncements about what they all believe. The claim that all religions believe in a hierarchy of being and in the design of the world by a designer is just wild guesswork, probably the uncritical projection of Christocentric assumptions.

But the generalization is not a genuine matter of empirical study and observation, because the recycling of the problematic category 'religion', which itself is a fundamental part of the problem, sets up a circularity that renders verification or falsification of the author's own claims impossible. Religions are not objects in the world. No one has ever seen a religion, anymore than anyone has ever seen a nation state or a society. We know from the detailed research of historians[1] that the idea of the nation state is a modern invention dating from around the end of the eighteenth century and made possible by the contingent arising of a number of contributory factors (though see my discussion below of Anthony D. Smith's sophisticated discussion of nations and nationalism). Why should we think any differently about 'religions'? What is the basis for these grandiose claims about 'religion' and 'religions'? How would anyone know enough about all these putative thought-worlds, also referred to by other problematic and much disputed terms such as 'faiths' and 'spiritual communities', to know that they all share essential characteristics that make them fundamentally different from non-religious secular views? And we should notice that, unlike Scott M. Thomas, another contributor whose interesting work I discuss in the next chapter, Kubálková never questions the changing historical usages of these English-language terms. She knows what they mean from the start, and her job is to reveal their shared metaphysical essence.

Further on we get the claim 'In the believer's view, the origins of religious experience are beyond the realm of human choice' (2003: 89). '[T]he believer' is a complete fiction, a myth. Who is 'the believer'? The author herself is the believer – she believes in her own wild fabrications. Besides, arguably there is an element of all experience that is beyond choice. When I look out of my window, I do not choose to have the visual experience of the tree-covered hills of Northern Kyoto, and the insistent ringing of the electronic bell at the railway crossing. Kubálková is not here making any kind of generalization based on systematic observation and the marshalling of evidence, and she is not succeeding in establishing that there exists an ontological separation between religious and non-religious experience.

There is also an assumption, slipped into the text without comment as though it is intuitively obvious and needs no theoretical justification, that belief in God and/or gods is a defining characteristic of 'religion'. We saw the same assumption made by Berman and Hitchens. Earlier I made the point that, even in the Anglophone tradition, the terms God and gods are complex, contested, and have been a cause of bloodshed. What, after all, is God, and how does God differ from gods? Are ancestors gods? Is the nation state a god? Is God the chief of the gods, or are the two terms so incompatible that for the believer in God then gods are irrational pagan figments of the imagination? Is God a real essence or a metaphor for a moral way of life, as some Christian theologians and philosophers have argued? But the search for an essence for religion is too important for these issues to be considered. It is another assumption, and this assumption is supported by another general claim, that 'sociologists of religion argue that creating or constructing gods is one of the human universals' (2003: 88). Durkheim argued in *The Elementary Forms of the Religious Life*[2] that belief in gods is not a universal. He explicitly rejected definitions based on belief in gods, and consequently defined religion in terms of the 'sacred'. The statement is simply left to stand. It is merely a hurriedly constructed stepping-stone to the next stage of Kubálková's metaphysical ambitions in determining the essence of the religious.

In further refining her metaphysical claims about the structure of the essence of religion, based on pseudo-empirical claims to know what all 'religious' believers think, Kubálková briefly considers the idea that 'paganism, nationalism and other ideologies have played a societal role comparable to that of religions … Soviet Marxism-Leninism is recognised as a secular religion; humanism has been described as a religion without God, and liberalism as Christianity without God' (2003: 88).[3] But she does not pursue this potentially fruitful line, perhaps because she senses that it might weaken her claim that religion and the secular are ontologically distinct. She merely uses this unanalysed statement to assert that this is not sufficient to identify *true religions*, a distinction which itself is strongly reminiscent of Christian claims that there is only one true religion and all those non-Christian practices that might seem distantly reminiscent of Christianity are not *true religion* but irrational superstitions, pagan barbarities. For Kubálková, religion is already intuited, in a way reminiscent of the ontological argument for the existence of God, which deduces from an *a priori* definition of 'God' that God must necessarily exist. In Kubálková's argument, religions exist *a priori*, and belief in God is deduced as an essential characteristic. Here she specifies the relevant religions as Judaism, Christianity and Islam. Suddenly the global and universal essence of religion is reduced to slightly more parochial proportions; we are only talking here about three so-called world religions.[4] But even here, in this minefield of contested categories, we cannot assume with Kubálková that Yahweh, Christ and Allah can all be unproblematically included together in the category 'God', belief in which can provide us with an essential characteristic of religion.

Apart from the difficulty of accepting that anyone could know empirically what is the essential characteristic of religions, there is also the circularity of starting with an intuitive assumption that one knows what religion is and what religions are, and then going on to search for the essence that makes them all exemplars of the same category. From here Kubálková then goes on to further demarcate the 'incommensurability of the positivist and religious understandings of the world ...' (2003: 90). Yet her own assertions about religion, religions and religious believers is itself closer to what she claims as a religious understanding of the world. The argument is completely circular, and based on an assertion of faith.

## Carsten Bagge Lausten & Ole Wæver

In their chapter 'In Defence of Religion: Sacred Referent Objects for Securitization' (Lausten and Wæver 2003), Carsten Bagge Laustsen and Ole Wæver make the interesting and potentially fruitful remark that 'IR is not the neutral observer it pretends to be; it is implicated by its own secularist self-perception' (2003: 175). However, this does not lead them to deconstruct religion and its supposed essential differences from politics and international relations. There are moments in their essay when I thought I might be reading a philosophically interesting move in this direction, as for example when they refer to 'the religion of politics' (2003: 165), which neatly unsettles both these categories. But such a project is not their main intention, which is to re-inscribe religion as separate and distinct.

For Laustsen and Wæver, religion has an essence. This belief is conveyed in many very explicit ways. They use expressions such as 'religion *as religion*', distinguishing it from 'religion *as community*' (2003: 151), 'the religious element in religion', the 'distinctly religious' (2003: 151), and the 'the essence of religious discourse' (2003: 152).

In Lausten and Wæver's view, 'faith', especially as theologized by Kierkegaard as 'the leap of faith', is the central issue that demarcates religion from other domains such as politics. 'Religion deals with the constitution of being through acts of faith' (2003: 174), and 'Religious discourse does not defend identity of community, but the true faith, our possibility to worship the right gods the right way and – in some religions – thereby have a chance of salvation' (2003: 151). What distinguishes religion from other 'referent objects' is 'faith' and 'being' (2003: 158). Faith is not essentially about power, as when, in discussing American foreign policy, they say: 'The new enemies are driven by faith, rather than power gains' (2003: 159).

Religion is also essentially characterized by 'fear and trembling', an expression for which Kierkegaard is famous (is fear and trembling not about power?). Religion also creates 'narratives about [the] abyss – about the giving of the word, the law, the book, and about God's withdrawal from the world' (2003: 155). Religion makes a radical distinction between the transcendent and the immanent, between 'the otherworldly realm' and this world (2003: 155), between 'sacred and profane', sacred being a defining characteristic of religious objects (2003: 157–8). Sacred objects are 'never just objects, persons or practices. They are spirit manifested in matter' (2003: 158). Religion, following both Kierkegaard and Bataille, is 'given by acts of hyperbolic madness' (2003: 157).

Yet it can easily be argued that none of these characteristics have much application, outside a quite tiny band of disciples of Kierkegaard, to the beliefs and practices normally described as 'religious' of millions of people around the world. Lausten and Wæver admit that:

> Numerous approaches to the study of religion exist. Among them, theology and philosophy constitute a systematic way of investigating religion, and this approach will be our prime context of reference. One cannot understand a phenomenon without considering the way this very phenomenon is described by those confronting it and practising it (2003: 152).

This implies that we already know who are the people who are truly practising 'religion', as defined by Kierkegaard's own specific version of nineteenth-century Protestant theology. But how many people in the world who, we are told by different theorists in a host of other writings, are religious would agree that they are really Kierkegaardian Protestants without realizing it? For Kierkegaard's view of true religion would exclude most Catholics, let alone Buddhists, Confucianists, Shintoists and so on. One also wonders if Kierkegaard would agree that 'religion' is a 'phenomenon', a thing, an object of secular analysis. It could surely be argued that the drift of this theology as faith in one God puts it in the realm of Christian truth, and both excludes it as a phenomenon and excludes millions of people who have multiple concepts of the legitimate object of their ritual homage.

Lausten and Wæver's choice of Kierkegaard's theology as their 'main approach to the study of religion' (2003: 152) is highly problematic. They claim that, though Kierkegaard (1813–55) was a 'distinctly nineteenth and twentieth century Protestant', his 'analytical distinctions can be used generally' (2003: 152).

But arguably this huge claim is itself an act of faith. Even within the Christian Protestant tradition, Kierkegaard does not define any kind of orthodox representation of the meaning of Christian truth. He is widely admired as an original and interesting thinker, but not more than, say, Paul Tillich or Karl Barth, both of whom were not only theologians but writers who had interesting (and conflicting) things to say about 'religion' and 'religions' as more general categories.

Deeply embedded in many versions of Protestant theology is the idea that Religion means Christian Truth, as revealed to us by Christ and as further revealed to us by the Holy Spirit through the reading of the Bible. There are no true religions outside this context. Catholicism was arguably the initial target of this Protestant critique, but clearly it has direct implications for the vast majority of the other practices and beliefs of humankind, and serious consequences for any analysis on the discourse on religion and religions. What was Kierkegaard's position on this? What would he have thought of the other 'religions' which Lausten and Wæver mention in passing? What would he have thought of theories of 'religion' which are casually extended to Islam, Hinduism, Judaism, or from God to 'gods' in the plural (2003: 152, 155)?[5]

Laustsen and Wæver do not seem to refer to Aquinas, the Catholic Church-State and its official theologies, any of the Prince Popes, nor Protestant theologians such as Luther, Calvin, Wesley, Jonathan Edwards, Paul Tillich and Karl Barth, to mention just a few at random. And how would all this help illuminate Gandhi or the Dalai Lama, who almost certainly would not think of 'religion' in Kierkegaardian terms? Are they to be excluded from the category of 'religion'? Or the people of Nepal who worship pre-pubescent girls as the living goddess (kumari)? Is caste and untouchability an essential feature of 'the religion Hinduism', a point much disputed by Indian courts in their various interpretations of the constitution? Or the Aborigines of Australia, whose view of the sacredness of the land would surely not fit into a Kierkegaardian Protestant theological paradigm? Yet in modern discourse the category 'religion' is widely used to refer to all these examples.

Neither do they mention theorists in the study of religion, which might include (to give just a few examples[6]) Herbert of Cherbury, who was a seventeenth-century Protestant of a radically different kind from Kierkegaard; David Hume, who some would argue was the first to conceptualize 'religion' as an object of naturalistic description and explanation, as in his *The Natural History of Religion*; the Sanskritist Max Müller, who is sometimes referred to as the father of the science of religion; C.P. Tiele; James George Frazer (*The Golden Bough*); Robertson Smith in his ground-breaking work on Semitic religion; Emile Durkheim; Mircea Eliade, who was one of the most influential writers on religion in the second half of the twentieth century; Clifford Geertz; Louis Dumont; and Jonathan Z. Smith. On the narrow and arbitrary choice of one Protestant theology, all of these theorists would be excluded as having 'religion' as their subject matter.

One tacitly critical reference is made to Peter L. Berger's *The Sacred Canopy*, but there is no proper discussion of this influential book (Berger is also mentioned on page 147 of Laustsen and Wæver's chapter). Berger has been one interesting voice in theoretical debates within sociology and religious studies. He is one of the very few exceptions to the general absence of references in this chapter to debates which have been published over the last few hundred years, and perhaps especially since the nineteenth century, about the problems of definition, the relations between theology and religious studies, and between these and the social sciences, the powerful and highly contested strain of phenomenology in the study of religion, the important contributions to the field made by anthropologists working in a wide variety of literate and non-literate societies, or specialists in the so-called world religions such as Islam, Hinduism, Buddhism, Sikhism, Confucianism, Shinto, Taoism, or the studies of African religions, religion in South America, so-called indigenous religions, and so on. Nor is there any mention of the arguments *against* essentialized definitions of religions, some of which draw on Wittgenstein's idea of family resemblances and are popular with many writers precisely because of the widely perceived impossibility of an essentialist definition of religion.

My own (published) view is that the term 'religion', which for centuries meant Christian truth, has been used so widely and indiscriminately in modern thinking that it has become a virtually empty category. The question then becomes, what drives these global discourses? But my arguments are contested, and rightly so, and would lose significant meaning if I did not attempt to bring them theoretically into relation with the traditions of theory and methodology which are so hotly debated in religious studies, sociology and anthropology. I would be talking in a vacuum, as though trying to reinvent the wheel. Yet without compunction Laustsen and Wæver can theorize religion on premises which have already been subjected to intense critique. Though Kierkegaard and Bataille are very interesting writers, and some of Laustsen and Wæver's discussion of them is also interesting, these discussions need to be located in a theoretical tradition if IR is to benefit from them. Laustsen and Wæver spend some time discussing Ninian Smart's seven dimensions of 'religion'. I myself have critiqued Smart's phenomenology of religion at length in my *Ideology of Religious Studies* (Fitzgerald 2000). In the present volume I would confine myself to only one observation. Like Laustsen and Wæver, I have questioned the problem of so-called pseudo-religions or quasi-religions such as Nazism and Nationalism, which fit many of the dimensions that Smart wishes to reserve for 'religions proper'. But, unlike them, I draw a radically different conclusion from these boundary cases. Whereas Laustsen and Wæver see this as a problem because it does not give us the hard and clear boundaries by which they desire to establish the essence of religion, I see so many boundary problems that the logic of Smart's approach leads to the conclusion that, as a descriptive and analytical category, 'religion' is entirely useless. I would ask Laustsen and Wæver to read a good introductory textbook to the history of theorizing about religion and religions.[7]

Throughout *Religion in International Relations: The Return from Exile* (Petito and Hatzopolous 2003), the binary opposition between 'religion' and the non-religious secular is transformed from a rhetorical construct born in specific historical interests, controversies and power contexts into an uncritical and universal presupposition. While in some papers there are attempts at critical historicization by authors such as Scott M. Thomas, some like Vendulka Kubálková and Carsten Bagge Lausten and Ole Wæver actually and explicitly theorize these supposed essences, while others merely assume the reality of the essential distinction and proceed to re-embed it in their descriptions and analyses.

# Anthony D. Smith

One of the outstanding essays in the *Millennium* journal (Petito and Hatzopolous 2000) is that by Anthony D. Smith, 'The "Sacred" Dimension of Nationalism' (Smith 2000). I have suggested at various points in this book that nationalism and devotion to the nation state could, according to widespread classificatory practices, itself be considered religious. But my purpose has not been to further embed the category 'religion' and its supposed distinction from the 'secular' into our descriptive and analytical repertoire, but to indicate how this distinction itself is a powerful mythological representation with a historical genesis made to appear as if in the objective nature of things. This is my main point of contention with Smith's careful and informed discussion of 'The Sacred Properties of the Nation'. Smith moves ambiguously backwards and forwards between the level of representations and the supposed factual level of empirical description.

At one level Smith seems to want to deconstruct a supposed essential difference between religion and secular nationalism by suggesting that nationalism is itself a new form of religion. His final sentence reads:

> [I]n its national manifestations, a new kind of intra-historical religion with its novel liturgies, symbols, and rituals provides the bond and inspiration for the citizens of the constituent national states that make up the contemporary international community (Smith 2000: 814).

I leave aside here the possibility of qualifying the last remark, viz. 'that *are imagined to* make up the contemporary international community'. Smith describes the nation as a 'sacred communion of its members' celebrated in rites, symbols and ceremonies (2000: 814 and passim). In this way he comes close to Durkheim. Smith quotes Durkheim's famous definition of religion, given near the beginning of the Elementary Forms:

'A religion is a unified system of beliefs and practices relative to sacred things, that is to say, things set apart and forbidden – beliefs and practices which unite into one single moral community called a Church, all those who adhere to them' (Smith 2000: 797; quoted from Durkheim 1912, *The Elementary Forms of the Religious Life*).

Smith comments:

From this perspective, much of what Durkheim wrote about the Arunta and other Australian aboriginal tribes applies with equal, if not greater force, to nations and nationalism. This comes out clearly in his discussion of society's tendency to create gods, even secular ones, as during the first years of the French Revolution, and of the totem as the flag or sign of the clan which evokes sacrifice on its behalf. (2000: 797)

Smith asks rhetorically (and including a quote from Durkheim):

Does this mean, then, that there is no essential difference 'between an assembly of Christians celebrating the principal dates of the life of Christ, or of Jews remembering the exodus from Egypt or the promulgation of the Decalogue, and a reunion of citizens commemorating the promulgation of a new moral and legal system or some great event in the national life?' For Durkheim's functional approach, there could be no real difference. Symbolisms may change, but as he himself put it, 'there is something eternal in "religion", because every society must remake itself periodically in a moral sense, and thereby uphold its identity through rites and ceremonies' (2000: 798).

But for Smith, Durkheim is in danger of collapsing too many distinctions that Smith wants to maintain. Durkheim 'fails to grasp the complexity of the relations between "religion" and "nationalism". In fact we often find considerable rivalry between "old" traditional religions and "new" nationalisms, even of the "religious" variety. There remain, after all, many adherents of traditional religions, and many religious sects, which are wary of, or hostile, to nationalism' (2000: 798).

Here we can see that, by imagining some nationalisms as having religious characteristics and others as having secular characteristics, Smith maintains his hold on something essential as the referent of religion and its distinction from the secular, an essence that takes different forms in old traditional religions and new religious nationalisms. Religion may continue in new forms, but according to Smith we need to distinguish between religion as such and the different forms it manifests.

The problem here is the assumed distinction between old traditional 'religions' and new 'religious nationalisms'. The problem is indicated in the way that the same word, 'religion', is being used to stand for two different things – two different power structures and the self-representations of the elites who legitimize the old and the new power structures – while the use of the same term obscures this. It implies that, between the old and the new power formations, something remained constant, albeit changed into a new form. But what is this 'religion' that at core remains the same referent? In what does the tension between traditional religions and modern religious nation-alisms consist, outside of the tensions between an existing and established order of power or its dominant representations, and a new one that challenges and threatens to replace the old one?

The problem is also in Durkheim, because Durkheim seems to want to say that the eternal element in 'religion' is really the eternal element in a 'society' which the 'religion' symbolically represents. In both cases, either 'religion' or 'society' is being essentialized, a core essence that is given renewed forms. But this use of language is arguably at the root of our problem of conceptu-alization. There is no eternal essence in 'a society', or in 'society' in general, except in the sense that this essence is invented at the level of rhetoric and myth. And the invention is that of elite myth-makers, propagandists and sociologists. The elite myth-makers and propagandists invent this essential core of continuity in order to legitimize the new order of power interests in terms of the old, or some selective construction of the old. And the sociologists take these myths and transform them into sociological theories based on an essentialized category of 'society'. The idea of 'a society', as one of an abstract class of societies, is largely the invention of sociologists who simultaneously have invented their own scientific secularity. An imagined category that they invented as part of modernity has become a series of problematic objects in the world that can be described and compared.

The same can be said of 'religion' and its supposed manifestation in 'religions'. There is no eternal core essence 'religion' which receives new forms except in the sense that myth-makers, propagandists and sociolo-gists invent them. The establishment of a new, 'modern' order of power will be made to seem legitimate through the appropriation and invention of 'traditions'. Much as the invention of religion is simultaneously the invention of the non-religious secular, so also the invention of tradition is the invention of modernity. So-called 'traditional religions' are then represented as becoming transformed into modern religious nationalisms. We act (and write) as though these imagined distinctions have an objective reality, and thereby organize our world accordingly. Yet when we come to look closely at these categories they none of them have any clear and distinct content. They form a system of parasitically imagined domains and entities with indistinct meanings.

Smith carries the burden of the descriptive and analytical distinctions between traditional religions, secular nationalisms and religious nationalisms. Yet so much of what he seems to want to say undercuts those very distinctions. Political transformations of religion (what is *not* political?), the messianization of politics, religious charisma, the gods of secular faith, 'the new religious faith' of nationhood as celebrated on Independence Day, Bastille Day, the anniversary of the October Revolution, ANZAC day, the annual Armistice Ceremony at the Cenotaph in Whitehall. What are these factors that are embedded in Smith's analysis as though they are distinct but come into problematic relations – the religious, the secular, the social and the political? In Smith's uses of 'political', what is meant other than power, or a specific power configuration, or a historically specific clash of power formations? It doesn't matter whether you talk about a traditional religion, a new religion, a secular nationalism, or a religious nationalism, or the old gods or the new gods, you are talking willy-nilly about different kinds of power formations or moral communities and their ideological legitimations representing the interests of different elites at different historical moments in time. If the secular is a transformation of religion, and if religion persists in a new form in secularity, then how are they distinguished? And why does it matter? If secular nation states have gods, then how do religious gods differ from secular gods? Why can we not say that 'gods' are symbolic representations of the order of power, and its hegemonic values, and that different orders of power generate different gods? What is the purpose in trying to force them into this predetermined, Anglophone religion–secular binary? For there is an inherent circularity between the categories whereby we represent our world, whether in elite propaganda or in the more sophisticated jargon of sociology, and the way we organize our affairs, or conduct foreign policy. Myths transform reified abstractions into the limiting conditions of our collective consciousness. Imaginings become alienated from our own productivity and stand over and against us as factual realities.

Smith distinguishes between three levels of analysis of the relationships between 'religion' and 'national identity'. The first or 'official' level posits 'a secular–religious spectrum'. He says:

> At one extreme, there are the outright 'secular nationalisms' of the French revolutionary or Turkish Kemalist variety, with their determined assaults on clerical elites and established religion; at the other end of the spectrum, the 'religious nationalisms' of the BJP in India or the Sharia-oriented regimes in several Muslim states. In between come the many shades of religiously inflected nationalisms, and the many mixed cases of religious–secular compromise in most national states, as well as the examples of powerful, well-organized oppositional national-religious movements like the Muslim Brotherhood or the Gush Emunim in Israel (2000: 800).

There is a deep ambiguity in these claims. Are they being offered as useful analytical distinctions or as descriptively factual? Is it a fact that the French Revolution was 'outright secular nationalism'? Given that he and Durkheim seem to believe that the French Revolution produced its own gods (and goddesses), that the principles of equality, liberty and fraternity are sacred, and that the new nation is replete with rituals, liturgies and ceremonies, then the term 'secular' is not clearly distinct from what we typically think of as religious, a point which Smith himself has made. He says:

> [T]he French Revolution itself ... became the prototype for a secular nationalism that saw the nation as the embodiment and beacon of liberty, reason and progress with a mission to liberate and civilize less fortunate peoples. This missionary ideal inspired French imperialism in Africa and Indochina, just as it swayed British imperial 'civilizing' reformers in India, as well as Americans in the Great Society with its millennial providential destiny. In all these cases, the community is itself invested with sacredness, as a moral communion of the faithful, and a clear line is drawn separating it from those outside and beneath. Inside that line the elect nation seeks salvation by fulfilling its great destiny and noble mission, while those outside toiling in darkness wait to receive its civilizing light and liberating gifts (2000: 805).

So is it true to say that the French Revolution constituted an assault on clerical elites and established religion? For one thing, the French Revolution assaulted not only clerical elites but the totality of the ancient regime, including the whole ideology of the estates of which the clerical elites were one sector. Equally important was the assault on the king and his family, on the nobility, and on the entire established apparatus of power in the Catholic church-state and its ideological legitimations. To say that the French Revolution constituted an assault on 'the established religion' requires a deconstruction of what 'religion' meant in the old regime. Religion meant not only clerical elites but the totality of the power relations of the French Catholic church-state as represented by the ideology of the ancient regime. More than this, the French Revolution was a significant transfiguration of the meaning of 'religion', a transfiguration which in its own way was also occurring in the recent new power formation of the United States of America and its rejection of the Anglican church-state of which the King of England was head. The meaning of religion was, in these revolutions, being transformed into a private right separated from the new non-religious state, later to be referred to, in another transformation of meanings, as 'the secular', that also produced the science of societies.

Smith lists the properties that go to make up modern nationalisms as Ethnic Election, Sacred Territory, Ethno-history, and National Sacrifice. The belief in Ethnic Election is the belief in the 'chosen people' (2000: 804). Smith usefully distinguishes two senses of a chosen people: missionary and covenantal. He gives both 'religious' and 'secular' examples of the missionary type of belief in a chosen people. The 'religious' type 'consists in the intense belief that the community has been chosen by the deity for a special religious task or mission, usually to defend the deity's representative or church on earth, or to convert the heathen to the "one and true" religion, or simply to expand the realm of the religion through territorial acquisitions' (2000: 804). He gives as examples the Frankish and Capetian kings of France fighting for Catholic Christendom against the Muslims or heathens; the Byzantine emperors and their Russian successor the tsars as guardians and warriors of the true faith; medieval Hungary fighting the Mongols and Ottomans ... in Catalonia during the *Reconquista*. He also gives two Muslim examples: the Arabs after their conversion to Islam, and the Shi'ite Persians under Safavid rule.

But in which sense were these 'religious' missions, as distinct from Catholic, or Orthodox Christian, or Muslim missions? None of these people would have been thinking in terms of a modern distinction between 'religion' and a non-religious secular. And none of them would have represented themselves as fighting for one religion against another. They were fighting for Christian Truth as against heresy and paganism. The word 'religion' would presumably have been unknown to any of them. No doubt the Christians made a Latinate distinction between the ecclesiastical and the temporal, but it is notable that, unlike modern 'secular' states, it was the arm of legitimate government – kings, emperors and tsars – that pursued these missions. It is not as if the rulers were secular in the modern sense of 'non-religious'. The Latin referent for secular usually stood for priests in contrast to *religiones*, the orders of friars, monks and nuns. If Christian kings and emperors were referred to as the secular powers, it would not have been in the modern sense of non-religious. Christianity was not 'a religion' among others, and it is unlikely that the Muslim powers imagined it that way either. The backward transmission of modern nuances distorts our understanding and representation of the past. Nor were these missions solely undertaken to spread a personal doctrine of salvation in the way that modern evangelical missionaries might do, even though such an individual soteriology can be taken as included. To be Christian was to be rational, to be a proper human being, to practise the disciplines of civility. This is why mass conversions were frequently the order of the day. To conquer other peoples was to establish a Christian sovereignty, to establish the reign of Christ on earth. Only Christian (or, in the case of Muslims, Islamic) rule could be considered legitimate.

It seems worth noting that all the examples of the 'religious' missionary type of nationalism are, with one exception, taken from Christian and Muslim examples – Iranian Shi'ites, and Protestant revivalists in the US. Should Khomeini be considered a 'religious' leader, with its implied separation from secular politics and the secular state? I do not know how these terms translate into Persian, but probably with some difficulty. The exception is the Bharatiya Janata Party (the BJP) in Hindu India. The choice of the BJP as an example of 'religious' as distinct from 'secular' nationalism is problematic, and may throw some light on the wider difficulties of distinguishing the religious from the secular according to the dominant modern sociological discourse which deploys these term as though they pick out some clear and stable descriptive content, often without knowing very much about the people they refer to. The assumption by Western scholars that Hindu nationalism is 'religious' nationalism is unreliable, since it shows no awareness of the contested meanings of these categories. Spokesmen for the BJP and Rashtriya Swayamsevak Sangh (RSS) have said that they are true secularists, and that Indian secularism must be based on the long, historical stream of Hindu convention. For example, L.K. Advani, at one time a member of the RSS and President of the BJP, said in an interview:

> Positive secularism flows from our commitment to national unity which is an article of faith for us and not just a slogan to be converted into slick spots for the TV. Our Constitution seeks to strengthen this unity by rejecting theocracy and by guaranteeing equality to all citizens, irrespective of their religion. These are two principal facets of secularism as our Constitution makers conceived them. For most politicians in the country, however, secularism has become just a device for garnering block minority votes. ... The BJP believes in Positive Secularism; the Congress-I and most other parties subscribe only to Vote Secularism. Positive Secularism means: justice for all, but appeasement of none (Advani 2007: 284–5).

Another influential spokeman for Hindutva nationalism was Atal Behari Vajpayee, who was a member of the RSS, entered the Jana Sangh, and was the first President of the new BJP between 1980 and 1986. He was also Prime Minister of India three times. I present some edited extracts from his 'The Bane of Pseudo-Secularism' (in Jaffrelot 2007: 315–18):

> Secular just means pertaining to this world ... Secular does not mean anti-religious or non-religious. In fact the people of India can never be secular in this sense. Secularism just means an impartial attitude of the State towards all modes of worship. The Jana Sangh champions the cause of such an impartial state and does not believe in adopting any one mode of worship as the religion of the State ... It is a matter of surprise that the party which declares its secularism from house tops and is the first to berate communalism not only compromises with communal elements for political ends but unashamedly supports minority demands in the guise of protecting minority interests. ... The solution of all problems of Bharat lies in arousing a strong sense of nationalism. Single-minded devotion to the nation and a readiness to sweat and if necessary also to give up everything can alone enable us to rise above sectarian, linguistic and religious considerations and behave like citizens of one great nation.

It can be seen from these passages that there is no easy identification of BJP or Hindutva nationalism with 'religion' as distinct from 'secular'. The very terms are contested. This becomes even more pertinent when we are reminded of the question of translation, for only educated elites speak and read English. Millions of Indians do not. In his 'Secularism, the Indian Concept', Vajpayee (2007) argues that there is a fundamental difference between the Western and the Indian meanings of 'secular':

> The temporal or political power of the State maintained its equipoise because of the teachings of the Acharyas. This balance was the result of the moral and altruistic outlook. We have had the tradition of discipline and not the rule by religious leaders ... The moral and material well being of the people can be ensured by the State acting according to Dharma. We find that Dharma is used in Indian thought in a much broader sense and in different contexts than the word 'religion', though often Dharma and religion are used as synonyms ... Dharma is also used in the sense of duty. Therefore, in the social context, Dharma is important. Dharma is the ensemble of the rules and regulations followed in various facets of human life of an individual and the society as a whole. ... We must realize the difference between Dharma and religion. Religion is related to certain definite beliefs ... Dharma is not entirely dependent upon beliefs. A person may or may not have any religious faith but he could still be called 'Dharmik'. That means he has good qualities. Essentially, Dharma is the way of life. ... 'Shatpath Brahmin' says that 'Dharma is the Ruler of a Ruler, the supreme authority lies in Dharma'. The Mahabharata also provides evidence that the king had to follow the authority of Dharma ... Mahatma Gandhi describes the correct attitude towards religion as 'Sarva Dharma Sambhava', equal respect to all religions. The concept of 'Sarva Dharma Sambhava' is somewhat different from the European secularism which is independent of religion ... We may say that the Indian concept of secularism is that of Sarva Dharma Sambhava ... Sarva Dharma Sambhava is not against any religion. It treats all religions with equal respect. And therefore it can be said that the Indian concept of secularism is more positive.

Vajpayee's strategy is to define a specific Indian sense of secularism by interpreting it according to *dharma* as a broad and ancient cultural concept of order more fundamental and inclusive than any specific 'religion'. According to him, and speaking with his strong identification with Hindutva nationalism, India already has its own tradition of secular order which should not be confused with specific religions but which adjudicates fairly and with tolerance between specific religions. His argument suggests that Hindu traditional culture is not religious but secular, being based on a concept of *dharmik* order that has governed all groups and all orders of power. The ruler has been as subject to *dharma* as the subject. Religions, by which he has Muslim, Sikh and other minorities in mind, are tolerated within the broad purvey of secular *dharma*. All who follow *dharma* are therefore by implication Hindu, even while continuing to practise their minority religion. Notice that he says that one can still be a good follower of *dharma* even if one does not follow any religion.

The objections to the basis for Hindu nationalism are obvious. Dalits and Muslims see *dharma* as central to Brahmanical ideology and caste. In one way or another, equating 'Hindu *dharma*' with shared ethnicity and making such an ideological category central to the demands and definition of the 'secular' state is a way to make Muslim and untouchable castes subordinated to Brahmin culture. But my purpose in quoting these politicians at length is to indicate how unstable and contested the religion–secular categories are, and how unreliable as ways of ordering our own view of the world. I do not know enough about Iran to be able to say whether or not similar debates about the meaning(s) of religion and secularism were taking place there. It would be surprising if they were not. But once the actual discourses on these categories have been historicized and contextualized in situations of power contestation, and the problems of translation taken into consideration, then the idea that they can provide us with useful descriptive and analytical categories for knowledge of what is in the world, reveals itself as a myth, an Anglophone ideology masquerading as a factual science.

I now turn to look in more detail at the work of one of the contributors to *Religion in International Relations: The Return from Exile*: Scott M. Thomas, who has been rightly and widely praised for his book *The Global Resurgence of Religion and the Transformation of International Religions* (Thomas 2005).

## Notes

1.    Ernest Gellner (1983); Eric Hobsbawm (1990); Benedict Anderson (1991).
2.    Emile Durkheim (2001).
3.    I have discussed these points, made by many authors, in detail throughout my *Ideology of Religious Studies* (Fitzgerald 2000).
4.    See, for instance, Tomoko Masuzawa (2005).
5.    I do not know the answer to these questions, but they surely need addressing.
6.    Within Religious Studies, one of the best-known recent critics of the field and its central category is Russell M. McCutcheon. See, for example, his *Manufacturing Religion* (1997), and *Critics Not Caretakers* (2001).
7.    One such I might recommend would be Ivan Strenski's well-researched and sophisticated introductory companion volumes: *Thinking About Religion: An Historical Introduction to Theories of Religion* (2006a), and *Thinking About Religion: A Reader* (2006b). Other good books are Seth D. Kunin (ed.) *Theories of Religion: A Reader* (2006), and Daniel L. Pals, *Seven Theories of Religion* (1996).

# Chapter 9

## Religion Resurging

Scott M. Thomas has been widely praised for his book *The Global Resurgence of Religion and the Transformation of International Relations* (2005). This is an ambitious book with many potentially fertile ideas. In his chapter (Thomas 2003) in Fabio Petito and Pavlos Hatzopolous' collection *The Return from Exile*, discussed in Chapter 8 of this volume, Thomas makes an interesting attempt to historically problematize the category of religion, with the added virtue of drawing on the insights of critical scholars from other disciplines, such as Talal Asad (2003: 47), John Bossy (2003: 47) and William T. Cavanaugh (2003: 27) to name only a few.[1] Referring to 'the modern invention of religion', he suggests that '[a]t issue is the meaning of religion in early modern Europe, and how we understand religion today' (Thomas 2003: 25). He refers to 'the invention of religion as part of the rise of western modernity' (2003: 28). He notices rightly that 'the rise of the modern state is the other part of the story ...' (2003: 27). He claims that:

> Most scholars of early modern Europe now recognise that the confusion over the role of religion and other political and socio-economic forces in the debate on the Wars of Religion was based on retrospectively applying a modern concept of religion – as a set of privately held doctrines or beliefs – to societies that had yet to make this transition (2003: 25).

That Thomas's aim seems to be a radical and critical questioning of the ideological functions of the religion and secular politics binary and much else that hangs on it appears to be made clear in the opening paragraph of the first chapter of his book:

> The concept of religion was invented as part of the political mythology of liberalism and now has emerged as a universal concept applicable to other cultures and civilizations. This understanding of religion is used to legitimate a form of liberal politics that considers the mixing of politics and religion to be violent and dangerous to reason, freedom, and political stability (Thomas 2005: 21).

Unfortunately Thomas continues the paragraph ambiguously, as though he is not quite sure whether or not he wants to critique the category of religion or simply make statements about religion as though religion had some objective existence in the world. Repeating the expression in his title, he continues:

> The global resurgence of religion, however, challenges the concepts of social theory that interpret public religion in this way. It challenges the idea that secular reason can provide a neutral stance from which to interpret religion, and it opens up the possibility of multiple ways of being 'modern', making 'progress', or being 'developed' … (2005: 21).

The radical pronouncements that appear here and there suggest that Thomas is concerned with the challenge that problematizing 'religion' as a category implies for International Relations as a 'secular' discipline – a problem because, if religion is a modern invention, as I think he rightly argues in places, then not only IR but everything that is conventionally (and juridically) placed in that category is logically and discursively dependent on 'religion' for its conceptualization. Thomas acknowledges the implications of this insight for the wider academy and much else (2005: 17).

But for most of the book, far from treating 'religion' as a rhetorical invention with a crucial part to play in the 'mythology of liberalism', and far from critiquing an understanding of 'religion' that constructs it as a real and present danger to liberal reason and freedom, Thomas energetically re-inscribes the category along with its ideological binary 'secular liberalism' as a fundamental organizing principle of his book. Even in the paragraph just quoted, Thomas moves from saying 'The concept of religion was invented as part of the political mythology of liberalism' to referring only two sentences later to 'The global resurgence of religion', as though there could be any such thing.

The author stays safely within the well-worn discursive conventions of the 'mythology of liberalism' that he also wants to critique, and in this way contributes to the rhetoric on religion and its implicit distinction from secular reason. I would suggest that his position remains unresolved because the conclusions he must draw are too radical. Too much is at stake. For the problem of the retrospective application of a modern concept 'as a set of privately held doctrines or beliefs', set apart from the non-religious state and so on, ineluctably implies the problem of the retrospective application of these other modern reified concepts such as 'socio-economic forces' which the modern concept of religion has made possible. If the modern secular state has depended for its conceptualization on the related concept of religion as a private right of faith in unseen mystical powers separated from the state, as in my view Thomas would be right to argue, then so have those modern discourses which construct 'political and socio-economic forces'.[2]

Thomas says that the 'persistence of secularization theory despite the global resurgence of culture and religion is rooted in modernization theory' (2005:

53). It is not clear whether Thomas is agreeing with Bellah or not when he cites him (Bellah) as describing secularization as a 'myth' (2005: 53). I think yes and no, because while Thomas seems from time to time to take the critical posture, his position is largely trapped within the same myth.

The entire secularization thesis is circular, a circularity built into the very ground-base of the so-called social scientific study of religion. Any modern domain that is represented as non-religious secular must logically depend on the modern invention of religion as if it is a separate domain with essentially different characteristics. Inversely, the modern invention of religion has been made possible by the parasitic modern invention of these putative non-religious secular 'forces'.

However, are these 'forces' that are classified in the modern way as non-religious 'secular' of an essentially different kind from the mystical or magical powers associated with 'religion'? We have seen wealthy people and poor people, bars of gold and stacks of paper (or nowadays digitized) money, and buildings called banks where they tend to accumulate or be exchanged. We have seen bank statements, inventories, bills of lading and other devices. We have seen people working in places called factories which produce goods that are traded in other places called shops, stores, showrooms, stalls, market places and that are shipped in trucks, ships, planes and trains. Yet no one has ever seen a 'socio-economic force'. Socio-economic forces are arguably themselves metaphysical postulates invented to direct, focus and explain what we do see and provide us with ways of acting in the world. Is there a discernibly *essential* difference between a socio-economic force and the healing powers attributed to the tombs of saints and sacralized kings? Socio-economic forces, like 'religions', look themselves to be objects of collective faith.

The two sides of the religion–secular binary are mutually parasitic, and therefore form one category of the collective imagination pretending to be two, distinguished from each other by reference to two different realities, the supernatural and the natural, or the metaphysical and the empirical, or faith as distinct from knowledge. The structure of the whole discourse in the final analysis is self-confirming and circular. From the position of one half of the binary – the secular – social scientists imagine that they are having a meaningful discussion about objects in the world called religions which on closer examination turn out to be the obverse side of the same dichotomous category; inverse images of what they suppose they are not – arbitrary demarcations of everything and anything that appears to be different from what they imagine characterizes their own secular position. I would argue that the whole enterprise is a conceptual illusion constructed by mirrors, an illusion which itself cannot be inferred from any number of empirical observations.

In contrast I argue that, for Thomas to take his critical insight to its logical conclusion, the fully interconnected myth of the religion–secular binary in its various guises needs to be taken whole, even if that means questioning our own positionality as secular citizens and academics, and upsetting modern faith-based orthodoxies such as social science and economics. The more we pursue this agenda, the more controversial it will become, because the issues are not merely intellectual and academic ones.

To go beyond the grand narrative also, in my own view, requires us to question belief in modern non-observable divinities such as socio-economic forces, capital, private property, self-regulating markets and the nation state. For these objects of modern devotion are disguised in the grand narrative of secular progress and rationality as commonplaces in accord with 'natural' reason. They are the objective realities that we find in the world and with which we must grapple. To deny these values in which we place our faith may be close to heresy, and not essentially different from heresy. In some societies it is a crime to burn a bank note or a national flag, for they both symbolically contain sacred mystical powers that are considered to keep the world or the nation from falling off its axis. Yet, like witches and their mystical powers, no one has ever seen capital, or private property, or self-regulating markets, or socio-economic forces, or nation states. Like witches, gods, the efficacy of the Mass, and other mystical powers and processes, these articles of modern faith are unavailable for empirical inspection. We act *as though* they exist, claim to find convincing evidence that they exist, and on the basis of such acts of faith we have collectively constructed a panoply of laws, theoretical models, bureaucratic procedures, and modes of regulation, enforcement and punishment that police the institutionalization of historically-contingent classifications and forms of life.

In the introduction to *The Global Resurgence*, Thomas reviews some of the historically recent events, including 9/11, that have had an impact on IR. This leads him to make assertions about religion that go in the opposite direction from the more searching and critical insights contained in the paragraphs reproduced at the beginning of this chapter. He says:

> The first theme indicated by these momentous events is the overall message of this book. There is a global resurgence of religion taking place throughout the world that is challenging our interpretation of the modern world – what it means to be modern – and this has implications for our understanding of how culture and religion influence international relations. ... [T]he global resurgence of religion taking place in the developed world ... is part of a larger crisis of modernity in the West. It reflects a deeper and more widespread disillusionment with a modernity that reduces the world to what can be perceived and controlled through reason, science, and technology, and leaves out the sacred, religion, or spirituality (2005: 10).

If this is the overall message of his book, as the author states, then it tends to contradict the more radical and interesting attempt to critique the central categories of description and analysis that are themselves fundamental to modernity. One of the sources of 'the crisis of modernity in the West' is the increasing recognition that Anglophone and more generally Europhone categories do not do the work of universal knowledge construction that has hitherto been assumed. If the fundamental dichotomous categories 'religion' and 'secular' are part of the problem in our understanding of the world, as Thomas rightly seems to claim, then those categories need to be bracketed and put into quarantine, not re-inscribed into the critique itself. The assertion that there is 'a global resurgence of religion taking place throughout the world' reads as a statement of fact, but the fact is constructed on the back of the very same problematic categories. Such a statement – and it is not an isolated example, for the problem pervades the whole book – confuses two different kinds of proposition: one that 'religion' has an objective existence and a resurging activity in the real world which must be recognised and noticed if we are to understand; the other that there is a powerful and widespread Anglophone discourse with persuasive power that constructs this illusion *as though* it described real events.

If my argument is correct, then the following claims at the end of Thomas's first chapter, concerning the meaning of 'postmodern', are burdened with problems of meaning. Thomas says:

[T]he global resurgence of religion cannot only be interpreted as a 'funda-mentalist' or 'anti-modern' reaction to the inevitable and inexorable spread of modernization and globalization ... the global resurgence of religion can be understood as ... part of a wider, already existing critique of global modernity, authenticity, and development. A postmodern perspective begins with a recognition that modernity's discontents have shown us that the Enlightenment's promise of freedom, autonomy, and meaning through rationality and knowledge has turned out to be a hollow one. It shares a basic insight with those artists, theologians, and cultural critics who recognise the limits to the disenchantment of the world, a trend foreseen by George Simmel over a century ago, who worried that the growing attachment to this 'world of things' would steadily devalue the human world ... For all these reasons the twentieth century may be the last modern century ... A truly multicultural international society is being formed for the first time, and finding out what it means to take cultural and religious pluralism seriously is one of the most important aspects of international politics in the twenty-first century (2005: 44–5).

First of all, if the term 'postmodern' has any useful and deconstructive deployment, I suggest it must at least indicate a critical methodological distancing ourselves from the very basic categories presupposed *by* the myth of modernity. Instead of remaining as conceptual tools in our descriptions and analyses, as they are in these sentences, they become the problematic focus of our critical attention. Then what can be meant by such an expression as 'cultural and religious pluralism'? How are we supposed to distinguish between culture and religion? Are 'culture' and 'religion' distinct from 'politics'? If 'the Enlightenment's promise of freedom, autonomy, and meaning through rationality and knowledge' is hollow, in what way is Thomas's claim about the resurgence of religion less hollow? What kind of evidence would we need to support his claim that a 'truly multicultural international society is being formed for the first time'?

What Thomas definitively classifies as resurgent 'religion' problematically includes 'charismatic Catholics and Catholic conservatives, evangelicals and Pentecostal Protestants, New Age spiritualists, Western Buddhists, and Japanese traditionalists ...' (2005: 10–11) One can understand the overwhelming sense of naturalness and inevitability in classifying Christian institutions, practices and movements as 'religion'. For historical reasons it seems counterintuitive to question that deployment. But, as I have already indicated in several places in the present volume, even this is problematic. Briefly, there is a historical Protestant tradition deriving from the Reformation that represents itself as Our Protestant Religion, meaning true religion in contradistinction to paganism, with the Catholic Church as paganism's prime example (the Whore of Babylon). But early modern rhetorical uses of 'religion' are profoundly different from the more recent discourse on religion and religions as universal, ubiquitous, and therefore as a neutral tool in the construction of secular knowledge. I have argued in *Discourse on Civility and Barbarity* (Fitzgerald 2007a) that religion as a discursive domain encompassed what subsequently came to be rhetorically constructed as distinct domains, both church and state. The idea of the state as a non-religious centre of rational governance that licenses 'religion' as a private right is surely itself part of the invention of modernity that Thomas has indicated when he says 'the rise of the modern state is the other part of the story ...'. The idea that 'religion' is equated solely with 'church', while the state is equated with secular 'politics', is not true of the dominant discourses of early modern England nor of Christendom generally; but is integral to the modern myth of religion and the non-religious secular.

It is true that, in early modern Anglophone Protestant discourse, the term 'religion' was sometimes applied to non-Christian practices as they were increasingly encountered in different parts of the world, for example in plantations and colonies, as England increased its overseas interests after the late sixteenth century. Presumably something similar was happening in other European languages, though these need to be researched in their own terms. However, I have argued that this deployment of the term when it occurred implied *false* religion, meaning an irrational substitute for true religion, Christian revelation.[3] This negative and perhaps ironic kind of usage did gradually develop into a more neutral discursive formation during the enlightenment and especially after the mid-nineteenth century with the foundation of the scientific study of religion by scholars such as Max Müller and C.P. Tiele. But even these were Protestant Christians, albeit liberals, who assumed that Protestant Christianity was the most rational and deepest truth of the meaning of human existence, and the 'religions of the world' were frequently constructed in European languages on the assumption that they were less than perfect revelations or interpretations of the one truth perfectly revealed for all time in the Bible and Jesus Christ. Thus, even in the attempt to found an objective academic discipline of religious studies since the nineteenth century, there has always existed this potential ambiguity between on the one hand the idea of religion as a neutral marker of a generic universal manifesting as specific 'religions', in principle in all human groups, and separated from non-religious practices, and on the other hand the older deployment of religion as Christian truth in contrast to idolatrous paganisms. (See my discussion in Chapter 11.)

If we consider, from a long-term perspective, the attempts by scholars to found an objective Science of Religion, we can see that the emergence of this theorized discourse on the religions of the world has coincided with the emergence of the discourse on the non-religious secular state, politics, economics and the secular university. On the surface, at least, in this newer discourse the binary opposite of 'religion' became the non-religious secular, a term that continues ambiguously to be applied in two analytically separable semantic contexts, on the one hand the non-religious domains, thus apparently displacing the older binary between Christian Truth and pagan irrationality, but on the other hand the secular priesthood, an ancient status which still survives within Catholicism and some traditions of Anglicanism. It would be strange to say in modern parlance that the secular priesthood was non-religious.

The continuity of some of the same terminology (religion, secular) has disguised the way that these two analytically separable discourses and their different meanings have shadowed each other, and how the claim to objective knowledge of religions continues an older Christian colonial hegemony in a new guise. These are logically two different discourses, but the terms 'religion' and 'secular', by providing a surface but credible appearance of continuity, have maintained ambiguity at different levels. In some evangelical Protestant missions registered in the US as religious charities under the constitutional separation of religion and the secular state, the language of the older discourse on true religion as against pagan idolatry is still resorted to by missionaries in the field.[4] In England, where the universities and the modern disciplines within them such as IR represent themselves as secular, or where the media polices the boundaries whenever the Bishops (now classified as 'religious', with a profoundly different nuance from the older term 'ecclesiastical') appear to be straying into 'politics', the situation at the level of the separation of church and state is notoriously less clear. That the coronation of the monarch is still enacted in a church by a priest, and includes the ancient sacred ritual of anointing, indicates the powerful survival of the older discourse in which the monarch's estate embodied in the commonwealth is a divine manifestation of the reign of Christ.[5] The monarch may have been referred to sometimes as 'secular', but more commonly as 'our sacred king' or our sacred queen. The attempt to separate 'sacred' from 'secular' and confine it to 'religion' is part of the modern discursive trick, for it simultaneously embeds the deeply unquestioned assumption that the world of capital, the nation state, private property, selfish individuals as rational maximizers, self-regulating markets, and the rest of secular modernity are simply the reality which rational moderns encounter.

If, following Thomas, we are to use the terminology of enchantment and disenchantment at all, then it is we who are producing and reproducing the discursive categories that construct this modern division. But are we not enchanted by capital and private property? Are we not enchanted by images of desire on the billboards and the media advertising? Are we not enchanted by the rituals of the US Presidency and the raising and lowering of the Stars and Stripes? Are we not enchanted by the flowing rhetoric of freedom, democracy and the liberation of all humans from tyranny? Modernity is surely its own kind of enchantment. The sociological conceit that the world became disenchanted due to the progress of scientific rationality, stripped of the illusions of magic and the mystical, is itself part of the construction of modernity.[6]

Thus, when Thomas claims that there is 'a global resurgence of religion taking place throughout the world', and links this with 9/11 and terrorism, he could be interpreted as re-inscribing both these analytically separable discourses on religion simultaneously. On the one hand by reproducing the rhetoric on religion as an essence that incarnates, or an agent that acts in the world, he is simultaneously constructing (by exclusion) the secularity of his own (IR) academic positionality – the very modernity that in other parts of the book he made us think he wanted to challenge. On the other hand, the link of religion with terror and irrationality feeds into an older Orientalism, one of Christian civility and rationality against pagan barbarity. And even if Thomas's theoretical intentions were clear, which unfortunately they are not, different readings are available for different readerships. Meanings that we as authors are not fully aware of are being continually transmitted, deployed and re-confirmed in the public arena.

Paganism might historically have been described as *irreligion* or as *anti-religion*, in the sense that paganism constitutes an irrational denial of the truth of Christian revelation, a denial inspired by Satan. But this is significantly different from the concept of *non-religious* secular, indicating how important it is to clarify the historically contextualized meanings of words.

Thomas includes Buddhism as resurgent, even though he qualifies it here with 'western'. Nevertheless, the Anglophone term Buddhism, along its Europhone equivalents, is itself a modern invention, and part of the more general modern invention of religion, religions and world religions (King 1999; Masuzawa 2005). Historically, Catholics and Protestants have considered Buddhism to be pagan, the work of the Devil (Gombrich 1988), and it is easy to establish that such categorization has been popular with Christian missionaries until surprisingly recently, and probably lurks as a conscious or unconscious assumption in much of the Anglophone discoursing on religion today.

*Western* Buddhisms, like Christianities of various kinds, may be classified as 'religions' by the non-religious secular state, but if Buddhists accept this classification at all, it might be because the state requires it. Is Buddhism a religion? Or is *buddha dhamma* a line of transmission of the truth discovered by Gotama Shakyamuni? I discussed the problems of trying to identify 'Buddhism' in South and East Asia in Chapter 4. I suggest it depends on who is using which words in which context and for what purposes. The ambiguity is present in India, where 'Buddhist' is constitutionally defined as a religious category. Yet several self-identifying Buddhist Dalits told me that the secular Republican Constitution is itself a Buddhist document because of the role played in its writing by Dr Ambedkar, the First Law Minister of India, whom many refer to as a Bodhisattva. One Israeli researcher of the Israel Vipassana Trust in Israel brings out some of the complexity of classification when he says:

[M]ost Israeli Dhamma practitioners do not see their identities, practices and associations as being religious. They claim that they practice Dhamma rather than Buddhism, or that Buddhism is not a religion. (Those who say that they practice Dhamma distinguish between Buddhism as a religion and Dhamma as not religious. Those who say they practice Buddhism refer to Buddhism as not religious.)[7]

Thomas may thus unintentionally be imposing this nomenclature on Buddhists for his own ideological (secular) purposes disguised as neutral or disinterested description, and tacitly confirming the legitimacy of state-enforced classifications.

To include Western Buddhists may therefore be problematic, unless the author is merely saying that specific Buddhist groups are classified by the state as 'religions'. This is significantly different from asserting that they *are* resurgent religions. And this problem seems even more dubious with the inclusion of what he refers to as 'Japanese traditionalists'. How do these fit into the same classificatory category, 'religion', as Western Buddhists and Pentecostal Christians, and all the multitude of other institutionalized practices that are collected together under this single Anglophone category from their different linguistic and cultural contexts? Why would it be any more appropriate to classify Japanese 'traditionalists' as 'religious' than members of the British National Front?

A moment's reflection suggests how astonishing it is that this procedure, whereby institutions and practices embedded in utterly different linguistic and cultural matrixes are all classified under the same Anglophone category, 'religion', a term which even in English is itself historically contested, ambiguous and unclear in meaning, should be so widely accepted that it seems counterintuitive to question it. This indicates the degree to which this ideological construction has been transformed through usage and the power of rhetoric into an intuitive commonplace that it would be eccentric (or danger-ously radical) to question. We surely have to strive to answer the pressing question about what drives us in our strange classificatory practices? Why do we feel compelled by some unquestioned intuition to place 'Buddhists' (itself a grand category of bewildering diversity) and 'Japanese traditionalists' into the same category as Imams, the Pope, or the Zande readers of chicken entrails, but to exclude the elaborate rituals of the City of London, the magic of socio-economic forces, or the mystifying powers of the nation state?

As if this is not problematic enough, Thomas imagines 'religion' as though it is one essence that can 'resurge' globally in different manifestations. It is thus part of the stuff that myths and metaphysics are made of. These categories are not themselves inductions from empirical observation, but the *a priori* categories of modernity still being asserted in a work that claims to question them. They are themselves the basis for a system of classification that constructs the sacred canopy of global capital.

Locating himself in postmodernity, the author says that 'Postmodernity challenges the idea that in our era there is still a grand narrative – the Western concept of modernity – a single overall character and direction to the meaning of progress, modernity, or development for all countries' (2005: 11).

If, however, this edifice of ideological modernity and progress is under-pinned and facilitated by the binary split between religion and the secular, a specific historical formation that claims universal application, then Thomas is committing himself to the grand narrative. For surely the modern invention and re-invention of religion and religions are themselves a significant part of the grand narrative of progress and rationality. There is a deep unresolved tension at the heart of Thomas's book, between on the one hand a radical reappraisal of 'religion' and its 'secular' binary as categories, or as two faces of the same category, and on the other hand his continued assertion of religion as an object or agent in the world, something that resurges and returns from exile and challenges its exclusion as a causal force in IR representations of world affairs.

That Thomas has not radically distanced himself from the grand narrative can be just about discerned in his fourth chapter, entitled 'The Soul of the World? Religious Non-State Actors and International Relations Theory'. I say 'just about discerned', because the grand narrative of modernity and progress does usually have some clearly discernible pathways, directions, signposts and prompts. But for this reader, admittedly naïve and untrained in the arcane arts of International Relations, I finished reading the chapter for the third time in a state of perplexity. I wonder if any real knowledge about the world has been conveyed to anyone, rather than an incoherent jumble of terms.

Perhaps this is unfair, because we do need terms that make useful distinctions, and Thomas is commendably and ambitiously striving to be comprehensive in his book. This may actually be his problem. He may be caught between two contradictory ambitions. One of his ambitions is to radically question the way the modern liberal West constructs its knowledge of the world, and to expose the way power and dominance become veiled behind illusions of objectivity and neutrality. The other ambition is to tell us all he can about the global resurgence of religion and the transformation of IR. These contradictory aims – the construction of knowledge and its simultaneous critique – may help to explain why so much of the prose confuses rather than clarifies.

The chapter 'examines a variety of types of religious non-state actors' (2005: 99), under section headings such as Substate Actors, Transnational Actors, Inter-Governmental Organizations, Transnational Religion, Epistemic Communities, Social Movements, and Global Civil Society. Like most of the book, this chapter is replete with statements, distinctions, descriptions, analyses and summaries in which categories with difficult-to-specify meanings such as religion, secular, politics, economics, and culture are intended to play a significant role. On the first one-and-a-half pages (2005: 97–8) of this chapter alone, that is to say in about 52 lines of text, all these expressions appear: 'the power of religion', 'the secular world of international relations', 'religious leaders, orders, and movements', 'religious non-state actors', 'main world religions', 'the global resurgence of religion', the 'evolving role of religion in international relations', 'social and religious changes', 'religious groups and communities', 'religion … rooted in particular types of faith communities', 'global religious subcultures or diaspora communities', 'the cultural, religious, and political landscape of world politics', 'religion as a global phenomena', 'faith communities around the world', and 'new religious movements'.

A major problem for the reader is to understand how terms such as 'religion' in the singular, 'religions' in the plural, 'new religious movements', religious changes, social changes (are religious changes not social changes?), faith communities and political landscapes (as for example in 'the political landscape of world politics') can be deployed to indicate clearly distinct, or partly distinct, or unseparated domains or processes. And this becomes of especial concern in the critical context that Thomas specified as part of his theoretical problematic, the modern invention of religion as part of modern liberal ideology and the corresponding invention of the modern non-religious nation state.

Let me make another, though connected, comment that at first may seem strange for one academic reviewing the work of another. This concerns the convention of referencing. In many if not most forms of academic production, it is rightly taken as a sign of accountability and thus legitimacy to back up one's statements with clear and frequent referencing. This is especially true in those contexts where one is aiming to criticise, amend and add to an already existing body of knowledge. However, in more philosophical or analytical contexts, where the main purpose is to look critically at what already exists as knowledge, to analyse how it has come to be put together in the way that it has, and to consider problems of meaning and epistemology, then references to authoritative sources outside the logic of the argument itself may become less urgent or necessary. It is in this context of referencing that the conflict of contradictory aims of Thomas's book shows up again. Is he trying to give us new and additional factual information about the resurgence of religion in the world? Or is he trying to question the liberal myth of modernity that has depended on the invention of religion and the secular nation state? In the chapter in question, containing roughly 22 pages dealing with complex issues in IR, there are 58 notes referencing approximately that number of books and articles. It is a commendable sign of wide and intense reading on difficult topics, a sign that indicates that Thomas is a serious scholar. My problem is a methodological one. If the central task is to critically problematize modern categories and the religious and secular domains that they authorize, then the texts which are taken to substantiate Thomas's claims constitute, for both reader and writer, a problem of monitoring at the very least! What are the purposes of all these authors? Are they providing additional grist to the mill for the discourse on religion's resurgence and its angry incarnation in reified entities such as Islam, Buddhism and Hinduism? Are these authors, or some of them, recycling the myths of modernity? Or are they all critical and deconstructive, aimed at exposing the ideological function of modern invented religion? How can the reader feel confident, short of reading every book herself, that all these cited authors share the same critical concern? For the modern discourse on religion and its relation to the invention of the secular state is pervasive, and not widely seen as a problem. Consequently it seems unlikely that many of the authors cited and quoted are even aware of the problem that Thomas suggested he was confronting.

The point that I am trying to make here is this. If one is seriously attempting to critique those categories that form the basis of modern assumptions about the world, then this immediately changes one's theoretical relationship to the vast majority of texts in the field. Very few authors writing from the perspective of IR, politics, economics or the social sciences take a critical approach to the basic categories that structure the field in which they are working. Most academics, like most politicians, journalists and judges, use terms like religion, secular, politics, state, economics and their adjectival forms as though their meanings are self-evident. Having adopted discursive formations in the normal way, and having pragmatic goals to achieve, it is not reasonable to expect them to have realised with Thomas that '[t]he concept of religion was invented as part of the political mythology of liberalism ...'. The vast majority of Anglophone and Europhone speakers will find such an idea as the modern invention of religion to be counter-intuitive. In such a situation of dense referencing it is unclear which authors really support which part of Thomas's theoretical aims. Thus the density of reading and referencing backfires, and tends to cloud the text rather than clarify it.

But this point that I make in passing is merely one additional angle on the fundamental problem in deciphering the author's text. The primary problem is with Thomas's own text itself. For the radical aim of critique that Thomas had led this reader to expect is betrayed on almost every page. Thomas wants to have it both ways. He wants to set himself up as a radical thinker with new ideas about the constitution of modernity and its implications for the state and international relations, as in his claim that '[a] postmodern perspective begins with a recognition that modernity's discontents have shown us that the Enlightenment's promise of freedom, autonomy, and meaning through rationality and knowledge has turned out to be a hollow one'. But at the same time he feels free to consolidate the mystifications of international relations by following the comfortable and well-worn discursive grooves of modern classifications.

Like all who have not dwelt on the issue, Thomas knows intuitively what are religions and who are religious leaders, and thus tacitly what and who are not. The Pope, Francis of Assisi, the Dalai Lama, Osama bin Laden – all are mentioned on the first page of the chapter:

> What is the power of religion and how does it operate in the secular world of international relations? The communist leaders in Poland and the Soviet Union discovered that the Pope had no army divisions but he had legions of followers. So did Francis of Assisi in his day, and so do the Franciscans and the Sufi orders, and the Dalai Lama and Osama bin Laden, and countless other religious leaders, orders, and movements in our time. How should we understand the meaning and influence of these religious non-state actors or non-governmental organizations (NGOs) in international relations today? (2005: 97).

But this statement ignores all the problems with the strategic deployment of unstable and contested terms in the context of modernity. The first point is that the opening sentence reifies 'religion' as a 'power' existing *in* the binary reification of 'the secular world'. This re-inscribes modern discourses as though they are describing objective reality. The Pope, who inherits from the Roman Emperor one of his official titles as *pontifex maximus,* and who traditionally has been referred to as both prince and priest, is here simply listed as a religious leader. Does this imply that he is not political? Or that he is ideally religious but actually, illegitimately, also political? This way of describing the Pope is surely part of the modern problem of classification that first separates religion and politics as two distinct essences and then is stymied on the vast range of marginal cases. Again, that the Dalai Lama is widely classified in English – and seems nowadays to classify himself – as a religious leader[8] does not therefore mean that he *is* a religious leader (whatever that might mean) but that Thomas and other agents of modern Anglophone liberal ideology choose to describe him in that way. It seems to be true that, when speaking in English, the Dalai Lama strategically describes himself as leader of the religion Tibetan Buddhism, but he is also presumably the leader of the Tibetan people considered as an 'ethnic' group with nationalist aspirations. But how does he represent himself in Tibetan? The expression 'Tibetan Buddhism' has been problematically constructed in modern history as a 'religion' that is an object of (Anglophone) secular description and analysis. In modern English terminology he might also be described as an ethnic leader or a national leader. But how are these different possible nomenclatures distinguished from each other? He is also widely regarded as the former head of state – head of a state in waiting[9] – of a colonized Chinese province that traditionally made no modern distinction between religious and political secular domains. The deployment of such terms is therefore part of the problematic of modernity.

The following news report indicates that claims and counter-claims about whether the Dalai Lama is truly a religious leader or not have serious implications for international diplomacy. It was published in the *Japan Times* (29 August 2009: p. 4) under the title 'Taiwan media warn Dalai Lama visit may hurt ties with China', and provided by the AFP-JIJI news agency:

> Taiwanese media warned Friday that President Ma Ying-jeou risked undermining the government's efforts to improve ties with China by approving a visit by the Dalai Lama.
>
> Ma on Thursday approved the trip by the Tibetan spiritual leader – scheduled from Sunday until Friday – whom Beijing accuses of trying to split Tibet from China, and opposes any foreign contact with him. 'The visit could plunge the already (typhoon) devastated Taiwan into a cross-strait political storm', said the United Daily News in an editorial. 'If Beijing would not leave the matter at that, the adjustments in cross-strait relations in the past year would be wasted.'
>
> The Taipei-based *China Times* said Ma would need to rebuild the hard-won trust with Beijing. 'We can imagine that Beijing is in shock as in return for its massive goodwill (Taiwan allows) the Dalai Lama's visit' it said, referring to China's 'national mobilization' for Taiwan's typhoon relief efforts. 'The Ma government would need to spend more efforts to rebuild trust across the Taiwan Strait.'
>
> However, the *Liberty Times* urged Ma to meet the Dalai Lama in order to stress the sovereignty of the island, which split from China in 1949 after a civil war. 'Taiwan and Tibet both suffer from China's aggression ... Ma should not be an accomplice for China's suppression of the Dalai Lama' by avoiding seeing him, it said. The visit was harshly criticised in Beijing, according to Chinese state media. Beijing regards Taiwan as part of its territory awaiting reunification – by force if necessary. 'The Dalai Lama is not a pure religious figure', an unnamed spokesman for China's Taiwan Affairs Office said, according to the official Xinhua news agency. 'Under the pretext of religion, he has all along been engaged in separatist activities.'

An additional short article, 'US backs visit' (Washington, AFP-JIJI), immediately followed this:

The United States on Thursday called the Dalai Lama a 'respected religious leader' and voiced hopes that his up-coming visit to Taiwan does not raise tensions between the island and China. China, branding the Dalai Lama a 'separatist' and 'not a pure religious figure', earlier Thursday condemned his plans to visit Taiwan, which Beijing considers part of its territory. But US State Department spokesman P.J. Crowley said that the Dalai Lama 'is an internationally respected religious leader. We believe that the Dalai Lama is a respected figure and he travels regularly, and we do not believe that this should result in increased tensions in the region,' Crowley told reporters.

This short news report is surely a potent illustration of the globalization of Anglophone discourse on the essential difference between the religious and the non-religious. It suggests how the language of 'religion' and its problematic relation to 'politics' has become part of the global rhetoric of power. The use of language here is striking. The policing of the boundaries between religion and politics is a matter of state power and even a contributory excuse for war. How the Dalai Lama is classified is crucial for whether or not he can be persuasively seen as a danger to power relations between states. Particularly striking is China's description of the Dalai Lama as 'not a pure religious figure', someone who under the guise of 'religion' is really involved in power politics, that is, in 'separatist activities'. His mask has been removed to reveal a counterfeit identity. As a rebuff, yet using the same rhetorical separation of religion and politics, the US agent refers to the Dalai Lama as 'an internationally respected religious leader' who should therefore be allowed to visit Taiwan without creating tensions. One can also note in passing the AFP-JIJI news agency's description, at the beginning of the article, of the Dalai Lama as a 'spiritual' leader, which is another term often used to indicate 'religious' as something which is essentially non-political and inoffensive. It implies that the Dalai Lama has no worldly desires concerning the liberation of Tibet.

A different example that might help to bring out the problem of whether a leader is religious, national, ethnic or none of these is that of the Emperor of Japan. The positionality of the Queen of England might also be included in such a critical analysis.

Thomas contrasts his list of religious leaders with the communist leaders in Poland and the Soviet Union. He does not stop to consider a point that has been made by innumerable commentators, that communism has so many of the attributes usually attributed to 'religion' that they cannot be essentially distinguished. Why are not the sanctified figures of Marx, Lenin and Stalin included as religious leaders? That in turn raises an issue about the role of the separation of irrational 'religion' from rational (positivistic) politics and economics in Leninism and Stalinism, a point I discuss in Chapter 11 of this volume.

Thomas uncritically adopts the orthodox distinction between religious and secular organizations and thus, instead of questioning the modern invention of religion and its ideological function in the construction of modernity, IR and the Grand Narrative, he reproduces it. The problematic categories that he claims are his critical concern turn out disappointingly to be the fundamental organizing principles of his own description and analysis. The text is full of references to 'world religions', the global resurgence of religion, new religious movements, 'the cultural, religious and political landscape of world politics' (a phrase that sounds more like a slogan than anything with serious powers of description or analysis), 'religious identity', 'religious diaspora community', 'religious INGO's', and so on and so forth. He unproblematically lists 'umbrella organizations representing the main world religions' (2005: 99) that merely follow official thinking. Without reproducing the full list, suffice it to say that they include the usual suspects: Bishops, Mennonites, Protestants, Penetcostals, Churches, Muslims, Hindus, Baptists, Evangelicals, and Jews. This kind of list is really a mantra or liturgical format sacralized by civil servants who act as ministers of the secular state.

The problems of meaning abound in this chapter. For example, on page 105 Thomas says:

> What may be distinctive about religious groups and communities ... stems from the way liberal modernity has invented religion as a body of ideas, doctrines or belief systems. When scholars attempt to determine causal beliefs or the causal capacity of religious ideas it is this concept of religion that is assumed.

I have already expressed agreement that a transformation in the meaning of religion occurred in the seventeenth century. But the problematic concept is being recycled even as it is being highlighted as a problem. For example, Thomas says that liberal modernity has invented religion, but he still does not hesitate to describe some groups, communities and ideas as religious. If we look carefully, then, we can actually observe the circularity and re-inscription in the quoted sentences. The discourse is like a computer virus that cannot be excised from the computer's functions.

A few pages earlier (page 101), in a discussion of the distinction between 'religious' and 'secular' INGOs (international non-governmental organizations), Thomas says:

> What distinguishes a religious INGO from a secular one is that its mission statement explicitly refers to religious faith as a motivation for its work, its personnel are related to some religious hierarchy or theological tradition, and it hires all or part of its staff on the basis of a creed or statement of faith ...

A moment's reflection shows that this statement has merely pushed the problem of meaning one step back. It is tautological. A religious INGO is defined by religious faith and religious hierarchy. But what is *religious* faith?

Indeed, what is *faith*? Here yet another problematic Anglophone concept is deeply embedded in a complex and contested Christian history – like 'soul'. 'Soul' is a term which Thomas, a glutton for punishment, flourishes up-front in the dramatic sub-title of the book, 'The Struggle for the Soul of the Twenty-First Century'. These terms are difficult if not impossible to translate without imposing Christian nuances on non-Christian languages. What constitutes faith or soul is contested greatly even in English! Yet 'faith' is given as a key criterion of the difference between the religious and the non-religious secular. Yet in ordinary language we use faith in many contexts, such as faith in the nation, faith in democracy, faith in the value of capital, faith in the methods of science, faith in the abilities of the US President, faith in the future, and faith in one's husband. The wide family of usages of 'faith' cannot be confined to one side of the religion–secular dichotomy.

This example of the re-inscription of the problematic term, or its substitution by other problematic terms, can also be seen when Thomas resorts to the distinction between the 'sacred' and the 'secular' to stand in for religion and politics. Discussing the rules, regulations and transparency of charitable giving and financial contributions to non-profit organizations, and in particular referring to the *hawala* system used by Muslim migrant workers, he says:

> [L]egal and accounting activity such as this has to be put in the larger context of religion and politics. The worlds of the sacred and the secular are not so easily divided in developing countries. It has to be realized that piety and protest, how the flow of grace and the flow of arms are related to each other, is not a new problem regarding non-state actors, and goes back to the colonial era (2005: 103).

I agree in general about the significance of the colonial context for the transformation of meanings and the invention of modern 'religion', the nation state and newly imagined domains such as 'politics' and 'economics'. I also agree that the flow of grace and the flow of arms are connected. I would suggest that the 'colonial era' is not so easily confined to the past, and that the contemporary re-inscription of these modern myths in IR and related disciplines could be seen as a continuation of cognitive imperialism by other means.

The use of 'sacred' here is an example. Here, 'sacred' is clearly supposed to stand in for 'religion', and 'secular' for 'politics'. So the separation is rhetorically inscribed in Thomas's paragraph in the first place. But then it is questioned, at least in 'developing countries'. In one sense this looks like an endorsement of the secularization thesis that the reader had assumed Thomas was questioning in this book. Development is implied to include an ability to distinguish between the religious and the secular, which in the secularization thesis is a sign of progress. But the logic of Thomas's more critical argument is that what sociologists such as Peter Berger have missed is that what they call secularization is really a process of inventing the modern binary while making it *look like* a discovery. By representing secularization as a progressive discovery of what there is in the world, rather than a new mythical construction with a powerful elective affinity with specific interests, then the secular positionality of the sociologist appears as the unavoidably commonplace and rational ground. It disappears into the background and thus becomes the master of persuasion.

Additionally, a look at the historical usages of 'sacred' and 'secular' problematizes this easy correlation. I have argued in my own work that 'sacred' in English has been used historically most frequently of the king, and that this usage was transferred stealthily to the 'king in parliament' (Fitzgerald 2007a). There are anyhow wide usages of 'sacred' to indicate practices, institutions, spaces, times and categories that are usually included in the 'secular' category. While it is true that the sacred is frequently used to stand for 'religion', it is also frequently used to stand for things that, in other contexts, are called secular. Is not the law of the land sacred?

Unfortunately one can find the problems indicated so far on almost every page of Thomas's book, and the further pursuit of them begins to seem arbitrary and random. Take his Chapter 5, 'Wars and Rumors of War? Religion and International Conflict'. The problem about what 'religion' is supposed to mean, and how religion is supposed to be articulated in relation to other categories such as politics, secular, culture, and ethnicity, presents problems of circularity, tautology and even banality:

> [R]eligion has been about war-making as much as it has been about peace-making. It has always had the capacity to reduce violence and to produce it (Thomas 2005: 121).

The banality in itself would not be a major problem. One would yawn and close the book. The major problem is that, under the guise of cutting-edge critique, in a work that will be widely distributed in the Anglophone world as the latest and smartest insights in International Relations, old clichés re-assert 'religion' as some force or agent in the world, mystically incarnated as the 'religions' 'Hinduism' and 'Buddhism' (2005: 121). We are still in the rhetorical mode of the secular Anglophone author making authoritative pronouncements about complex regions of the world that he seems to know little about. It is difficult to find much serious exploration of the modern history of the category 'world religions', of 'religion' as an Orientalist construct, how this category was invented, under what kind of colonial conditions, and what implications the invention of these reifications has for Thomas's thesis about the myths of liberal modernity. Despite moments of critical insight, this book is submerged in the conceits of liberal modernity.

One potential fertile source of ideas for Thomas is found in René Girard – one of the most frequently cited authors in his Chapter 5 – and the Girardian analysis of violence and mimetic desire. I do not pretend to be an expert on the work of Girard and am concerned here with Thomas's own use and representation of Girardian ideas. To what extent Girard himself supposed that concepts of sacrifice, scapegoat and mimetic desire are essentially 'religious' concepts can be pronounced on by Girardian specialists. Much of Thomas's discussion of Girard suggests that whatever may be said in terms of sacrifice and scapegoating about practices and institutions typically classified as 'religious' can be applied equally to those which are typically classified as 'secular'. If this is true, then it seems to this reader that the concept of mimetic desire and Girardian approaches to violence against both internal and external scapegoats may turn out to be as true of the violence of the secular state as of the violence of 'religious terrorists'.

If this is at least conceivable, it would be another potentially powerful strategy for subverting the illusion of the supposed essential differences between the irrational violence of religious others and the reasonable and reluctant violence of 'our' supposedly more developed secular regimes (see Cavanaugh 2009). Whether or not Girard himself would agree with this I do not know. But given Thomas's own statements about the need to historically problematize the invention of religion and its ideological function in legitimating the secular state, it is a problem for this reader to understand why he does not consistently pursue such a strategy, but continues to re-inscribe the categories of the discourse he seemed to want to deconstruct.

I do not have the expertise or the space to give a detailed explanation of Girard's theoretical concepts, and only intend to quote and paraphrase Thomas here so that readers not familiar with Girard can at least get the gist. My purpose is primarily to suggest how Thomas's use of Girardian concepts might apparently further his deconstructive critical agenda but in fact does not, or does so only ambiguously. Thomas says:

> Girard argues that the whole process of mimetic desire in culture and society is prone to violence and conflict ... If the models for what human beings desire – the ideas and objects of desire – are based on the desires and ideas they have learned from others, then the rivalry and competition with other human beings for the same objects of desire has the potential to cause violence and conflict ... If mimetic desire is oriented towards nonexclusive goods, such as learning a language or how to milk a cow, or plant maize, then imitation is peaceful and productive. If mimetic desire is oriented toward what are called exclusive goods or objects, whether they are intangible, such as status or prestige, great power, or hyper power status, or tangible goods like territory, the West Bank or Kosovo, or sexual objects, Helen of Troy, Marilyn Monroe, or Brad Pitt, then the inevitable result of imitation is rivalry, violence, and conflict ... (2005: 125–6).

Thomas indicates by these examples that, if this theory is true, then it is as true about the Western consumer capitalist societies within which we academics sell our books, have our feuds, and seek scapegoats as it is about all societies. On the other hand, he goes on:

> Girard's theory of sacrificial substitution shows that the underlying purpose of culture and religion is to accomplish what political scientists argue Hobbes's *Leviathan* was meant to accomplish – to help maintain order, restore harmony, and reinforce social cohesion ... Can those of us from the developed world, with stable governments, and a smoothly functioning judiciary imagine a world in which society is threatened by internal violence because of the absence of any social or political mechanisms or institutions to restrain or regulate violence and aggression? (2005: 129).

But is it not an act of violence to refer to poorer nations as the 'developing world', with its implication that we secular Westerners are already developed? I do not think Thomas intends this in a condescending way, and I believe he is rightly pointing to a radical problem in the constitution of many modern nation states in Africa. I am not an expert on Africa, and he may well be. Nor do I assume he is unaware of the colonial inheritance of these problems, whereby previously settled lifestyles of different groups with their own languages and customary forms of internal and external rules of exchange and established methods for settling disputes may have been disrupted by the colonial imposition of nation states with artificial boundaries. However, I am not clear that our own modern liberal democracies do not have their own practices of victimization and sacrificial violence, both internal and external. As I said, I am not an expert in Girardian theory. But could not the informal domestic violence practised against women and children in our own cultures be understood as part of the sacrifice needed to maintain the smooth functioning of male order? Could not the violence of US prisons and the long and frequent sentences handed down to black Americans be seen as an on-going sacrificial cult for the symbolic maintenance of white supremacy? Has the violence inflicted on indigenous Americans not had some similar functions? And what about the very real yet also symbolic violence of Guantanamo Bay, perpetrated against individuals who have not even been charged, let alone convicted, of any crime? For whom are our governments and court systems stable and smoothly-functioning?

One might also at least raise the possibility that the lethal violence of the US state and its allies unleashed in 'Shock and Awe', the military strategy employed in Iraq in 2003, was a kind of sacrificial violence perpetrated against a symbolic victim for the purposes of reasserting at the symbolic level the dignity and supremacy of the US after 9/11? I mention these kinds of issues because they might disrupt the assumption, more easily made by we white, middle-class academics, that our own systems of justice are smoothly-functioning and efficient.

It is in this possible context of considerations that I would question a too-easy distinction between us and them, we 'developed' moderns and those undeveloped people who have not achieved the advantages of liberal democracy. For it imports a value judgement based on the ideology of progress, an ideology inherent in the Euro-centric drive of the colonial era to dominate the world and impose a historically-specific hegemonic set of values as though they constitute the universal standard of civility and rationality. It may have been this very hegemonic drive that was partly the cause of the chaos of many African states. And it is a value judgement that may deflect from the question about for whom does Western liberal capitalism smoothly function? Whatever the declared or undeclared motive of the writer, the language of developed and undeveloped, like the language of failed states, too easily plays to the self-delusions of superior rationality, and the vision of ourselves as mature secular adults in contrast to the childish savages who sadly were left behind in the upward drive towards evolutionary enlightenment. I am not imputing to Thomas all these malign intentions, however; and I think he is correct to draw attention to the dreadful inequalities of opportunity and stability that afflict the world.

Another connected aspect of the liberal myth that Thomas wants to expose through the Girardian lens is 'the illusion of spontaneous desire', which is one of the illusory 'assumptions of liberal modernity, which sees agency, individuality, and spontaneity as the essence of society' (2005: 134). Thomas agrees with Girard's arguments that '[t]he notion of agency or autonomy, the idea that identity is "freely chosen", so dear to the conceptions of liberal modernity or liberal individualism that underlay the social construction of identity, is premised on what Girard calls the myth or illusion of spontaneous desire. It is the myth that individuals choose the objects of their own desire. Liberal modernity, with its abstract conception of the self, "overplays the role of the will in the conception of the self"' (2005: 131). Girard refers to this as 'the reigning ideology of the age'. It is surely an important part of it.

Girard's insight has important relevance for Thomas's critique of the illusions of Western liberal modernity. For Girard, or for Thomas if I have correctly understood him, identity is constructed through a triangular relationship between subject, object and imitated other. The desires of individuals and groups for things such as status, recognition, prestige and consumer objects is based on imitation of, and thus mediated by, other individuals and groups which have special significance to the identity of an individual or group. Desire – mediated desire, mimetic desire – works through attraction and repulsion (Thomas 2005: 132). This is why Girard calls his theory *mimetic*, since identity is based on similarity and difference. The hated or admired or envied other, whether internal or external, provides the focus for the cohesion of the group by projecting its own latent violence onto a potential sacrificial scapegoat.

So far we at least have no reason to suppose that these mechanisms apply only to groups classified in hegemonic English as 'religious', and are excluded from an analysis of the myth of the rational, peace-loving secular state. This potentially liberating implication of Girardian ideas is also to some extent present in the following paragraph, but we can see that, like a bad habit, 'religion' is hovering in the wings in an unholy alliance with 'culture', trying to insert its presumptuous self into the scheme like a computer virus:

> According to Girard, culture and religion originate in the need for societies or civilizations to keep mimetic rivalry in check so the kind of general crisis of order and collective violence that Hobbes described as man's natural condition in the state of nature does not happen. The way societies keep mimetic rivalry in check is by finding an outlet, a replacement for the cycle of reciprocal violence, or potential violence between antagonists that mimetic desire has produced. The outlet or replacement is through what Girard calls the scapegoat mechanism ... A society gains release from the collective violence that mimetic desire and rivalry produces by finding and blaming a scapegoat – a single victim or social group – to replace the violence between the antagonists in society. It is the scapegoat that helps save society from the devastating effects of collective violence (2005: 127).

These passages suggest that any society can be and needs to be thought about in this way, and that it applies as much to those societies and groups which are classified in Anglophone discourse as 'secular' as to those that are classified as 'religious'. Perhaps we can see a theory emerging here that helps us understand the massive violence of Western secular nation states? Indeed, to suppose that such a theory applies largely and specifically to those groups that become classified as 'religious terrorists' by the US State Department might itself feel like an act of symbolic violence against the Other. The general application of these Girardian ideas to all groups is pointed to in other passages. But the fuller insinuation of this passage could be that all societies are secular, and all have a 'religious' sacrificial cult. Thus 'religion' has a 'social function', which is to provide sacrifices that 'sacralize' and consequently channel the violence inherent in all social institutions. If this is the idea that Thomas wants to convey – and I admit I am not clear about what he does want to say here – then we are back with the functionalism of uncritical social science.

> [Girard] shows that the sacred is essential to the functioning of society because it alone can protect society from the destructive consequences of mimetic rivalry and violence. It is for this reason that all societies do not break out into violence or conflict all the time. ... According to Girardian theory the fatal penchant for internal violence in society – its dissensions, rivalries, jealousies, and quarrels, needs a sacrificial outlet, and it can only

be diverted by the intervention of a third party – the sacrificial victim or victims. The purpose of the scapegoat or sacrificial mechanism is to protect society from its own violence, to stem the rising tide of indiscriminate substitutions, and redirect the violence into proper, acceptable channels … The scapegoat mechanism turns Hobbes's war of all against all into a war of all against one – the victim or scapegoat. It is in this way that the problem of order and violence is resolved in domestic society and social cohesion is maintained (2005: 129).

The potential for insight here into the massive violence of the US state against other nations as well as on its own most vulnerable citizens must be great. Readers might feel at last that the spotlight is being turned on ourselves, so that, instead of projecting, in our use of language, our own violence onto the sacrificial violence of so-called 'developing nations', the very terminology itself arguably an act of victimization and aggression, we get a glimpse through the theoretical mirror into our own collective psyche. One of my worries here, though, is with the expression 'the sacred' and its supposed social functioning. Thomas seems to jump eagerly at any opportunity to reify a classificatory term into a metaphysical entity.

As I pick my way carefully though the buried landmines of ethnocentric classifications with which the whole section of Thomas's book is charged, I can extract many indications that Girard's theory, or Thomas's representation of Girard's theory, may provide fertile soil for self-critique. For example:

The scapegoat mechanism, from a Girardian perspective, is … part of the social order of any society, although the actual violence of the scapegoat mechanism becomes 'unveiled', and is more apparent at times of what Girardians call a 'sacrificial crisis' in society (2005: 132–3).

When I read these potentially enlightening and thought-provoking sentences, I found myself irresistibly pondering the mass terror and bloodiness of the invasions of Iraq and Afghanistan; the sacrifice of hundreds of thousands of 'liberated' Iraqis and of thousands of young men and women service personnel; and the new opportunities that resulted from this strategy for threats against Iran which quickly escalated the competition for nuclear weapons. But then my thoughts switched from the external Others to the internal scapegoats, to the domestic victims, sacrificed in the state's line of duty to protect those sacred temples of capital that we call banks and their magician-priests (such as the managers of hedge funds): failed mortgages and evictions, broken small businesses, rising mass unemployment, expanding prison populations, depression and drug addiction, offered up to the gods of capital and finance in the latest rush to save the banks and the financial sector. Surely there is the potential here for a theory that helps us to understand the violence of the 'secular' state against its most vulnerable citizens? Is not capitalism itself a vast sacrificial cult that feeds on internal as well as external othering?

Some of my own desires for critical collective self-reflection seem to be alluded to by Thomas:

> Girardians argue that what many of us call 'political stability' is when the violence of society is 'veiled violence', veiled by those institutions ... that provide an aura of moral legitimacy and respectability for violence ... [T]he precise boundaries of legitimate force [are] fiercely contested in all political systems – proper police behaviour, capital punishment, peaceful demonstrations, or the legitimacy of torture in interrogation by the French in Algeria, by the British during the Mau Mau uprising in Kenya in the 1950s, as well as by US armed forces in Iraq or Guantanamo Bay ... It is increasingly difficult to tell the difference between the – allegedly – 'good violence' or official violence of the state, and 'bad violence' of those individuals or social groups that oppose it. In this kind of world the boundary between force and violence is blurred. It becomes difficult to tell the difference between the police, thugs, comrades, warlords, criminals, or neighborhood gangs. In this kind of world, warlords have seats in the Serbian parliament, or the United States supports paramilitary forces in Guatemala or El Salvador, and it is at the heart of the confusion between groups that seek violent leverage in international relations through holy wars and terrorism, through guerrilla warfare, or wars of national liberation (2005: 133).

Thomas here really does seem to want to develop a theory which provides insight into the violence of the powerful so-called developed, secular nations as a strategy towards unpicking the myth of progress, freedom, rationality and tolerance.

I somehow can't help suspecting that the chaos in Africa to which Thomas rightly refers is related to the history of slavery, of colonially-imposed nation states, the destruction of complex societies which had built up the ritual processes which Thomas indicates are now frequently absent. It is of course pointless merely to wallow in regret about the past iniquities of European colonialism, provided we are completely clear that colonialism really has come to an end and is not continuing under a different guise. Here the Girardian idea of 'veiled violence' alluded to by Thomas might seem particularly relevant. Thomas is hinting at some way of bringing Girardian ideas of sacrifice, scapegoating, mimetic desire and violence, veiled and unveiled, into a fruitful theoretical relationship with the history of colonialism, the slave trade, the invasive destruction of indigenous forms of life, and the imposition of half-baked Euro-American institutions which deliver much less than they promise.

The idea of veiled violence seems powerful because it reminds us that the smoothly-functioning stability of human relations and efficiency of judicial processes that Thomas eludes to in nations that consider themselves to be developed is grounded on all sorts of different kinds of both veiled and unveiled violence. For this reader, one of the strong points about Thomas's use of these

Girardian ideas is that they could potentially liberate us from the self-serving myth of our own productivity and make us more aware that our own wellbeing is based on the sacrifices of cheap, exploited labour – not least that of women and children – in Africa and other places, not excluding the poor in our own streets.

Where is the veiled violence? Why, one place is in Thomas's own text! It is in the system of dominant representations recycled by powerful agencies such as the media and academia. The veiled violence lies in the myths of liberal capitalism, in the buried categories and embedded tropes that take on an air of irresistible common sense, of being in touch with reality while in effect constructing that reality. For myths to be powerfully real they only have to be believed and collectively acted upon.

Despite Thomas's laudable attempt to unearth these self-serving fictional devices, they continue to inhabit his text with stubborn persistence, and consequently confuse the reader. The following sentences show us not only the 'ambivalence of the sacred' but the ambivalence of theoretical intention:

> Girard's theory has provided an answer to the disturbing question posed at the beginning of this chapter, why is there such a paradox regarding religion and violence? ... The ambivalence of the sacred is rooted in the very nature of culture and religion. Culture and religion from the beginning have controlled violence through violence. Religion contains violence by effectively applying 'good' violence – the sacrificial mechanism – in order to control 'bad' (or profane) violence, the indiscriminate, reciprocal, or collective violence of society. Thus, from a Girardian perspective, the paradox of religion and violence that we see in war, ethnic conflict, and terrorism is caused by far more than what Charles Tilly's ideas people or what political or religious liberals often seem to suggest – religious militants who are simply misguided, and have misinterpreted religious texts in violent ways. The ambivalence of the sacred is rooted in the very complicity of the institutions of culture and religion with political power in the underlying violence on which any society's social cohesion, political order, and social stability are based (2005: 129–30).

I ask the reader first to notice the various reifications in this paragraph. It is very difficult for all of us to avoid the reifying effects of language, and when it is pointed out to us we may like to see reification as metaphorical thinking which is necessary for imaginatively transcending the range of the immediate into a wider context of referentiality. It is arguably an inherent feature of telling stories. However, metaphor easily becomes hypostatized as objective reality; narrative becomes myth; the metaphorical constructions of narrative become transformed into beliefs about the real. 'Culture and religion', twins which occur frequently in Thomas's fifth chapter with no explanation about what kind of relationship they have to each other, have a *nature*: their 'very nature' has something rooted in it, viz. 'the ambivalence of the sacred'. 'Culture and religion' are also a twin *agency*: it or they control violence, contain violence, and apply violence. And they have done this 'from the beginning', so they (or it) are eternal and unchanging in their essential nature and their incarnated functions. Surely this piece of representation is not essentially different in kind from what theologians do when they talk about God, the nature of God, the activities of the Holy Ghost, the incarnation of God in Christ, and the relation between God and the world? This piece of metaphysical theorizing about 'culture and religion' might be taken to justify the rabid media rhetoric about 'religious terrorism'. These essentialized agents are also complicit in 'political power', whatever the relationship is supposed to be between the 'culture and religion' twins, on the one hand, and 'political power' on the other.

Yet at the same time my own reading of this passage, in the wider context of Thomas's chapter as a whole, places his contradictory intention as a search for more fundamental causes of violence across the spectrum of all human groups, rather than those typically offered by modern liberal ideology as 'religious'. There are (or so we could read it) deep, collectively-generated forces of mimetic desire at work in all groups, and the mechanisms of self-identification in relation to a significant 'other', forces that cannot be explained in terms of individual spontaneously generated desire. The survival of any group depends on rituals of sacrifice that channel the violence inherent in all orders of power into regular, sacralized victimization. In this way violence can be both acknowledged and appeased, and the established system of group organization can continue without major breakdown. The sacrifice of the scapegoat transforms the on-going, day-to-day, routine violence of institutional life into a collectively recognized symbolic code. If this theory is true, then it seems to be true for all human groups, regardless of their classification as religious or nonreligious secular. Instead of regarding religion as an active agent in the world, with its own nature and intentions, we should see it as a category that facilitates the modern liberal myth of secular non-religious natural rationality.

In his concluding chapter, 'How Shall We Then Live?', Thomas says:

> We have seen that the global resurgence of religion challenges the idea that has been with us since the Enlightenment that there is some kind of neutral or privileged social space from which to evaluate values, beliefs, and practices of others in international society (2005: 247).

I have tried to show in this critique of Thomas's work that the very idea of a global resurgence of religion as a reified agent with essential characteristics and modes of action and incarnation re-inscribes the privileged presumption of a neutral, secular space from which Thomas classifies the practices of others. Thomas tells us that it is 'misleading ... to view the global resurgence of religion' in terms of extremism, fanaticism, fascism, terrorism, or fundamentalism, '... as if the global resurgence of religion is an aberration in an otherwise modern world' (2005: 248). But this is surely disingenuous. The very idea of a 'global resurgence of religion' implies an aberration: religion has been in exile, but is now returning with a vengeance to disrupt our modern world and our modern presumptions. The confusions that characterize the whole book tumble into view in his last chapter. Take the following paragraph:

> Postmodernity has challenged the idea that in our era Western modernity can determine the meaning of the overall character and direction of progress, modernity, or development for all countries. Our theories need to be able to account for the meaning and significance religious actors give for their social action. We have seen that so many of the concepts scholars have developed, and the hypotheses in which these concepts are framed, often rest on hidden, undeclared, and unstated assumptions about modernity and progress that are of doubtful resonance in view of the global resurgence of religion. This book has tried to grapple with the fact that rationalist approaches may be too embedded in the assumptions of Western modernity to fully understand the impact of culture and religion on international relations ... (2005: 248).

If the reader has been generous to me and has followed my critique so far, she will anticipate some of the contradictions in this characteristically opaque paragraph. What is postmodernity? Does Thomas believe that he speaks from a postmodern position? Could not postmodernity itself be included as an idea of Western modernity? If, as Thomas previously suggested, 'religion' is a modern invention along with the myth of the secular state and liberal modernity generally, then is he not himself driven by assumptions about modernity which underlie his own descriptive and analytical deployment of typically modern categories? There is semantic slippage (to put it politely) in the sentence where he challenges the idea that the idea that 'Western modernity can determine the meaning and overall character and direction of progress, modernity, or development for all countries.' What is actually being challenged here? He seems to be saying that progress, development and modernity are empirical facts, but that there are several of them, or several different kinds of them, and different countries can give their own meanings to these Anglophone concepts. But even if we could understand the meaning of this in English, one wonders how Thomas could know that there can be in principle as many meanings to these concepts as there are countries and languages. If every country can supply its own meaning to the idea of progress, then how meaningful could it be to talk about progress at all? The same point would hold for 'modernity' and 'development'.

Yet at the very moment that Thomas warns us not to be presumptuous, and to be aware of the hidden, unstated and undeclared assumptions underlying our own of concepts and theories, he himself in the same sentence assumes that he authoritatively knows who are the 'religious actors', apparently in advance of asking them if that is their own meaningful self-description. It sounds liberally generous and impressive to say 'our theories need to be able to account for the meaning and significance religious actors give for their social action' – in other words, we should let them speak for themselves. But who are we talking about? Has their been a single interview in any language, or any piece of evidence in Thomas's book about who does and who does not accept the designation 'religious actor'? Has their been a single piece of convincing evidence that such a thing as resurgent religion exists and that escapes the endless tautologies of modern assumptions that underlie Thomas's own theories? I would willingly refer to Thomas as a religious actor if only I could understand in which mystical forces his faith is invested.

## Notes

1.    Talal Asad (1993; 2003); William T. Cavanaugh (1995; 2000: ch. 10); John Bossy (1985; see also 1982).
2.    See for example the argument of Kathryn Sutherland in her introduction to her own edition of Adam Smith's *An Inquiry into the Nature and Causes of the Wealth of Nations* (1993). Sutherland points out that the modern term 'economics' did not exist in Smith's time. This raises the issue, relevant to the emergence of other modern categories such as 'religion', 'politics' and the secular state, why we have had to wait until the early nineteenth century the work of writers such as Jeremy Bentham, David Ricardo or Richard Whately for the development of a distinctively theorized field of economic science.
3.    See, for example, the points made by Sharada Sugitharaja on the construction of 'Hinduism' as a 'religion' in her paper 'Colonialism and Religion' (2010: 69–78) on discussed in chapter 11 of this book [p243].
4.    See the evidence in Carolyn Gallaher, 'The role of Protestant Missionaries in Mexico's Indigenous awakening' in Bulletin of Latin American Research, 26, 88–111.
5.    (see http://www.oremus.org/liturgy/coronation/cor1953b.html)
6.    Part of my problem with the work of Charles Taylor, in for example The Secular Age, is that he inscribes the enchanted-disenchanted binary into the distinction between modern and pre-modern. The Weberian idea that we moderns have disenchanted the world seems to me to be part of the myth which we should challenge. The enchantments may have changed, but I question the presumption that secular cognition is divested of enchantments. Our world is full of magical thinking, not least among bankers, politicians and academics.
7.    Joseph Loss (2010). Yet at the same time this is published in a journal that specializes in the study of religions, perhaps an unavoidable irony.
8.    See for example a recent article, 'Many faiths, one truth', published in the *International Herald Tribune* (with *Asahi Shinbun*) of 26 May

2010 in which the *Dalai Lama*, *Tenzin Gyatsu*, lists Buddhism, Islam, Christianity and Hinduism among the religions of the world, and claims that in their essence they all lead to the same truth.

9.    I here echo Naomi Goldenberg's expression for 'religions' as 'states in waiting'.

# Chapter 10

## The Politics of Secularism

Elizabeth Shakman Hurd's *The Politics of Secularism in International Relations* (2008) is focused and sustained in its attempt to critically historicize the religion–secular dichotomy as an ideological power formation deriving from Christendom and underpinning modernity. There are many reasons for saying this, but I stress four strands. One is her insight that the 'division between religion and politics is not fixed but rather socially and historically constructed'. Another is her helpful distinction between two different models of Euro-American secularism, which she refers to as *laïcism* (based on the French tradition) and *Judeo-Christian secularism* (typically instantiated by the US). The third is her detailed discussions of Turkey and Iran and relations between these two polities and Euro-America. The author usefully articulates Turkish Kemalism deriving from Ataturk and based on the French *laïcité* model. She points out that this dominant formation of secularism has been challenged recently not by 'Islamic fundamentalism' or a 'return' to Islamic law but by the AKP party in its attempt to refashion the secular in relation to Islam in a way which is not simply reducible to either *laïcism* or traditional Islamic law (see, for example, Hurd 2008: 71). In this way she adds to the growth of literature on modern secularisms outside Euro-America. Fourth is her recognition of the binary, mutually parasitic construction of an essentialized religion, 'Islam', as an irrational and backward Other against which European perceptions of its collective self as rational and progressive have been facilitated.

At times it seems as though her fundamental theoretical concern is with the relation between discursive categories and power. Thus, for example, she says '… the ability to represent Islam in a particular way is itself an exercise of power' (2008: 53). Where Euro-America is secular, rational, progressive and democratic, Islam is religious, irrational, backward and prone to tyrants and arbitrary dictatorships. These self-serving binary oppositions are therefore an exercise in power. It is in this context that the binary opposition between religious and secular domains can itself be seen as a modern Anglophone and more widely Europhone construct that orders the world in terms of a specific relationship of domination and subordination.

Hurd is aware of the circular and tautological nature of representations. In historically contextualizing the parasitic relationship between Euro-American self-images and images of Islam, she disclaims that she is saying anything substantive about Islam or its forms of governance:

[M]y subject is not Muslim belief, Islamic tradition, or the relationship between Islam and actual modes of governance in any particular country; it is European and American representations of Islam and how these representations have contributed to the constitution of different forms of secularist authority and the production of particular national identities through which these forms of secularism are expressed and articulated (2008: 53).

As Hurd has suggested, Anglophone or Europhone representations of non-European realities become dangerously distorting when the contested and contentious history of the categories in which they are framed is elided and concealed. Her own narratives of representation are conducted with critical awareness, in a way that is designed to illustrate rather than conceal the contested and problematic implications of modern categories. They are intended to show how Turkish and Iranian individuals and groups have taken up specific positions at specific moments in history in relation to Euro-American power, and to the rhetoric of progress and rationality. When she says '… my subject is not Muslim belief, Islamic tradition, or the relationship between Islam and actual modes of governance in any particular country …' I take her to mean that she only wishes to relate the least contentious historical 'facts' in a way that minimizes ideological presumption masquerading as objectivity, and that maximizes our awareness of the unstable categories under discussion. This is how I interpret Hurd when she refers to Scott and Hirschkind's reference to the 'ideological conditions that give point and force to the theoretical apparatuses employed to describe and objectify', in Hurd's case 'the secular and the religious' (2008: 2).

Like the work of Scott M. Thomas, considered in the previous chapter, Hurd's book represents a serious scholarly attempt at critical deconstruction. However, the ambiguities are there throughout her text. The first paragraph of the book indicates that, while intending to critique modern categories, including the religion-secular binary, and other categories such as politics are being recycled simultaneously into the text as though they are unproblematic descriptive and analytical concepts:

Religion is a problem in the field of international relations at two distinct levels. First, in recent years religious fundamentalism and religious difference have emerged as crucial factors in international conflict, national security, and foreign policy. This development has come as a surprise to many scholars and practitioners. Much contemporary foreign policy, especially in the United States, is being quickly rewritten to account for this change. Second, the power of this resurgence of religion in world politics does not fit into existing categories of thought in academic relations. Conventional understandings of international relations, focused on material capabilities and strategic interaction, exclude from the start the possibility that religion could be a fundamental organizing force in the international system (2008: 1).

Here can be found several examples of the ambiguity seen in Thomas's book. On the one hand, religion is a problem, which is a thoroughly ambiguous statement to make. Does Hurd mean that religion is a problem? Or that 'religion' is a problem? Does she mean that 'religion' is a problem as a dominant, Orientalist discourse, as in her point about representations of 'Islam' as a 'religion', and Muslims as religious, irrational, backward and prone to tyrants and arbitrary dictatorships, in contrast to Euro-America which is secular, rational, progressive, and democratic? The statement can be read in entirely different ways. But unfortunately the weight of interpretation in this paragraph tends to suggest that the religion Islam is the problem, rather than our discursive construction of it as such, with the implication that *they* are religious and irrational, whereas the United States is a secular and rational peace-maker in the world. My point is not to attribute bad intentions to Hurd, but to bring into view the way these ideological discourses work. When Hurd says that 'religious fundamentalism and religious difference' are causing problems in the world, the adjectival form 'religious' is used to describe fundamentalism and difference. This seems intended as a straight-forward statement of fact, and it will probably be read as such. Given the problematic of 'religion' as a discursive category, it surely follows that the distinction between religious and non-religious fundamentalism is also a problem.[1] There is at least arguably a kind of fundamentalism in the United States that does not separate neatly into the religion–secular binary. US foreign policy and its Shock and Awe military doctrine could be represented as a dreadful kind of fanaticism which does not divide easily into 'religious', 'political' and 'economic' motivations or descriptive categories. It might, for example, be described as a vast ritual of world purification involving human sacrifice.

Nor can it be clear what it is that 'does not fit into existing categories of thought in academic relations'. What descriptive and analytical weight hangs on 'religion' and 'politics' here? To say that 'the religious resurgence in world politics' does not fit into existing categories seems contradictory, because the words are being employed to construct the subject of the verb. The expression 'the resurgence of religion in world politics', like 'the global resurgence of religion' in the title of the book by Thomas, has the effect of reifying religion as though it is something that exists and even acts in the world.

These expressions which tacitly represent religion and politics as two separate and reified domains which do not fit well with each other is to construct the problem in the first place, and then to look for the solution. Such expressions do not fit well with something the author says on the same page:

'This book argues that these two problems are facets of a single underlying phenomenon: the unquestioned acceptance of the secularist division between religion and politics' (2008: 1).

Here, what Hurd refers to as the 'secularist division', which seems to be embedded descriptively in an expression such as 'this religious resurgence in world politics', is precisely what is critically at issue (2008: 1). It is unclear why the author should refer to it as a 'secularist' division when the idea of the 'secular', as much as the idea of generic 'religion', is generated *by* the division. What we need is an alternative narrative that accounts for the emergence of the total binary discourse.

One of the problems in Hurd's account (a problem widely shared by us all) is that 'politics', on the one hand, is universal, generic, transparent and self-evident; and yet on the other hand is a product of the modern, contested, historically-specific power discourse of the religion–secular binary. The continual swing between these assumptions, the dogmatic and the critical, can be seen in this passage:

> Secularism needs to be analyzed as a form of political authority in its own right, and its consequences evaluated for international relations. This is the objective of this book. My central motivating question is how, why, and in what ways does secular political authority form part of the foundation of contemporary international relations theory and practice, and what are the political consequences of this authority in international relations? (2008: 1)

I believe there is an important insight behind this statement, to the extent that international relations theory and practice is part of a specific configuration of power and is not constituted by pure disinterested description and analysis. Yet it still seems to me to re-hash the same problem. It seems as though Hurd's rhetorical question, formulated to express the central objective of her book, might amount to 'what are the political consequences for international relations theory and practice of secular political authority?' The term 'political' seems to cancel itself out. She continues:

> I argue, first, that the secularist division between religion and politics is not fixed but rather socially and historically constructed; second, that the failure to recognize this explains why students of international relations have been unable to properly recognize the power of religion in world politics; and, finally, that overcoming this problem allows a better understanding of crucial empirical puzzles in international relations, including the conflict between the United States and Iran, controversy over the enlargement of the European Union to include Turkey, the rise of political Islam, and the broader religious resurgence both in the United States and elsewhere (2008: 1).

If the division between religion and politics is not fixed, it implies that these categories do not have fixed meanings. They are strategic, rhetorical markers useful for states, politicians, academics, the media and other powerful interests to classify and differentiate according to the perceived needs of the moment. But the rhetorical construction is being recycled as factual description in the expression 'the power of religion in world politics' and 'the broader religious resurgence'. These criticisms may seem unfair and pedantic; however, I suggest that it is precisely through such ambiguities and slippages that rhetoric maintains its power to transform empty binaries with no clear meaning into apparently persuasive proclamations about the facts. Hurd herself shows part of this power game in her historical survey of the construction of Islam as irrational and barbaric religion as against the civility and rationality of the Eurocentric self. Equally one could argue that, ever since the struggles of nonconformists and Dissenters in the seventeenth century against the power of the church-state, minorities have availed themselves of the strategic discourse on religion and its assumed distinction from the non-religious, as a way of protecting their own traditions, by appealing to the constitutional rights of 'freedom of worship'. All these examples indicate that what counts as religion and what counts as secular is a matter of contestation and negotiation. In that case, how do expressions such as 'religious resurgence' and 'political consequences' work here? On the one hand the stated intention is to critically deconstruct these categories and the discourses within which they operate; yet at the same time the problematic terms are being used to describe the way the world is, without the reader knowing how the unfixed division is meant to work.

Hurd usefully suggests talking about secularism as a form of 'productive power' (2008: 1) which she derives from Michael Barnett and Raymond Duvall, and is defined as 'the socially diffuse production of subjectivity in systems of meaning and signification'. She continues: 'Secularism is a form of productive power that 'inheres in structures and discourses that are not possessed or controlled by any single actor" (2008: 1, quoting David Scott and Charles Hirschkind[2]).

The significance of this formulation is that it challenges the assumption that the secular is itself a simple given, a conformity to natural reason, the commonsense reality which enlightened moderns have arrived at progressively, a state of enlightenment divested of the metaphysical illusions of religion. By understanding the discourse on secularism as itself a form of productive power, it brings secularism into view as a project or ideology or power formation, after which it cannot remain veiled and hidden from critical sight, or as the transparent, neutral substratum of academic description and analysis.

Presumably one might argue that all collective representations constitute forms of productive power, differently configured but not necessarily essentialized into the religion–non-religion binary. Political economy, as theorized by the science of economics, is an integral part of the productive power of capital.

The exclusion of 'religion' from the constitution of 'the science of economics' places 'religion' at the epicentre of discursive productive power, though few economists would see it that way. To the degree that Hurd, Thomas and I can find agreement that we are engaged in the same critical project, then we are working on the production of collective representations ourselves, a critical deconstructive activity which achieves its productive power through negation. One of the most significant consequences of this insight that secularism is one among many historically and culturally generated forms of productive power is that it problematizes the religion–secular dichotomy by disembedding it from its mystified status of neutrality.

Religions can be viewed as bizarre objects and agents in the world only from a (non-religious) standpoint that is assumed to be normal, rational, self-evident, and in tune with commonsense reality. The idea that there are religions in the world causing problems such as fanaticism and terrorism, and threatening the peaceful authority of the secular state, is radically subverted when the 'secular' is brought into critical awareness as a discourse, a specific and competing configuration of power. I have myself argued that religious studies acts as an ideological state apparatus, in the sense that it authorizes the discourses which legitimize the power of the secular state and the secular rationality of capitalism while simultaneously disguising this function. Would Hurd (or Thomas) be prepared to say something similar about IR as an academic discipline?

If I have understood Hurd's intentions correctly, she is saying that both secularism and the category 'religion' together constitute a distinctively modern discursive binary that is mutual and parasitic. This binary is a productive power in that, on the one hand, religions are produced in the collective imaginary as distinct objects and agents in the world (Islam, Hinduism, Buddhism, Christianity, Sikhism etc.) which in their differences share some essential characteristics (faith in an unseen world, belief in God, metaphysical speculation, dogmatic authority); and on the other hand the secular is produced as natural rationality, the domain of common sense, of real power relations, of empirical knowledge. One of the features of this binary productive power is that, while the secular disappears into a background set of authoritative assumptions that seem universal and ahistorical (even though realized historically in the Enlightenment), religion appears as a problem, a hangover from a barbaric past, or an essentially different kind of ideology with disturbing features that threaten the real order of international relations. On this narrative, the Treaty of Westphalia changed all of that and religion was put on the back burner, exiled, tamed, domesticated, and the secular could finally flourish. This is what I take Hurd to mean when she says:

[I]n most accounts of international relations 'religion is thus essentially peripheral, and reflection on international politics is pursued as if it concerned an autonomous space that is not fundamentally disturbed by its presence' (2008: 3, with quote from Carlson and Owens; see her note 14).

I stress *if* I have understood Hurd's intentions correctly because I am confused about her intentions, particularly the logical level of analysis, and the logic of use of key terms, both here and in the book more widely. For example, she says:

> [T]his book presents an alternative to the assumption that religion is a private affair. This assumption is common in realist, liberal, and most constructivist international relations theory. Conventional wisdom has it that between 1517 and the Treaty of Westphalia in 1648 religion mattered in European politics. Since Westphalia, however, religion has been largely privatized. The idea behind this 'Westphalian presumption' is that religion had to be marginalized, privatized, or overcome by a cosmopolitan ethic to secure international order (2008: 3)

Here Hurd is critiquing an idea that she claims other people mistakenly hold. If Hurd is serious when she says that the division between religion and the non-religious secular is a historically conditioned power formation, then what could it mean to say that it is wrong to hold that 'religion is a private affair'? Whoever may or may not hold it, what kind of assumption is it? If it was taken literally it would be nonsense. Is its corrective the opposite claim that 'religion is a public affair'? These kinds of statements only make sense when 'religion' means Christian Truth, and should therefore be read as meaning that true religion or true Christianity consists of a private, personal and voluntary relationship of the individual with God, a relationship of the inner conscience of the believer which can claim no legitimate worldly power – power which is the prerogative of the state. She is surely talking about persuasive representations of 'religion' that have invented 'it' even as claims are made about it.

What does her expression 'the politics of secularism' (2008: 3, and in her book's title) mean? She means that secularism conceived as a neutral, given space which is not itself a product of control and power (2008: 4) is a false but deeply held assumption that has generally not been contested in international relations theory. To illustrate this, she quotes Brooks, apparently approvingly:

> Our foreign policy elites ... go for months ignoring the force of religion; then when confronted with something inescapably religious, such as the Iranian revolution or the Taliban, they begin talking of religious zealotry and fanaticism, which suddenly explains everything. ... We do not yet have, and sorely need, a mode of analysis that attempts to merge the spiritual and the material (2008: 4; note 21).

I am confused about the logical level at which categories such as religion, religious, spiritual and material, which ostensibly are being problematized, are being used here. The Iranian revolution and the Taliban are 'inescapably religious', and religion has or is a force which they ignore at their peril. But these are only inescapably religious if one is still mystified by the Anglophone rhetoric and not yet free through the critical unwinding of these tropes. Religion, religious, spiritual and material are four of the key terms at issue. There is slippage here between religion as a powerful Anglophone discourse which rightly needs to be critiqued in order to show that this is a historically constructed and unstable category parasitically connected to the category of the secular; and on the other hand a dogmatic assumption that the Iranian revolution and the Taliban are 'religious'. But to apply this category is to assume what is being questioned. One might ask, for example, if they are religious instead of political? Or are they both religious and political? If politics simply means power and control, then there is no real binary problem. Power is such a ubiquitous and general concept that to give it meaning it needs to be placed in a specific context. Without a specific and concrete context to give its use some content, then 'power' as 'politics' or 'politics' as 'power' remains a category at such an abstract level of deployment as to be virtually empty of content. If all human relations are in some sense and to some extent power relations, and if politics is simply exchangeable with power, then very little has been said.

On the other hand the modern domain of politics has emerged historically in the context of the modern invention of the non-religious 'secular'. But if politics means *secular non-religious politics* as constructed by Anglophone and more generally Europhone discourse, then we are still stuck in the binary that is being disembedded and critiqued. The ambiguity of the term 'politics' between the very general, ubiquitous notion of power on the one hand, and on the other the ideologically-loaded notion of non-religious secular power, seems to be the source of its illusionary magic.

Brooks is reported as saying that we need 'a mode of analysis that attempts to merge the spiritual and the material'. One can guess that she means a mode of analysis that does not presuppose the very dichotomy that is problematically presupposed in the discourse. And this is what I guess Hurd means, since she makes it very clear in other places that the discursive division or binary is itself the problem and we need a different theoretical formulation that does not recycle this binary vocabulary into the set of assumptions.

Hurd uses this quote to support her critical argument, but it isn't clear that the quoted passage does this, for the language is the problem. She says:

This book is structured around three sets of arguments that develop and illustrate my overarching claim that the traditions of secularism described here are an important source of political authority in international relations (2008: 4).

Again the ambiguity of 'politics'. Meaning power and control? Or carrying the arguably inescapable nuance of a constituent part of the secular domain, and as such an autonomous, neutral and given space that marginalizes religion and is therefore itself not religious? Hurd is both contesting the assumption of this neutral secular space and yet at the same time leaves it open for the reader to read politics as an expression of the space. If politics merely means power, then the problem seems less, but at the expense of content. But discourses on politics strongly contain the assumption that politics is non-religious, which reintroduces the problematic binary.

Take the following examples from chapter 8 of Hurd's book, which has as its title 'Religious Resurgence', a title strongly reminiscent of Scott Thomas and one that seems to presuppose that we could be clear *what* is resurging; or that might ambiguously be inviting us to feel puzzled by the expression. The author says: 'Religion and politics overlap and intersect in complex and multiple formations in different times and locations, composing political settlements that wax and wane in their influence' (2008: 134).

This formulation does not fundamentally problematize the categories religion and politics. It makes what sounds like a factual statement about two distinct, ahistorical domains that nevertheless have problematic relations (they 'overlap and intersect'). Yet in the very next sentence Hurd says 'Religion and politics do not belong to distinct domains.' But, in that case, how can we say they intersect and overlap? Furthermore, they have 'political' outcomes. But why not say that they have religious outcomes? If politics is a modern, secular (discursive) domain, then it is parasitic on religion (as a discourse). If politics is universal and ahistorical as 'power', then there is nothing especially modern about it. The contestable and slippery quality of these categories is reproduced whenever they are used descriptively and analytically. Therefore we cannot get a grip on their meaning, because there is always ambiguity. Yet this is the source of their rhetorical magic.

If religion is a modern discursive construct, then so is the non-religious, including International Relations as a discipline. One of the sources of power in modern contexts is surely, then, the discursively generated ideological binary division between religion and non-religion in the first place, for it is this division which transforms an imaginary domain into an irrefutable commonplace which IR experts (along with the majority of academics, politicians and journalists) have apparently not noticed until recently. When Hurd talks about 'forms of secularist authority and their relationship to religion', I assume her to mean something like 'discourses that construct "secular" authority and simultaneously construct "religion" as though these are essentially distinct phenomena which come into problematic contact'.

Hurd makes a useful analytical distinction between laicism and Judaeo-Christian secularism (2008: 5). Both are a 'productive modality of power' (2008: 53). Both are discursive traditions. Both 'defend some form of the separation of church and state' (2008: 5). However, they are different in certain respects:

With its origins in the French term *laïcité*, the objective of laicism is to create a neutral public space in which religious belief, practices, and institutions have lost their political significance, fallen below the threshold of political contestation, or been pushed into the private sphere. The mixing of religion and politics is regarded as irrational and dangerous. For modernization to take hold, religion must be separated from politics … laicism adopts and expresses a pretence of neutrality regarding the assumption that a fixed and final separation between religion and politics is both possible and desirable. This makes it difficult for those who have been shaped by and draw upon this tradition to see the limitations of their own conception of religion and politics. In other words, laicism presents itself as having risen above the messy debate over religion and politics, standing over and outside the melee in a neutral space of its own creation. The politics of laicism is more complex than is suggested by this alleged resolution (2008: 5).

The problem for the reader is to determine at what logical level the various uses of the terms are being used. If laicism claims (or is discursively constructed) to stand above both religion and politics, does this mean that laicism is discursively constructed as both non-religious and non-political? Somehow I would have thought that politics in France would be understood by French people to be a central expression of their secularity, and thus as being inseparable from it. In that case, how could laicism be seen as above politics? This may be a simple misunderstanding of mine, but I have tried to show that these categories seem to derive their productive power in part by their lack of stable meaning.

The second tradition of secularism that is influential in the international relations literature emphasizes the role of Christianity, and more recently Judeo-Christianity, as the foundation for secular public order and democratic political institutions. Unlike laicism, what I call Judeo-Christian secularism does not attempt to expel religion, or at least Judeo-Christianity, from public life. It does not present the religious–secular divide as a clean, essentialized, and bifurcated relationship, as in laicism. This form of secularism therefore seems counter-intuitive, at least at first. It corresponds only in part with Berger's authoritative definition of secularization as 'the process by which sectors of society and culture are removed from the domination of religious institutions and symbols.' For in this second trajectory of secularism, Euro-American secular public life is securely grounded in a larger Christian, and later Judeo-Christian, civilization. … Judeo-Christian dispositions and cultural instincts are perceived to have culminated in and contributed to the unique Western achievement of the separation of church and state. … Although sectors of Western society and culture have been partially removed from the domination of religious institutions and symbols à la Berger, political order in the West remains

firmly grounded in a common set of core values with their roots in Latin
Christendom (2008: 5–6).

I have argued elsewhere that Berger's definition is problematic precisely
because it assumes that we already know what is meant by religious institutions, and by the secular social and cultural space that he claims emerges into
view with their removal (Fitzgerald 2007a: 99) A connected point is that, if
it is true that the modern separation of church and state is today imagined as
the same as the modern separation of religion and politics, then the influence
of Judaeo-Christianity in the production of that separation, and the practical
fuzziness of the boundaries between them, does not undo the categorial
separation but presupposes it! The same distinction underlines both these
varieties of secularism; this suggests (and I think Hurd has partially made this
point in her reference to fuzzy boundaries) that the differences are more related
to the kind of disputes about how this boundary should be negotiated and
maintained in the French and US traditions, with their different relations to
Catholicism and Protestantism, and their different revolutionary histories and
traditions of enlightenment, rather than any more substantive disagreement (in
law and constitution for example) about the existence of the boundary itself.
    This point seems to be strengthened by Hurd's own observation that *both*
laicism and Judaeo-Christian secularism are present in US public discourse:

> These two varieties of secularist tradition worked together to fuel powerful
> American condemnations of the revolution and the representation of revolu-
> tionary Iran as a threat not only to American national interests but also to
> the foundations of American national identity itself. From 1979 onward, to
> stand for a secular (laicist, Judeo-Christian, or both) and democratic United
> States was to oppose an Islamic (theocratic, tyrannical) Iran (2008: 9).

Later, Hurd says: 'Elements of both laicism and Judeo-Christian secularism
compete and coexist in both European and American discourses on religion
and politics' (2008: 47).
    This suggests that what Hurd describes as two different traditions of
secularism could be read instead as an analytical distinction between two
strategically placed emphases within the historically emergent discourse on
religion and the secular. These emphases do not point to an *essential* difference
but share a crucial commonality in historical discourse (in reminding the
reader that this discussion is in English, I am leaving aside the problem – if it
is a problem – of translating French *laïcité* into 'laicism'). I suggest that, underlying both these emphases, in US Anglophone discourse at least, there lies a
common binary opposition that, in separating the 'religious' from the 'secular'
at the same time invents them. It is the invention of the non-religious that I
have suggested is as important as the invention of the religious, because it acts
to conceal the alternative view that dominant formations of modernity, such as

capitalism and nationalism, are not themselves essentially different from those practices classified as 'religions'. By disguising the arguable alternative view that capitalism and nationalism are mythical, faith-based ideologies with many resemblances to 'religions', it facilitates the illusion that they are somehow in clear contradistinction to religion, that is to say they are non-religious secular, in line with natural reason and common sense, and therefore in conformity with the real world, in the way that 'religions' are not. Both emphases derive from a modern, discursive construction that essentializes the distinction between the religious and the secular political domains in order to quarantine the latter from the perception that such a domain, too, is an arbitrary and historically contingent myth. It has been remarkably successful in this, as the history of IR apparently shows.

This essentialization may seem clearer in the variant that Hurd refers to as laicism, especially in its French version with its more dogmatic lines of inclusion and exclusion. I think Hurd intends to make this point when she says: 'The ambition to realize a pure, universal form of laicism that expels religion from politics is one of the hallmarks of modern French political order ...'. However, she then adds '... and has been achieved by legislating the relationship between the realm of the sacred and the realm of the profane' (2008: 54).

Here Hurd is apparently equating the 'sacred' with 'religion' and the 'profane' with the 'secular'. I have myself argued in various parts of this book, and also in some detail on the basis of an analysis of historical texts (Fitzgerald 2007a), that this equation is itself part of the modern ideological construction. Yet again, this passage ambiguously tends to undo the critical project that Hurd is engaged with. This identification itself is part of our shared problem.

The narrative that religion has been expelled from politics is presumably a rhetorical way of disguising their mutual discursive construction and essential distinction, which is the modern invention of the religion–non-religion binary. If, however, 'politics' is simply an ahistorical marker for 'power' relations, then I re-assert my claim that the older discourse on Religion as Christian Truth never did expel power, but legitimated it through the anointing of kings and the defence of the commonwealth. Is 'politics' an independent variable in Hurd's writing, or not? Can we assume we know what is meant by 'politics' and 'political order', or not? To make the assumption is also to make the assumption that it has a stable, universal referent that any normal, rational person, thinking in any language, would intuitively understand. But such an assumption merely makes 'politics' and 'political order' synonymous with the most abstract and empty word for 'power'! On the other hand, the critical line of Hurd's argument has been that both religion and secular politics have been constructed as a contested project of modernity, and it is their imagined separation into the religious and the non-religious secular domains respectively that constitutes them in modern ideology. To claim that 'religion' has been expelled from 'politics' is ambiguous to say the least, and is surely the kind of circular rhetoric that requires critical exposure.

In contrast, US Judaeo-Christian secularism appears on the face of it as more pragmatic, partially tolerating some interference of one domain in the functioning of the other. One aspect of the more pragmatic version that requires notice is that the presumption of the superior ground of secular rationality is softened, at least in some contexts, mainly by the sheer power of Christian evangelical contestation in the US. However, the idea that one domain can in strategic practice interfere beyond the boundaries of another domain still tacitly constructs their difference. The idea that their boundaries might be fuzzy does not eliminate the boundaries, but only takes the problem one step backwards, as a dispute about where the boundaries actually lie. US courts still have to make decisions about what constitutes a religious juridical person and what does not; and while the procedures and the criteria may be largely arbitrary and dependent on equally contestable categories, the simple fact of the procedures testifies to the institutionalized recognition, not only of the right of freedom of worship, but also of the importance of protecting the state from 'religion'.

An important part of Hurd's argument is that 'secularism' in both its forms has depended for its formation on a perceived opposition between European Christendom and Islam:

> Laicism and Judeo-Christian secularism, and the collective identities in which these traditions are embodied and through which they are expressed, have been consolidated in part through opposition to the idea of an antimodern, anti-Christian, and theocratic Islamic Middle East (2008: 49).

The construction of an essentialized 'Islam' as Other, as 'religion', as backward, as unprogressive, as theocratic, as arbitrary, as tyrannical and as irrational has made it possible to imagine Europe as secular, progressive, modern, democratic, and rational. Hurd points out that the theory of oriental despotism has been an important trope in the negative image of the Other.

Both varieties of Euro-American secularism participate in these oppositional structures, though there are significant nuances between them:

> [E]ach trajectory of secularism draws on a different set of historical representations of Islam: laicist assumptions contribute to depictions of Islam as a surmountable though formidable stumbling block to the rationalization and democratization of societies, whereas Judeo-Christian secularist assumptions lead to more ominous conclusions in which Islam is portrayed as a potential threat to the cultural, moral, and religious foundations of Western civilization ... (2008: 47).

A significant historical context for a modern, civilized and laicist French identity was the colonial adventure in Algiers with its 'differentiation of a civilized laicist colonizer from an uncouth, Islamic colonized Algeria' (2008:

55). French colonization was represented as a civilizing mission. Hurd does not much dwell on the relationship between colonialism and capitalism, but she gives us a brief insight into the power relations that underlay the civilizing mission in the power of the French state to 'gain a rotating reserve army of laborers necessary for building up the metropole' (2008: 55). The ideology worked well apparently, for 'The process of colonizing Algeria helped to consolidate both the tradition of modern French laicism and French republican ideals ... while excluding Muslims from these allegedly universal forms of identification' (2008: 55). Though the commitment to *laïcité* was in a formal sense established in the French Revolution, it became progressively established through the nineteenth century with the gradual erosion of Catholic power culminating in the law of 1905 'which ensured liberty of conscience, guaranteed the free exercise of religion (Article I), and acknowledged that the Republic would not recognize, remunerate, or subsidize any religious denomination (Article II)' (2008: 57).

Hurd argues that the gradual transformation of France into a secular Republic through the nineteenth century was not only due to the domestic struggle between the Church and the forces of liberalism, but that 'both contributed to and benefited from specific French colonial policies, in particular a more assertive and deliberate overseas colonial policy that developed after the military defeat of 1870 – the same year that France made Algeria an integral part of France with three departments French colonial representations of Algerian Muslims as nonsecular, uncivilized, and disorderly ... leading figure in French secularizing educational reforms of this era'. Ferry supported the 'obligation and duty that are imposed on all civilized people to make the signature of their representatives respected by all barbarous nations' (2008: 57, quoting Ferry).

Hurd tells an equally interesting and believable story about the construction of the myths of US manifest destiny. She has usefully summarized this process:

> The production of early American national identity as Christian, secular, and democratic was at least in part an effect of the attempt to differentiate a modern, republican Christian America from an antimodern, despotic Islamic Middle East. Long before any Muslims settled in the United States, Islam played an important role in the construction of American identity as Christian (later Judeo-Christian), secular, and democratic. This process of collective self-identification laid important cultural templates for powerful contemporary connections between American identity, manifest destiny, and Christianity ... These same templates contribute to American constructions of Muslim deviance at home and abroad, including contemporary notions of the 'rogue state', the Islamic terrorist, and the portrayal of Islam as a 'false religion' (2008: 63).

I have myself attempted to show how discourses on civility and barbarity have historically followed and helped to mould the changing contours of discourses on religion (Fitzgerald 2007a). The argument I developed in that book is a complex one and not easily summarized, though I have tried to indicate my own arguments in strategic response to the analysis of IR texts here. In the older discourse – which, as Hurd rightly suggests, still thrives – Religion has meant Christian Truth and has been opposed to pagan barbarity and irrationality. In the modern discourse, religion ostensibly developed a generic and neutral universality. In this discourse the opposite of religion is not pagan barbarity but secular non-religious rationality. Religions could therefore be scientifically studied from the superior secular standpoint of the Science of Religion, or sociology, or anthropology, or even biology. Here civility is possessed by those who have secular reason and therefore progress, whereas religion is the stigma of those barbarous and irrational others who believe in superstitions and who have absurd practices which need to be controlled and legislated by enlightened colonial administrations. However, in this modern discourse, especially in Protestant countries such as the US, Protestantism is also a rational form of personal faith which is consistent with secularism even where distinguished from it along the contours of the binaries: private to public; inner to outer; church to state; rational or non-rational faith in the unseen to scientific knowledge of the seen; and so on.

That these two analytically separable discourses both continue into the twenty-first century and are frequently imbricated in the other is evident from much that Hurd herself says and from much other evidence. In the final chapter of this volume I cite and quote Sharada Sugirtharajah (2010: 69–78) who has shown how, in the case of India, missionaries and Sanskritists, including those like Max Müller who founded the Science of Religion in the mid-nineteenth century, helped construct an imagined false religion Hinduism which was to be defeated by the higher rationality of Protestant Christian enlightenment.[3] Increasing colonial power encouraged the development of new, bureaucratic forms of classification from the available logic and categories of the Christian theological and philosophical traditions.

However, the needs of colonial classification cannot be cleanly separated from the power interests that drove empire and colonization in the first place. The most obvious elective affinity has been the representation of capital and corporate interests as the natural and inevitable outcome of human freedom, rational self-interest, democracy, freedom of markets, and the break-up of traditional forms of collective life. This is a power formation that appears to those in power as a transparent view of natural reason.

This point distinguishes both variations of modern ideology from the dominant meanings of 'secular' and 'religion' that have been defined histori-cally by a different and older discourse. In the older discourse the 'secular' institutions such as the secular priesthood were not 'non-religious' in the modern sense but were (and in so far as that discourse is still articulated, for example by the Catholic and Anglican Churches) encompassed by religion understood not as a private right but as the totalizing truth about the world. In that older discourse the secular and the religious were a nomenclature for different institutions or statuses within the overall organization of Christendom. If the 'religious orders' were considered closer to God because they had renounced the profane world to a greater extent than the celibate priesthood, this points not to the modern essentialization of two different ontological domains but to a *relative* degree of distance from God. In modern discourse, whether laicist or Judeo-Christian secularist, in both cases Anglophone (and more widely Europhone) 'religion' has been transformed from its meaning as Protestant (or Catholic) Christian Truth, policed since the sixteenth and seventeenth centuries by the church-states, to meaning a private, voluntary right to worship and association with no coercive powers and both separated from, and licensed by, the non-religious nation state.

Hurd says:

> The notion of the *saeculum* emerged in the thirteenth century in reference to a binary opposition within Christianity. Priests who withdrew from the world (*saeculum*) formed the religious clergy, while those who lived in the world formed the secular clergy. The term 'secular' was used in English, often with negative connotations, to distinguish clergy living in the wider world from those in monastic seclusion. In a second transformation, and by the sixteenth century, the term began to shed its affiliation with Godlessness and the profane; Keane notes that in this era 'the word "secular" was flung into motion and used to describe a world thought to be in motion. In this case, to "secularize" meant to make someone or something secular – converting from ecclesiastical to civil use or possession. By the end of the Thirty Years' War, secularization referred to the transfer of church properties to the exclusive control of the princes. Casanova describes this as the 'passage, transfer, or relocation of persons, things, functions, meanings, and so forth, from their traditional location in the religious sphere to the secular spheres'. This meaning of secularization predominated at the 1648 Peace of Westphalia and onward; on November 2, 1789, Talleyrand announced to the French National Assembly that all ecclesiastical goods were at the disposal of the French nation. In a third transformation and from the nineteenth century onward, secularism began to take on the meaning recognized in the vernacular today. It described a movement that was 'expressly intended to provide a certain theory of life and conduct without reference to a deity or a future life'. Coined officially by George Jacob Holyoake in 1851 ... the term secularism was at this time 'built into the ideology of progress' (2008: 13).

Though there may be some truth in this narrative, I would like to suggest a modified reading of the history of these categories. Despite the many authorities which Hurd lines up to underpin her claims in this one paragraph alone (in this case Jose Casanova, John Keane, T.N. Madan, Azam Tamimi), Hurd's history of the English word 'secular', while useful and insightful in some respects, is surely contestable in others. I found the clarification of the role of Kant's philosophy (Hurd 2008: 25ff) as a stage in the emergence of secularism, which draws considerably on the enlightening work of William E. Connolly, useful and significant; however, before we arrive there, there is some discussion of a longer historical trajectory that in my view still needs clarification. Beginning with Hurd's reference to thirteenth-century usage of Latin *saeculum*, she describes its relation to 'the religious' (in Latin *religiones*) as a binary opposition within Christianity. I would suggest some clarification: this is not a binary opposition in the same way that the modern Anglophone religion–secular dichotomy is a binary opposition. The distinction between God and the world was a theological distinction in which the world was created by God and was ultimately dependent on God. The distance between the sacred (ultimately God) and the profane was, and within the terms of that discourse still largely remains, a relative and context-dependent matter. Thus, for example, the distance between God and the profane human world was greater in Calvinism than in Catholicism, because Calvin abolished the miracle of the Mass and the ritual hierarchy of Rome and inaugurated a concept of the Fall so extreme that no action of repentance – no 'works' – could be efficacious in the restoration of a relationship with God. Salvation and damnation were predestined. It can be argued that this absolute Calvinist chasm between the world and God was a significant contribution to the emergence of something more than a relative sacred–profane distinction; it contributed to the idea – developing also as a rationale for the empirical sciences – that the world had little if anything essentially to do with God. The world could be studied, measured, and explained as a material system with its own causality.

This development in the natural sciences combined with the emergence of the new ideology of the state and politics, and with a transformation in the meaning of natural reason. In the older medieval Christian *imaginaire*, natural reason had been implanted by God in human understanding, and the world was rational because God had made it. However, with the emergence of modern binaries which radically distinguish between God and the world, religion and the secular, spirit and matter, and soul and body, rationality became formulated in terms of scientific knowledge as against faith, or in the pragmatic, problem-solving arbitrations of secular politics in distinction from the blind, unverifiable metaphysics of religion.

We can get a clearer idea of the difference between the modern essential-izing discourse on the religion–secular dichotomy, and the older relativity of the sacred–profane distinction, by considering some other possible examples of how they might have been applied in practice (I have discussed these and other examples in Fitzgerald 2007a.). The graveyard was a relatively sacred site, more sacred than the fields beyond but less sacred than the altar where Mass was enacted. Yet even here, the produce of the fields was considered relatively sacred in the sense that God is the ultimate cause of good crops, as the liturgy of Harvest Festival makes plain with the symbolic decoration of the church. Digging graves was a relatively profane and even polluting task, yet it took place within the sacred precincts of the graveyard; but digging a ditch to carry slops may have been profane in the more neutral sense that it was a functional occupation. However, even here, sermons and homilies of the sixteenth and seventeenth centuries make it clear that all work is, or ought to be, undertaken as service to God however humble, and such humble service is therefore in a sense sacralized by the church-state. One of the most sacred spaces in the land was the king's bedchamber, in the context of which only very high-ranking nobility could serve; whereas reception rooms in the palace were presumably less surrounded by protective taboos and prohibitions. The king's hunting grounds were sacred and protected by taboos and prohibitions, whereas the common land of the peasants was relatively profane, even though the right of common use was a sacred right hallowed by tradition. Parliament, where Lords Temporal and Ecclesiastical made and enacted the laws of the land, was a sacred space, hedged around by rituals, including the performance of Anglican communion, a space into which even the king's visits were increasingly restricted.

The secular priesthood were not *non-religious* in the modern sense, but only in the entirely different sense that they were not as close to God as those 'religious' who had in theory renounced living in the world. But the ideal of celibacy still marked the priesthood off as relatively special. The Pope and the king were both prince and priest, and in that older sense 'secular' – but still sacred. There was no notion that the secular were not Christian. Even the stronger sense of the profane as the rejection of God was itself a theological construct. Those in the service of Satan symbolically reversed the Christian order, for example by standing the Cross on its head or reciting the Lord's Prayer backwards. This is significantly different from the modern idea of neutral secularity. The fall of the angel was not a modern assertion of a world that does not require God as a hypothesis, a self-explanatory system of material causality and the pragmatic rationality of the secular state and politics. Satan was an angel, albeit an angel in reverse.

The distinction which Hurd points out between 'the religious' (the monastic orders which have renounced the world, also known in English as the Regulars, meaning monks, nuns and friars) and the secular clergy living in the world was in the first place a way of referring to distinct statuses within the church. The term 'secular' was also sometimes extended to civil authorities and statuses such as the king or prince and the civil courts. 'Civil' here did not mean non-religious in the modern sense. The ultimate responsibility of the civil courts was the hunting and punishment of heretics and traitors, technically distinct crimes but easily confused since to be a traitor was to go against the anointed king. The civil courts were distinguished from the ecclesiastical courts, not the religious courts. The term 'religion' was rarely used in English until after the Reformation, when it usually meant Protestant Christian Truth, and was proclaimed from time to time to propagandize the legitimacy of the break from Rome. Christian Truth did not exclude the secular or civil authorities and institutions but encompassed them. Arguably there was no concept of a non-religious institution, authority or truth until much later.

As it stands in Hurd's text (2008: 13), the quote from Casanova is therefore both circular and misleading. To say that 'secularization' referred to the transfer from 'the religious sphere to the secular spheres' by itself tells us nothing, since the key terms have to be contextualized, and such a statement leaves it wide open for modern meanings to be projected onto a different world. I suggest that such an expression – if it were conceivable at all in the seventeenth century – would have meant (as Hurd herself acknowledges) a transference from the religious orders to the secular priesthood, which is hardly a transfer from 'religion' to the 'secular' in the modern sense. Such an expression invites a retrospective projection of modern nuances onto a profoundly different semantic universe, in which 'secular' has developed the nuance of non-religious, and 'religion' has become neutrally pluralized as 'religions', a construction which allows eventually for the idea of Christianity being 'a religion', that is, one religion among others, which is an entirely modern discourse which was only emerging in the eighteenth century.

Hurd claims that 'This meaning of secularization predominated at the 1648 Peace of Westphalia ...'. She may be right about this, but which meaning? And I wonder how she knows this, and in which language is it written? I cannot find a single mention of 'secularization' in the English translation of that document provided online by Yale Law School Lillian Goldman Law Library (Avalon Project 2008). There are three uses of the term 'secular', and they are all predictably coupled with 'ecclesiastical', as in this clause:

> In the second place, the House of Hesse Cassel, and its Successors, shall retain, and for this purpose shall demand at any time, and when it shall be expir'd, the Investiture of his Imperial Majesty, and shall take the Oath of Fidelity for the Abby of Hitsfield, with all its Dependencys, as well Secular as Ecclesiastical, situated within or without his Territorys (as the Deanery of Gellingen) saving nevertheless the Rights possess'd by the House of Saxony, time out of mind (Avalon Project 2008).

This seems to indicate that, even after a hundred years of strife between Catholic and Protestant church-states, both secular and ecclesiastical authorities were still unquestionably deemed to be Christian institutions serving the purposes of Christian Truth. In England this was still true well into the early nineteenth century, despite the developments of scepticism, empiricism, industry, science, non-conformity, trade unionism, the early beginnings of feminism, and other fundamental aspects of the emergence of a new cosmology.

In the long run modernity does not depend on fundamental Christian doctrines such as creation, sacrifice, atonement, resurrection, judgement or obedience to the God-anointed Christian prince; but rather transforms them into optional extras that have no crucial bearing on the lives of citizens. Even so, the Coronation liturgy of Elizabeth II in 1953, which took place in Westminster Abbey, had as its central rite the anointing with oil. The Queen sat in the Chair of Edward the Confessor, who was both king and saint and whose tomb was for centuries the object of pilgrimage.

I do not deny that the Treaty of Westphalia appears retrospectively to have been a significant stage in the early formation of a world of sovereign nation states whose power relationships were to become the stuff of modern International Relations; nor that there was an idea of a process of 'secularization' at that time in the sense of the transference of church properties from the religious orders to the secular priesthood or the civil authorities. This would make sense in the case of the formation of Protestant church-states. But this was not a transfer from a 'religious' to a 'non-religious' domain in the modern sense. I cannot find any idea of the modern non-religious secular in that document. All the 'secular' authorities and institutions were Christian; the dispute was between different Christian confessions. This becomes clear in the following clause, where 'Religion' (mentioned five times in that translated document) clearly refers to Christian confession:

> That those of the Confession of Augsburg, and particularly the Inhabitants of Oppenheim, shall be put in possession again of their Churches, and Ecclesiastical Estates, as they were in the Year 1624. As also that all others of the said Confession of Augsburg, who shall demand it, shall have the free Exercise of their Religion, as well in publick Churches at the appointed Hours, as in private in their own Houses, or in others chosen for this purpose by their Ministers, or by those of their Neighbours, preaching the Word of God (Avalon Project 2008).

It is also clear that two Confessions are considered at the Treaty of Westphalia (Catholic and Lutheran):

> CVII.
> If any of those who are to have something restor'd to them, suppose that the Emperor's Commissarys are necessary to be present at the Execution of some Restitution (which is left to their Choice) they shall have them. In which case, that the effect of the things agreed on may be the less hinder'd, it shall be permitted as well to those who restore, as to those to whom Restitution is to be made, to nominate two or three Commissarys immediately after the signing of the Peace, of whom his Imperial Majesty shall chuse two, one of each Religion... (Avalon Project 2008).

That there are two religions (in the sense of two Confessions) does retrospectively suggest the beginnings of the emergence of a different logic of use, especially when other confessions such as the Calvinist are taken into account. However, this multiplication is still firmly established within an encompassing Christian Truth, and is nowhere near the modern generic usage that attributes a kind of ubiquitous universality to religion and religions, along with a ubiquitous universality to the non-religious secular.

It is also interesting to note that there does not appear to be a single instance of the word 'politics' in the English version of this document. There is one instance of the adjective 'politick':

CXXI.
That it never shall be alledg'd, allow'd, or admitted, that any Canonical or Civil Law, any general or particular Decrees of Councils, any Privileges, any Indulgences, any Edicts, any Commissions, Inhibitions, Mandates, Decrees, Rescripts, Suspensions of Law, Judgments pronounc'd at any time, Adjudications, Capitulations of the Emperor, and other Rules and Exceptions of Religious Orders, past or future Protestations, Contradictions, Appeals, Investitures, Transactions, Oaths, Renunciations, Contracts, and much less the Edict of 1629. or the Transaction of Prague, with its Appendixes, or the Concordates with the Popes, or the Interims of the Year 1548, or any other *politick* Statutes, or Ecclesiastical Decrees, Dispensations, Absolutions, or any other Exceptions, under what pretence or colour they can be invented; shall take place against this Convention, or any of its Clauses and Articles neither shall any inhibitory or other Processes or Commissions be ever allow'd to the Plaintiff or Defendant (Avalon Project 2008; emphasis added).

It can be seen in this passage that the adjective 'politick' qualifies 'statutes' and 'ecclediastical decrees, dispensations, absolutions ...' and thus makes no reference to any notion of a domain that might be construed as 'nonreligious' as distinct from 'religious'. In my own readings of historical documents, which of course can still be questioned by genuine experts in these historical periods, the noun 'politics' referring to a distinct domain separated from 'religion' is difficult to find before the late seventeenth century. Hurd herself rightly says that 'International relations theorists and practitioners need to reconsider the ontological and epistemological foundations of the discipline that govern what counts as politics in international relations. They need to rethink the assumptions about religion and politics embedded in the hypotheses and empirical tests of international relations scholarship' (Hurd 2008: 22). Yet only on the previous page she has said that she is investigating 'the political consequences of ... secularism in international relations ...' (2008: 21) in a form of words close to the title of the book, which re-inscribes politics as a descriptive and analytical category in her own text.

I have mentioned more than once in earlier chapters two historical examples of a clear, and I would suggest essentialized, discourse on 'politics' found in texts published in around 1680 by William Penn and John Locke respectively. I have argued elsewhere that, in English at least, an apparently crucial stage for the modern distinction between religion and politics is found here (see Fitzgerald 2007a). By distancing government from religion in the search for a higher ground of rational decision-making, then politics seems inevitably to be represented as itself non-religious. But the term 'secular' is not used in this context, and I would argue it is not used to refer to a non-religious domain until well into the nineteenth century (a point Hurd makes with her reference to Charles Holyoake in 1851).[4] And even in these late seventeenth-century uses, religion still referred mainly to Christian Truth, though retrospectively it can be argued that a generic idea of religions as ubiquitous and universal phenomena is beginning to emerge in the context of colonial expansion and the classificatory needs of colonial knowledge.[5] Yet well into the twentieth century, and arguably still today, the discourse on Religion as Christian truth and civility is still 'productive'.

In an interesting and useful discussion of Kant, which draws fruitfully on the work of William E. Connolly and some other writers, Hurd identifies the late eighteenth century as a crucial stage in the emergence of the modern religion–secular discourse. Though she is surely right to do so, I find it difficult to see how this stage of emergence fits in with her claims about the binary opposition of earlier centuries. A crucial question here is the way in which Kant, with his articulation of 'rational religion' (Hurd 2008: 25) clarified a long trajectory of shifting nuances in the emergent modern binary.

Hurd states clearly the importance of Kant in the development of a concept of generic Christianity that simultaneous enabled the articulation of a generic and universal presupposition of secular rationality that, she says, has foundational relevance for both Judaeo-Christian secularism and laicism:

> ... Kant laid a template for a generic form of Christianity that was intended to supersede sectarian faith. This template served as an important historical precursor of and political resource for later articulations of the forms of secularism described in this book ... To overcome sectarianism, Kant proposed elevating universal philosophy, or rational religion, to the position previously reserved for Christian theology ... As Connolly argues, the key to this Kantian rational religion is that it is anchored in a metaphysic of the supersensible that is presupposed by *any* agent of morality. 'Kant anchors rational religion in the law of morality rather than anchoring morality in ecclesiastical faith.' This allows Kant to retain the command model of morality from Augustinian Christianity while shifting the proximate point of command from the Christian God to the individual moral subject ... In this way, Kant's rational religion, although it seeks to displace Christian ecclesiastical theology, also shares several significant qualities with it (2008: 26).

Usefully citing and quoting Connolly, she identifies four common qualities shared by rational religion and ecclesiastical doctrine:

First, it places singular conceptions of reason and command morality above question. Second, it sets up (Kantian) philosophy as the highest potential authority in adjudicating questions in these two domains and in guiding the people towards eventual enlightenment. Third, it defines the greatest danger to public morality as sectarianism within Christianity. Fourth, in the process of defrocking ecclesiastical theology and crowning philosophy as judge in the last instance, it also delegitimates a place for several non-Kantian, nontheistic perspectives in public life (Connolly, quoted in Hurd 2008: 26).

Connolly (and Hurd) argues that forms of modern secularism adopted this matrix of assumptions but at the same time tended to let the 'metaphysical portfolio' (Connolly's expression) quietly slip out of sight. This, Hurd argues, 'describes laicism and, to a certain extent, Judeo-Christian secularism' (2008: 26). However, I feel that this strengthens my point that, though the distinction between these two different forms of secularism is useful in some contexts, for example in her discussion of Turkish Kemalism, it ought not to obscure the more fundamental point that underlying both these forms lies the emergence of a new common binary, clearly articulated in the late seventeenth century, developed by Kant and others in eighteenth-century Europe, a binary that found its way into the Bills of Rights and State Constitutions of some North American colonies and plantations, and eventually culminated in the US and French Constitutions and formulations of the universal rights of 'man'. While I would agree that the histories of the American and French Revolutions have to be studied on their own terms for the continuing emergence and articulation of these different forms of the religion–secular distinction, nevertheless the French, American, German, Scottish and English Enlightenments shared crucial ideological features. Some aspects of Hurd's discussion of Kant seem to point to this.

Hurd claims that 'Secularism refers to a public settlement of the relationship between politics and religion' (2008: 12). But this seems a strained formulation which, while neat and pithy, is not clearly meaningful. Has the relationship between politics and religion been settled? To put it in this way might be to invite a misunderstanding similar to that which is conveyed in the modern sociological concept of secularization, which is that the idea that 'politics' and 'religion' as two separate domains with problematic relations was already conceptualized but required clarification and agreement, whereas it might surely be truer to say that this modern binary was itself only in the long-term process of emergence. As with so many writers, there is a constant slippage between treating 'religion' and 'politics' as two pre-existing domains found universally but given different degrees of clarity in their recognition; and treating these as modern discourses which invent new domains by giving old terms new meanings (or, as with 'politics' and 'economics', virtually inventing new terms). When Hurd goes on to say that, in contemporary Europe and the United States, the 'secular is associated with the worldly or the temporal ...'

(2008: 13), there is the danger that the reader will impute the same meanings to 'worldly' and 'temporal' as was meant in these earlier centuries, a point I have already laboured to make.

I have argued earlier in this chapter and in other places in this book that the discourses on the modern religion–secular binary should be analytically distinguished from the older discourses on the sacred and the profane. This distinction might be helpful in Hurd's stated aim: 'The principle substantive objective of this book is to deconstruct the secular–theological oppositional binary and open the way for religiopolitical possibilities that are structured less antagonistically, softening the rigid oppositions that often characterize the assumptions brought to the study and practice of both secularism and religion' (2008: 17). Whereas the modern discourses on the religion–secular distinction are (as Hurd acknowledges here) sharply drawn, and, I argue, are constructed rhetorically as essentially different, the older discourse on the sacred and profane was less an oppositional than a relational category indicating degrees of distance from God.

I would suggest (and have argued in this book in, for example, Chapter 8 in a discussion of Anthony D. Smith's essay) that the ubiquitous modern usage of the term 'society' and its adjectival form 'social' also needs critical attention. Discussing 'methods and assumptions' (2008: 16ff), Hurd says:

> I argue on the one hand in favor of the view that people and institutions are social constructions in a pervasive sense of the term, while on the other hand acknowledging that this assumption of the constructed character of being is itself profoundly contestable. My approach to social construction gives priority 'not to a disengaged subject in its relation to independent objects, but to historically specific discursive practices within which people are engaged prior to achieving a capacity to reflect upon them.' Humans engage with each other and with the world within previously established contexts that help to constitute us and the objects represented to and by us. As Barnett and Duval argue, 'constitutive relations cannot be reduced to the attributes, actions, or interactions of pregiven actors. Power, accordingly, is irreducibly social (2008: 17; the first of Hurd's quotes in this extract is from Connolly).

There is much in this paragraph with which I agree. The problem is the term 'social', as in 'social constructions', or the phrase 'irreducibly social'. For 'social' is another of those categories which has been significantly transformed in meaning by social science, especially since the early nineteenth century and the invention of sociology by Saint Simon and Comte. Could we, for example, say that 'society', 'societies' in the plural, and 'the social' are themselves modern social constructions? This would indeed bring us hard and fast against the circularity of our ideological representations. There is a history to the terms social, society and the pluralized 'societies'[6] which needs to be contextualized in historical relationship with modern categories such as 'religions', 'nations', 'politics', 'economics', the secular and so on. One of the outstanding features of these terms is the way they have been constructed as singularities, reified entities, things that exist in the world with clear boundaries. If interrogating these categories is a significant part of our collective endeavour, then we have to avoid recycling them into our own texts as though they are unproblematic descriptive and analytical categories. When we talk about 'social constructions', we may be in danger of substituting one set of reified entities (for example, the concept of individual selves existing in a pre-existent relationship with individual objects which Hurd is rightly critiquing) with another set, 'societies'.

I do, however, appreciate Hurd for her imaginative and deliberate use of the term 'faith' when she describes her own faith 'that animates this study', and her connection of this laudably subversive usage with Gramsci whom she quotes as saying 'all commitments pose an element of belief – that is, an active conviction and commitment – that one could interpret as religious' (2008: 17).

It seems to me that her usage here is in line with common usage, and that such common usage subverts the rhetorical construction of the essential difference between 'religion' and other practices which are usually classified as 'secular' in the sense of nonreligious. She also has many interesting things to say about atheism, about Deleuzean metaphysics and about Spinoza's monism (2008; 19–20)

Though I disagree with the implied assumption that 'the social' is less problematic than 'individualism' or 'materialism', I agree with Hurd's general thrust when she says:

> [T]he combination of individualism and materialism that underlies both neorealism and neoliberalism in international relations, which assumes that the structure constraining state behavior derives from the aggregation of properties of the actors such as the distribution of power, technology and geography, is also problematic. It disregards the social construction of subjectivity by assuming that social actors are preconstituted and downplays or ignores the social processes through which material factors gain meaning for actors. My approach therefore comes closest to ... Barnett and Duvall's concept of 'productive power', insofar as it emphasizes the elusive yet significant context within which social production of subjectivity takes place (2008: 20).

I also agree with Hurd when, in agreement with Talal Asad, she says (quoting from Scott and Hirschkind) that the secular must be approached 'not simply in terms of the doctrinal separation of religious and political authority but as a concept that has brought together sensibilities, knowledges, and behaviours in new and distinct ways' (2008: 21), and that her own approach to secularism attempts (in her own words) 'to capture the histories, sensibilities, and habits that are carried and transformed by and through collective secularist norms, identities and institutions' (2008: 21).

Hurd's arguments are especially concerned with analysing public discourse in the US and Europe, and with relations between France and North Africa, the European Union and Turkey, and the United States and Iran (2008: 21). But she then goes on to say: 'This study takes the collective cultural, religious, and political pulse of the United States and Europe vis-à-vis secularism, Islam and Judeo-Christianity from a position that strives to achieve critical distance from the collective cultural formations and authoritative traditions under study' (2008: 21).

This statement once again brings us hard up against the problem of our critical inquiry, because key terms here such as cultural, religious, political, are themselves contested categories from which she wants to critically distance herself. The re-inscription of categories that Hurd simultaneously (and in my view rightly) wishes to problematize can also be found in this paragraph where she critiques the clash of civilizations narrative:

> ... in which religion is seen as a fixed source of communal unity and identity that generates conflict in international politics ... [A]t least two considerations emerge ... The first is that the attempt to identify something called 'religion' and to assign it a stable and unchanging role in 'politics', whether domestic or international, is a questionable move that is called into question through a genealogy of the secular. The second is that elements of religion always escape such attempts to represent, define, and confine religion to particular roles, spaces, and moments in politics (2008: 24–5).

In this passage, her second point tends to undermine her first one, because if (as I think she rightly says) there is no fixed meaning for these categories, then how would she know that 'elements of religion always escape such attempts' in relation to politics? To avoid these tendencies to recycle the terms which are being critically problematized, we need (and I believe this is Hurd's theoretical desire) to develop a different vocabulary and a different narrative within which to situate our own problematic positionality. How can we extricate ourselves from the terms of established discourse when those terms continually appear and re-appear as categorical markers of our own critical arguments?

There are any number of examples of this confusion between religion, politics and other categories as the target of critique on the one hand, while on the other hand their recycling into the text as descriptive and analytical categories.

Much of the discussion continues with this kind of ambiguity. For example, well into the book Hurd still says that there is 'good evidence for the resurgence. It is now unsustainable to claim that religion plays no significant role in international relations' (2008: 134). But how can we assess such evidence about 'religion' when the purpose of the book is to show that there is no clear meaning or empirical referent to the key term? She goes on to talk about 'religious politics' and the 'politicization of religion around the world in recent decades', hoping to find a pseudo-solution to the inherent ambiguity and contradictoriness of the categories by merging them or hyphenating them. Yet, going on a little further, she reverts to critique: '"religious resurgence" is a term that relies upon particular secularist epistemological assumptions … it is a dispute over the very terms of the debate that structure the discussion of religion and politics … Secularist assumptions prestructure our understanding of religious resurgence. Conventional assumptions about what religion is and how it relates to politics determine the kinds of questions deemed worth asking about the "return of religion"' (2008: 135). There is thus a constant slippage between the critical problematization of key modern categories and their uncritical re-inscription into the terms of Hurd's text itself. The whole discourse is circular, and arguably has to be, for it is itself a metaphysics based on an act of faith. Reverting to a metaphor I used earlier in the book, Hurd is here like the fly caught in glue (as we all are), dancing from one category to the other in an attempt to find a sure basis for critique and escape. We are all in that situation; but I suggest that we have to learn that reliance on the existing problematic categories for descriptive and analytical purposes will maintain the circularity we wish to subvert.

## Notes

1.    Tariq Ali, in *The Clash of Fundamentalisms* (2003), comes close to critically removing this distinction between 'our rational secularity' and 'their irrational religiosity', though I do not think this is a particular issue for him at the explicit, theoretical level.
2.    David Scott and Charles Hirschkind, in their 'Introduction: The Anthropological Skepticism of Talal Asad' to Scott and Hirschkind 2006.
3.    See also David Chidester (1996) for the colonial invention of religion on the frontiers of southern Africa.
4.    According to Waterman, Richard Whately appears to have been the first economist to characterize economics as a *secular* science in his *Introductory Lectures of 1831* as Drummond Professor of Political Economy; see my discussion in Chapter 11.
5.    See my analysis of the work of Samuel Purchas in this regard (Fitzgerald 2007a).
6.    See John Bossy (1982, 1985).

# Chapter 11

## *Some Further Theoretical Implications*

In this book I have looked closely at a number of texts that are broadly concerned with international relations written by economists, social scientists and IR specialists. Some of the texts are explicitly concerned with the ideological construction of modernity and the key categories that constitute modernity. As such they represent attempts at critical deconstruction. In some cases this deconstructive method invites the view that International Relations itself, as a supposedly non-religious secular discipline, is part of the problem of modernity, rather than the solution. Yet at the same time, such texts or their authors are ambiguous about their real purpose, because they continue to re-inscribe the problematic categories in the construction of their own texts. This reveals a conflict between, on the one hand, an intention to go on constructing supposed knowledge about the world, and on the other hand radically questioning any knowledge which is produced through the descriptive and analytical deployment of those same categories. Speaking for myself, 'religion' and 'religions' have provided a place to begin, in part because I myself come from a Religious Studies background (as explained in some detail in Chapter 4), and it was from that starting point that I became increasingly sceptical of the validity of 'religion' as a descriptive and analytical category. Part of my problem was that there seemed no clear way of distinguishing between what constitutes 'religion', or a 'religious' practice or experience, and what, say, a political or economic one. It was from the research and living experiences described there that I began to see that 'religion' is not a standalone category, but is deeply involved in a series of binary oppositions constructing imaginary domains which are mutually parasitic, and none of which have any clear referents. Religion and politics is one of those binaries, and at a more general level so is religion and secular. This line of inquiry has put me in a critical relationship with Religious Studies, and more broadly, the social sciences, on the grounds that, rather than producing valid disinterested knowledge about the world, writers in these disciplines are recycling the fundamental ideological terms of modernity, and are thus engaged in an ideological project which appears as objective knowledge. As such, they or we are mystifyingly perpetuating the myths of religion, of the secular, and more generally of modernity.

It was in particular the language used about religion by some writers in IR that first drew my attention to that discipline and its imagined self-constitution as a secular academic domain. The idea that 'religion' could be an object in the world taking on different forms in specific so-called 'religions' such as Islam, Hinduism and Christianity, and as such having an impact on secular nation states, immediately struck me as a myth, or the mythical use of language. This perception becomes even stronger when authors transform 'religion' into a universal, malign and irrational agent stalking the globe and causing chaos. In this mythical narrative of religion as an intentional agent with its own volition and moods I saw a demon of modernity threatening the rational order of the secular gods, the liberal capitalist nation states which inhabit and act in the realm of the really real.

I hope to have shown by a close analysis of a range of texts how, even where an author has the stated objective of deconstructing the myth of liberal modernity, the key terms continue to be recycled like a computer virus, deeply resistant to removal. This tension and conflict between the critical deconstructive project on the one hand, and the desire to produce yet more knowledge on the basis of these same classificatory paradigms, seems to be at the heart of some of the texts which I have analysed. For example, the absence of religion (its exile) can either be revealed as a rhetorical deployment making possible the simultaneous imagining of a non-religious, empirical secular discipline such as IR. Or it can be an object of faith and belief, as in the narrative of its 'resurgence' and 'return from exile'. In the latter case, the secular ground of reason which is deemed to frame IR and the social sciences, instead of being an integral part of the myth, becomes the unassailable ground of rational analysis from which religion, politics and national states can be objects of knowledge.

The secularity of academics in secular universities cannot legitimately remain as an unexamined background of assumed objectivity as though our productions of knowledge are innocent and disinterested. I have argued that secularity is a modern ideology that becomes camouflaged through the operation of various rhetorical tricks. Obviously I do not believe that these tricks are conscious. To imagine so would be contradictory to a major part of my argument. It is precisely our collective ability to invent myths and then believe in them as though they are descriptions of reality given in experience that buries from view their contested historical origins and transforms them into commonplaces. Though the study of 'religion' is only one secular speciali-zation among many, 'religion' as a category and a discourse is fundamental to the whole ideological enterprise. The modern invention of religion, its reifi-cation into an impossible-to-define something which incarnates universally in the 'religions' of all human groups, languages and periods of history, is a key to the dominant ideology of the secular. Without such a category, there could be no concept of the non-religious. But the reverse is also true.

That these categories have no essential meaning is unsurprising unless one believes that categories are more than conventions of classification, necessary to think with, but historically and linguistically specific, and even within one language subject to shifts in usage and meaning. But some general categories are contingently more powerful than others. Moreover, the categories with which I have been concerned in this book do not stand alone but form binaries: religion–secular; god–world; spirit–matter; faith–knowledge; metaphysics–empiricism; divine–human; theology–politics; and so on. Written constitutions, such as those of the US, France and India to take just three examples, are major sites for the modern proclamation of this reigning belief system. They transform the *imaginaire* of the modern nation state into the natural order of things, and we believers collectively invest this modern 'god' with enormous power and clothe it in an aura of sanctity. Yet at the same time the history of court interpretations, for example concerning what can be legitimately included in the clauses on religious freedom and what cannot, vividly illustrate the historically obvious, which is that there is no such thing as a religious as distinct from a non-religious practice apart from what powerful agencies determine.

As some of the writers discussed in this book have insightfully pointed out, it has been the ability to imagine 'religion' as absent that has been a condition for the imagining of secular universities and nation states. At its most powerful the myth of the nation state generates nationalism, a collective emotion of an extreme and even fanatical kind that can mobilize armies and demand the ultimate sacrifice. In some ways like the Christian God that dominated an earlier ideological formation, the state appears to us as a special kind of unquestionable fact about the order of things within which we find ourselves. The state stands over and against us as a reified object or agent that alienates us from our own creation, and which we venerate through the performance of a range of ritualized obediences.

Put in this way, the modern nation state shares many resemblances with those beliefs and practices that we usually classify as 'religion' or 'religious'. Yet to acknowledge this and to refer to our veneration of the nation as our religion would be to expose a fundamental contradiction that the myth cannot resolve. As the range of practices and institutions which can be classified as religious widens, its distinctiveness becomes correspondingly weaker. When the practices and institutions normally classified as 'secular' are also included – as in the idea of secularism as a religion – then the category loses its point. For the myth produces not only nation states but other god-like substances which we also worship and which have a different cultic logic. One of these is technological progress and the mastery of 'nature'.[1] Another is the pre-existing and pre-theorized individual and the myth of freedom. Another is capital as theorized (or theologized) by political economy.

The jurisdictions of capital and the nation state seem most obviously in conflict, since capital is imagined to transcend the boundaries of nation states and chafes at the restrictions of national governments. But the basic category that is deployed to legitimate all these modern gods is natural secular reason. And natural secular reason has been made possible by the invention of supernatural religion. Here we can find the outer circular edges of our faith structure, with all its logical problems and contradictions.

It has been a general criticism of the texts considered so far in this book that, in critiquing 'religion', the tacit non-religious secularity of the position of the various authors has either remained unexamined or at least not been clarified effectively. I myself receive a salary from a secular university and teach 'religion' as a special subject, and yet the logic of my ideas puts me in a problematic relation to both 'religion' and to the secularity of the secular university. This is my objective situation, and it is one of contradiction. It seems to me to be a fact that the ideology of religious studies continues to be widely reproduced and those of us in the critical religion tendency are a small minority. We have a growing but still marginal impact on the special field of religious studies, and our views make even less impact outside religious studies. Even within the field, there is a deep resistance to even considering our views among many scholars, who still seem to think that their main obligation is to continue teaching and publishing descriptions of religions and religious practices, without much considering the unintended consequences of that classificatory impulse. In national and international religious studies conferences, for instance, the various panels on 'critical theory' are merely a tolerated branch encompassed by the overall project of reproducing the dominant discourse on 'religion' as though nothing has been disturbed over the past 140 years since Max Müller gave his Science of Religion lectures. And though in the last 20 years or so the theoretical paradigm of the *sui generis* 'nature' of religion stemming from Eliade has lost its appeal, the gap has been plugged by alternative theories, such as family resemblance definitions of religion or biological claims in psychology for an inherited 'religious' gene.[2]

The more recent interest of biologists and social psychologists in 'religion' indicates that the problem is much wider than religious studies. Religious studies scholars who reify 'religion' and 'religions' are only in their own way doing what anthropologists, social scientists and many others across the secular academy do. The root problem is that valid knowledge is financed and legitimated by the secularity of the secular university. To critique religion as a category unsettles and makes problematic the legitimacy of secular reason. It is not so different from heresy, because it strikes at the roots of an entire system of meaning, and threatens to expose the myth of secular reason as an entire ideological apparatus of the power of modernity. There is an understandable anxiety that reason itself is being questioned. Though one might look for allies in Marxist, feminist and postcolonial writers, as a generalization such writers assume a secular worldview themselves. If it is true, as I claim, that the critique of 'religion' must simultaneously be a critique of its parasitic binary opposite the 'secular', then our lack of impact is not surprising. One is unlikely to make many friends by arguing that the religion–secular binary is an ideological basis for mystifying 'natural reason', and thus questioning modern formations of knowledge and power in general.

## The Critique of Political Economy

Let me stress again that my experience of researching in India and living in Japan, my interest in some forms of what for shorthand I will here call 'Buddhist' practice,[3] and my attempt (however limited and imperfect) to think outside a Eurocentric framework, were as fundamental to my arguments about the ideology of the religion–secular binary as any other element. I do, however, believe that Marx and the critical tradition of Marxism still provide some powerful tools, albeit Eurocentric ones, by which the issues can be strategically framed. I wish to stress that I am not an uncritical Marxist 'believer'. Significant strands of Marx and Marxism – for example, Lenin – reify and idealize the secular scientific with disastrous results. The science of dialectical materialism is itself a mystification, even though it seems to be not greater than the mystifying belief in naturally self-maximizing individuals or in naturally self-regulating markets, or in the belief in progress and the end of history shared by liberal political economists. On the other hand, rather than sharing Robert Nelson's characterization of Marx as hopelessly illogical and bombastic – 'a social misfit' (2001: 30) – I see Marx as a passionate human being who cared about justice and who had some peculiarly penetrating insights into the way in which the exploitation and commodification of fellow human beings for another's own profit becomes disguised in theories of political economy as natural, inevitable, reasonable and even liberating.

It is generally known that Adam Smith shared with many people of his time – and perhaps many still today – a belief in the natural and inevitable progress of human rationality through stages of development.[4] As societies develop to a higher stage of production, then people begin to enter the market as 'free' agents who maximize their own rational interests. But this raises a problem of historical transition from the earlier stage of inherited ownership and serfdom – a stage that also included variable degrees of independent self-subsistence – to the higher stage of the free and rational participation in capitalist markets. James M. Buchanan, who was awarded the 1986 Nobel Prize in Economics, expresses the view that markets are 'spontaneous' and as such they are 'discovered':

> The great scientific discovery of the eighteenth century was that of the spontaneous coordination properties of the market economy. If persons are left to act in their own interests, whatever these may be, within a legal framework of private property and contract ... the wealth of a nation will be maximally enhanced, if this wealth is defined in terms of the evaluations that individuals, themselves, place on goods and services. The market economy is, in this

sense, 'efficient,' but more importantly, because the market, in its totally decentralized fashion, carries out the allocative-distributive function, any need for collectivized or politicized management of the economy is obviated. The 'natural' proclivity of the scientifically uninformed is to think that, in the absence of management, chaos must result. The task of economic science, or more appropriately, of political economy, became, and remains after more than two centuries, one of conveying the general understanding of the coordinating properties of markets in increasingly complex institutional reality.

This central idea of 'order without design,' or consequences that are not within the intent or choices of any person or group, was indeed a discovery of momentous proportion, and, in retrospect, we should be able to appreciate the genuine excitement that was shared by the classical political economists (Buchanan 2007).

I believe historically the ideas of 'order without design' and 'spontaneous coordination' were derived from theology; that is, order without apparent design, though in fact God's providence acts as the hidden hand to bring things to equilibrium and 'spontaneous coordination'. The notion that markets have spontaneous properties that were 'discovered' may turn out to be a rather over-simplified and perhaps even mystified view of the origins of modern capitalism. For one thing, it seems to ignore the violence that has accompanied the propagation of the doctrine of free markets. According to Michael Perelman, Marx argued that the origins of 'free markets' were not 'free' at all but required the intervention, often violent and deliberate, of a sustained series of measures that benefited powerful groups and individuals at the expense of vulnerable people. One of the key ideas in Marx's critique of political economy concerned the processes of primitive accumulation, which was necessary for the creation of wage labour. Perelman has produced evidence that:

> To make sure that people accepted wage labor, the classical political economists actively advocated measures to deprive people of their traditional means of support. The brutal acts associated with the process of stripping the majority of the people of the means of producing for themselves might seem far removed from the laissez-faire reputation of classical political economy. In reality, the dispossession of the majority of small-scale producers and the construction of laissez-faire are closely connected, so much so that Marx, or at least his translators, labeled this expropriation of the masses as 'primitive accumulation' (Perelman 2000: 1).

Perelman produces considerable evidence that most of the early classical political economists ...

... strongly advocated policies that furthered the process of primitive accumulation, often through subterfuge. While energetically promoting their laissez-faire ideology, they championed time and time again policies that flew in the face of their laissez-faire principles, especially their analysis of the role of small-scale, rural producers ... [T]he underlying development strategy of the classical political economists was consistent with a crude proto-Marxian model of primitive accumulation, which concluded that nonmarket forces might be required to speed up the process of capitalist assimilation in the countryside. This model also explains why most of the classical political economists expressed positions diametrically opposed to the theories usually credited to them ... classical political economy advocated restricting the viability of traditional occupations in the countryside to coerce people to work for wages (2000: 2–3).

The classical political economists showed a 'keen interest in driving rural workers from the countryside and into factories, compelling workers to do the bidding of those who would like to employ them, and eradicating any sign of sloth.'

There is a strong argument that the basic theoretical assumptions of political economy came more or less directly from Christian moral theology and the concerns of Christian moralists during the seventeenth and eighteenth centuries.[5] Waterman, for instance, has shown in detail how the belief in naturally self-maximizing individuals acting for their own interest, and the belief in natural equilibrium of markets, derived from theological concerns about the nature of God's Providence in an increasingly harsh and competitive world characterized by cupidity and selfishness (Waterman 2008). However, Richard Whately appears to have been the first economist to characterize economics as a *secular* science in his *Introductory Lectures of 1831* given as Drummond Professor of Political Economy: '... political economy is a scientific enterprise that affords "secular" knowledge, or knowledge of Nature, whereas theology is a *religious* enterprise that affords "sacred" knowledge, or knowledge of God' (Waterman 2008: 132).[6] I suppose that Whately crystallized in conscious language what had slowly been emerging in a more tacit way in the thinking of theologians and moral philosophers. As Waterman put it: 'Whately's demarcation of "science" from "theology" marked the beginning of a sea change in the theological context of scientific and scholarly thinking. Although it was necessarily implicit in eighteenth-century natural theology – else how could science be recruited as independent evidence for a deity? – it was only implicit.' Before that point, the distinction between theology and natural science that seems so natural to us today was not clearly made, and was indeed only gradually being developed.

Newton published his *Philosophiae Naturalis Principia Mathematica* 'with an eye upon such Principles as might work with considering Men for the belief of a Deity' (Newton, quoted in Waterman 2008: 127). Waterman points out that eighteenth-century natural theology was dominated by Newtonian thought. He gives as one example a textbook written by Colin Maclaurin – *An*

*Account of Sir Isaac Newton's Philosophical Discoveries* – which was used in the training of Anglican priests, and which was required reading at Cambridge and the Scottish universities. This work 'showed that Newton's cosmology not only demonstrates the existence and attributes of God – as Newton himself believed – but also leads to a belief in an afterlife and a view of this life as a state of probation, which thus prepares us for the study of scripture' (2008: 127 viz (2008: 127). These ideas influenced Adam Smith, who lectured in Natural Theology at Glasgow University. Newtonian natural theology 'reinforced' the ideas 'of Providence or Nature, and that of equilibrium', which became fundamental to economics as a secular science. I infer that Smith's belief in the 'hidden hand' regulating markets derives from this belief in the Providence of God.

In the desire to found a new theorized field of economics which would legitimate new forms of ownership, profit and exploitation of labour, the theological origins of such basic metaphysical or at least non-empirical notions as 'naturally' selfish individuals and self-regulating markets were gradually forgotten. This seems to parallel the 'forgetting' of the origins of the imagined non-religious state which some of the writers in IR discussed in this book are now attempting to recover. It seems that the emergence of a discourse on political economy as a secular (non-religious) science in the nineteenth century was pre-dated by the earlier emergence of the idea of governance and 'politics' as separate from 'religion'. The first sustained challenge of which I am aware to the dominant assumption that religion (understood as Christian Truth) encompassed governance came in the seventeenth century. I have pointed out before in this book that the distinction of the civil authority and its laws and powers from privatized 'religion' was clearly made by both Locke and Penn in 1680's. (Use of the term 'secular' to refer to the non-religious domain of political power, however, apparently had to wait until the mid-nineteenth century.) Penn, Locke and Newton were all contemporaries. England remained a Christian church-state until well into the nineteenth century and the idea of the radical separation of religion and governance continued in England only as a subordinated discourse of non-conformity. However, it had greater success in North America for reasons I have explored elsewhere (Fitzgerald 2007a).

The modern invention of economics as the domain of natural human rational action deriving from self-interest and competition for scarce resources did not only derive from issues in Christian moral theology. It has been parasitic on, and at the same time instrumental in, the discursive transformation of religion as Christian truth into a different, modern myth of religion and religions. The transformations in the meanings of terms like 'religion' and 'the secular' can in my view only be understood in the context of colonialism and the needs of colonial administrators and apologists to classify, for purposes of domination and exploitation, an expanding world of non-Christian practices and institutions. It is only in such a context that we can understand why it was in the seventeenth, eighteenth and nineteenth centuries that Christian theology began to formulate the problems in terms that could lead to the emergence of political economy in the first place.

Like science, technology, politics and the state, the domain of economics is dependent on metaphysical beliefs not derivable from empirical observation but clothed in an aura of neutral, non-ideological factuality. Capital and markets are not themselves things that can be observed in the world, but powerful myths that act as charters for action or as metaphysical presuppositions on which economic theories are founded. This process of mystification of economic theory requires a forgetting of the historical connections with theology so that its claims can appear to be in accordance with the order of things. It also requires a forgetting of its origins in the rationalization of power in colonial contexts. It also requires – as argued by Perelman – amnesia about the violence and sustained process of primitive accumulation. Perelman has further argued that what is termed 'primitive accumulation' was not a once-and-for-all phase which is now behind us. Summarizing one of the purposes of his chapter on the subject, he says:

> Most discussions of primitive accumulation address the subject as a shorthand expression for describing the brutality of the initial burst of capitalism. In contrast, this chapter makes the case for treating primitive accumulation as an essential theoretical concept in analyzing the ongoing process of capitalist accumulation (2000: 4).

His arguments evoke the thought that colonization has been a vast project of 'primitive accumulation' by European and North American power since the Spanish and Portuguese began colonizing Latin America. In this light, political economy appears as an ideology for transforming power interests and the exploitation of human labour (including slavery) and other resources as an inevitable aspect of progress and development. Thus in the modern invention of economics as a secular science we can see the ideological operation of the religion–secular binary. Issues of values and morality in the exercise of power are marginalized from the workings of 'natural' development and the myth of 'free markets'.

It may be that Milton Friedman is right in his influential book, *Capitalism and Freedom* (1962), in which he argues that freedom and democracy can only be achieved once the irrational clutter of traditional collective controls has been removed, or reduced to a necessary minimum, and individuals are liberated to follow their natural self-interests in free markets of exchange. This powerful and influential view suggests that it is in such an *imaginaire* of globalized liberal capitalism that women and other relatively powerless subjects can achieve true democratic equality of opportunity. After all, one thrust of his argument is that the interferences of the state apparatus should be reduced as far as possible to let ordinary people rather than traditional elites decide what is good for them. This looks like a grass-roots-level theory of democracy that demystifies history and tradition, and allows ordinary people like you and me to decide. If it is true that the modern state is another ideological mystification of male power[7], then it might arguably also be true that Friedman's theorization of liberal economics and a minimal state implies greater power to individual women as well as men.

As against Friedman, Naomi Klein's recent book *The Shock Doctrine (2007)* gives a great deal of evidence that Friedman and his students have acted as advisers to some of the worst recent (male) dictators – Pinochet in Chile being only one notorious example. On this argument, if it is true, the theory and the *de facto* practice are badly at odds. It would mean that, apart from the rhetoric, the institutionalization of the doctrines of the Chicago School of Economics has been exemplified, not by an appeal to the democratic processes of consensus decision-making, but by violent, top-down coups and the imposition of military repression.

I am not here going to attempt to assess the evidence of Klein's (2007) allegations:[8] her book contains 59 pages of reference sources. But the weight of her case increases in the context of Perelman's arguments concerning primitive accumulation. Klein is not concerned with the modern invention of religion and the consequent myth of economics as a factual science that describes natural processes. But I believe my argument adds a dimension worth considering. Friedman and his disciples see themselves as instructors in economic realities. If Klein's arguments are right, they could therefore justify their collusions with dictators as a temporary expediency. This would also seem consistent with Perelman's arguments about the continued violence of 'primitive accumulation' as a necessary and on-going process for the construction of markets. On their assumed powers of prediction, once 'natural' markets have been given a chance to get started then the power of a dictator will turn out to be only a provisional necessity, and will naturally be replaced by the dictates of the markets.

I suggest that the confidence in the rightness of Friedman's views, shared by his disciples, derives from the mystification of economics as a natural, secular science based on empirical facts, which in turn depends on its tacit distinction from religious faith. Yet arguably there is no *essential* difference between faith in Friedman and faith in 'religion'. It is an ideological illusion which economic 'science' both depends on and reproduces.

Friedman is an influential writer, not only at the theoretical level, but also within the ruling classes of US imperial power. His ideas have relevance for what kind of institutions universities should be and how they should be funded, and we should debate openly and democratically both their virtues and their vices – just as we should do the same for any other major economic theorist such as Marx, Hayek or Keynes. But as someone influenced by Marx's ideas of the role of ideology, not only to *challenge* liberal economics effectively, but even to *understand* it properly, seems to me to require a demystification of secular scientific rationality and consequently a demystification of the discursive separation of the religion–secular binary. Those who buy Friedman's arguments will defend, tooth and nail, the superiority of secular social science and biological reality against the supposed mystifications of 'religious faith'. I argue that liberal economics is a powerful myth – the myth of natural reason and the 'discovery' of free markets[9]. But there are no empirical observations that will finally settle the issue. My argument, too, has accumulated various pieces of evidence, but in the final analysis it too rests on rhetorical persuasion.

My point here is to try to imaginatively connect the gradual and uneven transformation of the meaning of 'religion' with the corresponding invention of the non-religious domain of natural reason through emergent ideologies of the state, politics and political economy. As discourses on the state, politics and economics emerged gradually and with increasing power, so the category 'religion' was progressively transformed in meaning.

However, it was not only theories of individual liberty and free markets that emerged. Theories of socialism also gained strength, focused more on 'equality' than on 'liberty'. And this is part of my problem with 'the socialist left', which is that, being constituted by the same ideological configuration that it hopes to overcome, it recycles a different version of a more fundamental modern ideological paradigm which is shared by anti-Marxist theorists of political economy.

We are all constrained by and within the categories and discourses that configure dominant myths. An obvious question is, if you deconstruct the religion–secular myth intellectually, so what? Where do you go from there? What ground do you think you stand on? This is an especially relevant question for me, for two reasons. One is that I get my salary from a secular university and publish my work in secular academic publications. The other is that it is in the logic of my argument itself to entirely reject the illusion that a so-called progressive elite can engineer a revolution on behalf of other people.

Thus, on the one hand I deliberately and systematically criticise what appears to me to be a powerful myth which transforms an ideology of secular reason into common sense and consequently embeds a destructive and exploitative concept of human nature as though it is ahistorical, and given in the nature of things. Yet on the other hand I cannot offer any positive strategy in the form of an alternative paradigm.

The dilemma for anyone in a similar situation is well illustrated in the debate between Michel Foucault and Noam Chomsky televised in The Netherlands in 1971, a crucial part of which can be viewed online at YouTube (Chomsky 2006). Chomsky was explaining his arguments in favour of what he referred to as anarcho-syndicalism as some kind of goal for democratic, social transformation. Foucault countered that any contemporary vision of a future society characterized by freedom from the coercions of the state, and from the monopoly of power by a dominant class, would itself necessarily incorporate the categories and conceptions that inform the contemporary configuration. Until there is a genuine revolutionary moment, the dominant ideological assumptions will continue to shape consciousness at different levels of awareness. Thus authoritarianism would likely become reproduced under the guise of anarcho-syndicalism. The primary task is necessarily the continued and persistent critique of all current institutions in order to demystify their apparent neutrality (including the universities and the schooling system) and make conscious the power relations that they hide. Chomsky countered in turn that, while he recognised that risk, and agreed entirely on the critical project, it was a necessary risk given the then current destruction of Vietnam and other parts of Indo-China by US imperial power. Chomsky offered Foucault the two alternatives: either wait for the maximally right moment to challenge the power of the state and the vested interests served by apparently neutral institutions, and meanwhile allow the lethal bombing of Vietnam to continue; or organize peaceful revolutionary action now. He had chosen the latter. The debate ended at that point. Nealon discusses Edward Said's criticisms of Foucault, and his (Said's) citation of the Chomsky–Foucault debate. In that debate and elsewhere, Foucault questions a revolutionary goal based on concepts of 'justice' and 'human nature'. 'Justice', for example, "in itself is an idea which in effect has been invented and put to work in different societies as an instrument of certain economic and political power or as a weapon against that power"; and "I think that to imagine another system is to extend our participation in the present system" (quoted in Nealon, 1993:65).[10]

My own strategy has been the more negative one of deconstructing the religion–secular binary and its various substitute binaries, in the belief that through such a deconstructive process a space can be opened up for an alternative democratic vision to emerge. I am not aware that either Michel Foucault or Noam Chomsky has been specifically focused on this issue of the modern invention of religion. I have huge respect for Chomsky as a moral exemplar, and think of him in some ways as a great contemporary prophet, in the sense that a prophet holds up a moral mirror to those in power and challenges them to account for their own iniquities. There is a moral principle here that, rather than projecting the other as the source of the problem, classifying them as irrational 'religious' fanatics, and attempting to bomb them into submission, we should in the first place examine our own fanatical dogmatism, and our own institutionalized lust for power and profit. Fundamentally I agree with his ethical stand, and think his analysis of the workings of powerful institutions such as the media, the state and the corporations is convincing. But I think he has missed the function of the modern invention of 'religion' in the mystified legitimation of secular state rationality and corporate power. On the issue of 'religion' he seems to have fairly orthodox secularist views. Yet he himself seems to me to be one of those individuals whose moral and intellectual achievements tacitly subvert the distinction between the religious and the political. His commitment to truth and to human emancipation is neither 'religious' nor 'political' in the ideologically-loaded senses of these modern categories.

Later in this chapter I suggest that there is a possible ambiguity in Marx's own thinking around the referent for 'religion', an ambiguity that in Lenin's writing becomes an explicit proclamation of the superior rationality of 'secular' science. Yet many critics of Marx have tried to claim that Marxism itself is a kind of pseudo-religion – see, for example, Bertrand Russell (1961) and, more recently, Robert Nelson (2001). Contrary to this, I hope to persuade the reader that there is a valid and productive reading of Marx's powerful critique of ideology that situates him in a subversive relationship to the religion–secular binary. Though he himself was caught up in the ambiguous and unstable terminology of the times, his ideas on alienation and mystification also suggest powerful tools for unravelling the function of the religion–secular binary in making the reason of political economy seem 'natural'. So rather than merely signalling some general agreement with 'the left' rather than 'the right' (a dubious distinction and probably part of our problem), I also want both to add to the arguments and to reframe them.

## Orientalism and Postcolonial Studies

I argued, on the basis of a close reading of a few texts (see previous chapters), that the ideological characteristics of university practices tend to be elided, as though theorizing about religion is an innocent, neutral or technical matter of specialization with no implications for wider issues of power. But I also noted that some specialists in International Relations have made an attempt to broach the modern ideological invention of religion and the corresponding *imaginaire* of the secular state. Thomas, for example, also suggests provocatively that the formation of IR itself may have depended on the 'invention' of religion and its exile from power into privatization. I have suggested that, if he took this argument to its logical next step, he would turn his full attention to the critique of IR as an ideological formation in the service of the modern liberal state, and the secular academy more widely, as itself part of a modern discursive configuration. But this in turn would require greater visibility of Thomas's own theoretical and moral positionality. This is more easily said than done. Like the rest of us, and for understandable reasons, Thomas and Hurd tend to remain effaced from their texts and to present their arguments in a formal and impersonal way. This would be in contrast to Connolly, who, in his essay *Why I am not a Secularist* (1999), combines a sophisticated and detailed knowledge of Euro-American philosophies with a trenchant but thoughtful statement of his own positionality.

The difficulty of clearly stating the element of moral commitment in the construction of the dominant categories of modernity is sometimes evident in postcolonial studies and critical theory. Academic writers such as myself are compromised by our own dependence on our positions in secular universities. The work of a writer such as Robert Young, in *Postcolonialism: An Historical Introduction* (2001), might be taken as one of a number of exceptions to this tendency.[11] But I am not aware that such a critical position extends to an analysis of the way the modern colonial invention of religion and religions has been instrumental in transforming secular ideological discourse into natural reason. Postcolonial theory and critical studies are widely taught and read in universities in the UK and North America, and at the formal level these encourage a critical analysis of power. But though the positionality of the writer can often be inferred, it is power displaced and distanced 'out there' in the past, in the historical colonialism of Christian Europe, or in the contemporary neocolonialism of US foreign policy. It is not necessarily brought to bear on the immediate context of the secular university, and thus to the function of 'religion' in the ideological mystification of neutral and disinterested knowledge.

Edward Said himself (like Noam Chomsky, and indeed like Judith Butler, Friedrich Hayek or Milton Friedman) has frequently exposed his position in public on the moral and immoral uses of power, and on the practical means for challenging what he believes are the immoral uses of power. But, as a famous public intellectual, he could derive some protection from his location in a prestigious university, and from the public outrage that would presumably have resulted if he had been offered early retirement as a result of restructuring and downsizing. Most of us cannot be assured of such protection, and tend to distance our own moral commitment behind the conventions of academic objectivity and self-effacement. We fear that our work will be dismissed as too subjective, polemical, insufficiently scholarly and objective, or too 'political'.

These academic productions and debates, though critical in the sense that they expose the way knowledge disguises power, have tended themselves to remain within the boundaries of secular knowledge production, theoretically anti-imperialist but functionally neutral and changing little at home. The postcolonial and Saidean critique of Euro-American 'knowledge' of the oriental Other has not generated much democratic, inter-disciplinary debate within the academy about the function of the *secularity* of secular universities as ideological state apparatus,[12] or as agencies in reproducing and legitimating dominant power structures.

## Religious Studies, Orientalism and International Relations

As the IR specialist Robert Bosco (2009, and discussed in chapter 3 of this book) has pointed out, a minority critical wing of religious studies has trenchantly combined postcolonial theory with a deconstruction of religion as an orientalist category of classification.[13] Writers in religious studies have been able to combine historical and ethnographic research with a critique of the ideological formation of their own discipline. Such writers expose themselves to the criticism that, by so doing, they threaten the credibility of their own departments and their jobs as a consequence. I have no doubt that challenging the legitimacy of religious studies and its central category can damage the brand name and the marketing image of religious studies and comparative religion, even though it can also result in the development of innovative new courses which are popular with students. To propose that we reformulate the institutional space in which we are employed in a way consistent with the logic of my own research and ideas does not make for popularity or promotion opportunities. To critically interrogate 'religion' as itself an ideological category is also to question the 'non-religious secular' that defines the university. Given that 'religion' and 'politics' are categories that are uncritically deployed, not only in the politics and religion departments, but throughout the humanities and social sciences, even those who claim to have read Nietzsche and Foucault tend to stand aloof from such a project.

Much of the critique of religious studies (and by implication IR and the social sciences) as a discipline inevitably involves the moral issues about representation by privileged academics of those 'subalterns' who cannot answer back,[14] or who, because of unequal power relations, are unable to represent themselves. These issues have been much discussed in critical religion. However, since the IR writers discussed here do not show much awareness of this literature (just as I am short on knowledge of many important debates within IR), and since I hope to engage with specialists in IR, I will briefly indicate a crucial nineteenth-century stage in the formation of the Science of Religion by Christian missionary scholars of India which is quite widely debated by religion specialists themselves.[15]

One issue for the European scholar-missionaries working on India was whether or not there was any 'religion' in India. In one sense they thought there was, but in another sense not. The Christian concept of natural religion (as distinguished from Revelation) suggested that God had implanted in Adam and Eve and all their descendents an awareness of His divine transcendental reality. With the Fall from the Garden of Eden (located in 1603 by Samuel Purchas in the region that is present-day Iraq) and the subsequent dispersal of their descendents at the time of the Flood and the Tower of Babel, this God-consciousness had become drastically ameliorated and attenuated, degenerating into the superstitions found around the world. Only through the Christian Revelation could lost humanity be restored to a proper understanding of the will of God, and thus saved. The practices observed in India were thus taken to be religion only in a parodic sense. If religion meant Christian Truth, then these were not religion in any proper sense.

The colonial encounters, and the need to subjugate, control and exploit the indigenous peoples, confronted the Christian consciousness with hermeneutical and classificatory problems. This had been true since the Spanish and Portuguese had first encountered the Amerindian peoples. The question about whether or not the indigenous peoples had 'religion' (understood as a primal consciousness of God) became a problem of representing, describing, interpreting and classifying their bizarre and barbaric practices. This was a momentous process for indigenous peoples themselves because it implied for their conquerors the question whether or not they were fully rational or even human. This was also a pressing issue for the court theologians and lawyers of the Spanish king, because the use of indigenous Amerindians as slave labour could only be justified if they could be classified as irredeemably irrational and thus sub-human – as a kind of 'natural slave', to use Aristotle's formulation (see Pagden 1982; and a discussion in Fitzgerald 2007a: ch. 4). By the time of the nineteenth century the inevitable use of Christian categories to organize colonial data was becoming transformed into a 'science' of objective knowledge. Similarly, slavery and various forms of bonded labour, which had been sanctified by the Christian church-state, became transformed into wage-labour and indentured servitude sanctified by the new 'science' of liberal economics.

Sharada Sugirtharajah's paper 'Colonialism and Religion' (2010: 69–78) raises the broad question about the purpose and motivation of representations of others:

> No doubt genuine scholarly curiosity and interest in other cultures have played a vital role in the production of knowledge, but the question is what kind of knowledge is produced and for whom, and what purpose is it meant to serve (Sugirtharajah 2010: 76).

She is more specifically concerned with the hermeneutical strategies of nineteenth-century Protestant Indologists such as Max Müller, Monier Monier-Williams and Horace Wilson, and Protestant missionaries such as William Ward and John Nicol Farquhar. She points out that 'some of the ideological and hermeneutical underpinnings of the 19th century western engagement with "Hinduism" continue to inform the present academic study and representation of Hinduism' (2010: 71).

William Ward (1817), a Baptist missionary quoted by Sugirtharajah, refers to *The Religion of the Hindoos* in his book's title, and to their 'religious ceremonies':

> 'The reader will perceive, that in all these religious ceremonies not a particle is found to interest or amend the heart; no family bible ... no domestic worship; no pious assembly ... No standard of morals to repress the vicious; no moral education in which the principles of virtue and religion may be implanted in the youthful mind. Here everything that assumes the appearance of religion, ends ... in an unmeaning ceremony, and leaves the

heart cold as death to every moral principle' (Sugirtharajah 2010, quoted from Ward 1817).

As Sugirtharajah points out, the crucial idea here is that, while the 'religion of the Hindoos' might have the appearance of religion, it is false religion and therefore not really religion at all. It can also be pointed out that, while questioning whether or not the Hindus have 'religion' according to the paradigm of Christian Truth, Ward is simultaneously classifying their practices as 'religious', which is a further indication of the ambiguous emergence of 'religion' as an 'objective' or neutral scientific category from Christian theological terminology.

H.H. Wilson (1862) stated that 'The task that has been proposed to the members of the University is twofold. They are invited to confute the falsities of Hinduism, and affirm to the conviction of a reasonable Hindu the truths of Christianity' (Sugirtharajah 2010: 74, quoted from Wilson 1862). The purpose of studying and teaching Hinduism is to 'know what they are' so that they can be converted from their 'superstition' and 'ignorance' to Christianity (Sugirtharajah 2010: 75).

Monier-Williams was Boden Professor of Sanskrit at the University of Oxford. This professorial chair had for its object the study of Sanskrit and (or for the purposes of) 'the conversion of the natives of India to Christianity'. Writing in 1879, he said:

No one can travel in India and shut his eyes to the benefits conferred on its inhabitants by English rule. In fact, our subjugation of the country affords an exemplification of the now trite truth that the conquest of an inferior race by a superior, so far from being an evil, is one of the great appointed laws of the world's progress and amelioration (Sugirtharajah 2010: 71, quoted from Monier-Williams 1879).

Monier-Williams believed that India was given to the British to 'be elevated, enlightened and Christianized'.

Max Müller shared a Protestant and missionary interest in representing 'Hinduism' for Europeans. Müller was one of the earliest scholars to explicitly found 'the Science of Religion' in his *Introduction to the Science of Religion* in 1873. He was a philologist and a Sanskritist, and was a great and productive translator of Indian texts such as the Veda and the Vedanta. His 'scientific' philological theories are at least tacitly dependent on Christian myths of the Fall from a pristine God-consciousness. He claims this is evidenced in the very earliest Vedic texts, and that later texts and the contemporary Indian superstitions are indicated by a degenerating 'disease of language'. As Sugirtharajah points out, Müller spoke in favour of the colonization of India, including its cultural and intellectual colonization, and saw at least one of the purposes of Sanskrit scholarship in terms of 'discovery and conquest' (2010: 69, quoting from Müller 1873).

One of the things that becomes clear in Sugirtharajah's paper is that Christian theological colonial commitments found their way into the formation of the 'scientific study of religion' as neutral and disinterested classification. Sugirtharajah points out that these men were 'keen to show that Hinduism is not a religion but at the same time tend to classify it as a religion' (2010: 73–4). Thus it seems that, theologically and morally, Hinduism is ambiguously not a religion or merely an appearance of religion, but according to scientific classification it is a religion. This seems to me to well illustrate the confusion of two discourses on religion that need to be analytically separated – one, the discourse on religion understood as Christian Truth and civility as against the barbarity of paganism; and the other, religion as a generic and neutral object of knowledge for secular scholarship.

I do not mean to imply that India alone provided the source for the colonial invention of religion. David Chidester, in *Savage Systems* (1996; see also Chidester 2000, 2007), has shown how 'religion' as a generic modern category, and the field of religious studies which claims to specialize in it, were constructed on the frontiers of colonized Africa and in the context of the power relations that existed there. His historical research shows how religion or the absence of religion changed strategically in the way that missionaries and other colonial representatives used the term for purposes of colonial conquest and administration. He also shows how metropolitan theorists in London or Oxford used contradictory and inaccurate evidence derived second- or third-hand from African reportage in various ways to construct a largely mythical category of 'religions' that in turn passed into academic discourse.

## The Global Resurgence of Religion

In her book *The Invention of World Religions* (2005) Tomoko Masuzawa has shown how the modern idea of 'world religions' emerged in the nineteenth and early twentieth centuries from a variety of sources, not least the industry of many scholars and missionaries, including those such as Max Müller and C.P. Tiele, who were the founding fathers of the Science of Religion. I myself have also critiqued the category of world religions in previous publications. However, I have been more concerned with the modern category of religion and religions that is *presupposed* in the idea of world religions. Müller, Tiele and others engaged in debates about which religions were truly world religions, and which were merely religions confined to the context of a specific group. One can see this preoccupation continuing much more recently in the work of a religious studies scholar such as the late Ninian Smart. The general idea has been that only some religions are able to cross the boundaries of specific groups and become planted like seeds in the soils and different climatic conditions of a variety of different cultures – to use a metaphor that seems to lend itself to this kind of debate. Needless to say, for nineteenth-century

Christian scholars, Christianity was the archetypal world religion, because it is defined as the true revelation of God. Two other 'religions' seemed dubiously to qualify: Buddhism and Islam. For Smart, the paradigmatic 'religions' appear to have been Christianity and Buddhism.

However, prehaps in contrast to Masuzawa, my own concern has been to show that, regardless of whether or not we classify a religion as a world religion or merely as a 'religion', it is crucial to notice what is happening to other categories which are being invented and transformed through the same complex historical processes. I have tried to show that this modern category has been mutually parasitic on the invention of the non-religious secular, and the specific disciplinary formation of the secular in politics, economics, education and law. When the nineteenth-century scholar missionaries were developing the work of writers going back to the sixteenth century, they were inventing not only religion, religions and world religions, but the modern non-religious secular. One feature of the general trajectory of these divided domains has been essentialization. Religion is inscribed in modern discourses as essentially different from the state, politics and economics, with different functions, ends, characteristics and epistemologies.

The idea that some 'religions' can be transported and translated by missionaries from one place to another lends itself to a reified image which, even if only intended as a metaphor, can easily lapse into a rhetorical habit of misplaced concreteness. As discussed in the present book, recent rhetoric on religion and religions has even invested 'religions' with agency, as if they have a kind of autonomous existence and purpose.

In this book I have given examples of what I mean by the modern myth of religion as it is constructed academically. Especially since 9/11, journal articles and books by IR specialists have reflected a serious concern with what has been named 'the return from exile' of religion and 'the resurgence of religion in international relations'.

The two apparently contradictory images of 'religion' in public discourse that have been popularized by the media, by politicians, and by some academics, have gathered new strength since the 1980s, and especially since 9/11. Of course, many academics who theorize those practices and institutions conventionally demarcated as 'religions' or as 'religious' will rightly deny that they work with such crude exaggerations. They will point out that they are concerned with detailed expert knowledge of religious traditions, or of the religious aspects of human life. And some of those will go further, and point out that they use their specialist and complex knowledge to question and problematize the deployment of this category, showing how it fails to fit non-European ways of organizing the world. But, as far as I know, few of these more critical scholars have drawn attention to the parallel and parasitic problem of the translation of non-religious secular classification into non-European languages. Nor have they explicitly problematized their own secular positionality in the university.

Mark Juergensmeyer is one of the scholars of religious studies cited in the IR books I have been discussing. He is Director of Global and International Studies and a professor of sociology and religious studies at the University of California, Santa Barbara. He is also a recent President of the American Academy of Religion, which is the largest academic institution in the world for the promotion of the study of 'religion' and 'religions'. He is author or editor of 15 books, many of which promote the myth of global conflict between religious and secular beliefs and practices. Juergensmeyer is therefore an influential but uncritical inscriber of the religion–secular binary as though it were a fact of nature rather than an ideological construct. He is also responsible for promoting the myth of religious violence. I suggest that, unintentionally, he gives authority to the essentializing *imaginaire* that makes this conflict possible.

Sometimes Juergensmeyer sounds puzzled by his own preconception of the distinctions between religious and non-religious nations, or between religious and non-religious terrorists. At one point in his provocatively titled *The New Cold War? Religious Nationalism confronts the Secular State* (1993), a work that is widely cited and quoted in IR, he argues that secular nationalism and religion are equivalent in terms of both structure and function within their respective contexts. For example, one characteristic that they share is that:

> They both serve the ethical function of providing an overarching framework of moral order, a framework that commands ultimate loyalty from those who subscribe to it … For this reason I believe the line between secular nationalism and religion has always been quite thin. Both are expressions of faith, both involve an identity with and a loyalty to a large community, and both insist on the ultimate moral legitimacy of the authority vested in the community (Juergensmeyer 1993: 16).

This insight, that religion and secular nationalism have significantly shared characteristics, might have led him to seriously question an assumed essential difference between them. Could we not be talking about a whole range of human beliefs and practices with various kinds of overlapping and shared elements? This de-essentialization of religion and its distinction from the secular – as in the distinction between religious and secular nationalisms, or religious and secular violence – requires a shift from the language of objectivity to the language of discourse. If, for example, policy-makers in Washington could understand that the religion 'Islam' and its supposed opposition to secular rationality are as much products of the Western imagination as anything else, then the dreadful threat that Islam seems to pose to Western democracy can be deconstructed and replaced by more specific and localized problems such as conflicts of interests that are negotiable.

But Juergensmeyer fails to make this move in any consistent way, and unfortunately he then proceeds to discuss a whole range of different kinds of movements in the world by placing them into the rhetorically-inscribed conflicting boxes, the religions and the seculars, the religions and the non-religions, claiming to be able to make a significant analytical distinction between religious and secular nationalisms, or religious and secular terrorisms, or religious and secular ideologies.[16]

This tendency to the reification and essentialization of religion appears throughout Juergensmeyer's work. It is relevant to look at some of Juergensmeyer's other published titles to see the processes of reification and essentialization at work:

- *The Oxford Handbook of Global Religions* (2006)
- 'From Bhindranwale to Bin Laden: The Rise of Religious Violence' (2004)
- *Terror in the Mind of God: The Global Rise of Religious Violence* (2002)
- *Gandhi's Way: A Handbook of Conflict Resolution* (2002)
- *The New Cold War? Religious Nationalism Confronts the Secular State* (1994)
- *Violence and the Sacred in the Modern World* (1992)

These titles inscribe the presuppositions that religions exist in the world and that some of these are 'global', distinct from non-global ones but part of the same distinct family; and that there is a special kind of violence: religious violence, with its implied essential difference from non-religious violence, and 'religious' nationalism, with its implied distinction from non-religious nationalism in the expression used in the title of his 1993 book, 'Religious nationalism confronts the secular state'. In this way we can see how the idea of the non-religious or secular state is also inscribed as a domain which is somehow just there, as though it were a part of the natural order of things.

I mentioned that Juergensmeyer does discuss the problem; indeed, he wrestles with it in various attempts to demarcate the characteristics that define their essential differences. In this he is the inheritor of a long tradition in religious studies and anthropology that is concerned with the proper definition of religion and the qualities that demarcate religion from the putative non-religious domains of human life. One of the fascinating features of this definitional obsession is how many of them are in direct contradiction of each other. But this theoretical worry does not apparently inhibit him from further propagation of the myth. He says in the opening summary of his article 'Is Religion the Problem?' (Juergensmeyer 2004):

In the rubble following the collapse of the World Trade Center towers in the violent assault of September 11 lies the tawdry remnants of religion's innocence. In those brief horrifying moments our images of religion came of age. Religion was found in bed with terrorism. Whatever bucolic and tranquil notions we may have had were rudely replaced by those that were tough, political, and sometimes violent. Is this the fault of religion? Has its mask been ripped off and its murky side exposed – or has its innocence been abused? Is religion the problem or the victim?

From Juergensmeyer's own summary and from the article's title itself, we can immediately notice a number of tropes that I have alluded to throughout this book. There is an unmistakable tendency to talk about religion as though it is a thing or even an agent with an essentially different nature from politics. Is religion a problem or a victim? Religion is innocent and tranquil (or so we imagined); religion was found in bed with terrorism; religion wears a mask; behind its mask religion is really not religion at all, but something quite different: it is tough, political and violent; religion has a murky side. The inescapable impression that is conveyed by these expressions is that religion is something we encounter in the world, something that acts in the world, something with its own autonomous nature, and, while we may be mistaken about its real identity, there seems to be no doubt that it has one.

Readers might feel that it is unfair to take the wording of Juergensmeyer's summary as his considered view, either that expressed in the article or in his work more widely, especially if he is being ironic or writing with his tongue in his cheek. But I don't think there is any real evidence that Juergensmeyer has an ironic view of his work.

When Juergensmeyer grasps such a critical point and then backs off from it, reverting to an analytical and descriptive dependence on the same problematic, essentializing discourse, one is surely justified in trying to identify unconscious and indirect motives and interests that may be driving this entrenched discourse that pervades academia and public rhetoric. I am raising a question here about how we might explain the metaphysical compulsion which today globally exists to represent the world in terms of religion and the non-religious secular. My own suggestion has been that the modern invention of generic religion, which in its ideal form ought to be private, non-political and harmless, but which sometimes reveals a different face as barbaric, irrational, violent and concerned with power, is the very condition for inscribing 'our' secular civility as being in accordance with reason and common sense.

## Is the Present Writer Positioned in the 'Secular' or the 'Religious' Domain?

The question of secularism has been greatly discussed by people such as Jurgen Habermas, Charles Taylor, Talal Asad, William E. Connolly, Zaheer Baber, Rajeev Bhargava, T.N. Madan, Ashis Nandy, Partha Chatterjee, Akeel Bilgrami, Stanley J. Tambiah, and many others.[17] To engage with these writers who (apart, perhaps, from Asad) are working from within different paradigms to mine, would make this book longer and more complex, and would detract from my own specific focus and method. Even Talal Asad, who shares some of the same theoretical reference points as me, and whose work has a strong relationship to anthropology as well as history, has a very different starting point and trajectory towards similar and overlapping ground – in his detailed concern with the history of Islam for example.

How much any writer can say, or wants to say, about his or her own commitments concerning moral and immoral uses of power in international relations will partly depend on the purpose of their argument. Marx said (and I see it as a serious philosophical statement, and not as a slogan) that 'The philosophers have merely interpreted the world. The point is to change it.' Not every book, chapter or paper can deal with everything at once, and there are limits to the possibility of critique in any context. Not all of us feel able or willing to fall into what may be a trap of making explicit pronouncements about the morality of, say, British colonization of India, or contemporary US foreign policy in Iraq and the Middle East, or the practices of multinational corporations. Some intellectuals such as Edward Said, Judith Butler, Milton Friedman and Noam Chomsky can combine seriously researched data with philosophical sophistication and explicit positions on international relations and foreign policy. But there comes a time when a critical mass of opinion across and within disciplines begins to gather shape, and at such a point there may be a responsibility on some of us to try to articulate positions nearer to home. This is what I take IR writers such as Scott Thomas and Elizabeth Shakman Hurd to be broaching within their discipline, combined with a tentative and modest interdisciplinarity.

## Marx on Religion and Secularity

My own critique of discourses on 'religion' is partly an experiment in applying critical Marxist theories of mystification and alienation to the modern 'secular' academy. However, as already mentioned, there are various parts of Marx's theory that I reject; anyway my analysis is not straightforwardly Marxist but derives from other sources too. I touched on these in the background sketch of my own research trajectory earlier in the book (see Chapter 4), but it may be helpful if I briefly mention some of these again here. One observation is that there is a strong family resemblance between Christianity, Marxism and liberal capitalism as faith-based soteriologies, by which I mean doctrines of human liberation, both individual and collective.[18] Yet, of these, only Christianity is normally classified as a religion. Sometimes Marxism is described as a 'pseudo-religion' or a 'quasi-religion', or a religion-like phenomenon.[19] But liberal capitalism is rarely referred to as a religion as far as I know, and I have offered reasons for this throughout this book.

Another source lies in the observation of anomalies in the classification of religious and secular practices. I gave as one example that theorized practices of empirical investigation and experiment such as yoga or vipassana meditation are normally not classified as 'sciences'[20] but as 'religious' practices or as parts of the 'religions' Hinduism and Buddhism. But these are Anglophone classifications, not indigenous Sanskritic or Pali ones. This in turn draws attention to the colonial invention of Hinduism and Buddhism as religions by orientalists, scholar missionaries, East India Company servants and colonial administrators.[21] The invention of Indian religion was foundational to the formation of religious studies. My critique of discourses on religion is therefore partly derived from the postcolonial and orientalist critique of the colonial constructions of world religions. However, one problem with these critiques is that they rarely draw critical attention to the way that the invention of these religions is simultaneously the invention of their own 'secular' positionality.

A further source of doubts about the universality of religion and its distinction from the secular came from living in Japan, to where I still frequently travel. I have already discussed some of these in Chapter 4. My arguments about Japan can be found in other publications and there is no space to pursue them here.

So, while influenced by critical Marxism, my arguments are also rooted in other theoretical, epistemological and experiential sources that Marxism, as a European intellectual tradition, cannot be expected to explain satisfactorily. But I do think the critical traditions of Marxism provide some powerful tools for understanding the world. Or to put that in another way, though Marxist thought is in many ways itself Eurocentric, it also contains the possibility of self-critique, and can therefore contribute to the subversion of Eurocentric assumptions.

## Critical and Positivistic Legacies of Marx

Since the demise of Soviet socialism, the Marxist legacy has lost a great deal of its appeal as an alternative to liberal capitalism as a way of construing the world. I suggest that one significant reason for this is that Marx has been uncritically interpreted as a 'secular scientific' philosopher by some of his most powerful interpreters such as Lenin, and has thus been placed by its supporters as well as its critics as a competitor within the same ideological space as 'secular' liberal capitalism. If the critics of liberal capitalism critiqued the pretensions to objective scientific knowledge of economics and the social sciences in general, whether of the 'left' or the 'right', then I believe a more fundamental critique of ideology could be achieved. This would imply abandoning one's own claim to a superior kind of the same secular epistemology, and shifting the critique to secularism itself as a mystifying ideology. And to do this would require looking again at 'religion', and noticing that this is itself a modern invention that has the ideological function of mystifying the secular as 'natural' rationality. Such a shift in positionality makes possible not only a critique of the rationalistic pretensions of the secular capitalist state, but also of the secular socialist state.

Yet the critique of the category religion and its supposed distinction from the secular is in some significant ways consistent with a critical reading of Marx. The central aspect of Marxist philosophy that has influenced my deconstruction of 'religions' as imaginary objects of scientific knowledge has been the role of ideologies and their ability to transform and disguise power relations as the inevitable and natural order of things. Marx by and large treated 'religion' as part of ideology in general. I would suggest that he and Engels, and later Lenin, had a fairly static concept of religion, in the sense that 'religion' refers in their writing mainly to Judaeo-Christian theism or Trinitarianism, the myths of the heavenly family, and the ideological role of Christian church-states. This is unsurprising since in the nineteenth century the predominant meaning of 'religion' was Christian truth in its various Catholic, Orthodox, Anglican, or more generally Protestant variations, and the encompassing authority supposed to derive from that truth.

On the other hand Marx lived in an era when discourses on the generic category religion were becoming increasingly visible. One context for the reification of religion and religions as objects of knowledge was the colonial one: a problem for missionaries, orientalists, colonial administrators and others in the classification and control of non-Christian peoples and their practices. A simultaneous context was the rise to dominance of science, technology, and the discourse on non-religious secular rationality, and the distinction between 'facts' and 'values'. We have already seen earlier in this chapter that Richard Whately was the first to make explicit the claim, in 1831, that economics is a secular science in the sense of non-religious. It was in around 1850 that Charles Holyoake founded the Secular Society, thus marking the gradual but continuing transformation of a category (secular) from its predominant older use to refer to a branch of the clergy. It was during this period that sociology was developed by Auguste Comte as the scientific study of 'societies'. And it was not long after this that Max Müller and others such as C.P. Tiele founded the Science of the Study of Religion, crystallizing authoritative theorizations of religions and world religions. The Science of Religion was one of a series of historical moments, stretching back to the seventeenth century, which formalized the discursive shift.

It would therefore not be surprising if there were ambiguity in Marx's use of 'religion'. After all, the Temple to the Goddess of Reason emerged during the French Revolution. Comte founded his own version of this. The founders of the Science of Religion were mainly Protestant missionary-scholars whose descriptions and analyses of religions, despite being described as scientific, were explicitly embedded in theological premises.

Marx's main referent for religion as a form of ideology was Christianity. But, given the ambiguity between the two discourses on religion just indicated, he probably sometimes used the category in a more generic sense as well. That is a matter of Marxist exegesis and I do not intend to try to settle that point here. I have myself attempted an analysis of the historical trajectory of the Anglophone discourses on religion, and have argued that these two fundamentally different, analytically separable discourses are and have been commonly elided. Both of these discourses were operating in the nineteenth century and earlier, and still do so today (Gallaher 2007: 97).[22] These discourses are sometimes more and sometimes less clearly distinguished depending on the agency and context in which they were and still are being reproduced. These discourses can be and have been easily confused due to the rhetorical usage of the same words 'religion' and 'secular', a usage which acts to disguise their very different implications and outcomes.

Certainly Marx was impressed by the natural sciences, and he apparently asked Darwin to endorse *Kapital*. Furthermore, he seems to have had a belief in a science of the laws of history, though what kind of science he believed that might be is open to debate. This does not in itself mean that Marx was a positivist, and indeed it seems reasonable to hold that his critical theory of ideology points in the other direction from positivism, which is to say that what in any given historical context is considered as authoritative knowledge is a function of the ruling ideology, and in the long run and more or less indirectly corresponds to the interests of the dominant class and the mystification of actual power relations.

I would suggest that Marx's theorization of ideology reduces the importance of any possible distinction between a religious and a non-religious secular ideology. The general point in Marxian analysis is to focus on ideal constructions of knowledge dominant in a historical era, and to show how these serve the interests of the status quo. By masking real relations of production and power, a dominant ideology legitimates the status quo and makes it seem inevitable. This aspect of Marx has undoubtedly influenced my own approach to deconstructing the religion–secular binary. In more contemporary terms, the myths of neo-liberal capitalism such as free markets, the supposedly free and naturally self-interested individual, the realization of democracy in the formal equality of the legal and political domains, and the belief in inevitable progress towards universal enlightenment and prosperity, are all aspects of the dominant ideological discourse of today. The legitimating function of the media and the role of the social sciences and such genres as travel writing in disguising the power of representation as objective knowledge are all part of the ideological configuration. This mystification of knowledge is well embedded into our secular academic practices. Gramsci's concept of hegemony further helps us to understand how it is that those of us who are alienated from the products of our own labour (and this applies as much to academic production as to other forms of production) continue, not merely to accept our own alienated condition, but to actively conform to it.

Marx was profoundly concerned with human liberation from historically constructed conditions of existence, particularly the capitalist production regime of his time. Marxism is a soteriological praxis aimed at the end of history through the liberation of human consciousness from ideological illusions. In this, it shares some important family resemblances with both Christianity and liberal capitalism. As soteriologies that are not themselves inductively derivable from empirical observation, all three ideologies could easily be classified as religions. They are all based on acts of faith in a metaphysically speculative endpoint in history. Both Marxism and liberal capitalism share many family resemblances to what are typically thought of as 'religions', despite claims made by their respective devotees that they are not religious but scientific.

As a generalization, there seems to be little attention given in the Marxist traditions to the critical deconstruction of the religion–secular binary. This may partly derive from the misplaced desire to formulate Marxism as 'scientific', which has as one consequence the reification of religion as an essentially distinct domain of displaced fantasy and metaphysical speculation. There has been comparatively little specific critique of the transformations in ideological discourses of religion and religiosity, taking these as problematic categories and not just self-evident aspects of the world picked out by neutral description. In short, and making a generalization, what most Marxist writers have done is to assume that religions are generic forms of mystification which offer an escape from the 'real' world of material relations, and then to make claims about how they function as part of the ideological superstructure more generally. What they have generally failed to do is to notice that 'religions' are modern inventions that simultaneously legitimate a mystified secular domain.

## Marxist-Leninism

Lenin's version of socialism, which became institutionalized in the Soviet State, and which claimed Marx as its founding saint, can be seen to have adopted a structurally similar distinction between religion and the secular as liberal capitalism. When Lenin thought about religion, it was the Orthodox church that he typically had in mind, and his critique of religion was a critique of the power of the Orthodox Church and its ideological mystification of the Czarist church-state. As a basis for opposition, Lenin derived from his reading of Marx and Engels a positivistic understanding of scientific rationality, applying it to the laws of history. His belief that secular rationality can produce objective knowledge and analysis of the human condition mirrors the Enlightenment faith in reason that also underlies liberal capitalism. The essential distinction between religion and science, and between religion and the rational non-religious state, was clearly stated by Lenin in 1904, when he expresses his hostility towards 'religion' but also asserts that it is a private right:

Religion must be declared a private affair. In these words socialists usually express their attitude towards religion. But the meaning of these words should be accurately defined to prevent any misunderstanding. We demand that religion be held a private affair so far as the state is concerned. But by no means can we consider religion a private affair so far as our Party is concerned. Religion must be of no concern to the state, and religious societies must have no connection with governmental authority. Everyone must be absolutely free to profess any religion he pleases, or no religion whatever, i.e., to be an atheist, which every socialist is, as a rule. Discrimination among citizens on account of their religious convictions is wholly intolerable. Even the bare mention of a citizen's religion in official documents should unquestionably be eliminated. No subsidies should be granted to the established church nor state allowances made to ecclesiastical and religious societies. These should become absolutely free associations of like-minded citizens, associations independent of the state. Only the complete fulfillment of these demands can put an end to the shameful and accursed past when the church lived in feudal dependence on the state, and Russian citizens lived in feudal dependence on the established church, when medieval, inquisitorial laws (to this day remaining in our criminal codes and on our statute-books) were in existence and were applied, persecuting men for their belief or disbelief, violating men's consciences, and linking cosy government jobs and government-derived incomes with the dispensation of this or that dope by the established church. Complete separation of Church and State is what the socialist proletariat demands of the modern state and the modern church. ... Our Programme is based entirely on the scientific, and moreover the materialist, world-outlook. An explanation of our Programme, therefore, necessarily includes an explanation of the true historical and economic roots of the religious fog. Our propaganda necessarily includes the propaganda of atheism; the publication of the appropriate scientific literature, which the autocratic feudal government has hitherto strictly forbidden and persecuted, must now form one of the fields of our Party work.

V. I. Lenin, Socialism and Religion, *Novaya Zhizn*, No. 28, December 3, 1905, available at Marxists Internet Archive, http://www.marxists.org/archive/lenin/works/1905/dec/03.htm

It is clear that, when Lenin was talking about 'religion' here, he was referring mainly to the Orthodox Czarist confessional state, and was not using the term in the modern generic sense. On the other hand it is also clear that he was rhetorically reformulating the meaning of 'religion'. What he calls the feudal state is permeated by Orthodox Christianity, such that the church is not fundamentally distinct from the state. His rhetoric transforms religion into a private right guaranteed by the secular, scientific, socialist state. He is saying, this is what religion is at the moment (i.e. in 1904), and this is what it ought to be. He is rhetorically both demanding and assuming an essential distinction between the feudal superstitions of religion tacitly understood as the illegitimate involvement of the Orthodox Church in the state, and scientific rationality which includes economics and is the basis of the transformation of society. Having made this essentialized rhetorical distinction, it is likely, given the diverse peoples included in the Soviet empire, that 'religion' floated in meaning between the Orthodox Church and a more generic classification. I could find only two clauses concerning 'religion' in the 1918 Constitution of the Russian Soviet Federated Socialist Republic, which was adopted by the Fifth All-Russian Congress of Soviets on 10 July 1918:

13. For the purpose of securing to the workers real freedom of conscience, the church is to be separated from the state and the school from the church, and the right of religious and anti-religious propaganda is accorded to every citizen.
...
21. The Russian Socialist Federated Soviet Republic offers shelter to all foreigners who seek refuge from political or religious persecution.

But this brevity is not much different than that of the 1st Amendment to the US Constitution. In this sense of an essential separation between 'religion' understood as a private right and a voluntary association, and the secular state founded on non-religious scientific principles, Lenin is following the same distinction already invented in the Enlightenment, and enshrined by the American and French Revolutions. He goes on to demand:

Our propaganda necessarily includes the propaganda of atheism; the publication of the appropriate scientific literature, which the autocratic feudal government has hitherto strictly forbidden and persecuted, must now form one of the fields of our Party work. We shall now probably have to follow the advice Engels once gave to the German Socialists: to translate and widely disseminate the literature of the eighteenth-century French Enlighteners and atheists.[23]

The French enlightenment thinkers were also mainly preoccupied by 'religion' in the sense of Christianity, Judaeo-Christian monotheism, and the dominant church-states of Europe, whether Catholic universalism or Protestant national church-states. Yet (as already pointed out in the discussion of Marx's positionality in the nineteenth century) information about the practices and institutions of non-Christian peoples in colonies and potential colonies in different parts of the world were of course increasing in volume in the eighteenth century, and one way of expressing this is to say that generic religions were being invented (the term 'Hinduism', for example, was apparently first used around 1787 by the East India Company servant and evangelist Charles Grant',[24] and thus an ambiguous discourse of 'religion' was also developing. On the one hand it referred to the dominant ideology of Christendom and Europe in which the confessional church-states were perceived to shackle free enquiry and were the main target of Enlightenment critique. On the other hand the process of creating the non-religious rationality of the enlightenment was simultaneously creating religion and religions as generic objects of secular knowledge. Over a hundred years later, Lenin was continuing that enlightenment process, though in the specific context of early twentieth-century Russia and the Orthodox Czarist church-state. Lenin inherited the Marxist critique of the Enlightenment as a bourgeois enterprise. Scientific rationality is only partial until it comes to uncover the dialectical laws of history.

In short, Marxist-Leninist philosophers and servants of socialism are (or claimed to be) scientific, even more scientific than the bourgeois founders of the scientific societies of France, Germany, England, Holland and Scotland. The point for my purposes is that the theories that guide Marxist-Leninism are clearly held to be essentially different from those suffering the delusions of 'religious faith'.

As such, the argument between the apologists of Soviet state socialism and those of liberal democratic capitalism was not fundamentally about the distinction between the rationality of secular knowledge and the irrationality of religious faith. The argument was about which concept of secular knowledge is the most correct or fully developed. Both systems in one way or another have been historically founded on the assumption of secular rationality as essentially distinct from religion. And both systems are founded on rhetoric that transforms an ancient meaning of Religion as Christian Truth encompassing the church-state (whether Catholic, Orthodox or Protestant national) into a generic 'other' class of essentially separated and distinct practices to be found in all societies. Both Lenin and the earlier Enlightenment thinkers, through the power of rhetoric and an elective affinity with powerful interests, strategically fostered the religious–secular binary as a basis of modernity.

Thus Soviet state socialism, like liberal capitalism – which are both equally discourses constitutive of modernity – embedded into its constitution the rhetoric that secular science (including economics and theories of the state) is essentially different from 'religion'. Religion was thus an object of secular, scientific knowledge. Religion was required to be an object of knowledge in order that people and practices consequently classified as 'religious' could be identified, tolerated, licensed or eliminated. It is this problematic ideological process that is taken to be a rational base for our own knowledge production, with special departments of religious studies to study religions, and other departments to study politics, societies, states, systems of exchange, International Relations and so on. But the meanings we attribute to all these categories is the product of power struggles, competing claims to superior knowledge of the world, competition over the control of territories and resources such as oil and labour, and revolutions.

In contrast to the Leninist and Stalinist cults which disappeared in the 1980s, the European and North American governments that operate within the *imaginaire* of secular liberal capitalism do not persecute or eliminate those who are classified by the secular courts as religious (but see Wenger 2005). Or, rather, they do not eliminate those whom they classify as religious provided those classified accept the classification system within which their right to exist is determined. Those institutions and practices classified as religious are permitted to exist and even flourish provided they offer no serious challenge to the dominant status quo; and that their beliefs conform to the virtues as defined by secular nation states and their constitutions. These include that they are voluntary, peace-loving, non-profit-making, obey the laws of the secular state, and do not seriously challenge capital or the representative system of democracy. In liberal capitalist democracies, only those classified as religious who seem to pose an ideological threat (e.g. they challenge the system of classification itself) are delegitimized, especially if they can be strategically placed into the category of 'religious nationalists' or 'religious terrorists', with all the attendant implications of irrational barbarism. One of the deep and largely unquestioned assumptions communicated below the radar screen by these procedures is that the state, and the capitalist corporate interests which the state represents, is in conformity with natural reason. But I suppose that an analogous ideological process operated to make the Soviet State appear to its founders and managers in much the same light, in accordance with natural reason.

The point about this generalization is that both liberal capitalist and state socialist regimes do (or have done in the past) embed a fundamental distinction between secular rationality and objective knowledge on the one hand, and 'religion' as something of an essentially different order. There will doubtless be differences historically in the ways that state policy has been implemented towards those who are classified as 'religious'. The differences between liberal capitalism and state socialism were not fundamentally about the distinction between the secular scientific rational and the religious irrational, but about whose secular knowledge is most accurate.

In both these cases, therefore – that is, in both Marxist-Leninist socialism and liberal capitalism – there seems to me to be a fundamental separation at the ideological level between the realm of values and the realm of facts. It is just that they disagree what the facts are, or how the facts should be interpreted. In both cases, economics is taken as expressive of the fundamentals of human existence, even though the cases operate on competing theories. This would be despite those tendencies in the rhetorical denunciations of both sides in the Cold War to morally denounce the other's system of economics and state organization. The Cold War rhetoric of Soviet politicians and powerful state agencies accused the US and the West generally of being deficient in the principle of equality and the just distribution of wealth. The US agents accused the Soviets of denying individual liberty. Both of these values (equality and liberty) had been powerfully proclaimed by Enlightenment thinkers and by the revolutionaries and the US and French Constitutions of the late eighteenth century. These claims of moral superiority and human concern have tended to obscure the observations of critics of both systems that, in both, human value has been essentially separated from the theorized representations of economics and politics, which in turn appear as inevitably in conformity with the 'real world' of some supposed natural reality.

This appeal to the realm of social scientific facts would seem to be a contradiction of the larger implications of Marx's theory of alienation, that this separation of human value from production and capital is itself an ideological illusion which serves the interests of the owners of capital (including the owners of human capital as wage labour) at the expense of those of us who are alienated from control over our own production. Like other wage earners, academics are simultaneously both aware and unaware that they are alienated from their own productivity. Even if (and perhaps for good reasons) we do not describe ourselves as Marxists, it is difficult not to see the power of Marx's theory of alienation, and Gramsci's theory of hegemony, as ways of explaining this 'see and yet not see' facility of human consciousness.

As should already be only too clear from reading this book, my critical analysis of discourses on 'religion' is simultaneously a critique of 'secularism'. I want to show how the modern construction of religion and religions tacitly transforms a specific ideological formation with origins in modern history into an assumption about the immutable order of things. Secularism has been widely defended, morally and intellectually. Powerful arguments have been produced in favour of the modern nation state, including representative government and the protection of the rights of minorities against persecution. The knowledge production of secular universities has also been defended. But I think secular rationality needs uprooting academically from its disguise of neutrality and disinterestedness, and seen as a discourse which legitimates particular formations of power. One way of doing this is through a critical reading of Marx. But there are some serious qualifications that have to be made too.

## The Hegelian Dialectic and the End of History

Much of the debate between Marxists and liberal capitalists is and has been tacitly framed by secularist assumptions, and yet simultaneously it has been an argument about the end of history. As we have seen, Lenin explicitly intended to found a secular socialist republic. He was able to do this by appealing to a positivistic strand in the thought of Marx and Engels, and by claiming that socialism, including the dialectical laws of history, is scientific and non-religious. He followed the Enlightenment constructions of rationality by framing 'religion' as a source of mystification and oppression. In this way he reproduced a reification of religion structurally similar to those of the liberal capitalists and the Western social sciences.

In that sense I am positioned against both sides of the argument. As I already suggested – but it seems a point worthy of repetition – the argument between Marxist-Leninists and liberal capitalists was not fundamentally about the legitimacy of 'secular' knowledge as against 'religious' belief, but about which of two scientific theories of 'society' and 'economics' is better and truer. The differences between the actual policies towards minorities and practices deemed 'religious' in liberal capitalist and socialist states is important, and I have no interest in minimizing them. But that point does not substantially affect my argument that the formation of both Western capitalist and socialist polities has constitutionally and ideologically been predicated on the division between these two parasitically-invented domains.

On the other hand, a more critical reading of Marx can help the argument that the imaginary confinement of 'religion' and its separation from the imaginary secular state or 'free markets' is simultaneously the modern invention of both. In my argument the religion–secular binary is fundamental to the mystification of power relations and thus operates as a basis of modern ideology. Ideological myths – both socialist and liberal capitalist – appear as neutral and objective knowledge.

Francis Fukuyama (1992) thought the final dialectic was between socialism and liberal capitalism.[25] I suggest that this misreads the situation. If we are to use the language of the Hegelian dialectic at all, it might be said that the synthesis – we might tentatively refer to it as the postcolonial synthesis[26] – is between imagined 'religion' and imagined 'secular' civility. But the history that this brings to an end is that mythical history which represents Eurocentric categories as the achievement of universal enlightenment. Ironically, such a dialectical synthesis liberates us from Hegel's Eurocentric discourse. It requires the subversion of the imaginary and alienating split of the religion–secular binary which is deeply implicated in European colonial power formations, and on which the myths of both state socialism and liberal capitalism depend. Fukuyama's Hegelian metaphysics itself indicates that liberal capitalism is conceived as an act of faith, a teleology and a soteriology. It is thus not essentially different from Christianity or Marxist-Leninism. Fukuyama is a liberal capitalist theologian.

The state of the world indicated by the International Relations experts discussed in previous chapters, including all the conflicts that are classified as 'religious' terrorism and 'religious' nationalism, and the mystified representations of violent secular states as reasonable, peace-loving and only reluctantly violent, requires a new *imaginaire* and a shift in classifications if a new paradigm is to emerge. If the end of history means anything, then it means the end of Eurocentric mythic history and its faith in the gods of modernity, and that has not arrived.

# Notes

1.  See, for example David F. Noble, *The Religion of Technology: the Divinity of Man and the Spirit of Invention* (1999).
2.  See Ann Taves (2009).
3.  Especially meditation, a practice marginalized in the secular university as a 'religious' or a 'spiritual' practice, whereby the challenge of its deconstructive epistemological implications can be generally ignored as philosophically unimportant or even eccentric.
4.  Adam Smith [1776] (1993).
5.  Waterman assigns the origin of the ideas of Providence or nature, equilibrium and 'self-love', which were adopted by anglophone economic thinkers, to French moral theologians such as Boisguilbert and from there to the Physiocrats (2008: 127/8)
6.  Whateley is quoted as saying: "That Political-Economy should have been complained of as hostile to Religion, will probably be regarded a century hence ... with the same wonder, almost approaching incredulity, with which we at the present day hear of men's having sincerely opposed, on religious grounds, the Copernican system...." (Waterman, 2008:132). This early 19th century claim that economics is as scientific as the Copernican system is strongly reminiscent of the claim of Eli Berman, discussed in a previous chapter of this book (p146), that the Chicago economist Iannacone's insight – that an efficient religious sacrifice allows people to demonstrate their commitment – may be science of the kind in which Galileo was engaged when he made experiments from the Tower of Pisa to disprove Aristotle (p146)
7.  The feminist writer Catherine MacKinnon has produced one of the strongest versions of this argument: "Feminism has no theory of the state ... What is state power? Where, socially, does it come from? How do women encounter it? What is the law for women? How does law work to legitimate the state, male power, itself? Can law do anything for women? Can it do anything about women's status?...... The question for feminism is: what is this state, from women's point of view? The state is male in the feminist sense: the law sees and treats women the way men see and treat women. The liberal state coercively and authoritatively constitutes the social order in the interests of men as a gender – through its legitimating norms, forms, relation to society, and substantive policies." Catherine A. MacKinnon, *Toward a Feminist Theory of the State*, Harvard University Press, 1991; chapter 8, found at http://fair-use.org/catharine-mackinnon/toward-a-feminist-theory-of-the-state/chapter-8
8.  Klein's allegations have been hotly disputed by a member of the Cato Institute. See Johan Norberg, 'The Klein Doctrine: the Rise of Disaster Polemics', *Cato Institute Briefing Papers* No. 102, 14 May 2008. My

problem with Norberg's response is his unwillingness to engage in any critical self-reflection, as though everything in Klein's book is pure invention. Even if there are anomalies in the way she presents her evidence, it does not seem to occur to Norberg that Klein's allegations make a great deal of sense of many other representations of US Imperial power.

9.  James Buchanan, in his article 'The Triumph of Economic Science: Is Fukuyama Wrong? And if so, Why?' (2007), uses the expression 'discovery of free markets' five times. He uses expressions such as the following to characterize sceptics: 'the scientifically uninformed', 'the presumptive arrogance of intellectuals who claimed to know something about the economic process' and 'an unreasoned public attitude … relatively immune to either empirical or logical argument'.

10.  Jeffrey T. Nealon, *Postmodernism after Deconstruction*, 1993 Ithaca, NY: Cornell University Press. See also the interesting discussion of this debate by James Miller, *The Passion of Foucault*, Harvard University Press, 1993:200/3.

11.  There are several historians whose work is germane to the issues of power, and who combine serious research knowledge with a critical stance and pretty clear indications of authorial positionality. One is Eric Wolf, *Europe and the People Without History* [1982] (1997). There is still an issue, however, about the critical theorization of the ideological role of academics in modern universities. In religious studies, Russell M. McCutcheon has clearly articulated some of the issues in his *Manufacturing Religion: The discourse on sui generis religion and the politics of nostalgia* (1997) and *Critics not Caretakers* (2003).

12.  I take this way of thinking about the disguised ideological agencies from Althusser's 'Ideology and Ideological State Apparatuses: Notes Toward an Investigation', in *Lenin and Philosophy and Other Essays* (1971).

13.  There is a now a large religious studies literature informed by post-colonial and orientalist paradigms. One author who combines these with knowledge of Sanskrit, of the history of India, the history of the Anglophone category of religion, and a committed positionality, is Richard King, *Orientalism and Religion: Postcolonial Theory, India and 'The Mystic East'* (1999).

14.  See D. Chakrabarty (2000).

15.  See also David Chidester, *Savage Systems* (1996) for a powerful analysis of the origins of religious studies on the frontiers of colonial south Africa.

16.  See Fitzgerald 2000: 106–18, for a detailed analysis; see also Cavanaugh (1995, 2000), and Richard King (2007).

17.  An excellent reader that includes articles by many of these authors, much of it concerned with the debate in India, is Rajeev Bhargava (ed.), *Secularism and its Critics* (1998).

18. I have written about this issue in relation to Dr B.R. Ambedkar, the leader of India's untouchables and Dalits, the first Law Minister of India in Nehru's cabinet, and the chairman of the Constitutional Committee that wrote the Republican Constitution of India. Ambedkar was a powerful opponent of Gandhi. I have analysed Ambedkar's thoughts about religion, politics and liberation, and the various idioms which he used. Before his death in 1956 he took *diksha* in Nagpur and entered *buddha dhamma*.

19. I have questioned these terms in *The Ideology of Religious Studies* (Fitzgerald 2000).

20. Though they might be referred to as 'folk science' to distinguish them from real science.

21. I am well aware that this was not a one-way process of imposition by colonialists, but that these essentializing discourses were produced through a collaboration with Indian scholars from the high, literate classes. But it was nevertheless a colonial project, and much of the work depended on translating texts into European languages.

22. For one example, a US-based Protestant missionary in Mexico recently told a researcher that her strategy was 'impacting lostness'; see Carolyn Gallaher, 'The role of Protestant Missionaries in Mexico's indigenous awakening' (2007). The 'awakening' seems ambiguously to be about the awakening not only to Christian Truth, but also to free commodity and labour markets.

23. Lenin's reference note here says: 'See Frederick Engels, 'Flüchtlings-Literatur', *Volksstaat*, Nr, 73 vom 22.6.1874'.

24. See Geoffrey Oddie, *Imagined Hinduism: British Missionary Constructions of Hinduism*, [New Delhi: Sage, 2006:pp68ff.])

25. I take it that Francis Fukuyama's 'end of history' in his *The End of History and the Last Man* (1992, first published as an essay in *The National Interest*: 'The End of History?' (Fukuyama 1989) is a Hegelian dialectic with secular liberal capitalism rather than the Prussian State as the final synthesis. Fukuyama believed that the final dialectical struggle was between socialism and liberal capitalism. My point is that the secular is not the end of anything, because it does not stand on its own feet, but is conceptually parasitic on 'religion'.

26. I say 'tentatively', because the term 'postcolonial' is itself ambiguous, being read by many people as if it refers to a further historical development in time, which in turn invited a further re-inscription of Eurocentric 'progress'.

# Bibliography

Advani, L.K. (2007) 'Extract from an Interview of L.K. Advani' in Jaffrelot pp. 282–88.

Advani, L.K. (2007) 'Extract from The Ayodhya Movement' in Jaffrelot 289–98.

Ali, T. (2003) *The Clash of Fundamentalisms*, London: Verso.

Aloysius, G. (1997) *Nationalism without a Nation in India*, Place: Oxford University Press.

Aloysius, G. (2010) *The Brahminical Inscribed in the Body-politic*, New Delhi: Critical Quest.

Althusser, Louis (1971). 'Ideology and Ideological State Apparatuses: Notes Toward an Investigation', in *Lenin and Other Essays*, New York & London: Monthly Review Press.

Ambedkar, B.R. (1945) *What Gandhi and the Congress Have Done to the Untouchables*, Bombay: Thakur & Co.

Ambedkar, B.R. (1982) [1936] *Annihilation of Caste*, Jalandhar: Bheem Patrika Publications.

Anderson, Benedict (1991) *Imagined Communities: Reflections on the Origin and Spread of Nationalism*, London: Verso.

Asad, Talal (1993) *Genealogies of Religion: Discipline and Reasons of Power in Christianity and Islam*, Baltimore and London: Johns Hopkins University Press.

Asad, Talal (2001) 'Reading a Modern Classic: W.C. Smith's The Meaning and End of Religion', *History of Religion* 40(3), 205–22.

Asad, Talal (2003) *Formations of the Secular: Christianity, Islam, Modernity (Cultural Memory in the Present)*, missing text.

Avalon Project (2008) *Peace of Westphalia (1648)* Yale Law School Lillian Goldman Law Library, available online at http://avalon.law.yale.edu/17th_century/westphal.asp/ (accessed 7 June 2011).

Balagangadhara, S. N. (1994). "The Heathen in his Blindness..." *Asia, the West, and the Dynamic of Religion*. Leiden, New York: E. J. Brill.

Banton, E.M. (ed.) (1966) *Anthropological Approaches to the Study of Religion*, London: Tavistock Publications.

Barghava, Rajeev (ed.) (1998) *Secularism and Its Critics,* Delhi: Oxford University Press.

Benjamin, Walter [1921]. *Capitalism as Religion*, [translation of fragment 74 from Vol.VI of Gesamelte Schriften, edited by Rolf Tiedemann and Herman Schweppenhauser, avaliable at http://www.rae.com.pt/Caderno_wb_2010/Benjamin%20Capitalism-as-Religion.pdf

Berger, Peter (1973) *The Social Reality of Religion*, Harmondsworth: Penguin Books. (Originally published as *The Sacred Canopy*, 1967).

Berger, Peter (ed.) (1999) *The Desecularization of the World: Resurgent Religion and World Politics*. Washington, DC: Ethics and Public Policy Center and Wm. B. Eerdmans Publishing Company.

Berman, Eli (2009) *Radical, Religious and Violent: The New Economics of Terrorism*. Cambridge, Mass: The MIT Press.

Bloch, E., Keppens, M. and Hegde, R. (eds) (2010) *Rethinking Religion in India: the Colonial Construction of Hinduism* London & NY: Routledge.

Bosco, Robert M. (2009) 'Persistent Orientalisms: the concept of religion in international relations', *Journal of International Relations and Development*, 12, 90–111.

Bossy, John (1982) 'Some Elementary Forms of Durkheim', *Past and Present*, 95, 3–18.

Bossy, John (1985) *Christianity in the West, 1400–(1700)* Oxford: Oxford University Press.

Braun, Willi and McCutcheon, Russell (eds) (2000) *Guide to the Study of Religion*, Continuum Press.

Breen, John (2010) '"Conventional Wisdom" and the Politics of Shinto in Postwar Japan', *Politics and Religion*, IV (1) – Spring, 68–82. Available online at http://www.politicsandreligionjournal.com/images/pdf_files/engleski/volume4_no1/5%20-%20john%20breen.pdf/ (accessed 7 June 2011).

Bruce, Steve (2003) *Religion and Politics*, Polity Press.

Buchanan, James M. (2007) 'The Triumph of Economic Science: Is Fukuyama Wrong? And if so, Why?', kaikeikensain Board of Audit Japan, Dai nana go tokubetsu kikou No.7 special contribution. Available online at http://www.jbaudit.go.jp/effort/study/mag/7-1.html/ (accessed 7 June 2011).

Cannadine, David (2001) *Ornamentalism: How the British Saw Their Empire*, Oxford: Oxford University Press.

Carrette, Jeremy (2007) *Religion and Critical Psychology: Religious Experience in the Knowledge Economy*, London & New York: Routledge.

Carrette, Jeremy and King, Richard (2005) *Selling Spirituality: the Silent Takeover of Religion*, London & New York: Routledge.

Cavanaugh, William T. (1995) '"A fire strong enough to consume the house": the wars of religion and the rise of the state', *Modern Theology*, 11, 397–420.

Cavanaugh, William T. (2007) 'Colonialism and the Myth of Religious Violence', in T. Fitzgerald (ed.), *Religion and the Secular; Historical and Colonial Formations*, London: Equinox.

Cavanaugh, William T. (2009) *The Myth of Religious Violence*, Cambridge: Cambridge University Press.

Chakrabarty, D. (2000) *Provincializing Europe: postcolonial thought and historical difference*, Place: Princeton University Press.

Chidester, David (1996) *Savage Systems: Colonialism and Comparative Religion in Southern Africa*, Place: University of Virginia Press.

Chidester, David (2000) 'Colonialism', in W. Braun and Russell T. McCutcheon (eds), *Guide to the Study of Religion*, London and New York: Cassell.

Chidester, David (2007) 'Imperial Inventions of Religion in Colonial Southern Africa', in T. Fitzgerald, *Religion and the Secular: Historical and Colonial Formations*, London: Equinox.

Chomsky, Noam (2006) *The Foucault–Chomsky Debate: On Human Nature*, Introduction by John Rajchman, Place: New Press. The debate can be viewed online at http://www.youtube.com/watch?v=WveI_vgmPz8&feature=related and http://www.youtube.com/watch?v=S0Saqrx gJvw&feature=related (accessed 7 June 2011).

Connolly, William E. (1999) *Why I am not a Secularist*, Minnesota: University of Minnesota Press.

Cooper, G. (1988) 'North American Traditional Religion', in S.R. Sutherland *et al.*, *The World's Religions*, London: Routledge; pp. 873–82.

Dale, Peter N. (1991) *The Myth of Japanese Uniqueness*, Place: Macmillan Palgrave.

Dowd, Douglas (2000) *Capitalism and its Economics: A Critical History*, London and Sterling, VA: Pluto Press.

Dumont, Louis (1980) *Homo Hierarchicus: the Caste System and its Implications*, Chicago and London: Chicago University Press.

Dumont, Louis (1986) *Essays on Individualism*. Chicago: University of Chicago Press.

Durkheim, Emile (2001) [1912] *The Elementary Forms of the Religious Life*, trans. Carol Cosman, ed. Mark S. Cladi, Oxford: Oxford University Press.

Evans-Pritchard, E.E. (1937) *Witchcraft, Oracles and Magic among the Azande*, Oxford: Clarendon Press.

Fitzgerald, T. (1993) 'Japanese Religion as Ritual Order', *Religion*, 23, 315–41.

Fitzgerald, T. (1994a) 'Marathawada ni mirareru no Bukkyo' (Village Buddhism in Marathawada), in Masao Naito (ed.), *Kasuto seido to hisabetsumin (Untouchability and the Caste system)*, Tokyo: Akashi Shoten.

Fitzgerald, T. (1994b) 'Shukyo no Saisei to Ambedkar no Bukkyô' ('Religious Renewal' and Ambedkar Buddhism), in Shigeharu Tanabe (ed.), *Ajia no Shûkyô no saisei (Religious Renewals in Asia)*, Kyoto: Kyoto University Press.

Fitzgerald, T. (1994c) 'Buddhism in Maharahstra: a Tripartite Analysis' in A.K.Narain & D.C. Ahir (eds.) Dr. Ambedkar, Buddhism and Social Change, Delhi: BR Publishing Corporation

Fitzgerald, T. (1995) Review article: 'Things, thoughts and people out of place: P. Swanson *et al.* (eds), *Religion and Society in Modern Japan*, Berkeley: Asian Humanities Press, 1993', *Japanese Journal of Religious Studies*, 22(1–2), 201–17.

Fitzgerald, T. (1996a) 'From Structure to Substance: Ambedkar, Dumont and Buddhism', *Contributions to Indian Sociology* (CIS), 30(2), 273–88.

Fitzgerald, T. (1996b) 'Religion, Philosophy and Family Resemblances', *Religion*, 26, 215–36.

Fitzgerald, T. (1997) 'Ambedkar Buddhism in Maharashtra', *Contributions to Indian Sociology* (CIS). 31(2), 225–51.

Fitzgerald, T. (1999a) 'Ambedkar, Buddhism and the concept of Religion', in S.M. Michael (ed.), *Dalits in Modern India: Essays in Honour of Stephen Fuchs*, New Delhi: Vistaar Publications; pp. 118–34.

Fitzgerald, T. (1999b) 'Politics and Ambedkar Buddhism in Maharashtra', in Ian Harris (ed.), *Buddhism and Politics in 20th Century Asia*, London and New York: Pinter (Cassells Academic Press); pp. 79–104.

Fitzgerald, T. (1999c) 'The Mariai Village Festival in Maharashtra', in Masakazu Tanaka (ed.), *Living with Shakti: Gender, Sexuality and Religion in South Asia*, Senri Ethnological Series no. 50, Osaka: National Museum of Ethnology; pp. 169–92.

Fitzgerald, T. (2000) *The Ideology of Religious Studies*, New York: Oxford University Press.

Fitzgerald, T. (2002) '"Religion" and "the Secular" in Japan: problems in history, social anthropology and religious studies', *Japan Anthropology Workshop (JAWS) Newsletter*, September, available online in *Electronic Journal of Contemporary Japanese Studies (EJCJS)* at http://www.japanesestudies.org.uk/discussionpapers/Fitzgerald.html/ (accessed 7 June 2011).

Fitzgerald, T. (2003) 'Playing language games and performing rituals: religious studies as ideological state apparatus', *Method and Theory in the Study of Religion*, 15(3), 209–54.

Fitzgerald, T. (2004) 'Analysing sects, minorities and social movements: the case of Dr. Ambedkar and Dalits', in Surendra Jondhale and Johannes Beltz (eds), *Changing the World: Dr Ambedkar, Buddhism and Social Change in India*, New Delhi: Oxford University Press.

Fitzgerald, T. (2007a) *Discourse on Civility and Barbarity: A Critical History of Religion and Related Categories*, London and New York: Oxford University Press.

Fitzgerald, T. (ed.) (2007b) *Religion and the Secular: Historical and Colonial Formations*, London: Equinox.

Foucault, M. (2006) *The Foucault–Chomsky Debate: On Human Nature*, Introduction by John Rajchman, NY: The New Press. The debate can be viewed online at http://www.youtube.com/watch?v=WveI_vgmPz8&feature=related and http://www.youtube.com/watch?v=S0Saqrx gJvw&feature=related (accessed 7 June 2011).

Fox, Jonathan (2004) 'The Rise of Religious Nationalism and Conflict: Ethnic Conflict and Revolutionary Wars, 1945–2001', *Journal of Peace Research*, 41(6), 715–31.

Friedman, Milton (1962) *Capitalism and Freedom*, Chicago: University of Chicago Press.

Frykenberg, R. 1989. "The Emergence of Modern 'Hinduism' as a concept and as an institution: a reappraisal with special reference to South Asia" in G-D. Sontheimer & H. Kulke (eds.), 1989. Hinduism Reconsidered, New Delhi: Manohar.

Fukuyama, Francis (1989) 'The End of History?', *The National Interest*, Publishing details.

Fukuyama, Francis (1992) *The End of History and the Last Man*, New York: Free Press.

Gallaher, Carolyn (2007) 'The role of Protestant Missionaries in Mexico's indigenous awakening', *Bulletin of Latin American Research*, 26, 88–111.

Geertz, Clifford (1966) 'Religion as a Cultural System', in E.M. Banton (ed.) *Anthropological Approaches to the Study of Religion*, London: Tavistock Publications; 1–46.

Gellner, Ernest (1983) *Nations and Nationalism*, Ithaca, NY: Cornell University Press.

Goenka, (2003) 'Pure Attention', *Buddha Dharma: The Practitioner's Quarterly*, (Spring). Available online at http://archive.thebuddhadharma.com/issues/2003/spring/goenka_pure_attention.html/ (accessed 7 June 2011).

Gombrich, Richard (1988) *Theravada Buddhism: A Social History from Ancient Benares to Modern Colombo*, Place: Routledge.

Goodchild, Philip (2002) *Capitalism and Religion: the Price of Piety*, London: Routledge.

Goody, Jack R. (1961) 'Religion and Ritual: the Definitional Problem', *British Journal of Sociology*, 15, 142–63.

Gyatsu, Tenzin (the Dalai Lama) (2010) 'Many faiths, one truth', *International Herald Tribune* (with Asahi Shinbun), 26 May.

Hardacre, Helen (1989) *Shinto and the State 1868–1988*, Princeton NJ: Princeton UP

Hardy, F. (1983) *Viraha-Bhakti: the Early History of Krsna Devotion in South India*, NY: OUP.

Hardy, F. (1990) *The World's Religions: The Religions of Asia*, London & NY: Routledge.

Harvey, David (2010) *A Companion to Marx's Capital*, Verso.

Haynes, Jeffrey (2007) *An Introduction to International Relations and Religion*, Pearson Longman

Hitchens, Christopher (2007) *God is Not Great: How Religion Poisons Everything*, Crows Nest, N.S.W.: Allen & Unwin.

Hobsbawm, E.J. (1990) *Nations and Nationalism since 1780: Programme, Myth, Reality*, Cambridge: Cambridge University Press.

Hopkfe, Lewis M. and Woodward, Mark R. (2004) *Religions of the World*, Place, NJ: Pearson Prentice Hall.

Hume, David (1957) [1757] *The Natural History of Religion*, H.E. Root (ed.), Place: Stanford University Press.

Hurd, Elizabeth Shakman (2008) *The Politics of Secularism in International Relations*, Place: Princeton University Press.

Isomae, Junichi (2007). 'The Formative Process of State Shinto in relation to the Westernization of Japan: the concepts of 'religion' and 'shinto' ', in T. Fitzgerald, 2007b 93–103.

Jaffrelot, C. (ed.) (2007) *Hindu Nationalism: A Reader*, Delhi: Permanent Black.

Jefferson, Thomas (1786) *Virginia Statute of Religious Freedom*. Transcription available online at http://www.virginiamemory.com/docs/BillofRights.pdf/ (accessed 7 June 2011).

Juergensmeyer, Mark (1991) 'Sacrifice and Cosmic War', *Journal of Terrorism and Political Violence*, 3(3), 101–17.

Juergensmeyer, Mark (1993) *The New Cold War? Religious Nationalism confronts the Secular State*, Berkeley, CA: University of California Press.

Juergensmeyer, Mark (2000) *Terror in the Mind of God: The Global Rise of Religious Violence*, Berkeley, CA: University of California Press.

Juergensmeyer, Mark (2004) 'Is Religion the Problem?', Paper 21, Orfalea Center for Global and International Studies, University of California, Santa Barbara, available online at http://escholarship.org/uc/item/4n92c45q/ (accessed 7 June 2011).

King, Richard (1999) *Orientalism and Religion: postcolonial theory, India and the 'Mystic East'*, Place: Routledge.

King, Richard (with Jeremy Carrette) (2005) *Selling Spirituality: the Silent Takeover of Religion*, London and New York: Routledge.

King, Richard (2007) 'The association of "religion" with violence: reflections on a modern trope', in John R. Hinnells and Richard King (eds), *Religion and Violence in South Asia: Theory and Practice*, Place: Routledge; pp. 226–57.

King, Richard (2010) 'Colonialism, Hinduism and the Discourse of Religion', in E. Bloch *et al.* (eds), *Rethinking Religion in India: the Colonial Construction of Hinduism*, Place: Routledge.

Klein, Naomi (2007) *The Shock Doctrine*, Harmondsworth: Penguin.

Klostermaier, Klaus K. (1994) *A Survey of Hinduism*, Albany, NY: SUNY Press.

Kubálková, Vendulka (2003) 'Toward an International Political Theology', in F. Petito and P. Hatzopolous (eds), *Religion in International Relations: The Return from Exile*, New York and Basingstoke: Palgrave Macmillan; pp. 79–105; also published in Fabio Petito and Pavlos Hatzopolous (eds), 'Religion and International Relations', *Millennium Journal of International Relations* [Special Issue], 29(3) (2000), pp. 675–704.

Kunin, S.D. (ed.) (2006) *Theories of Religion: A Reader*, Place: Edinburgh University Press.

Kuroda, Toshio (1981) 'Shinto in the History of Japanese Religion', *Journal of Japanese Studies*, 7/1, p1-21.

Laustsen, Carsten Bagge and Wæver, Ole (2003) 'In Defence of Religion: Sacred Referent Objects for Securitization', in F. Petito and P. Hatzopolous (eds), *Religion in International Relations: The Return from Exile*, New York and Basingstoke: Palgrave Macmillan; also published in Fabio Petito and Pavlos Hatzopolous (eds), 'Religion and International Relations', *Millennium Journal of International Relations* [Special Issue], 29(3) (2000) 705–40.

Lindisfarne, Nancy, (see also Tapper) 2002, "Starting from Below: Fieldwork, Gender and Imperialism Now", The Richards Lecture, sponsored by the Centre for Cross-Culture Research on Women and Gender, Queen Elizabeth House, University of Oxford, 22nd May, 2002, http://users.ox.ac.uk/~cccrw/working%20papers/richards2002.pdf.

Locke, John (1689) *A Letter concerning Toleration*, 2nd edition, London: Publisher.

Loss, Joseph (2010) 'Buddha-Dhamma in Israel: Explicit Non-Religious and Implicit Non-Secular Localization of Religion', *Nova Religio: The Journal of Alternative and Emergent Religions*, 13(4), 84–105.

Loy, David (1997). 'The Religion of the Market', *Journal of the American Academy of Religion* 65/2, 275–90.

Lynch, Owen (1969) *The Politics of Untouchability*, New York: Columbia University Press.

MacKinnon, Catherine (1991) *Towards a Feminist Theory of the State*, Place: Harvard University Press.

McCutcheon, Russell (1997) *Manufacturing Religion: The Discourse on Sui Generis Religion and the Politics of Nostalgia*, New York: Oxford University Press.

McCutcheon, Russell (2001) *Critics not Caretakers: Redescribing the Public Study of Religion*, New York: SUNY Press.

McCutcheon, Russell (2003) *The Discipline of Religion: Structure, Meaning, Function*, London and New York: Routledge.

McCutcheon, Russell (2007) '"They Licked the Platter Clean": On the Co-Dependency of the Religious and the Secular', *Method and Theory in the Study of Religion*, 19, 173–99.

Madison, James (1786) *Virginia Statute of Religious Freedom*. Transcription available online at http://www.virginiamemory.com/docs/BillofRights.pdf/ (accessed 7 June 2011).

Mandair, Arvind-Pal S. (2009) *Religion and the Spectre of the West: Sikhism, India, Postcoloniality, and the Politics of Translation*, Place: Columbia University Press.

Masuzawa, Tomoko (2005) *The Invention of World Religions*, Chicago and London: University of Chicago Press.

Midgley, Mary (1985) *Evolution as a Religion*, London and New York: Routledge.

Miller, James (1993) *The Passion of Foucault*, Harvard University Press.

Monier-Williams, M. (1879) *Modern India and the Indians*, 3rd edition, London: Trüber & Co.

Moore, R. Laurence (1995) *Selling God: American Religion in the Marketplace of Culture*, Oxford & NY: Oxford University Press.

Müller, F. Max (1873) *Introduction to the Science of Religion*, London: Longmans Green.

Mullins, Mark, Shimazono Susumu & P. Swanson (eds) 1993. *Religion and Society in Japan*, [Nanzan Studies in Asian Religions], Berkeley, Calif: Asian Humanities Press.

Narain, A. K. & D.C. Ahir (eds) *Dr. Ambedkar, Buddhism and Social Change*, Delhi: BR Publishing Corporation.

Nealon, Jeffrey T. (1993) *Postmodernism after Deconstruction*, Ithaca, NY: Cornell University Press.

Nelson, Robert H. (2001) *Economics as Religion: from Samuelson to Chicago and Beyond*, Place: Pennsylvania State University Press.

Noble, David F. (1999) *The Religion of Technology: the Divinity of Man and the Spirit of Invention*, Harmondsworth: Penguin.

Norberg, Johan (2008) 'The Klein Doctrine: the Rise of Disaster Polemics', *Cato Institute Briefing Papers* No. 102, 14 May.

Oddie, G.A. (2006) *Imagined Hinduism: British Protestant Missionary Constructions of Hinduism, 1793–1900*, New Delhi: Sage

Pals, Daniel L. (1996) *Seven Theories of Religion*, Oxford: Oxford University Press.

Parrinder, G. (1970) *Avatar and Incarnation: A Comparison of Indian & Christian Beliefs*, London: Faber & Faber.

Parrinder, G. (1972) *Upanishads, Gita, and Bible: A Comparative Study of Hindu and Christian Scriptures*, London: Harper & Row.

Penn, William (1680) *The Great Question to be Considered by the King, and this approaching Parliament, briefly proposed, and modestly discussed: (to wit) How far Religion is concerned in Policy or Civil Government, and Policy in Religion? With an Essay rightly to distinguish these great interests, upon the Disquisition of which a sufficient Basis is proposed for the firm Settlement of these Nations, to the Most probable satisfaction of the Several Interests and Parties therein. [By one who desires to give unto Caesar the things that are Caesar's, and to God the things that are God's.]* Microfiche. National Library of Scotland.

Perelman, Michael (2000) *The Invention of Capitalism: Classical Political Economy and the Secret History of Primitive Accumulation*, Durham, NC and London: Duke University Press.

Petito, Fabio and Hatzopolous, Pavlos (eds) (2000) 'Religion and International Relations', *Millennium Journal of International Relations*, Special Issue 29(3).

Petito, Fabio and Hatzopolous, Pavlos (eds) (2003) *Religion in International*

*Relations: The Return from Exile*, New York and Basingstoke: Palgrave Macmillan.

Plattner, Stuart (1989) *Economic Anthropology*, Stanford: Stanford University Press.

Purchas, Samuel (1626/1613) *Purchas, his Pilgrimage; or, Relations of the World and the Religions observed in all Ages*, London.

Ram, Nandu (ed.) (2008) *Ambedkar, Dalits and Buddhism*, New Delhi: Jawaharlal Nehru University in collaboration with Manak Publications.

Rodrigues, Valerian (2005) *Dalit–Bahujan Discourse*, New Delhi: Critical Quest.

Russell, Bertrand, (1961) [1946] *History of Western Philosophy*, London: George Allen and Unwin.

Said, Edward (1978) *Orientalism: Western Concepts of the Orient*, Harmondsworth: Penguin.

Saler, Benson (2000) *Conceptualizing Religion: Immanent Anthropologists, transcendent natives, and unbounded categories*. New York: Berghahn.

Scott, D. and Hirschkind, C. (eds) (2006) *Powers of the Secular Modern: Talal Asad and His Interlocutors*, Stanford: Stanford University Press.

Smith, Adam [1776] (1993) *An Inquiry into the Nature and Causes of the Wealth of Nations*, Introduction by Kathryn Sutherland, Oxford: Oxford University Press.

Smith, Anthony D. (2000) 'The "Sacred" Dimension of Nationalism', in Fabio Petito and Pavlos Hatzopolous (eds), 'Religion and International Relations', *Millennium Journal of International Relations* [Special Issue], 29(3) (2000) 791–814.

Smith, D.E. (1998) 'India as a Secular State., in Rajeev Bhargava (ed), *Secularism and Its Critics*, Delhi: Oxford University Press; pp. 177–233.

Smith, J.E. (1994) *Religions and Quasi-Religions: Humanism, Marxism and Nationalism*, Basingstoke: Macmillan.

Smith, Jonathan Z. (1998) 'Religion, Religions, Religious', in Mark C. Taylor (ed.) *Critical Terms for Religious Studies*, Chicago and London: University of Chicago Press; pp. 269–84.

Smith, W.C. (1978) *The Meaning and End of Religion*, London: SPCK.

Smith, W.C. (1983) 'The Modern West in the History of Religion', *Presidential Address at the American Academy of Religion Annual Meeting*.

Sontheimer, G-D & H. Kulke (eds) (1989) *Hinduism Reconsidered*, New Delhi: Manohar

Spiro, Melford (1966) 'Religion: Problems of Definition and Explanation', in E.M. Banton (ed.) *Anthropological Approaches to the Study of Religion*, London: Tavistock Publications; pp. 85–126.

Strenski, Ivan (2006a) *Thinking About Religion: An Historical Introduction to Theories of Religion*, Oxford: Blackwell.

Strenski, Ivan (2006b) *Thinking About Religion: A Reader*, Oxford: Blackwell.

Strenski, Ivan (2010) *Why Politics Can't Be Freed From Religion*, Oxford: Wiley-Blackwell.

Sugirtharajah, Sharada (2010) 'Colonialism and Religion', in E. Bloch *et al.* (eds), *Rethinking Religion in India: The colonial construction of Hinduism*, Place: Routledge; pp. 69–78.

Sutherland, Kathryn (1993) 'Introduction', Adam Smith: *An Inquiry into the Nature and Causes of the Wealth of Nations*, Oxford: OUP.

Tapper, Nancy (see also Lindisfarne) (1987) 'Nature and Gender: An Anthropological Perspective', *King's Theological Review*, Volume X, No.2, 45–51.

Taves, Ann (2009) *Religious Experience Reconsidered: A Building-Block Approach to the Study of Religion and Other Special Things*, Place: Princeton University Press.

Taylor, Charles (2007) *A Secular Age*, Cambridge, Mass: Harvard University Press.

Taylor, Mark C. (1998) *Critical Terms for Religious Studies*, University of Chicago Press.

Thomas, Scott M. (2000) 'Taking Religious and Cultural Pluralism Seriously: The Global Resurgence of Religion and the Transformation of International Society', in Fabio Petito and Pavlos Hatzopolous (eds), 'Religion and International Relations', *Millennium Journal of International Relations* [Special Issue], 29(3) (2000) 815–42.

Thomas, Scott M. (2003) 'Taking religious and cultural pluralism seriously', in Fabio Petito and Pavlos Hatzopolous (eds), *Religion and International Relations: The Return from Exile*, New York: Palgrave; pp. 21–54.

Thomas, Scott M. (2005) *The Global Resurgence of Religion and the Transformation of International Religions*, Place: Palgrave Macmillan.

Turner, Victor (1966) 'Colour Classification in Ndembu Ritual', in E. M. Banton (ed.) *Anthropological Approaches to the Study of Religion*, London: Tavistock Publications; pp. 47–84.

Vajpayee, Atal Behari (2007) 'The Bane of Pseudo-Secularism', in C. Jaffrelot (ed.) *Hindu Nationalism: A Reader*, Delhi: Permanent Black; pp. 315–17.

Von Stietencron, H. (1989) "Hinduism: on the proper use of a deceptive term', in Sontheimer & Kulke (eds)

Ward, William (1817) *A View of the History, Literature, and Religion of the Hindoos*, London: Black, Parbury and Allen.

Waterman, A.M.C. (2008) 'The Changing Theological Context of Economic Analysis Since the Eighteenth Century', *History of Political Economy*, 40, 121–42.

Weber, Max (1963) *The Sociology of Religion*, [trans. by Ephraim Fischoff] Boston: Beacon Press.

Wenger, Tisa (2005) '"We are guaranteed Freedom": Pueblo Indians and the Category of Religion in the 1920's', *History of Religions*, 45(2), 89–113.

Wenger, Tisa (2009) *We Have a Religion: the 1920's Pueblo Indian Dance Controversy and American Religious Freedom*, Chapel Hill, NC: University of North Carolina Press.

Williams, David (1994) *Japan: beyond the end of history*, London and New York: Routledge.

Wilson, Bryan (1990) 'New Images of Christian Community', in John McManners (ed.) *The Oxford History of Christianity*, Oxford and New York: Oxford University Press.

Wilson, H.H. (1862) *Essays and Lectures chiefly on the Religion of the Hindus*, London: Trüber & Co.

Winch, Peter (1970) 'Understanding a Primitive Society', in B. Wilson (ed.), *Rationality*, New York: Harper & Row; pp. 78–111.

Wolf, Eric R. (1997) [1982] *Europe and the People Without History*, Place: University of California Press.

Young, Robert (2001) *Postcolonialism. An Introduction*, Malden, MA and Oxford: Blackwell.

Zelliot, Eleanor (1966) 'Buddhism and Politics in Maharashtra', in D.E. Smith (ed.), *South Asian Politics and Religion*, Princeton: Princeton University Press; pp. 191–212. Reprinted in E. Zelliot (1992) *From Untouchable to Dalit*; pp. 126–49.

Zelliot, Eleanor (1972) 'Gandhi and Ambedkar: A Study in Leadership', in J.M. Mahar (ed.), *The Untouchables in Contemporary India*, Boulder, CO: University of Arizona Press. Reprinted in E. Zelliot (1992) *From Untouchable to Dalit*; pp. 150–83.

Zelliot, Eleanor (1977) 'The Psychological Dimension of the Buddhist Movement in India', in G.A. Oddie, *Religion in South Asia*, Delhi: Manohar; pp. 119–44.

Zelliot, Eleanor (1992) *From Untouchable to Dalit: Essays on Ambedkar Movement*. New Delhi: Manohar.

# Index